CENSORED

30th anniversary edition

CENSORED 2007

The Top 25 Censored Stories

PETER PHILLIPS & PROJECT CENSORED

INTRODUCTION BY ROBERT JENSEN
CARTOONS BY TOM TOMORROW

SEVEN STORIES PRESS

New York / London / Melbourne / Toronto

Seven Stories Press
140 Watts Street
New York, NY 10013
www.sevenstories.com

In Canada: Publishers Group Canada, 250A Carlton Street, Toronto, ON M5A 2L1

In the U.K.: Turnaround Publisher Services Ltd., Unit 3, Olympia Trading
Estate, Coburg Road, Wood Green, London N22 6TZ

In Australia: Palgrave Macmillan, 627 Chapel Street, South Yarra VIC 3141

College professors may order examination copies of Seven Stories Press titles
for a free six-month trial period. To order, visit www.sevenstories.com/textbook/
or fax on school letterhead to 212.226.1411.

ISSN 1074-5998

9 8 7 6 5 4 3 2 1

Book design by Jon Gilbert

Cover images:
Computer training room © Jeff Leung
Network cabling 1 © Chris Hellyar
Cybercop © John Overmyer
United States Censorship © Charles Alexander Moffat
Computer behind barbed wire © Marc Lemire

Printed in the U.S.A.

Contents

CARL JENSEN, PH.D.
Founder of Project Censored

IN DEDICATION TO:

You, the who picking this book up
to the writers, contributors, evaluators, researchers, judges
dedicated to all who seek awareness

this public service
founded by Dr. Carl Jensen who, with a first class, launched a project
in response to a question a professor couldn't answer
sparking an investigation, this book is an invitation
30 years research of what the media was and wasn't covering

the project of Project Censored thus began bubbling
with a mission to educate about the role of an independent media
in a free and democratic society

so to its readers, supporters, contributors
a revolution of under-covered history is chronicled in these editions of
Censored News
written by journalists, synopsized by students, edited by a volunteer staff
this 30 years is thanks to you

in the world wide—classroom—community
we honor journalists by highlighting and awarding their reporting
while training seasons of students who stretch their minds through
semesters
interns in their turn learn that democracy is action
and to the dedicated staff, working volunteers, editors, mentors
who go over and beyond because of the cause
and to the director who dedicates himself
activism is activated in his hands-on teaching
through a project that makes happen the printing of this book

9

local approachable going global organization
filled in these pages, this ongoing project, part of the media
reform movement
made of a small staff and director keeping doors open out of two
tiny class rooms
created office space in a university—in response to a question
producing this book and its award ceremony
as part of the alternative solution

that's why with your support
it is our privilege and opportunity to present you with
what has for 30 years and still is
part of democracy in action, please view this attraction
Project Censored presents you with
The News That Didn't Make The News

—Joni Wallent

Preface

by Peter Phillips and Project Censored

Imagine real news as media information that contributes to the lives and socio-political understandings of working people. Such news informs, balances, and awakens society. Real news speaks truth to power and challenges the hegemonic top-down corporate entertainment news systems. Real news empowers and keeps key segments of working people in the United States tuned in, informed and active.

For thirty years Project Censored has been reporting the real news that corporate media refuses to cover. We find those cutting edge challenging news stories, not liberal-sanitized Democrat news, or whitewashed money-incrusted Republican news, or PR-manipulated, corporate released news. No, we like the real news that builds movements for social change. Real news keeps the 15 percent of us who are innovators in society aware of our power and our ability to influence positive change. Project Censored real news is about stimulating social activism in our daily lives, and making each act deliberate and heart-centered. Real news reports to the center of self, and helps us find a core for shared action. Real news organizes movement towards human betterment, shapes policy for equality, and stands in the faces of the neo-con global dominance power brokers.

Real news cannot be measured with Arbitron ratings. It is not there for the selling of materialism, or capitalist propaganda. It is not there for grandiose nationalism. Nor is it there to provide entertaining stimulation to the self alienated. Real news can only be measured through its success in building democracy, stimulating grassroots activism, and motivating resistance to top-down institutions. Democratic activism underlies the purpose, reason, and message of free speech. True Democrats empowered with real news are insubordinate and challenging. Power is rooted in the people and the leaders will follow where we choose to go.

Welcome to *Censored 2007*, our thirtieth anniversary edition. This is a book to keep as a permanent resource. It is our largest and most complete volume to date, packed full of real news and analysis of corporate media failures.

Chapter One, "The Top Twenty-five Most Censored News Stories of the Year," is our feature effort that some 200 faculty and students spent thousands of hours researching. Chapter Two follows with updates on censored stories from our 2006 volume. A key centerpiece of the 2007 edition is Chapter Three, "Thirty Years of Censored News," which updates each of the number one stories since our founding in 1976.

Chapter Four, "Junk Food News," has a new twist this year, as in-depth reviews of the most frivolous news stories are contrasted with important real news from the same time periods.

Andrew Roth, the new Associate Director of Project Censored, supervised the research for Chapter Five, "Media Democracy in Action," which includes powerful updates on media reform, Municipal Wi-Fi, Alternative Weeklies, Voces Unidades!, Sierra Club Chronicles and The ACLU Freedom Files.

Ben Frymer, assistant professor sociology, coordinated the research work on Chapter Six, covering FCC telecommunications reforms and the corporate push to deregulate the Internet. Chapter Six includes updates of the maps on corporate media ownership in the U.S.

Censored 2007's Chapters Seven, Eight, and Nine include contributions from Bob Burton and Diane Farsetta, Center for Media and Democracy (PR Watch), Julie Hollar, Janine Jackson and Hilary Goldstein with FAIR, and Wendy Ginsberg and Molly Zapp with the Index on Censorship (London). They provide a comprehensive review of the state of the media in the U.S. and the world.

Chapters Ten, Eleven, and Twelve are original research studies conducted by faculty and students at Sonoma State University. We examine the corporate media's increasing favoritism toward the global dominance group's agenda of military control of the world. Separate studies on Associated Press bias and gay and lesbian media visibility are new additions to Project Censored's continuing academic research on important media issues.

Chapter Thirteen is a special report on Japan's news media by Tomoomi Mori, a doctoral student in the Faculty of Social Studies at Doshisha University in Kyoto, Japan.

In Chapter Fourteen Edward S. Herman and David Peterson provide an in-depth analysis of Milosevic's death as seen through the propaganda system of corporate media news, and Robert A. Hackett and William K. Carroll analyze the importance of the emerging media democracy movement in Chapter Fifteen.

Welcome to our thirtieth anniversary edition of *Censored*.

Acknowledgments

Project Censored is managed through the Department of Sociology in the School of Social Sciences at Sonoma State University. We are an investigative sociology and media analysis project dedicated to journalistic integrity and the freedom of information throughout the United States.

Over 250 people were directly involved in the production of this year's *Censored 2007*. University and program staff, students, faculty, community experts, research interns, guest writers, and our distinguished national judges all contributed time, energy, and money to make this year's book an important resource for the promotion of freedom of information.

I want to personally thank those close friends and intimates who have counseled and supported me through another year of Project Censored. Most important, my wife MaryLia, who as my lover, friend, and partner provides daily consultative support to Project Censored. The men in the green oaks breakfast group, Noel Byrne, Bob Butler, Bob Klose, Derrick West, Colin Godwin, and Bill Simon, are personal advisors and confidants who help with difficult decisions. A special thanks also to Carl Jensen, founder of Project Censored, and director for twenty years. His continued advice and support are very important to the project. Tricia Boreta and Kate Sims are Project Censored coordinators and associate administrators. Their dedication and enthusiasm are greatly appreciated.

A big thanks goes to the people at Seven Stories Press. They are more than a publishing house, but rather have become close friends who help edit our annual book in record time and serve as advisors in the annual release process of the "Most Censored Stories." Publisher Dan Simon is dedicated to building democracy in America through knowledge and literature. He deserves full credit for assembling an excellent support crew including: Jon Gilbert, Ria Julien, Phoebe Hwang, Anna Lui, Crystal Yakacki, Theresa Noll, Ruth Weiner, Lars Reilly, Tara Parmiter, George Mürer and interns: Lauren Hougen, Sinan Schwarting, Anastassia Fisyak, and Jason Spears.

Thanks also to Bill Mokler and the sales staff at Consortium Books, who will see to it that every independent bookstore, chain store, and wholesaler in the U.S. are aware of *Censored 2007*. Thanks to Hushion House, our distributors in Canada, as well as Turnaround Publishers Services Ltd. in Great Britain and Tower Books in Australia.

We especially thank and welcome Novi Mondi Media in Italy for translating and distributing the *Censored* yearbooks in Italian and Spanish.

Thank you to Robert Jensen who wrote the introduction to the *Censored 2007* edition. Robert is a Project Censored national judge.

Thanks also to the authors of the most censored stories for 2007, for without their often-unsupported efforts as investigative news reporters and writers, the stories presented in *Censored* would not be possible.

Our guest writers this year are Julie Hollar, Janine Jackson, Hilary Goldstein, Wendy Ginsberg, Molly Zapp, Edward S. Herman, David Peterson, Andrew Sloan, James J. Dean, Andrew Roth, Robert A. Hackett, Bill Carroll, Bob Burton, Diane Farsetta, Tomoomi Mori, and Ben Frymer. They represent a unique combination of scholars, journalists, and activists dedicated to media freedom through a diversity of news and opinion. Thank you to each and all for your unique contribution to *Censored 2007*.

This year's book again features the cartoons of Tom Tomorrow. "This Modern World" appears in more than ninety newspapers across the country. We are extremely pleased to use Tom Tomorrow's wit and humor throughout the book.

Our national judges, some of whom have been involved with the Project for thirty years, are among the top experts in the country concerned with First Amendment freedoms and media principles. We are honored to have them as the final voice in ranking the top twenty-five best *Censored* stories.

An important thanks goes to our financial donors including: The Sonoma State University Instructionally Related Activity Fund, the School of Social Sciences at Sonoma State University, and especially the over 4,000 individuals who purchase books and send us financial gifts each year. You are our financial base who continue to give year after year to this important student-run media research project.

This year we had over 100 faculty/community evaluators assisting with our story assessment process. These expert volunteers read and rated the nominated stories for national importance, accuracy, and credibility. In April, they participated with over 100 students in selecting the final top twenty-five stories for *Censored 2007*.

Most of all, we need to recognize the Sonoma State University students, in the Spring 2006 Media Censorship class and the Fall 2005 Sociology of Media class, who worked thousands of hours nominating and researching some 300 under-published news stories. Students are the principle writers of the censored news synopses in the book each year. Over eighty students served as interns for the project, working on various teams including: public relations, web design, news story research, office support, events/fund raising, and broadcast production. Student education is the most important aspect of Project Censored, and we could not do this work without the dedication and effort of our student interns.

An extremely special thank you to Joni Wallent for coordinating the Project Censored thirtieth anniversary dinner on March 11, 2006.

Chris Bachelder, David Abbott, and Adam Armstrong, advised by Erica Wilcher, comprise the Website Team. The Project Censored web site www.projectcensored.org, has expanded under their supervision with over 20,000 people a day logging on to Project Censored in 2005–2006.

Lastly, I want to thank our readers and supporters from all over the United States and the world. Hundreds of you nominated stories for consideration as the best censored news story of the year. Thank you very much!

PROJECT CENSORED STAFF

Peter Phillips, Ph.D.	Director
Andrew Roth, Ph.D.	Associate Director
Carl Jensen, Ph.D.	Director Emeritus and Project Advisor
Tricia Boreta	Coordinator/Editor
Katie Sims	Coordinator/ Broadcast Team/ Editor
Suze Cribbs	Events Coordinator
Joni Wallent	Public Relations Team Leader
Jennifer Page	Student Office Assistant
Rachael Olea-Lizarraga	Student Office Assistant
Larissa Heeren	Teaching Assistant
David Abbott	Teaching Assistant/Editor
Charlene Jones	Teaching Assistant/Editor

SPRING & FALL 2005 & 2006 INTERNS AND COMMUNITY VOLUNTEERS

David Abbott, Kathryn Albergate, Lesley Amberger, Ian Aragon, Sean Arlt, Adam Armstrong, Jimmy Bailon, Chris Bacheldar, Melanie Bourassa, Joe Butwill, Sandy Brown, Lew Brown, Suze Cribbs, Kelly Decosta, Isaac Dolido, Kelly Fabela, Brian Fuchs, Charlotte Goodman-Smith, Margaux Hardy, Zoe Huffman, Matt Johnson, Charlene Jones, Bailey Malone, Peter McArthur, Kristine Medeiros, Sandy Murphy, Attila Nagy, Lindsey San Martin, Rachel Olea-Lizarraga, Ambrosia Pardue, Ned Patterson, Lauren Powell, Fabrice Romero, Dan Randall, Sarah Randle, Nick Ramirez, Jessica Rodas, Theodora Ruhs, Vincent Ryan, Michelle Salvail, Jacob Shifrine, Andrew Sloan, Bridget Thornton, Margo Tyeck, Celeste Vogler, Joni Wallent, Brittany Walters, Yuri Wittman

STUDENT RESEARCHERS IN SOCIOLOGY OF MEDIA CLASS, FALL 2005

Chris Bachelder, Sara Christianson, Lisa Dobias, Kelly Fabela, Matt Frick, Deanna Haddock, Pla Her, Zoe Huffman, Lauren Kelly, Adam Lesh, William Martin, Brian Murphy, Karen Nosek, Rafael Perez, Gary Phillips, Kim Quinn, Lani Ready, Cole Ryan, Michelle Salvail, Andrew Sloan, Daniel Turner, Nicole Vaticano

STUDENT RESEARCHERS IN SOCIOLOGY OF MEDIA CENSORSHIP CLASS, SPRING 2006

Christine Baird, Rachel Barry, Matt Beavers, Rachelle Cooper, Isaac Dolido, Brett Forest, Brian Fuchs, Deyango Harris, Sean Hurley, Michael Januleski, Peter McArthur, Heidi Miller, Monica Moura, Caitlyn Peele, Lani Ready, Jessica Rodas, Destiny Stone, Arlene Ward, Courtney Wilcox

INDEPENDENT RESEARCH TEAM

Bridget Thornton, Lew Brown, Andrew Sloan, Celeste Vogler, Sarah Randle, Brian Fuchs, Zoe Huffman, Fabrice Romero

PROJECT CENSORED 2006 BROADCAST SUPPORT

Ryssa Tamho, Erich Trieselmann, Dora Ruhs, Dan Randall, Paul Sarran, Michael Litle, Charlotte Goodman-Smith, Sandy Brown, John Bertucci, Ian Aragon

RESEARCH GROUP FOR THIRTY YEARS OF CENSORED NEWS CHAPTER

Sonoma State University, Hutchins School of Liberal Studies Weapons of Mass Distraction class, Professors Stephanie Dyer and Ben Frymer
Student Researchers: Audra Anderson, Lindsey Babb, Crystal Blackford, Vanessa Bonaventure, Ashli Cassara, Emily Chavez, Dana Dayanovitch, Walt Donaldson, Mike Fanning, Jenna Goll, Alexandria Grey, Amanda Halpin, Shauna King, Malia Lytle, Kristen McCarty, Julee Melhus, Sandra Moore, Mariah Morris, Sandy Murphy, Katie O'Connell, Mike Olivera, Theresa Petrellese, Benjamin Reilly, Ashley Rice-Kiener, Erin Roehm, Carolyn Rojas, Sarah Short, Danielle Spridgen, and Stacy Williams.

PROJECT CENSORED 2006 NATIONAL JUDGES

ROBIN ANDERSEN, associate professor and chair, Department of Communication and Media Studies, Fordham University

RICHARD BARNET, author of fifteen books and numerous articles for *New York Times Magazine, The Nation,* and *The Progressive*

LIANE CLORFENE-CASTEN, cofounder and president of Chicago Media Watch; award-winning journalist with credits in national periodicals such as *E Magazine, The Nation, Mother Jones, Ms., Environmental Health Perspectives, In These Times,* and *Business Ethics;* author of *Breast Cancer: Poisons, Profits, and Prevention*

LENORE FOERSTEL, Women for Mutual Security, facilitator of the Progressive International Media Exchange (PRIME)

ROBERT HACKETT, professor, School of Communication, Simon Fraser University; Co-director of News Watch Canada since 1993; author of *Democratizing Global Media: One World, Many Struggles* (Co-Edited With Yuezhi Zhao), and *Remaking Media: The Struggle To Democratize Public Communication* (With William K. Carroll)

CARL JENSEN, professor emeritus communication studies, Sonoma State University; founder and former director of Project Censored; author of *Censored: The News That Didn't Make the News and Why* and *20 Years of Censored News*

ROBERT JENSEN, professor of journalism at the University of Texas at Austin; author of *The Heart of Whiteness: Confronting Race, Racism and White Privilege* and *Citizens of the Empire: The Struggle to Claim Our Humanity*

SUT JHALLY, professor of communications and executive director of the Media Education Foundation, University of Massachusetts

NICHOLAS JOHNSON,* professor, College of Law, University of Iowa; former FCC Commissioner (1966-1973); author of *How to Talk Back to Your Television Set*

RHODA H. KARPATKIN, president of Consumers Union, non-profit publisher of *Consumer Reports*

CHARLES L. KLOTZER, editor and publisher emeritus, *St. Louis Journalism Review*

NANCY KRANICH, past president of the American Library Association (ALA)

JUDITH KRUG, director of the Office for Intellectual Freedom, American Library Association (ALA); editor of *Newsletter on Intellectual Freedom, Freedom to Read Foundation News,* and *Intellectual Freedom Action News*

MARTIN LEE, investigative journalist, media critic and author; an original founder of Fairness and Accuracy in Reporting in New York; former editor of *Extra Magazine*

DENNIS LOO, associate professor of sociology at California State Polytechnic University, Pomona; Co-editor of *Impeach the President: The Case Against Bush and Cheney*

WILLIAM LUTZ, professor of English, Rutgers University; former editor of *The Quarterly Review of Doublespeak;* author of *The New Doublespeak: Why No One Knows What Anyone's Saying Anymore*

JULIANNE MALVEAUX, PH.D., economist and columnist for King Features and Pacifica radio talk show host

MARK CRISPIN MILLER, professor of media ecology, New York University; director of the Project on Media Ownership

JACK L. NELSON,* professor emeritus, Graduate School of Education, Rutgers University; author of sixteen books, including *Critical Issues in Education,* and author of more than 150 articles

MICHAEL PARENTI, political analyst, lecturer, and author of numerous books, including *The Culture Struggle, Superpatriotism, The Assassination of Julius Caesar, A People's History of Ancient Rome, The Terrorism Trap, September 11 and Beyond,* and *Democracy for the Few*

BARBARA SEAMAN, lecturer; author of *The Greatest Experiment Ever Performed on Women: Exploding the Estrogen Myth, The Doctor's Case Against the Pill, Free and Female: Women and the Crisis in Sex Hormones,* and other books; cofounder of the National Women's Health Network

NANCY SNOW, professor, College of Communications, California State University-Fullerton; Senior Fellow, USC Center on Public Diplomacy; Adjunct Professor, University of Southern California, Annenberg School for Communication; author of *Propaganda, Inc., Information War,* and co-editor with Yahya R. Kamalipour of *War, Media and Propaganda*

NORMAN SOLOMON, syndicated columnist on media and politics; co-author of *Target Iraq: What the News Media Didn't Tell You;* executive director of the Institute for Public Accuracy

SHEILA RABB WEIDENFELD,* president of D.C. Productions, Ltd.; former press secretary to Betty Ford

*Indicates having been a Project Censored judge since our founding in 1976

IN MEMORIAM

Dr. George Gerbner, University of Pennsylvania;

Rabbi Michael Robinson, Project Censored Community Evaluator; and

Richard Barnet, co-founder of Washington's Institute for Policy Studies

MEDIA FREEDOM FOUNDATION

PROJECT CENSORED: 501-C-3 / Board of Directors

Carl Jensen, Noel Byrne, Rick Williams, Mary Lia, Bill Simon, Peter Phillips

PROJECT CENSORED EDITORIAL BOARD

Carolyn Epple, Charlene Tung, Dorothy Freidel, Francisco Vazquez, Greta Vollmer, Jeanette Koshar, Mary Gomes, Michael Ezra, Myrna Goodman, Patricia Kim-Rajal, Philip Beard, Rashmi Singh, Rick Luttmann, Ronald Lopez, Stephanie Dyer, Thom Lough, Tim Wandling, Tony White, Dr. Gary Evans, Andrew Roth, Ben Frymer, Wingham Liddell, Dr. April Hurley, and Karilee Shames

PROJECT CENSORED 2005 & 2006 FACULTY, STAFF, AND COMMUNITY EVALUATORS

Melinda Barnard, Ph.D. Communications
Philip Beard, Ph.D. Modern Languages
Jim Berkland, Ph.D. Geology
Stephen Bittner, Ph.D. History
Barbara Bloom, Ph.D. Criminal Justice Admin
Andrew Botterell, Ph.D. Philosophy

Maureen Buckley, Ph.D. Counseling
Elizabeth Burch, Ph.D. Communications
Noel Byrne, Ph.D. Sociology
James R. Carr, Ph.D. Geology
Yvonne Clarke, M.A. University Affairs
Liz Close, Ph.D. Nursing (Chair)
Lynn Cominsky, Ph.D. Physics/Astronomy
G. Dennis Cooke, Ph.D. Zoology
Bill Crowley, Ph.D. Geography
Victor Daniels, Ph.D. Psychology
Laurie Dawson, Ph.D. Labor Education
James Dean, Ph.D. Sociology
Randall Dodgen, Ph.D. History
Stephanie Dyer, Ph.D. Cultural History
Carolyn Epple, Ph.D. Anthropology
Gary Evans, M.D.
Michael Ezra, Ph.D. Chemistry
Tamara Falicov, M.A. Communication Studies
Fred Fletcher, Community Expert Labor
Dorothy (Dolly) Freidel, Ph.D. Geography
Patricia Leigh Gibbs, Ph.D. Sociology
Robert Girling, Ph.D. Business Econ
Mary Gomes, Ph.D. Psychology
Myrna Goodman, Ph.D. Sociology
Scott Gordon, Ph.D. Computer Science
Karen Grady, Ph.D. Education
Diana Grant, Ph.D. Criminal Justice Admin
Velma Guillory-Taylor, Ed.D. American Multicultural Studies
Chad Harris, M.A. Communication Studies
Laurel Holmstrom, M.A. Academic Programs (English)
Jeffrey Holtzman, Ph.D. Environmental Sciences
Sally Hurtado, Ph.D. Education
Pat Jackson, Ph.D. Criminal Justice Admin.
Tom Jacobson J.D., Environmental Studies & Planning
Sherril Jaffe, Ph.D. English
Paul Jess, Community Expert Environmental Law
Cheri Ketchum, Ph.D. Communications
Patricia Kim-Rajal, Ph.D. American Culture
Mary King M.D. Health

Paul Kingsley, M.D.
Jeanette Koshar, Nursing
John Kramer, Ph.D. Political Science
Heidi LaMoreaux, Ph.D. Liberal Studies
Virginia Lea, Ph.D. Education
Wingham Liddell, Ph.D. Business Administration
Jennifer Lillig Whiles, Ph.D. Chemistry
Thom Lough, Ph.D. Sociology
John Lund, Business & Political Issues
Rick Luttmann, Ph.D. Math
Robert Manning, Peace Issues
Regina Marchi, M.A. Communication Studies
Ken Marcus, Ph.D. Criminal Justice Admin.
Perry Marker, Ph.D. Education
Elizabeth Martinez, Ph.D. Modern Languages
David McCuan, Ph.D. Political Science
Phil McGough, Ph.D. Business Admin.
Eric McGuckin, Ph.D. Liberal Studies
Robert McNamara, Ph.D. Political Science
Andy Merrifield, Ph.D. Political Science
Jack Munsee, Ph.D. Political Science
Ann Neel, Ph.D. Sociology
Catherine Nelson, Ph.D. Political Science
Leilani Nishime, Ph.D. American Multicultural Studies
Linda Nowak, Ph.D. Business
Tim Ogburn, International Business
Tom Ormond, Ph.D. Kinesiology
Wendy Ostroff, Ph.D. Liberal Studies
Ervand M. Peterson, Ph.D. Environmental Sciences
Keith Pike, M.A. Native American Studies
Jorge E. Porras, Ph.D. Modern Languages
Jeffrey T. Reeder, Ph.D. Modern Languages
Michael Robinson, Rabbi, Religion
Rick Robison, Ph.D. Library
R. Thomas Rosin, Ph.D. Anthropology
Richard Senghas, Ph.D. Anthropology/Linguistics
Rashmi Singh, Ph.D. American Multicultural Studies
Cindy Stearns, Ph.D. Women's Gender Studies
John Steiner, Ph.D. Sociology

Greg Storino, American Airlines Pilot
Meri Storino, Ph.D. Counseling
Elaine Sundberg, M.A. Academic Programs
Scott Suneson, M.A. Sociology/Political Sci.
Laxmi G. Tewari, Ph.D. Music
Karen Thompson, Ph.D. Business
Suzanne Toczyski, Ph.D. Modern Languages
Carol Tremmel, M.A. Extended Education
Charlene Tung, Ph.D. Women's Gender Studies
David Van Nuys, Ph.D. Psychology
Francisco H. Vazquez, Ph.D. Liberal Studies
Greta Vollmer, Ph.D. English
Alexandra (Sascha) Von Meier, Ph.D. Environmental Sciences
Albert Wahrhaftig, Ph.D. Anthropology
Tim Wandling, Ph.D. English
Tony White, Ph.D. History
John Wingard, Ph.D. Anthropology
Craig Winston, J.D. Criminal Justice
Richard Zimmer, Ph.D. Liberal Studies

SONOMA STATE UNIVERSITY SUPPORTING STAFF AND OFFICES

Ruben Arminana, President, Sonoma State University and staff
Eduardo Ochoa, Chief Academic Officer and staff
Carol Blackshire-Belay, Vice Provost Academic Affairs
Elaine Leeder, Dean of School of Sciences and staff
Erica Wilcher, Administrative Manager
Katie McCormick. Operations Analyst
Connie Lewsadder, Dean's Assistant
William Babula, Dean of School of Arts and Humanities
Barbara Butler and the SSU Library Staff
Paula Hammett, Social Sciences Library Resources
Jonah Raskin and Faculty in Communications Studies
Susan Kashack, Jean Wasp and staff in SSU Public Relations Office

I would like to offer a special thank you to Dean of Social Sciences
Elaine Leeder and Dean's assistant Connie Lewsadder for their help

leading and organizing the Fund Development Committee. I want to express my gratitude also to committee members Andrea Neves, Michael Hamm, Dr. Edward Spencer, Judy Aquiline, Elaine Wellin, and Alice Chang.

Colleagues in the Sociology Department: Noel Byrne, Kathy Charmaz, Myrna Goodman, Melinda Milligan, James Dean, Theresa Ciabattari, Andrew Roth, Thom Lough, Elaine Wellin, Madeleine Rose, and department coordinators Lisa Kelley-Roche and Katie Musick.

Thanks also to our ongoing supportive friends in the Sonoma State community: Cecilia O'Brian, Peter Flores, Linda Williams, Bruce Berkowitz, Jerry Uhlig, Mo Llanes, Martha Ezell, Henry Amaral, Bill Bayley, Rod Baraz, Angela Hardin, Katie Pierce, Kamen Nikolov, John Wright, John Connole, Angelo Vera, and Nadir Vissanjy.

The Project Censored crew (SSU faculty, students, and PC staff).

Introduction

by Robert Jensen

For thirty years, Project Censored has collected the crucial stories that the mainstream corporate news media largely ignore and celebrated the smaller, scrappier news outlets that chase down those neglected truths. The stories in the project's volumes cover a range of subjects so broad that it is difficult to herd them into simple categories, but a pattern emerges that can help us understand why the dominant corporate media so often fail in their core mission of holding the powerful accountable.

Corporate journalists agree that they should serve as watchdogs on power but bristle, of course, at the suggestion that they fail to do that. In a society in which enormous power is concentrated in a militarized state and predatory corporations, the task for journalists is clear: "ruthless criticism of the existing order," to borrow a phrase from a famous nineteenth-century journalist, Karl Marx. But more often toothless than ruthless, today's supposed journalistic watchdogs in the mainstream end up being more bark than bite.

What constrains corporate journalists in their mission? In his propaganda model, Edward Herman identified key factors: the very structure of media corporations and advertising revenue of the news business, as well as the so-called practices of "objective" journalism that, paradoxically, hamper the news media in the pursuit of truths that matter most and make mainstream journalism less objective in a deeper sense of the term.

Herman pointed out that another powerful force shaping contemporary corporate journalism is the ideological limits within which journalists work. In other words, one of the most important things to remember about American journalists is that they are Americans—educated and socialized into a certain set of beliefs that are widely accepted in the halls of power and the intellectual institutions that serve power in the United States.

What are the key components of this dominant U.S. ideology? There are three core ideas that are like the water we swim in—claims taken to be obvious and beyond question, unless one makes a concerted effort to analyze and challenge this "conventional wisdom." Most corporate journalists either have internalized these ideological statements or are not willing to contest them, which helps explain what is—and, just as important, what isn't—in the country's daily newspapers, news magazines, and television news shows. At the core of this American ideology are assertions that:

1. capitalism is the natural way to organize an economy and, therefore, inevitable;
2. the United States, unique among nations, is inherently benevolent in its foreign and military policy, and
3. any political solutions that are "viable," and hence worthy of consideration, are defined by the platforms of the Democratic and Republican parties.

To identify these ideas as core ideology is not to suggest that all dissenting ideas have been eliminated in the United States and that no one thinks outside these limits. There are political groups presenting alternative visions, but they are largely pushed to the margins and are rarely present in what we might call the visible political spectrum—the range of people, groups, and ideas that are allowed consistent and respectful access to mainstream forums, including the corporate media. The United States is, after all, not a fascist state, but a liberal (in the Enlightenment sense of the term), pluralist, capitalist democracy. In such states, social control is achieved primarily by manipulation of public opinion, with coercion and violence used sparingly (but always available in reserve for crisis periods).

So, this critique of corporate journalism is no conspiracy theory that suggests a small cabal is controlling the public mind. It's an analysis of how the vehicles for educating and amusing people (schools, universities, journalism, and entertainment media) tend to replicate this dominant ideology and keep the majority of the population away from "dangerous" ideas. Anyone who has worked within these institutions knows there is some freedom to resist, but that the system of rewards and punishments for intellectual workers keeps the vast majority in line.

So, how do these ideological tenets affect journalism?

BUSINESS AND ECONOMICS

The dominant assumption about corporate capitalism in the United States is not simply that it is the best among competing economic systems, but that it is the only sane and rational way to organize an economy in the contemporary world. Especially after the demise of the Soviet Union, corporate journalists see no reason to challenge that assumption. As a result, virtually all discussion of business and economics ignores the fact that in much of the world these ideas are still the subject of lively debate. While U.S. journalists are allowed to police the worst offenses of corporations in capitalism—especially when other powerful institutions identify such abuses, such as in the case of the Enron scandal—the fundamental justice, or injustice, of the system is off the table for investigation and discussion.

It's difficult to point to the problems with the coverage of ideas about alternative economic orders in the United States because there is almost no such coverage. So, perhaps this part of the U.S. ideology has been most evident the past year in corporate media coverage of other countries where the debate goes on, such as Venezuela. Despite the fact that President Hugo Chavez was democratically elected and is more popular in his country than President Bush is in the United States, Chavez is routinely referred to in the U.S. media as a "strongman" or "autocrat." This likely is because journalists cannot conceive of a leader who speaks of "socialism for the twenty-first century" as anything but a Soviet-style dictator. The barely concealed hostility to Chavez in the U.S. press would be laughable if it weren't so deadly serious; the possibility of U.S. military action against Venezuela is real, and part of the process of creating public support for such actions is demonizing foreign leaders, with the help of the news media.

FOREIGN AND MILITARY POLICY

That demonization process is possible in large part because of the second ideological assumption, about the inherent benevolence of the United States in its dealings around the world. This is an extension of the "city upon the hill" metaphor that has always anchored the self-conception of not only U.S. elites but also much of the public. The idea is that the U.S. was not only the world's first democracy but, when it had the capacity to project power outside its borders, the vehicle for democratizing the world. In that worldview, U.S. actions are presumed to be morally justified. If the effects of U.S. policy end up being not so benevolent, any unpleasant consequences are written off as the result of well-intentioned policies that were flawed either because of inadequate planning or poor execution. For example, the U.S. attack on South and North Vietnam, Laos, and Cambodia (what we call the Vietnam War) that left 3–4 million dead was portrayed by corporate journalists primarily as the unintended result of naiveté and honest mistakes, not a vicious campaign to destroy a nation attempting to break out of the U.S. sphere of influence.

Likewise, when the stated rationales (weapons of mass destruction and ties to terrorist groups) for the disastrous 2003 invasion and ongoing occupation of Iraq were proved to be false, journalists were quick to accept that "intelligence failures" had led Bush planners to mistaken assumptions about the threat Iraq posed. The corporate news media then followed the lead of the Washington elite and accepted that the new goal of U.S. politicians and planners was democratizing the Middle East. The more plausible explanation—that the administration officials manipulated intelligence to justify a war they had long planned to fight—was politely avoided in mainstream news media. Search the corporate media for any extended discussion of what is obvious to the vast majority of the world: That the invasion was part of a sixty-year project of extending and deepening U.S. control over the strategically crucial oil and gas resources of the Middle East and Central Asia. You'll be searching a long time.

POLITICS

One of the reasons that search for an alternative point of view would be so exhausting is because in the post-World War II period, Republicans and Democrats have been largely united in the goal of expanding U.S. dominance around the world. While there are sometimes disagreements—within the two parties as well as between them—about the appropriate strategy and tactics to maintain this U.S. empire, the lack of any serious mainstream opposition to this project means that corporate journalists will almost always fall in line behind those offering this conventional wisdom.

This also can play out in similar fashion in domestic policy. For example, as health-care costs increase and people without insurance scramble to cope, one sensible option is scrapping the United States' inefficient system of private insurance in favor of some sort of universal health-care insurance run by the federal government. But we are told by journalists that this "single-payer" system is not viable. Why? Because the heavy hitters in both major parties reject it. The fact that public opinion polls show a majority of Americans support some type of government-endorsed health system to provide universal coverage is apparently irrelevant to discussions of what is politically viable—that concept is defined by politicians and the big-money donors who fund them.

No matter what the specific subject of the stories cataloged by Project Censored, a common theme in them is a rejection of the conventional wisdom. These stories don't adopt these ideological assertions, but instead challenge them. The stories about business and economics don't treat the abuses of corporations as an aberration from an otherwise healthy system, but instead examine modern industrial capitalism's ethic of amoral greed and the displacement of human and ecological costs of production onto the public and the commons. Stories on foreign and military policy dare to ask honest questions about the motivation of U.S. planners and the consequences of an imperial system. The sources used and solutions examined in these stories don't stop with the elites in the major parties.

This volume reminds us that the core mission of journalism in a democracy doesn't change: That ruthless criticism of the existing order, a monitoring of powerful institutions, the watchdog role of the press. The energy and commitment of the staff and students who produce Project Censored demonstrate that such journalism is possible.

Robert Jensen worked as a reporter and editor at corporate newspapers for a decade before earning a doctorate at the University of Minnesota and signing on as a journalism professor at the University of Texas at Austin. He is the author of *The Heart of Whiteness: Race, Racism, and White Privilege* and *Citizens of the Empire: The Struggle to Claim Our Humanity* (both from City Lights Books), and *Writing Dissent: Taking Radical Ideas from the Margins to the Mainstream* (Peter Lang). His writing is available online at http://uts.cc.utexas.edu/~rjensen/index.html and he can be reached at rjensen@uts.cc.utexas.edu.

THIS MODERN WORLD

by TOM TOMORROW

CHAPTER I

The Top Censored Stories of 2005 and 2006

by Peter Phillips, Tricia Boreta, Kate Sims, and Project Censored

For thirty years Project Censored has released an annual list of the most important news stories not covered by the corporate media in the United States. Here again is our release of the news that didn't make the news—a compilation of the best examples of journalism that the corporate media marginalized.

As we finalize our number one story, Internet neutrality coverage is finally picking up steam. Yet, coverage at this time is very much too little, too late. The issue has been discussed in the media democracy movement for over a year, but was generally ignored by the corporate media until the last days of the latest congressional hearings in June 2006. Even then, the media disregarded the overwhelming, one-sided spending of multi-millions of dollars for lobbying by vested interests in the telecom industry that stand to gain from the negation of Internet neutrality.

Democracy doesn't work when last-minute sound bites take the place of important public debate and comprise the bulk of information that could be available to the American electorate. A functioning democracy requires that issues be covered and discussed months and even years before critical decisions are made in Congress and other decision-making bodies. We need time for review and analysis of critical issues, not confusing, minute-long news blips.

We have a long way to go in building a media system in the U.S. that supports a healthy democratic process. Our efforts are but one piece of a larger dynamic of citizen-based democracy. Each piece is important as it works to build strategies that validate the core American values of freedom, equality, and accountability. We invite you to turn off corporate news and act with your communities to find independent sources of information that feed your democratic souls and build cooperative human societies.

1

Future of Internet Debate Ignored by Media

Sources:
Buzzflash.com, July 18, 2005
Title: "Web of Deceit: How Internet Freedom Got the Federal Ax, and Why Corporate News Censored the Story"
Author: Elliot D. Cohen, Ph.D.

Student Researchers: Lauren Powell, Brett Forest, and Zoe Huffman
Faculty Evaluator: Andrew Roth, Ph.D.

Throughout 2005 and 2006, a large underground debate raged regarding the future of the Internet. More recently referred to as "network neutrality," the issue has become a tug of war with cable companies on the one hand and consumers and Internet service providers on the other. Yet despite important legislative proposals and Supreme Court decisions throughout 2005, the issue was almost completely ignored in the headlines until 2006.[1] And, except for occasional coverage on CNBC's *Kudlow & Kramer*, mainstream television remains hands-off to this day (June 2006).[2]

Most coverage of the issue framed it as an argument over regulation—but the term "regulation" in this case is somewhat misleading. Groups advocating for "net neutrality" are not promoting regulation of internet content. What they want is a legal mandate forcing cable companies to allow internet service providers (ISPs) free access to their cable lines (called a "common carriage" agreement). This was the model used for dial-up internet, and it is the way content providers want to keep it. They also want to make sure that cable companies cannot screen or interrupt internet content without a court order.

Those in favor of net neutrality say that lack of government regulation simply means that cable lines will be regulated by the cable companies themselves. ISPs will have to pay a hefty service fee for the right to use cable lines (making internet services more expensive). Those who could pay more would get better access; those who could not pay would be left behind. Cable companies could also decide to filter Internet content at will.

On the other side, cable company supporters say that a great deal of time and money was spent laying cable lines and expanding their speed and quality.³ They claim that allowing ISPs free access would deny cable companies the ability to recoup their investments, and maintain that cable providers should be allowed to charge. Not doing so, they predict, would discourage competition and innovation within the cable industry.

Cable supporters like the AT&T-sponsored Hands Off the Internet website assert that common carriage legislation would lead to higher prices and months of legal wrangling. They maintain that such legislation fixes a problem that doesn't exist and scoff at concerns that phone and cable companies will use their position to limit access based on fees as groundless. Though cable companies deny plans to block content providers without cause, there are a number of examples of cable-initiated discrimination.

In March 2005, the FCC settled a case against a North Carolina-based telephone company that was blocking the ability of its customers to use voice-over-Internet calling services instead of (the more expensive) phone lines.⁴ In August 2005, a Canadian cable company blocked access to a site that supported the cable union in a labor dispute.⁵ In February 2006, Cox Communications denied customers access to the Craig's List website. Though Cox claims that it was simply a security error, it was discovered that Cox ran a classified service that competes with Craig's List.⁶

COURT DECISIONS

In June of 1999, the Ninth District Court ruled that AT&T would have to open its cable network to ISPs (*AT&T v. City of Portland*). The court said that Internet transmissions, interactive, two-way exchanges, were telecommunication offerings, not a cable information service (like CNN) that sends data one way. This decision was overturned on appeal a year later.

Recent court decisions have extended the cable company agenda further. On June 27, 2005, The United States Supreme Court ruled that cable corporations like Comcast and Verizon were not required to share their lines with rival ISPs (*National Cable & Telecommunications Association vs. Brand X Internet Services*).⁷ Cable companies would not have to offer common carriage agreements for cable lines the way that telephone companies have for phone lines.

According to Dr. Elliot Cohen, the decision accepted the FCC assertion that cable modem service is not a two-way telecommunications offering, but a one-way information service, completely overturning the 1999 ruling. Meanwhile, telephone companies charge that such a decision gives an unfair advantage to cable companies and are requesting that they be released from their common carriage requirement as well.

LEGISLATION

On June 8, the House rejected legislation (HR 5273) that would have prevented phone and cable companies from selling preferential treatment on their networks for delivery of video and other data-heavy applications. It also passed the Communications Opportunity, Promotion, and Enhancement (COPE) Act (HR 5252), which supporters said would encourage innovation and the construction of more high-speed Internet lines. Internet neutrality advocates say it will allow phone and cable companies to cherry-pick customers in wealthy neighborhoods while eliminating the current requirement demanded by most local governments that cable TV companies serve low-income and minority areas as well. [8]

Comment: As of June 2006, the COPE Act is in the Senate. Supporters say the bill supports innovation and freedom of choice. Interet neutrality advocates say that its passage would forever compromise the Internet. Giant cable companies would attain a monopoly on high-speed, cable Internet. They would prevent poorer citizens from broadband access, while monitoring and controlling the content of information that can be accessed.

Notes
1. "Keeping a Democratic Web," *The New York Times*, May 2, 2006.
2. Jim Goldman, Larry Kudlow, and Phil Lebeau, "Panelists Michael Powell, Mike Holland, Neil Weinberg, John Augustine and Pablo Perez-Fernandez discuss markets," Kudlow & Company CNBC, March 6, 2006.
3. http://www.Handsofftheinternet.com.
4. Michael Geist, "Telus breaks Net Providers' cardinal rule: Telecom company blocks access to site supporting union in labour dispute," *Ottawa Citizen*, August 4, 2005.

5. Jonathan Krim, "Renewed Warning of Bandwidth Hoarding," *The Washington Post*, November 24, 2005.
6. David A. Utter, "Craigslist Blocked By Cox Interactive," http://www.Webpronews.com, June 7, 2006.
7. Yuki Noguchi, "Cable Firms Don't Have to Share Networks, Court Rules," *Washington Post*, June 28, 2005.
8. "Last week in Congress / How our representatives voted," *Buffalo News* (New York), June 11, 2006.

UPDATE BY ELLIOT D. COHEN, PH.D.

Despite the fact that the Court's decision in *Brand X* marks the beginning of the end for a robust, democratic Internet, there has been a virtual MSM blackout in covering it. As a result of this decision, the legal stage has been set for further corporate control. Currently pending in Congress is the "Communications Opportunity, Promotion, and Enhancement Act of 2006"(HR 5252), fueled by strong telecom corporative lobbies and introduced by Congressman Joe Barton (R-TX). This Act, which fails to adequately protect an open and neutral Internet, includes a "Title II—Enforcement of Broadband Policy Statement" that gives the FCC "exclusive authority to adjudicate any complaint alleging a violation of the broadband policy statement or the principles incorporated therein." With the passage of this provision, courts will have scant authority to challenge and overturn FCC decisions regarding broadband. Since under current FCC Chair Kevin Martin, the FCC is moving toward still further deregulation of telecom and media companies, the likely consequence is the thickening of the plot to increase corporate control of the Internet. In particular, behemoth telecom corporations like Comcast, Verizon, and AT&T want to set up toll booths on the Internet. If these companies get their way, content providers with deep pockets will be afforded optimum bandwidth while the rest of us will be left spinning in cyberspace. No longer will everyone enjoy an equal voice in the freest and most comprehensive democratic forum ever devised by humankind.

As might be expected, none of these new developments are being addressed by the MSM. Among media activist organizations attempting to stop the gutting of the free Internet is The Free Press (http://www.freepress.net/), which now has an aggressive "Save the Internet" campaign.

2

Halliburton Charged with Selling Nuclear Technologies to Iran

Source:

GlobalResearch.ca, August 5, 2005
Title: "Halliburton Secretly Doing Business With Key Member of Iran's Nuclear Team"
Author: Jason Leopold

Faculty Evaluator: Catherine Nelson, Ph.D.
Student Researchers: Kristine Medeiros and Pla Herr

According to journalist Jason Leopold, sources at former Cheney company Halliburton allege that, as recently as January of 2005, Halliburton sold key components for a nuclear reactor to an Iranian oil development company. Leopold says his Halliburton sources have intimate knowledge of the business dealings of both Halliburton and Oriental Oil Kish, one of Iran's largest private oil companies.

Additionally, throughout 2004 and 2005, Halliburton worked closely with Cyrus Nasseri, the vice chairman of the board of directors of Iran-based Oriental Oil Kish, to develop oil projects in Iran. Nasseri is also a key member of Iran's nuclear development team. Nasseri was interrogated by Iranian authorities in late July 2005 for allegedly providing Halliburton with Iran's nuclear secrets. Iranian government officials charged Nasseri with accepting as much as $1 million in bribes from Halliburton for this information.

Oriental Oil Kish dealings with Halliburton first became public knowledge in January 2005 when the company announced that it had subcontracted parts of the South Pars gas-drilling project to Halliburton Products and Services, a subsidiary of Dallas-based Halliburton that is registered to the Cayman Islands. Following the announcement, Halliburton claimed that the South Pars gas field project in Tehran would be its last project in Iran. According to a BBC report, Halliburton, which took thirty to forty million dollars from its Iranian operations in 2003, "was winding down its work due to a poor business environment."

However, Halliburton has a long history of doing business in Iran, starting as early as 1995, while Vice President Cheney was chief executive of the company. Leopold quotes a February 2001 report published in the *Wall Street Journal*, "Halliburton Products and Services Ltd., works behind an unmarked door on the ninth floor of a new north Tehran tower block. A brochure declares that the company was registered in 1975 in the Cayman Islands, is based in the Persian Gulf sheikdom of Dubai and is "non-American." But like the sign over the receptionist's head, the brochure bears the company's name and red emblem, and offers services from Halliburton units around the world." Moreover mail sent to the company's offices in Tehran and the Cayman Islands is forwarded directly to its Dallas headquarters.

In an attempt to curtail Halliburton and other U.S. companies from engaging in business dealings with rogue nations such as Libya, Iran, and Syria, an amendment was approved in the Senate on July 26, 2005. The amendment, sponsored by Senator Susan Collins R-Maine, would penalize companies that continue to skirt U.S. law by setting up offshore subsidiaries as a way to legally conduct and avoid U.S. sanctions under the International Emergency Economic Powers Act (IEEPA).

A letter, drafted by trade groups representing corporate executives, vehemently objected to the amendment, saying it would lead to further hatred and perhaps incite terrorist attacks on the U.S. and "greatly strain relations with the United States primary trading partners." The letter warned that, "Foreign governments view U.S. efforts to dictate their foreign and commercial policy as violations of sovereignty often leading them to adopt retaliatory measures more at odds with U.S. goals."

Collins supports the legislation, stating, "It prevents U.S. corporations from creating a shell company somewhere else in order to do business with rogue, terror-sponsoring nations such as Syria and Iran. The bottom line is that if a U.S. company is evading sanctions to do business with one of these countries, they are helping to prop up countries that support terrorism—most often aimed against America.

UPDATE BY JASON LEOPOLD
During a trip to the Middle East in March 1996, Vice President Dick Cheney told a group of mostly U.S. businessmen that Congress should ease sanctions in Iran and Libya to foster better relationships, a statement that, in hindsight, is completely hypocritical considering the Bush administration's foreign policy.

"Let me make a generalized statement about a trend I see in the U.S. Congress that I find disturbing, that applies not only with respect to the Iranian situation but a number of others as well," Cheney said. "I think we Americans sometimes make mistakes . . . There seems to be an assumption that somehow we know what's best for everybody else and that we are going to use our economic clout to get everybody else to live the way we would like."

Cheney was the chief executive of Halliburton Corporation at the time he uttered those words. It was Cheney who directed Halliburton toward aggressive business dealings with Iran—in violation of U.S. law—in the mid-1990s, which continued through 2005 and is the reason Iran has the capability to enrich weapons-grade uranium.

It was Halliburton's secret sale of centrifuges to Iran that helped get the uranium enrichment program off the ground, according to a three-year investigation that includes interviews conducted with more than a dozen current and former Halliburton employees.

If the U.S. ends up engaged in a war with Iran in the future, Cheney and Halliburton will bear the brunt of the blame.

But this shouldn't come as a shock to anyone who has been following Halliburton's business activities over the past decade. The company has a long, documented history of violating U.S. sanctions and conducting business with so-called rogue nations.

No, what's disturbing about these facts is how little attention it has received from the mainstream media. But the public record speaks for itself, as do the thousands of pages of documents obtained by various federal agencies that show how Halliburton's business dealings in Iran helped fund terrorist activities there—including the country's nuclear enrichment program.

When I asked Wendy Hall, a spokeswoman for Halliburton, a couple of years ago if Halliburton would stop doing business with Iran because of concerns that the company helped fund terrorism she said, "No."

"We believe that decisions as to the nature of such governments and their actions are better made by governmental authorities and international entities such as the United Nations as opposed to individual persons or companies," Hall said. "Putting politics aside, we and our affiliates operate in countries to the extent it is legally permissible, where our customers are active as they expect us to provide oilfield services support to their international operations.

"We do not always agree with policies or actions of governments in every place that we do business and make no excuses for their behaviors. Due to the long-term nature of our business and the inevitability of political and social change, it is neither prudent nor appropriate for our company to establish our own country-by-country foreign policy."

Halliburton first started doing business in Iran as early as 1995, while Vice President Cheney was chief executive of the company and in possible violation of U.S. sanctions.

An executive order signed by former President Bill Clinton in March 1995 prohibits "new investments (in Iran) by U.S. persons, including commitment of funds or other assets." It also bars U.S. companies from performing services "that would benefit the Iranian oil industry" and provide Iran with the financial means to engage in terrorist activity.

When Bush and Cheney came into office in 2001, their administration decided it would not punish foreign oil and gas companies that invest in those countries. The sanctions imposed on countries like Iran and Libya before Bush became president were blasted by Cheney, who gave frequent speeches on the need for U.S. companies to compete with their foreign competitors, despite claims that those countries may have ties to terrorism.

"I think we'd be better off if we, in fact, backed off those sanctions (on Iran), didn't try to impose secondary boycotts on companies . . . trying to do business over there . . . and instead started to rebuild those relationships," Cheney said during a 1998 business trip to Sydney, Australia, according to Australia's *Illawarra Mercury* newspaper.

3
Oceans of the World in Extreme Danger

Source:
Mother Jones, March/April 2006
Title: "The Fate of the Ocean"
Author: Julia Whitty

Faculty Evaluator: Dolly Freidel, Ph.D.
Student Researcher: Charlene Jones

Oceanic problems once found on a local scale are now pandemic. Data from oceanography, marine biology, meteorology, fishery science, and glaciology reveal that the seas are changing in ominous ways. A vortex of cause and effect wrought by global environmental dilemmas is changing the ocean from a watery horizon with assorted regional troubles to a global system in alarming distress.

According to oceanographers the oceans are one, with currents linking the seas and regulating climate. Sea temperature and chemistry changes, along with contamination and reckless fishing practices, intertwine to imperil the world's largest communal life source.

In 2005, researchers from the Scripps Institution of Oceanography and the Lawrence Livermore National Laboratory found clear evidence the ocean is quickly warming. They discovered that the top half-mile of the ocean has warmed dramatically in the past forty years as a result of human-induced greenhouse gases.

One manifestation of this warming is the melting of the Arctic. A shrinking ratio of ice to water has set off a feedback loop, accelerating the increase in water surfaces that promote further warming and melting. With polar waters growing fresher and tropical seas saltier, the cycle of evaporation and precipitation has quickened, further invigorating the greenhouse effect. The ocean's currents are reacting to this freshening, causing a critical conveyor that carries warm upper waters into Europe's northern latitudes to slow by one third since 1957, bolstering fears of a shut down and cataclysmic climate change. This accelerating cycle of cause and effect will be difficult, if not impossible, to reverse.

Atmospheric litter is also altering sea chemistry, as thousands of toxic compounds poison marine creatures and devastate propagation. The ocean has absorbed an estimated 118 billion metric tons of carbon dioxide since the onset of the Industrial Revolution, with 20 to 25 tons being added to the atmosphere daily. Increasing acidity from rising levels of CO_2 is changing the ocean's PH balance. Studies indicate that the shells and skeletons possessed by everything from reef-building corals to mollusks and plankton begin to dissolve within forty-eight hours of exposure to the acidity expected in the ocean by 2050. Coral reefs will almost certainly disappear and, even more worrisome, so will plankton. Phytoplankton absorb greenhouse gases, manufacture oxygen, and are the primary producers of the marine food web.

Mercury pollution enters the food web via coal and chemical industry waste, oxidizes in the atmosphere, and settles to the sea bottom. There it is consumed, delivering mercury to each subsequent link in the food chain, until predators such as tuna or whales carry levels of mercury as much as one million times that of the waters around them. The Gulf of Mexico has the highest mercury levels ever recorded, with an average of ten tons of mercury coming down the Mississippi River every year, and another ton added by offshore drilling.

Along with mercury, the Mississippi delivers nitrogen (often from fertilizers). Nitrogen stimulates plant and bacterial growth in the water that consume oxygen, creating a condition known as hypoxia, or dead zones. Dead zones occur wherever oceanic oxygen is depleted below the level necessary to sustain marine life. A sizable portion of the Gulf of Mexico has become a dead zone—the largest such area in the U.S. and the second largest on the planet, measuring nearly 8,000 square miles in 2001. It is no coincidence that almost all of the nearly 150 (and counting) dead zones on earth lay at the mouths of rivers. Nearly fifty fester off U.S. coasts. While most are caused by river-borne nitrogen, fossil fuel-burning plants help create this condition, as does phosphorous from human sewage and nitrogen emissions from auto exhaust.

Meanwhile, since its peak in 2000, the global wild fish harvest has begun a sharp decline despite progress in seagoing technologies and intensified fishing. So-called efficiencies in fishing have stimulated unprecedented decimation of sealife. Long-lining, in which a single boat sets line across sixty or more miles of ocean, each baited with up to 10,000 hooks, captures at least 25 percent unwanted catch. With an estimated 2 billion hooks set each year, as much as 88 billion pounds of life a year is thrown back to the ocean either dead or dying. Additionally, trawlers drag nets across every square inch of the continental shelves every two years. Fishing the sea floor like a bulldozer, they level an area 150 times larger than all forest clearcuts each year and destroy seafloor ecosystems. Aquaculture is no better, since three pounds of wild fish are caught to feed every pound of farmed salmon. A 2003 study out of Dalhousie University in Nova Scotia concluded, based on data dating from the 1950s, that in the wake of decades of such onslaught only 10 percent of all large fish (tuna, swordfish) and ground fish (cod, hake, flounder) are left anywhere in the ocean.

Other sea nurseries are also threatened. Fifteen percent of sea-grass beds have disappeared in the last ten years, depriving juvenile fish, manatees, and sea turtles of critical habitats. Kelp beds are also dying at alarming rates.

While at no time in history has science taught more about how the earth's life-support systems work, the maelstrom of human assault on the seas continues. If human failure in governance of the world's largest public domain is not reversed quickly, the ocean will soon and surely reach a point of no return.

Comment: After release of the Pew Oceans Commission report, U.S. media, most notably *The Washington Post* and National Public Radio in 2003 and 2004, covered several stories regarding impending threats to the ocean, recommendations for protection, and President Bush's response. However, media treatment of the collective acceleration of ocean damage and cross-pollination of harm was left to Julia Whitty in her lengthy feature. In April of 2006, *Time Magazine* presented an in-depth article about earth at "the tipping point," describing the planet as an overworked organism fighting the consequences of global climate change on shore and sea. In her *Mother Jones* article, Whitty presented a look at global illness by directly examining the ocean as earth's circulatory, respiratory, and reproductive system.

Following up on "The Last Days of the Ocean," *Mother Jones* has produced "Ocean Voyager," an innovative web-based adventure that includes videos, audio interviews with key players, webcams, and links to informative web pages created by more than twenty organizations. The site is a tour of various ocean trouble spots around the world, which highlights solutions and suggests actions that can be taken to help make a difference.

UPDATE BY JULIA WHITTY

This story is awash with new developments. Scientists are currently publishing at an unprecedented rate their observations—not just pre-dictions—on the rapid changes underway on our ocean planet. First and foremost, the year 2005 turned out to be the warmest year on record. This reinforces other data showing the earth has grown hotter in the past 400 years, and possibly in the past 2,000 years. A study out of the National Center for Atmospheric Research found ocean temperatures in the tropical North Atlantic in 2005 nearly two degrees

Fahrenheit above normal; this turned out to be the predominant catalyst for the monstrous 2005 hurricane season—the most violent season ever seen.

The news from the polar ice is no better. A joint NASA/University
of Kansas study in *Science* (02/06) reveals that Greenland's glaciers
are surging towards the sea and melting more than twice as fast as ten
years ago. This further endangers the critical balance of the North
Atlantic meridional overturning circulation, which holds our climate
stable. Meanwhile, in March, the British Antarctic Survey announced
their findings that the "global warming signature" of the Antarctic is
three times larger than what we're seeing elsewhere on Earth—the
first proof of broadscale climate change across the southern continent.

Since "The Fate of the Ocean" went to press in *Mother Jones* magazine, evidence of the politicization of science in the global climate
wars has also emerged. In January 2006 NASA's top climate scientist, James Hansen, accused the agency of trying to censor his work.
Four months later, Hansen's accusations were echoed by scientists at
the National Oceanic and Atmospheric Administration, as well as by
a U.S. Geological Survey scientist working at a NOAA lab, who
claimed their work on global climate change was being censored by
their departments, as part of a policy of intimidation by the anti-sci-
ence Bush administration.

Problems for the ocean's wildlife are escalating too. In 2005, biol-
ogists from the U.S. Minerals Management Service found polar bears
drowned in the waters off Alaska, apparent victims of the disappearing ice. In 2006, U.S. Geological Survey Alaska Science Center
researchers found polar bears killing and eating each other in areas
where sea ice failed to form that year, leaving the bears bereft of food.
In response, the International Union for the Conservation of Nature
and Natural Resources revised their Red List for polar bears—
upgrading them from "conservation dependent" to "vulnerable." In
February, the U.S. Fish and Wildlife Service announced it would
begin reviewing whether polar bears need protection under the
Endangered Species Act.

Since my report, the leaders of two influential commissions—the
Pew Oceans Commission and the U.S. Commission on Ocean
Policy—gave Congress, the Bush administration, and our nation's gov-
ernors a "D+" grade for not moving quickly enough to address their
recommendations for restoring health to our nation's oceans.

Most of these stories remain out of view, sunk with cement boots in the backwaters of scientific journals. The media remains unable to discern good science from bad, and gives equal credence to both, when they give any at all. The story of our declining ocean world, and our own future, develops beyond the ken of the public, who forge ahead without altering behavior or goals, and unimpeded by foresight.

4

Hunger and Homelessness Increasing in the U.S.

Sources:

The New Standard, December 2005
Title: "New Report Shows Increase in Urban Hunger, Homelessness"
Author: Brendan Coyne

OneWorld.net, March 2006
Title: "U.S. Plan to Eliminate Survey of Needy Families Draws Fire"
Author: Abid Aslam

Faculty Evaluator: Myrna Goodman, Ph.D.
Student Researchers: Arlene Ward and Brett Forest

The number of hungry and homeless people in U.S. cities continued to grow in 2005, despite claims of an improved economy. Increased demand for vital services rose as needs of the most destitute went unmet, according to the annual *U.S. Conference of Mayors Report*, which has documented increasing need since its 1982 inception.

The study measures instances of emergency food and housing assistance in twenty-four U.S. cities and utilizes supplemental information from the U.S. Census and Department of Labor. More than three-quarters of cities surveyed reported increases in demand for food and housing, especially among families. Food aid requests expanded by 12 percent in 2005, while aid center and food bank resources grew by only 7 percent. Service providers estimated 18 percent of requests went unattended. Housing followed a similar trend, as a majority of cities reported an increase in demand for emergency shelter, often going unmet due to lack of resources.

As urban hunger and homelessness increases in America, the Bush administration is planning to eliminate a U.S. survey widely used to improve federal and state programs for low-income and retired Americans, reports Abid Aslam.

President Bush's proposed budget for fiscal 2007, which begins October 2006, includes a Commerce Department plan to eliminate the Census Bureau's Survey of Income and Program Participation (SIPP). The proposal marks at least the third White House attempt in as many years to do away with federal data collection on politically prickly economic issues.

Founded in 1984, the Census Bureau survey follows American families for a number of years and monitors their use of Temporary Assistance for Needy Families (TANF), Social Security, Medicaid, unemployment insurance, child care, and other health, social service, and education programs.

Some 415 economists and social scientists signed a letter and sent it to Congress, shortly after the February release of Bush's federal budget proposal, urging that the survey be fully funded as it "is the only large-scale survey explicitly designed to analyze the impact of a wide variety of government programs on the well being of American families."

Heather Boushey, economist at the Washington, D.C.–based Center for Economic and Policy Research told Abid Aslam, "We need to know what the effects of these programs are on American families . . . SIPP is designed to do just that." Boushey added that the survey has proved invaluable in tracking the effects of changes in government programs. So much so that the 1996 welfare reform law specifically mentioned the survey as the best means to evaluate the law's effectiveness.

Supporters of the survey elimination say the program costs too much at $40 million per year. They would kill it in September and eventually replace it with a scaled-down version that would run to $9.2 million in development costs during the coming fiscal year. Actual data collection would begin in 2009.

Defenders of the survey counter that the cost is justified as SIPP "provides a constant stream of in-depth data that enables government, academic, and independent researchers to evaluate the effectiveness and improve the efficiency of several hundred billion dollars in spending on social programs," including homeless shelters and emergency food aid.

UPDATE BY ABID ASLAM

As of the end of May 2006, hundreds of economists and social scientists remain engaged in a bid to save the U.S. Census Bureau's Survey of Income and Program Participation (SIPP). Ideologically diverse users describe the survey as pioneering and say it has helped to improve the uptake and performance of, and to gauge the effects on American families of changes in public provisions ranging from Medicaid to Temporary Assistance to Needy Families and school lunch programs.

A few journalists took notice because users of the data, including the Washington-based Center for Economic and Policy Research (CEPR), which spearheaded the effort to save SIPP, chose to make some noise.

By most accounts, the matter was a simple fight over money: the administration was out to cut any hint of flesh from bureaucratic budgets (perhaps to feed its foreign policy pursuits) but users of the survey wanted the money spent on SIPP because, in their view, the program is valuable and no feasible alternative exists or has been proposed.

That debate remains to be resolved. Lobbyists expect more legislative action in June and among them, CEPR remains available to provide updates.

But is it just an isolated budget fight? This is the third time in as many years that the Bush administration has tried—and in the previous two cases, failed under pressure from users and advocates—to strip funding for awkward research. In 2003, it had tried to kill the Bureau of Labor Statistics (BLS) Mass Layoff Statistics report, which detailed where workplaces with more than fifty employees closed and what kinds of workers were affected. In 2004 and 2005, it had attempted to drop questions on the hiring and firing of women from employment data collected by the BLS. Hardly big-ticket items on the federal budget, the mass layoffs reports provided federal and state social service agencies with data crucial for planning even as it chronicled job losses and the so-called "jobless recovery." The women's questionnaire uncovered employment discrimination.

In other words, SIPP and the BLS programs are politically prickly. They highlight that, regardless of what some politicians and executives might say, economic and social problems persist and involve real people whose real needs remain to be met.

This calls to mind the old line about there being three kinds of lies: lies, damn lies, and statistics. To be convincing, they must be broadly consistent. If the numbers don't support the narrative, something simply must give. With the livelihoods, life chances, and rights of millions of citizens at stake, these are more than stories about arcane budget wrangles.

5

High-Tech Genocide in Congo

Sources:
The Taylor Report, March 28, 2005
Title: "The World's Most Neglected Emergency: Phil Taylor talks to Keith Harmon Snow"

Earth First! Journal, August 2005
Title: "High-Tech Genocide"
Author: Sprocket

Z Magazine, March 1, 2006
Title: "Behind the Numbers: Untold Suffering in the Congo"
Authors: Keith Harmon Snow and David Barouski

Faculty Evaluator: Thom Lough, Ph.D.
Student Researchers: Deyango Harris and Daniel Turner

The world's most neglected emergency, according to the UN Emergency Relief Coordinator, is the ongoing tragedy of the Congo, where six to seven million have died since 1996 as a consequence of invasions and wars sponsored by western powers trying to gain control of the region's mineral wealth. At stake is control of natural resources that are sought by U.S. corporations—diamonds, tin, copper, gold, and more significantly, coltan and niobium, two minerals necessary for production of cell phones and other high-tech electronics; and cobalt, an element essential to nuclear, chemical, aerospace, and defense industries.

Columbo-tantalite, i.e. coltan, is found in three-billion-year-old soils like those in the Rift Valley region of Africa. The tantalum extracted from the coltan ore is used to make tantalum capacitors, tiny components that are essential in managing the flow of current in electronic devices. Eighty percent of the world's coltan reserves are found in the Democratic Republic of Congo (DRC). Niobium is another high-tech mineral with a similar story.

Sprocket reports that the high-tech boom of the 1990s caused the price of coltan to skyrocket to nearly $300 per pound. In 1996 U.S.-sponsored Rwandan and Ugandan forces entered eastern DRC. By 1998 they seized control and moved into strategic mining areas. The Rwandan Army was soon making $20 million or more a month from coltan mining. Though the price of coltan has fallen, Rwanda maintains its monopoly on coltan and the coltan trade in DRC. Reports of rampant human rights abuses pour out of this mining region.

Coltan makes its way out of the mines to trading posts where foreign traders buy the mineral and ship it abroad, mostly through Rwanda. Firms with the capability turn coltan into the coveted tantalum powder, and then sell the magic powder to Nokia, Motorola, Compaq, Sony, and other manufacturers for use in cell phones and other products.

Keith Harmon Snow emphasizes that any analysis of the geopolitics in the Congo, and the reasons for why the Congolese people have suffered a virtually unending war since 1996, requires an understanding of the organized crime perpetrated through multinational businesses. The tragedy of the Congo conflict has been instituted by invested corporations, their proxy armies, and the supra-governmental bodies that support them.

The process is tied to major multinational corporations at all levels. These include U.S.-based Cabot Corp. and OM Group; HC Starck of Germany; and Nigncxia of China—corporations that have been linked by a United Nations Panel of Experts to the atrocities in DRC. Extortion, rape, massacres, and bribery are all part of the criminal networks set up and maintained by huge multinational companies. Yet as mining in the Congo by western companies proceeds at an unprecedented rate—some $6 million in raw cobalt alone exiting DRC daily—multinational mining companies rarely get mentioned in human rights reports.

Sprocket notes that Sam Bodman, CEO of Cabot during the coltan boom, was appointed in December 2004 to serve as President Bush's Secretary of Energy. Under Bodman's leadership from 1987 to 2000, Cabot was one of the U.S.'s largest polluters, accounting for 60,000 tons of airborne toxic emissions annually. Snow adds that Sony's current Executive Vice President and General Counsel Nicole Seligman was a former legal adviser for Bill Clinton. Many who held positions of power in the Clinton administration moved into high positions with Sony.

The article "Behind the Numbers," coauthored by Snow and David Barouski, details a web of U.S. corruption and conflicts of interest between mining corporations such as Barrick Gold (see Story #21) and the U.S. government under George H. W. Bush, Bill Clinton, and George W. Bush, as well as U.S. arms dealers such as Simax; U.S. defense companies such as Lockheed Martin, Halliburton, Northrop Grumman, GE, Boeing, Raytheon, and Bechtel; "humanitarian" organizations such as CARE, funded by Lockheed Martin, and International Rescue Committee, whose Board of Overseers includes Henry Kissinger; "Conservation" interests that provide the vanguard for western penetration into Central Africa; and of course, PR firms and news outlets such as the *New York Times*.

Sprocket closes his article by noting that it's not surprising this information isn't included in the literature and manuals that come with your cell phones, pagers, computers, or diamond jewelry. Perhaps, he suggests, mobile phones should be outfitted with stickers that read: "Warning! This device was created with raw materials from central Africa. These materials are rare, nonrenewable, were sold to fund a bloody war of occupation, and have caused the virtual elimination of endangered species. Have a nice day." People need to realize, he says, that there is a direct link between the gadgets that make our lives more convenient and sophisticated—and the reality of the violence, turmoil, and destruction that plague our world.

UPDATE BY SPROCKET

There are large fortunes to be made in the manufacturing of high-tech electronics and in selling convenience and entertainment to American consumers, but at what cost?

Conflicts in Africa are often shrouded with misinformation, while U.S. and other western interests are routinely downplayed or omitted by the corporate media. The June 5, 2006, cover story of *Time*, entitled "Congo: The Hidden Toll of the World's Deadliest War," was no exception. Although the article briefly mentioned coltan and its use in cell phones and other electronic devices, no mention was made of the pivotal role this and other raw materials found in the region play in the conflict. The story painted the ongoing war as a pitiable and horrible tragedy, avoiding the corporations and foreign governments that have created the framework for the violence and those which have strong financial and political interests in the conflict's outcome.

In an article written by Johann Hari and published by *The Hamilton Spectator* on May 13, 2006, the corporate media took a step toward addressing the true reason for the tremendous body count that continues to pile up in the Democratic Republic of Congo: "The only change over the decades has been the resources snatched for Western consumption—rubber under the Belgians, diamonds under Mobutu, coltan and casterite today."

Most disturbing is that in the corporate media, the effect of this conflict on nonhuman life is totally overlooked. Even with a high-profile endangered species like the Eastern lowland gorilla hanging in the balance, almost driven to extinction through poaching and habitat loss by displaced villagers and warring factions, the environmental angle of the story is rarely considered.

The next step in understanding the exploitation and violence wrought upon the inhabitants of central Africa, fueled by the hunger for high-tech toys in the U.S., is to expose corporations like Sony and Motorola. These corporations don't want protest movements tarnishing their reputations. Nor do they want to call attention to all of the gorillas coltan kills, and the guerrillas it feeds.

It is time for our culture to start seeing more value in living beings, whether gorillas or humans, than in our disposable high-tech gadgets such as cell phones. It is time to steal back a more compassionate existence from the corporate plutocracy that creates destructive markets and from the media system that has manufactured our consent.

It is not just a question of giving up cell phones (though that would be a great start). We must question the appropriation of our planet in the form of a resource to be consumed, rather than as a home and community to be lived in.

"High-Tech Genocide" and other articles about cell phone technology are available by contacting the author: sprocket@riseup.net.

UPDATE BY KEITH HARMON SNOW

War for the control of the Democratic Republic of Congo—what should be the richest country in the world—began in Uganda in the

1980s, when now Ugandan President Yoweri Museveni shot his way to power with the backing of Buckingham Palace, the White House, and Tel Aviv behind him.

Paul Kagame, now president of Rwanda, served as Museveni's Director of Military Intelligence. Kagame later trained at Fort Leavenworth, Kansas, before the Rwandan Patriotic Front (RPF)— backed by Roger Winter, the U.S. Committee on Refugees, and the others above—invaded Rwanda. The RPF destabilized and then secured Rwanda. This coup d'etat is today misunderstood as the "Rwanda Genocide." What played out in Rwanda in 1994 is now playing out in Darfur, Sudan; regime change is the goal, "genocide" is the tool of propaganda used to manipulate and disinform.

In 1996, Paul Kagame and Yoweri Museveni, with the Pentagon behind them, launched their covert war against Zaire's Mobutu Sese Seko and his western backers. A decade later, there are 6 or 7 million dead, at the very least, and the war in Congo (Zaire) continues.

If you are reading the mainstream newspapers or listening to National Public Radio, you are contributing to your own mental illness, no matter how astute you believe yourself to be at "balancing" or "deciphering" the code.

News reports in *Time Magazine* ("The Deadliest War In The World," June 6, 2006) and on CNN ("Rape, Brutality Ignored to Aid Congo Peace," May 26, 2006) that appeared at the time of this writing are being interpreted by conscious people to be truth-telling at last. However, these are perfect examples filled with hidden deceptions and manipulations.

For accuracy and truth on Central Africa, look to people like Robin Philpot (*Imperialism Dies Hard*), Wayne Madsen (*Genocide and Covert Operations in Africa, 1993–1999*), Amos Wilson (*The Falsification of Consciousness*), Charles Onana (*The Secrets of the Rwanda Genocide—Investigation on the Mysteries of a President*), Antoine Lokongo (www.congopanorama.info), Phil Taylor (www.taylor-report.com), Christopher Black ("Racism, Murder and Lies in Rwanda"). World War 4 Report has published my reports, but they are inconsistent in their attention to accuracy, and would as quickly adopt the propaganda, and have done so at times.

It is possible to collect little fragments of truth here and there— *never* counting on the mainstream system for this—but one must beware the deceptions and bias. In this vein, the elite business journal *Africa Confidential* is often very revealing. Some facts can be gleaned from www.DigitalCongo.net and *Africa Research Bulletin*.

Professor David Gibb's book *The Political Economy of Third World Intervention: Case of the Congo Crises* is an excellent backgrounder that identifies players still active today (especially Maurice Tempelsman and his diamonds interests connected to the Democratic Party). Ditto *King Leopold's Ghost* by Adam Hocshchild, but—exemplifying the expedience of "interests"—remember that Hocshchild never tells you, the reader, that his father ran a mining company in Congo. Almost ALL reportage is *expedient*; one needs take care their propensity to be deceived.

Professor Ruth Mayer's book *Artificial Africas: Colonial Images in the Times of Globalization* is a particularly poignant articulation of the means by which the "media" system distorts and manipulates all things African. And, never forget www.AllThingsPass.com.

Also hoping to correct the record and reveal the truth, the International Forum for Truth and Justice in the Great Lakes of Africa (www.veritasrwandaforum.org), based in Spain, and co-founded by Nobel Prize nominee Juan Carrero Seraleegui, is involved in a groundbreaking lawsuit charging massive crimes against humanity and acts of genocide were committed by the now government of Rwanda.

6

Federal Whistleblower Protection in Jeopardy

Source:
Public Employees for Environmental Responsibility website
Titles: "Whistleblowers Get Help from Bush Administration," December 5, 2005
    "Long-Delayed Investigation of Special Counsel Finally Begins," October 18, 2005
    "Back Door Rollback of Federal Whistleblower Protections," September 22, 2005
Author: Jeff Ruch

Faculty Evaluator: Barbara Bloom, Ph.D.
Student Researchers: Caitlyn Peele and Sara-Joy Christienson

Special Counsel Scott Bloch, appointed by President Bush in 2004, is overseeing the virtual elimination of federal whistleblower rights in the U.S. government.

The U.S. Office of Special Counsel (OSC), the agency that is supposed to protect federal employees who blow the whistle on waste, fraud, and abuse is dismissing hundreds of cases while advancing almost none. According to the Annual Report for 2004 (which was not released until the end of first quarter fiscal year 2006) less than 1.5 percent of whistleblower claims were referred for investigation while more than 1000 reports were closed before they were even opened. Only eight claims were found to be substantiated, and one of those included the theft of a desk, while another included attendance violations. Favorable outcomes have declined 24 percent overall, and this is all in the first year that the new special counsel, Scott Bloch, has been in office.

Bloch, who has received numerous complaints since he took office, defends his first thirteen months in office by pointing to a decline in backlogged cases. Public Employees for Environmental Responsibility (PEER) Executive Director Jeff Ruch says, ". . . backlogs and delays are bad, but they are not as bad as simply dumping the cases altogether." According to figures released by Bloch in February of 2005 more than 470 claims of retaliation were dismissed, and not once had he affirmatively represented a whistleblower. In fact, in order to speed dismissals, Bloch instituted a rule forbidding his staff from contacting a whistleblower if their disclosure was deemed incomplete or ambiguous. Instead, the OSC would dismiss the matter. As a result, hundreds of whistleblowers never had a chance to justify their cases. Ruch notes that these numbers are limited to only the backlogged cases and do not include new ones.

On March 3, 2005, OSC staff members joined by a coalition of whistleblower protection and civil rights organizations filed a complaint against Bloch. His own employees accused him of violating the very rules he is supposed to be enforcing. The complaint specifies instances of illegal gag orders, cronyism, invidious discrimination, and retaliation by forcing the resignation of one-fifth of the OSC headquarters legal and investigative staff. The complaint was filed with the President's Council on Integrity and Efficiency, which took no action on the case for seven months. PEER was one of the groups who co-filed the complaint against Bloch and Ruch wants to know, "Who watches the watchdogs?"

This is the third probe into Bloch's operation in less than two years in office. Both the Government Accountability Office and a U.S. Senate subcommittee have ongoing investigations into mass dismissals of whistleblower cases, crony hires, and Bloch's targeting of gay employees for removal while refusing to investigate cases involving discrimination on the basis of sexual orientation.

The Department of Labor has also gotten on board in a behind-the-scenes maneuver to cancel whistleblower protections. If it succeeds, the Labor Department will dismiss claims by federal workers who report violations under the Clean Air Act and the Safe Drinking Water Act. General Counsel for PEER, Richard Condit says, "Federal workers in agencies such as the Environmental Protection Agency function as the public's eyes and ears . . . the Labor Department is moving to shut down one of the few legal avenues left to whistleblowers." The Labor Department is trying to invoke the ancient doctrine of sovereign immunity, which says that the government cannot be sued without its consent. The Secretary of Labor's Administrative Review Board recently invited the EPA to raise a sovereign immunity defense in a case where a woman was trying to enforce earlier victories. Government Accountability Project General Counsel Joanne Royce sums up major concerns: "We do not want public servants wondering whether they will lose their jobs for acting against pollution violations of politically well-connected interests."

UPDATE BY JEFF RUCH

With the decline in oversight by the U.S. Congress and the uneven quality of investigative journalism, outlets such as the U.S. Office of Special Counsel become even more important channels for governmental transparency. Unfortunately, under the Bush-appointed Special Counsel, this supposed haven for whistleblowers has become a beacon of false hope for thousands.

Each year, hundreds of civil servants who witness problems ranging from threats to public safety to waste of tax funds find that their reports of wrongdoing are stonewalled by the Office of Special Counsel (OSC). Consequently, these firsthand accounts of malfeasance are not investigated and almost uniformly never reach the public's attention.

The importance of this state of affairs is that the actual workings of federal agencies are becoming more shrouded in secrecy and disinformation. Americans are less informed about their government and less able to be in connection with the people who actually work for them—the public servants.

In a recent development, employees within the OSC have filed a whistleblower complaint about the Special Counsel, the person who is supposed to be the chief whistleblower defender. After several months delay, the Bush White House assigned this complaint to the Inspector General for the Office of Personnel Management for review. This supposedly independent investigation has just begun in earnest, nearly one year after the complaint was filed.

Also, the Government Accountability Office (GAO) issued a report in May 2006 blasting the Bush-appointed Special Counsel for ignoring competitive bidding rules in handing out consultant contracts. GAO also recommended creating an independent channel whereby Office of Special Counsel employees can blow the whistle on further abuses by the Special Counsel.

In another recent development, PEER's lawsuit against the Special Counsel to force release of documents concerning crony hires has produced more, heavily redacted documents showing that these sole source consultants apparently did no identifiable work. Ironically, the PEER suit was filed under the Freedom of Information Act, a law that the Special Counsel is also charged with policing.

And in a new annual report to Congress, OSC (stung by criticism about declining performance) has, for the first time, stopped disclosing the number of whistleblower cases where it obtained a favorable outcome. Consequently, it is impossible to tell if anyone is actually being helped by the agency.

PEER's web page on the Office of Special Counsel has posted all developments since this story and also allows a reader to trace the story's genesis.

7

U.S. Operatives Torture Detainees to Death in Afghanistan and Iraq

Sources:

American Civil Liberties Website, October 24, 2005
Title: "U.S. Operatives Killed Detainees During Interrogations in Afghanistan and Iraq"

TomDispatch.com, March 5, 2006
Title: "Tracing the Trail of Torture: Embedding Torture as Policy from Guantanamo to Iraq"
Author: Dahr Jamail

Community Evaluator: Rabbi Michael Robinson, Ph.D.
Student Researchers: Michael B. Januleski Jr. and Jessica Rodas

The American Civil Liberties Union (ACLU) released documents of forty-four autopsies held in Afghanistan and Iraq October 25, 2005. Twenty-one of those deaths were listed as homicides. The documents show that detainees died during and after interrogations by Navy SEALs, Military Intelligence, and Other Government Agency (OGA).

"These documents present irrefutable evidence that U.S. operatives tortured detainees to death during interrogation," said Amrit Singh, an attorney with the ACLU. "The public has a right to know who authorized the use of torture techniques and why these deaths have been covered up."

The Department of Defense released the autopsy reports in response to a Freedom of Information Act request filed by the ACLU, the Center for Constitutional Rights, Physicians for Human Rights, Veterans for Common Sense, and Veterans for Peace.

One of forty-four U.S. military autopsy reports reads as follows: "Final Autopsy Report: DOD 003164, (Detainee) Died as a result of asphyxia (lack of oxygen to the brain) due to strangulation as evidenced by the recently fractured hyoid bone in the neck and soft tissue hemorrhage extending downward to the level of the right thyroid cartilage. Autopsy revealed bone fracture, rib fractures, contusions in mid abdomen, back and buttocks extending to the left flank, abrasions, lateral buttocks. Contusions, back of legs and knees; abrasions on knees, left fingers and encircling to left wrist. Lacerations and superficial cuts, right 4th and 5th fingers. Also, blunt force injuries, predominately recent contusions (bruises) on the torso and lower extremities. Abrasions on left wrist are consistent with use of restraints. No evidence of defense injuries or natural disease. Manner of death is homicide. Whitehorse Detainment Facility, Nasiriyah, Iraq."

Another report from the ACLU indicates: "a 27-year-old Iraqi male died while being interrogated by Navy Seals on April 5, 2004, in Mosul, Iraq. During his confinement he was hooded, flex-cuffed, sleep deprived and subjected to hot and cold environmental conditions, including the use of cold water on his body and head. The exact cause of death was 'undetermined' although the autopsy stated that hypothermia may have contributed to his death."

An overwhelming majority of the so-called "natural deaths" covered in the autopsies were attributed to "arteriosclerotic cardiovascular disease" (heart attack). Persons under extreme stress and pain may have heart attacks as a result of the circumstances of their detainments.

The Associated Press carried the story of the ACLU charges on their wire service. However, a thorough check of LexisNexis and ProQuest electronic data bases, using the keywords ACLU and autopsy, showed that at least 95 percent of the daily papers in the U.S. did not bother to pick up the story. The *Los Angeles Times* covered the story on page A4 with a 635-word report headlined "Autopsies Support Abuse Allegations." Fewer than a dozen other daily newspapers including: *Bangor Daily News*, Maine, page 8; *Telegraph-Herald*, Dubuque, Iowa, page 6; *Charleston Gazette*, page 5; *Advocate*, Baton Rouge, page 11; and a half dozen others actually covered the story. The *Pittsburgh Post-Gazette* and the *Seattle Times* buried the story inside general Iraq news articles. *USA Today* posted the story on their website. MSNBC posted the story to their website, but apparently did not consider it newsworthy enough to air on television.

Janis Karpinski, U.S. Brigadier General Commander of the 800th Military Police Brigade, was in charge of seventeen prison facilities in Iraq during the Abu Ghraib scandal in 2003. Karpinski testified January 21, 2006 in New York City at the International Commission of Inquiry on Crimes against Humanity Committed by the Bush administration. Karpinski stated: "General [Ricardo] Sanchez [commander of coalition ground forces in Iraq] signed the eight-page memorandum authorizing a laundry list of harsh techniques in interrogations to include specific use of dogs and muzzled dogs with his specific permission." Karpinski went on to claim that Major General Geoffrey Miller, who had been "specifically selected by the Secretary of Defense to go to Guantanamo Bay and run the interrogations operations," was dispatched to Iraq by the Bush administration to "work with the military intelligence personnel to teach them new and improved interrogation techniques." When asked how far up the chain of command responsibility for the torture orders for Abu Ghraib went, Karpinski said, "The Secretary of Defense would not have authorized without the approval of the Vice President."

UPDATE BY DAHR JAMAIL

This story, published in March 2006, was merely a snapshot of the ongoing and worsening policy of the Bush administration regarding torture. And not just time, but places show snapshots of the criminal policy of the current administration—Iraq, like Guantánamo Bay, Cuba, Bagram Air Force Base in Afghanistan, and other "secret" U.S. military detention centers in Eastern European countries are physical examples of an ongoing policy which breaches both international law and our very constitution.

But breaking international and domestic law has not been a concern of an administration led by a "president" who has claimed "authority" to disobey over 750 laws passed by Congress. In fact, when this same individual does things like signing a secret order in 2002 which authorized the National Security Agency to violate the Foreign Intelligence Surveillance Act by wiretapping the phones of U.S. citizens, and then goes on to allow the secret collection of the telephone records of tens of millions of Americans, torture is but one portion of this corrupted picture. This is a critical ongoing story, not just because it violates international and domestic law, but this state-sanctioned brutality, bankrupt of any morality and decency, is already coming back home to haunt Americans. When U.S. soldiers are captured in Iraq or another foreign country, what basis does the U.S. have now to ask for their fair and humane treatment? And with police brutality and draconian "security" measures becoming more real within the U.S. with each passing day, why wouldn't these policies be visited upon U.S. citizens?

While torture is occasionally glimpsed by mainstream media outlets such as the *Washington Post* and *Time Magazine*, we must continue to rely on groups like the Center for Constitutional Rights in New York City, Human Rights Watch, and Amnesty International who cover the subject thoroughly, persistently, and unlike (of course) any corporate media outlets.

Since I wrote this story, there continues to be a deluge of information and proof of the Bush administration continuing and even widening their policy of torture, as well as their rendering prisoners to countries which have torturing human beings down to a science.

All of this, despite the fact that U.S. laws prohibit torture absolutely, clearly stating that torture is never, ever permitted, even in a time of war.

To stay current on this critical topic, please visit the following websites regularly:

http://www.amnesty.org/
http://www.hrw.org/
http://www.ccr-ny.org/v2/home.asp

8

Pentagon Exempt from Freedom of Information Act

Sources:

The New Standard, May 6, 2005
Title: "Pentagon Seeks Greater Immunity from Freedom of Information"
Author: Michelle Chen

Newspaper Association of America website, posted December 2005
Title: "FOIA Exemption Granted to Federal Agency"

Community Evaluator: Tim Ogburn
Student Researchers: Rachelle Cooper and Brian Murphy

The Department of Defense has been granted exemption from the Freedom of Information Act (FOIA). In December 2005, Congress passed the 2006 Defense Authorization Act which renders Defense Intelligence Agency (DIA) "operational files" fully immune to FOIA requests, the main mechanism by which watchdog groups, journalists and individuals can access federal documents. Of particular concern to critics of the Defense Authorization Act is the DIA's new right to thwart access to files that may reveal human rights violations tied to ongoing "counterterrorism" efforts.

The rule could, for instance, frustrate the work of the American Civil Liberties Union (ACLU) and other organizations that have relied on FOIA to uncover more than 30,000 documents on the U.S. military's involvement in the torture and mistreatment of foreign detainees in Afghanistan, Guantanamo Bay, and Iraq—including the Abu Ghraib scandal.

Several key documents that have surfaced in the advocacy organization's expansive research originate from DIA files, including a 2004 memorandum containing evidence that U.S. military interrogators brutalized detainees in Baghdad, as well as a report describing the abuse of Iraqi detainees as violations of international human rights law.

According to Jameel Jaffer, an ACLU attorney involved in the ongoing torture investigations, "If the Defense Intelligence Agency can rely on exception or exemption from the FOIA, then documents such as those that we obtained this last time around will not become public at all." The end result of such an exemption, he told *The New Standard*, is that "abuse is much more likely to take place, because there's not public oversight of Defense Intelligence Agency activity."

Jaffer added that because the DIA conducts investigations relating to other national security-related agencies, documents covered by the exemption could contain critical evidence of how other parts of the military operate as well.

The ACLU recently battled the FOIA exemption rule of the CIA in a lawsuit over the agency's attempt to withhold information concerning alleged abuse of Iraqi detainees. The CIA's defense centered on the invocation of FOIA exemption, and although a federal judge ultimately overrode the rule, Jaffer cited the case as evidence of "exemption creep"—the gradual stretching of the law to further shield federal agencies from public scrutiny.

According to language in the Defense Authorization Act, an operational file can be any information related to "the conduct of foreign intelligence or counterintelligence operations or intelligence or security liaison arrangements or information exchanges with foreign governments or their intelligence or security services."

Critics warn that such vague bureaucratic language is a green light for the DIA to thwart a wide array of legitimate information requests without proper justification. Steven Aftergood, director of the research organization Project on Government Secrecy, warns, "If it falls in the category of 'operational files,' it's over before it begins."

Thomas Blanton, director of the National Security Archive, adds, "These exemptions create a black hole into which the bureaucracy can drive just about any kind of information it wants to. And you can bet that Guantánamo, Abu Ghraib-style information is what DIA and others would want to hide."

The Newspaper Association of America reports that, due to lobbying efforts of the Sunshine in Government Initiative and other open government advocates, congressional negotiators imposed an unprecedented two-year "sunset" date on the Pentagon's FOIA exemption, ending in December 2007.

UPDATE BY MICHELLE CHEN

The DIA, the intelligence arm of the Department of Defense, has been a source for critical information on the Pentagon's foreign operations as well as the DIA's observations of the conduct of other branches of the military. Its request for immunity from the FOIA last year was not the first attempt to shield its data from members of the public, but it did come at a time that the government's antiterror fervor was beginning to crest.

Open-government groups warn that such an exemption from FOIA requests, which the Central Intelligence Agency already enjoys, would close off a major channel for information in a government bureaucracy already riddled with both formal and informal barriers of secrecy. The Pentagon's request alarmed groups like the ACLU, which has relied heavily on such data to build cases regarding torture and abuse of detainees in Iraq.

Since the article was published, the language proposed for the Defense Department budget for fiscal year 2006 was adopted.

The bill specifically refers to the immunity of "operational files," though this is somewhat ambiguously defined.

Another development in this issue over the past year is that secrecy and intelligence gathering have become intense domestic political issues. As a result, heightened public attention to the gradual rollback on open-government laws is beginning to stir some congressional action in the form of hearings and investigative reports, not just related to classified information per se but also the new quasi-classified categories that have cropped up since September 11.

Earlier this year, the Pentagon initiated a department-wide review of FOIA practices, though it is unclear whether this internal evaluation will lead to actual changes in how information is disclosed or withheld from public purview.

For more on this issue, see:

The Project on Government Secrecy, a watchdog group run by the American Federation of Scientists: http://www.fas.org/sgp/congress/2006/index.html

The National Security Archives at George Washington University, which has an extensive collection of FOIA documents and has issued numerous reports and studies on government secrecy and FOIA policies: http://www.gwu.edu/~nsarchiv/nsa/foia.html

The ACLU website: http://www.aclu.org/torturefoia/released/042005/

The GPO website: http://frwebgate.access.gpo.gov/cgi-bin/getdoc .cgi?dbname=109_cong_bills&docid=f:s1042pp.txt.pdf

The Pentagon's review of FOIA practices: http://www.defenselink .mil/pubs/foi/DoD_FOIA_Review.pdf

9

The World Bank Funds Israel-Palestine Wall

Sources:
Left Turn, Issue #18
Title: "Cementing Israeli Apartheid: The Role of World Bank"
Author: Jamal Juma'

Al-Jazeerah, March 9, 2005
Title: "U.S. Free Trade Agreements Split Arab Opinion"
Author: Linda Heard

Community Evaluator: April Hurley, M.D.
Student Researchers: Bailey Malone and Lisa Dobias

Despite the 2004 International Court of Justice (ICJ) decision that called for tearing down the Wall and compensating affected communities, construction of the Wall has accelerated. The route of the barrier runs deep into Palestinian territory, aiding the annexation of Israeli settlements and the breaking of Palestinian territorial continuity. The World Bank's vision of "economic development," however, evades any discussion of the Wall's illegality.

The World Bank has meanwhile outlined the framework for a Palestinian Middle East Free Trade Area (MEFTA) policy in their most recent report on Palestine published in December of 2004, "Stagnation or Revival: Israeli Disengagement and Palestinian Economic Prospects."

Central to World Bank proposals are the construction of massive industrial zones to be financed by the World Bank and other donors and controlled by the Israeli Occupation. Built on Palestinian land around the Wall, these industrial zones are envisaged as forming the basis of export-orientated economic development. Palestinians imprisoned by the Wall and dispossessed of land can be put to work for low wages.

The post-Wall MEFTA vision includes complete control over Palestinian movement. The report proposes high-tech military gates and checkpoints along the Wall, through which Palestinians and exports can be conveniently transported and controlled. A supplemental "transfer system" of walled roads and tunnels will allow Palestinian workers to be funneled to their jobs, while being simultaneously denied access to their land. Sweatshops will be one of very few possibilities of earning a living for Palestinians confined to disparate ghettos throughout the West Bank. The World Bank states:

> "In an improved operating environment, Palestinian entrepreneurs and foreign investors will look for well-serviced industrial land and supporting infrastructure. They will also seek a regulatory regime with a minimum of 'red tape' and with clear procedures for conducting business. Industrial Estates (IEs), particularly those on the border between Palestinian and Israeli territory, can fulfill this need and thereby play an important role in supporting export based growth."

Jamal Juma' notes that the "red tape" which the World Bank refers to can be presumed to mean trade unions, a minimum wage, good working conditions, environmental protection, and other workers' rights that will be more flexible than the ones in the "developed" world. The World Bank explicitly states that current wages of Palestinians are too high for the region and "compromise the international competitiveness" even though wages are only a quarter of the average in Israel. Juma' warns that on top of a military occupation and forced expulsion, Palestinians are to be subjects of an economic colonialism.

These industrial zones will clearly benefit Israel abroad where goods "Made in Palestine" have more favorable trade conditions in international markets. IPS reporter Emad Mekay, in February 2005, revealed the World Bank's plan to partially fund Palestinian MEFTA infrastructure with loans to Palestine. Israel is not eligible for World Bank lending because of its high per capita income, but Palestine is. Mekay quotes Terry Walz of the Washington-based Council for the National Interest, a group that monitors U.S. and international policy towards Israel and the Palestinians: "I must admit that making the Palestinians pay for the modernization of these checkpoints is an embarrassment, since they had nothing to do with the erection of the separation wall to begin with and in fact have protested it. I think the whole issue is extremely murky."[1]

Mekay goes on to note that this is the first time the World Bank appears ready to get actively involved in the Israeli occupation of Palestinian land. Former World Bank president James Wolfensohn rejected this possibility last year. Neo-conservative Paul Wolfowitz was, however, confirmed as president of the World Bank on June 1, 2005.

In breach of the ICJ ruling, the U.S. has already contributed $50 million to construct gates along the Wall to "help serve the needs of Palestinians."

Linda Heard reports for Al-Jazeerah that the U.S. is currently pushing for bilateral Free Trade Agreements (FTAs) with various Arab states, including members of the Gulf Cooperation Council (GCC), as part of a vision for a larger Middle East Free Trade Agreement. President Bush hopes the MEFTA will encompass some twenty regional countries, including Israel, and be fully consolidated by 2013.

Many in the region are suspicious of the divisive trend of bilateral agreements with the U.S. and worry that the GCC will end up with small, fragmented satellite economies without any leverage against world giants. Prince Saud Al-Faisal, the Saudi foreign minister, stated, "It is alarming to see some members of the GCC enter into separate agreements with international powers . . . They diminish the collective bargaining power and weaken not only the solidarity of the GCC as a whole, but also each of its members."

Note

1. Emad Mekay, "World Bank and U.S.: Palestinians Should Pay for Israeli Checkpoints," *IPS*, February 25, 2005.

UPDATE BY JAMAL JUMA'

"Cementing Israeli Apartheid: The Role of the World Bank" was written last summer as part of Stop the Wall's campaign efforts to widen attention of those horrified by the construction of the 700 km long wall around Palestinian cities and villages. It aimed to expose the vicious mechanism of control, exploitation, and dispossession devised by the Occupation, but moreover the activities of the international community in safeguarding the Wall and making Palestinian ghettos sustainable.

It opens a chapter in a story that no one wants to hear: the globalization of apartheid in the Occupation of Palestine. Zionism has its own racist interest in ghettoizing 4 million Palestinians in the West Bank and Gaza and securing the judaization of Jerusalem. It ensures a Jewish demographic majority and ethnic supremacy over as much of Palestine as possible, working against all UN resolutions and the recent ICJ ruling on the Wall.

Within this project it finds allies in the international community keen to exploit cheap Palestinian labor locked behind Walls and gates. The degree to which Zionism and the international community—headed by the World Bank—work together with the aim of controlling every aspect of Palestinian life has become increasingly evident since the *Left Turn* article.

The Palestinian Authority's (PA) role is reduced to the administrators of the Bantustans. The Palestinian people resoundingly said no to Bantustans at the ballot boxes last January.

While the Bank's initial responsibility was to devise economic policies for the sustainability of a Palestinian Bantu-State, the institution is now facilitating efforts to ensure that Palestinians cannot interfere in the plans of the Occupation and the international community. The World Bank is gearing up to take over the payrolls of various Palestinian institutions, should the PA not comply with Zionist and global interests.

While global IFIs meticulously plan the financial and material survival and political control of the ghettos, Ehud Olmert offers the slogan of "Final Borders" to describe the project. In legitimizing the Wall, annexing Jerusalem, increasing the number of settlers, and denying the mere existence of the refugees, Olmert finds a willing accomplice in the Bank and its policy makers in Washington, who look to cash in on the Bantu-State.

The Palestinian people will never accept the plan, so it is hoped that they will be starved into it. But we will not kneel down. After dozens of massacres, killings, arrests, and almost sixty years of life in the Diaspora, surrender is too high a price to pay. We are not asking for outside institutions to provide us with bread, but to comply with their duties under international law and support our struggle for justice and liberation.

None of the horrific realities of life in Palestine are apparent in the headlines and doublespeak of mass media and international diplomacy, where our ghettoization is called "state-building." International complicity with Israeli apartheid is dressed up as "humanitarian aid." Palestinians are supposed to be grateful for gates in the Wall so they can be funneled between ghettos.

Just like Olmert's schemes with the White House, the media shuns and neglects the rights and voices of Palestinians. Neither the daily killing of our people, nor the destruction of our homes, the dispossession of our farmers, or the sufferings of 6 million refugees make headlines. The consumers of mainstream media outlets are left to discuss the diatribe of "peace" and "borders," disputed between the protagonists of our oppression, while the racism, ethnic cleansing, and ghettoization continue.

More information on the issue is to be found at our website: http://www.stopthewall.org

10

Expanded Air War in Iraq Kills More Civilians

Sources:

The New Yorker, December 2005
Title: "Up in the Air"
Author: Seymour M. Hersh

TomDispatch.com, December 2005
Title: "An Increasingly Aerial Occupation"
Author: Dahr Jamail

Community Evaluator: Robert Manning
Student Researcher: Brian Fuchs

There is widespread speculation that President Bush, confronted by diminishing approval ratings and dissent within his own party as well as within the military itself, will begin pulling American troops out of Iraq in 2006. A key element of the drawdown plans not mentioned in the President's public statements, or in mainstream media for that matter, is that the departing American troops will be replaced by American airpower.

"We're not planning to diminish the war," Seymour Hersh quotes Patrick Clawson, the deputy director of the Washington Institute, whose views often mirror those of Dick Cheney and Donald Rumsfeld. "We just want to change the mix of the forces doing the fighting—Iraqi infantry with American support and greater use of airpower."

While battle fatigue increases among U.S. troops, the prospect of using airpower as a substitute for American troops on the ground has caused great unease within the military. Air Force commanders, in particular, have deep-seated objections to the possibility that Iraqis will eventually be responsible for target selection. Hersh quotes a senior military planner now on assignment in the Pentagon, "Will the Iraqis call in air strikes in order to snuff rivals, or other warlords, or to snuff members of their own sect and blame someone else? Will some Iraqis be targeting on behalf of al-Qaeda, or the insurgency, or the Iranians?"

Dahr Jamail reports that the statistics gleaned from U.S. Central Command Air Forces (CENTAF) indicate a massive rise in the number of U.S. air missions—996 sorties—in Iraq in the month of November 2005.

The size of this figure naturally begs the question, where are such missions being flown and what is their size and nature? It's important to note as well that "air war" does not simply mean U.S. Air Force. Carrier-based Navy and Marine aircraft flew over 21,000 hours of missions and dropped over twenty-six tons of ordnance in Fallujah alone during the November 2004 siege of that city.

Visions of a frightful future in Iraq should not overshadow the devastation already caused by present levels of American air power loosed, in particular, on heavily populated urban areas of that country. The tactic of using massively powerful 500 and 1,000 pound bombs in urban areas to target small pockets of resistance fighters has, in fact, long been employed in Iraq. No intensification of the air war is necessary to make it commonplace. Jamail's article provides a broad overview of the air power arsenals being used against the people of Iraq.

A serious study of violence to civilians in Iraq by a British medical journal, *The Lancet*, released in October 2004, estimated that 85 percent of all violent deaths in Iraq are generated by coalition forces (see *Censored 2006*, Story #2). 95 percent of reported killings (all attributed to U.S. forces by interviewees) were caused by helicopter gunships, rockets, or other forms of aerial weaponry.[1] While no significant scientific inquiry has been carried out in Iraq recently, Iraqi medical personnel, working in areas where U.S. military operations continue, report that they feel the "vast majority" of civilian deaths are the result of actions by the occupation forces.

Given the U.S. air power already being applied largely in Iraq's cities and towns, the prospect of increasing it is chilling indeed. As to how this might benefit the embattled Bush administration, Jamail quotes U.S. Air Force Lieutenant Colonel Karen Kwiatkowski:

> "Shifting the mechanism of the destruction of Iraq from soldiers and Marines to distant and safer air power would be successful in several ways. It would reduce the negative publicity value of maimed American soldiers and Marines, would bring a portion of our troops home and give the Army a necessary operational break. It would increase Air Force and Naval budgets, and line defense contractor pockets. By

the time we figure out that it isn't working to make oil more secure or to allow Iraqis to rebuild a stable country, the Army will have recovered and can be redeployed in force."

Note

1. Les Roberts, et al., "Mortality Before and After the 2003 Invasion of Iraq," *The Lancet*, October 29, 2004.

UPDATE BY DAHR JAMAIL

Eleven days after this story about the lack of reportage in the corporate media about the U.S. military's increasing use of air power in Iraq, the *Washington Post* ran a story about how U.S. air strikes were taking an increasing toll on civilians. Aside from that story, the *Washington Post*, along with the *New York Times*, remain largely mute on the issue, despite the fact that the U.S. use of air strikes in Iraq has now become the norm rather than being used in contingencies, as they were in the first year of the occupation. Needless to say, corporate media television coverage has remained the same as it did prior to the publishing of this story—they prefer to portray a U.S. occupation of Iraq sans warplanes dropping bombs in civilian neighborhoods.

This story remains a critical issue when one evaluates the occupation of Iraq, for the number of civilians dying, now possibly as high as 300,000 according to Les Roberts, one of the authors of the famous Lancet Report, only continues to escalate. This is, of course, due in large part to U.S. war planes and helicopters dropping bombs and missiles into urban areas in various Iraqi cities.

It is also important when one looks at the fact that more than 82 percent of Iraqis now vehemently oppose the occupation, because one of the biggest recruiting tools for the Iraqi resistance is U.S. bombs and missiles killing the innocent. Years from now when a corporate media outlet decides to break down and acknowledge that the level of anti-American sentiment in Iraq is as high (or higher) than it is anywhere in the world, and asks the mindless question, "Why do they hate us?" one will only need to look towards the indiscriminate use of air power on the Iraqi population.

This story was not difficult to write for two reasons: the first was that any reporter in Iraq with eyes and ears knows there is a vast amount of air power being projected by the U.S. military. Secondly, thanks to the Internet, statistics on sorties are readily available to anyone willing to look. Googling "CENTAF" brings up several "Air Power Summary" reports, where one is able to find how many missions, and what type, are being flown each month in Iraq, as well as other countries.

To monitor the number of Iraqi civilians being killed by these missions, along with other deaths caused by the U.S. occupation of Iraq, the Iraqi Mortality Survey published in the prestigious British *Lancet* medical journal, albeit eighteen months out of date and a highly conservative estimate by the authors admission, remains by far and away the most accurate to date.

One thing is for certain, and that is the longer the failed U.S. occupation of Iraq persists, the more U.S. air power will be used—a scenario that closely resembles that of the shameful Vietnam War.

11

Dangers of Genetically Modified Food Confirmed

Sources:

The Independent, May 22, 2005
Title: "Revealed: Health Fears Over Secret Study in GM Food"
Author: Geoffrey Lean

Organic Consumers Association website, June 2, 2005
Title: "Monsanto's GE Corn Experiments on Rats Continue to Generate Global Controversy"
Authors: GM Free Cymru

The Independent, January 8, 2006
Title: "GM: New Study Shows Unborn Babies Could Be Harmed"
Author: Geoffrey Lean

Le Monde and *Truthout*, February 9, 2006
Title: "New Suspicions About GMOs"
Author: Herve Kempf

Faculty Evaluator: Michael Ezra, Ph.D.
Student Researchers: Destiny Stone and Lani Ready

Several recent studies confirm fears that genetically modified (GM) foods damage human health. These studies were released as the

World Trade Organization (WTO) moved toward upholding the ruling that the European Union has violated international trade rules by
stopping importation of GM foods.

➤ Research by the Russian Academy of Sciences released in
December 2005 found that more than half of the offspring of rats fed
GM soy died within the first three weeks of life, six times as many as
those born to mothers fed on non-modified soy. Six times as many
offspring fed GM soy were also severely underweight.

➤ In November 2005, a private research institute in Australia,
CSIRO Plant Industry, put a halt to further development of a GM pea
cultivator when it was found to cause an immune response in laboratory mice.[1]

➤ In the summer of 2005, an Italian research team led by a cellular
biologist at the University of Urbino published confirmation that
absorption of GM soy by mice causes development of misshapen
liver cells, as well as other cellular anomalies.

➤ In May of 2005 the review of a highly confidential and controversial Monsanto report on test results of corn modified with Monsanto
MON863 was published in *The Independent/UK*.

Dr. Arpad Pusztai (see *Censored 2001*, Story #7), one of the few
genuinely independent scientists specializing in plant genetics and
animal feeding studies, was asked by the German authorities in the
autumn of 2004 to examine Monsanto's 1,139-page report on the
feeding of MON863 to laboratory rats over a ninety-day period.

The study found "statistically significant" differences in kidney
weights and certain blood parameters in the rats fed the GM corn as
compared with the control groups. A number of scientists across
Europe who saw the study (and heavily-censored summaries of it)
expressed concerns about the health and safety implications if
MON863 should ever enter the food chain. There was particular concern in France, where Professor Gilles-Eric Seralini of the University
of Caen has been trying (without success) for almost eighteen
months to obtain full disclosure of all documents relating to the
MON863 study.

Dr. Pusztai was forced by the German authorities to sign a "declaration of secrecy" before he was allowed to see the Monsanto rat feeding study, on the grounds that the document is classified as "CBI" or
"confidential business interest." While Pusztai is still bound by the

declaration of secrecy, Monsanto recently declared that it does not object to the widespread dissemination of the "Pusztai Report."[2]

Monsanto GM soy and corn are widely consumed by Americans at a time when the United Nations' Food and Agriculture Organization has concluded, "In several cases, GMOs have been put on the market when safety issues are not clear."

As GMO research is not encouraged by U.S. or European governments, the vast majority of toxicological studies are conducted by those companies producing and promoting consumption of GMOs. With motive and authenticity of results suspect in corporate testing, independent scientific research into the effects of GM foods is attracting increasing attention.

Comment: In May 2006 the WTO upheld a ruling that European countries broke international trade rules by stopping importation of GM foods. The WTO verdict found that the EU has had an effective ban on biotech foods since 1998 and sided with the U.S., Canada, and Argentina in a decision that the moratorium was illegal under WTO rules.[3]

Notes

1. "GM peas cause immune response—A gap in the approval process?" http://www.GMO-Compass.org, January 3, 2006.
2. Arpad Pusztai, "Mon863-Pusztai Report," http://www.GMWatch.org, September 12, 2004.
3. Bradley S. Clapper, "WTO Faults EU for Blocking Modified Food," *Associated Press*, May 11, 2006.

12

Pentagon Plans to Build New Landmines

Source:
Inter Press Service, August 3, 2005
Title: "After 10-Year Hiatus, Pentagon Eyes New Landmine"
Author: Isaac Baker

Human Rights Watch website, August 2005
Title: "Development and Production of Landmines"

Community Evaluator: Scott Suneson
Student Researchers: Rachel Barry and Matt Frick

The Bush administration plans to resume production of antipersonnel landmine systems in a move that is at odds with both the international community and previous U.S. policy, according to the leading human rights organization, Human Rights Watch (HRW).

Nearly every nation has endorsed the goal of a global ban on antipersonnel mines. In 1994 the U.S. called for the "eventual elimination" of all such mines, and in 1996 President Bill Clinton said the U.S. would "seek a worldwide agreement as soon as possible to end the use of all antipersonnel mines." The U.S. produced its last antipersonnel landmine in 1997. It had been the stated objective of the U.S. government to eventually join the 145 countries signatory to the 1997 Mine Ban Treaty, which bans the use, production, exporting, and stockpiling of antipersonnel landmines.

The Bush administration, however, made an about-face in U.S. antipersonnel landmine policy in February 2004, when it abandoned any plan to join the Mine Ban Treaty, also known as the Ottawa Convention. "The United States will not join the Ottawa Convention because its terms would have required us to give up a needed military capability," the U.S. Department of State's Bureau of Political-Military announced, summing up the administration's new policy, "The United States will continue to develop non-persistent anti-personnel and anti-tank landmines."

HRW reports that, "New U.S. landmines will have a variety of ways of being initiated, both command-detonation (that is, when a soldier decides when to explode the mine, sometimes called 'man-in-the-loop') and traditional victim-activation. A mine that is designed to be exploded by the presence, proximity, or contact of a person (i.e., victim-activation) is prohibited under the International Mine Ban Treaty."

To sidestep international opposition, the Pentagon proposes development of the "Spider" system, which consists of a control unit capable of monitoring up to eighty-four hand-placed, unattended munitions that deploy a web of tripwires across an area. Once a wire is touched, a man-in-the-loop control system allows the operator to activate the devices.

The Spider, however, contains a "battlefield override" feature that allows for circumvention of the man-in-the-loop, and activation by the target (victim).

A Pentagon report to Congress stated, "Target Activation is a software feature that allows the man-in-the-loop to change the capability of a munition from requiring action by an operator prior to being detonated, to a munition that will be detonated by a target. The Chairman, Joint Chiefs of Staff, and the Service Chiefs, using best military judgment, feel that the man-in-the-loop system without this feature would be insufficient to meet tactical operational conditions and electronic countermeasures."

The U.S. Army spent $135 million between fiscal years 1999 and 2004 to develop Spider and another $11 million has been requested to complete research and development. A total of $390 million is budgeted to produce 1,620 Spider systems and 186,300 munitions. According to budget documents released in February 2005, the Pentagon requested $688 million for research on and $1.08 billion for the production of new landmine systems between fiscal years 2006 and 2011.

Steven Goose, Director of HRW Arms Division, told Project Censored that Congress has required a report from the Pentagon on the humanitarian consequences of the "battlefield override" or victim-activated feature of these munitions for review before approving funds. Though production was set for December of 2005, Congress has not, as of June 2006, received this preliminary Pentagon report.

If the Spider or similar mine munitions systems move forward, a frightening precedence will be set. At best the 145 signatories to the Ottawa Convention will be beholden to the treaty, which forbids assistance in joint military operations where landmines are being used. At worst, U.S. production will legitimize international resumption of landmine proliferation.

Steven Goose warns, "If one doesn't insist on a comprehensive ban on all types and uses of antipersonnel mines, each nation will be able to claim unique requirements and justifications."

UPDATE BY ISAAC BAKER

Landmines are horrific weapons. And, naturally, news stories about the terror they inflict upon human beings—mainly civilians—are gritty and disturbing if they are truthful. Especially when it's your own government that's responsible.

And given the mainstream media's typical service to power, this story didn't make many headlines.

But the potential ramifications of the U.S. government resuming production of landmines are overwhelming. And since the average

American can't depend on many media to inform them of the horrific things their government is doing, concerned people must take it upon themselves to put their government in its place.

We all must ask ourselves: Do we want our government—the body that theoretically represents we, the people—spending millions upon millions of dollars on these destructive weapons? Are we comfortable with sitting back and letting our government produce weapons that kill and maim civilians?

Or will we coalesce and let the powerful know that we will not stand for this gross disregard for human life and international opinion?

It's our responsibility to stop the abuses of power in our country. And if we do not confront our government on this issue, I believe, the blood of the innocents will be on all of our hands.

For more information on how to get involved please visit: http://www.hrw.org and http://www.banminesusa.org or www.icbl.org

13

New Evidence Shows Dangers of Roundup

Sources:
Third World Resurgence, No. 176, April 2005
Title: "New Evidence of Dangers of Roundup Weedkiller"
Author: Chee Yoke Heong

Faculty Evaluator: Jennifer Whiles, Ph.D.
Student Researchers: Peter McArthur and Lani Ready

New studies from both sides of the Atlantic reveal that Roundup, the most widely used weedkiller in the world, poses serious human health threats. More than 75 percent of genetically modified (GM) crops are engineered to tolerate the absorption of Roundup—it eliminates all plants that are not GM. Monsanto Inc., the major engineer of GM crops, is also the producer of Roundup. Thus, while Roundup was formulated as a weapon against weeds, it has become a prevalent ingredient in most of our food crops.

Three recent studies show that Roundup, which is used by farmers and home gardeners, is not the safe product we have been led to trust.

A group of scientists led by biochemist Professor Gilles-Eric Seralini from the University of Caen in France found that human placental cells are very sensitive to Roundup at concentrations lower than those currently used in agricultural application.

An epidemiological study of Ontario farming populations showed that exposure to glyphosate, the key ingredient in Roundup, nearly doubled the risk of late miscarriages. Seralini and his team decided to research the effects of the herbicide on human placenta cells. Their study confirmed the toxicity of glyphosate, as after eighteen hours of exposure at low concentrations, large proportions of human placenta began to die. Seralini suggests that this may explain the high levels of premature births and miscarriages observed among female farmers using glyphosate.

Seralini's team further compared the toxic effects of the Roundup formula (the most common commercial formulation of glyphosate and chemical additives) to the isolated active ingredient, glyphosate. They found that the toxic effect increases in the presence of Roundup 'adjuvants' or additives. These additives thus have a facilitating role, rendering Roundup twice as toxic as its isolated active ingredient, glyphosate.

Another study, released in April 2005 by the University of Pittsburgh, suggests that Roundup is a danger to other life-forms and non-target organisms. Biologist Rick Relyea found that Roundup is extremely lethal to amphibians. In what is considered one of the most extensive studies on the effects of pesticides on nontarget organisms in a natural setting, Relyea found that Roundup caused a 70 percent decline in amphibian biodiversity and an 86 percent decline in the total mass of tadpoles. Leopard frog tadpoles and gray tree frog tadpoles were nearly eliminated.

In 2002, a scientific team led by Robert Belle of the National Center for Scientific Research (CNRS) biological station in Roscoff, France showed that Roundup activates one of the key stages of cellular division that can potentially lead to cancer. Belle and his team have been studying the impact of glyphosate formulations on sea urchin cells for several years. The team has recently demonstrated in *Toxicological Science* (December 2004) that a "control point" for DNA damage was affected by Roundup, while glyphosate alone had no effect. "We have shown that it's a definite risk factor, but we have not evaluated the number of cancers potentially induced, nor the time frame within which they would declare themselves," Belle acknowledges.

There is, indeed, direct evidence that glyphosate inhibits an important process called RNA transcription in animals, at a concentration well below the level that is recommended for commercial spray application.

There is also new research that shows that brief exposure to commercial glyphosate causes liver damage in rats, as indicated by the leakage of intracellular liver enzymes. The research indicates that glyphosate and its surfactant in Roundup were found to act in synergy to increase damage to the liver.

UPDATE BY CHEE YOKE HEONG

Roundup Ready weedkiller is one of the most widely used weedkillers in the world for crops and backyard gardens. Roundup, with its active ingredient glyphosate, has long been promoted as safe for humans and the environment while effective in killing weeds. It is therefore significant when recent studies show that Roundup is not as safe as its promoters claim.

This has major consequences as the bulk of commercially planted genetically modified crops are designed to tolerate glyphosate (and especially Roundup), and independent field data already shows a trend of increasing use of the herbicide. This goes against industry claims that herbicide use will drop and that these plants will thus be more "environment-friendly." Now it has been found that there are serious health effects, too. My story therefore aimed to highlight these new findings and their implications to health and the environment.

Not surprisingly, Monsanto came out refuting some of the findings of the studies mentioned in the article. What ensued was an open exchange between Dr. Rick Relyea and Monsanto, whereby the former stood his grounds. Otherwise, to my knowledge, no studies have since emerged on Roundup.

For more information look to the following sources:
Professor Gilles-Eric, criigen@ibfa.unicaen.fr
Biosafety Information Center, http://www.biosafety-info.net
Institute of Science in Society, http://www.i-sis.org.uk

14

Homeland Security Contracts KBR to Build Detention Centers in the U.S.

Sources:

New America Media, January 31, 2006
Title: "Homeland Security Contracts for Vast New Detention Camps"
Author: Peter Dale Scott

New America Media, February 21, 2006
Title: "10-Year U.S. Strategic Plan for Detention Camps Revives Proposals from Oliver North"
Author: Peter Dale Scott

Consortium, February 21, 2006
Title: "Bush's Mysterious 'New Programs'"
Author: Nat Parry

Buzzflash, February 13, 2006
Title: "Detention Camp Jitters," February 13, 2006
Author: Maureen Farrell

Faculty Evaluator: Gary Evans, M.D.
Student Researchers: Sean Hurley and Caitlyn Peele

Halliburton's subsidiary KBR (formerly Kellogg, Brown and Root) announced on January 24, 2006 that it had been awarded a $385 million contingency contract by the Department of Homeland Security to build detention camps in the United States.

According to a press release posted on the Halliburton website, "The contract, which is effective immediately, provides for establishing temporary detention and processing capabilities to augment existing Immigration and Customs Enforcement (ICE) Detention and Removal Operations (DRO) Program facilities in the event of an emergency influx of immigrants into the U.S., or to support the rapid development of new programs. The contingency support contract provides for planning and, if required, initiation of specific engineering, construction and logistics support tasks to establish, operate and maintain one or more expansion facilities."

What little coverage the announcement received focused on concerns about Halliburton's reputation for overcharging U.S. taxpayers for substandard services.

Less attention was focused on the phrase "rapid development of new programs" or what type of programs might require a major expansion of detention centers, capable of holding 5,000 people each. Jamie Zuieback, spokeswoman for ICE, declined to elaborate on what these "new programs" might be.

Only a few independent journalists, such as Peter Dale Scott, Maureen Farrell, and Nat Parry have explored what the Bush administration might actually have in mind.

Scott speculates that the "detention centers could be used to detain American citizens if the Bush administration were to declare martial law." He recalled that during the Reagan administration, National Security Council aide Oliver North organized the Rex-84 "readiness exercise," which contemplated the Federal Emergency Management Agency rounding up and detaining 400,000 "refugees" in the event of "uncontrolled population movements" over the Mexican border into the U.S.

North's exercise, which reportedly contemplated possible suspension of the Constitution, led to a line of questioning during the Iran-Contra Hearings concerning the idea that plans for expanded internment and detention facilities would not be confined to "refugees" alone.

It is relevant, says Scott, that in 2002 Attorney General John Ashcroft announced his desire to see camps for U.S. citizens deemed to be "enemy combatants." On February 17, 2006, in a speech to the Council on Foreign Relations, Defense Secretary Donald Rumsfeld spoke of the harm being done to the country's security, not just by the enemy, but also by what he called "news informers" who needed to be combated in "a contest of wills."

Since September 11 the Bush administration has implemented a number of interrelated programs that were planned in the 1980s under President Reagan. Continuity of Government (COG) proposals—a classified plan for keeping a secret "government-within-the-government" running during and after a nuclear disaster—included vastly expanded detention capabilities, warrantless eavesdropping, and preparations for greater use of martial law.

Scott points out that, while Oliver North represented a minority element in the Reagan administration, which soon distanced itself from both the man and his proposals, the minority associated with COG planning, which included Cheney and Rumsfeld, appear to be in control of the U.S. government today.

Farrell speculates that, because another terror attack is all but certain, it seems far more likely that the detention centers would be used for post-September 11-type detentions of rounded-up immigrants rather than for a sudden deluge of immigrants flooding across the border.

Vietnam-era whistleblower Daniel Ellsberg ventures, "Almost certainly this is preparation for a roundup after the next September 11 for Mid-Easterners, Muslims and possibly dissenters. They've already done this on a smaller scale, with the 'special registration' detentions of immigrant men from Muslim countries, and with Guantánamo."

Parry notes that *The Washington Post* reported on February 15, 2006 that the National Counterterrorism Center's (NCTC) central repository holds the names of 325,000 terrorist suspects, a fourfold increase since fall of 2003.

Asked whether the names in the repository were collected through the NSA's domestic surveillance program, an NCTC official told the *Post*, "Our database includes names of known and suspected international terrorists provided by all intelligence community organizations, including NSA."

As the administration scoops up more and more names, members of Congress have questioned the elasticity of Bush's definitions for words like terrorist "affiliates," used to justify wiretapping Americans allegedly in contact with such people or entities.

A Defense Department document, entitled the "Strategy for Homeland Defense and Civil Support," has set out a military strategy against terrorism that envisions an "active, layered defense" both inside and outside U.S. territory. In the document, the Pentagon pledges to "transform U.S. military forces to execute homeland defense missions in the . . . U.S. homeland." The strategy calls for increased military reconnaissance and surveillance to "defeat potential challengers before they threaten the United States." The plan "maximizes threat awareness and seizes the initiative from those who would harm us."

But there are concerns, warns Parry, over how the Pentagon judges "threats" and who falls under the category of "those who would harm us." A Pentagon official said the Counterintelligence Field Activity's TALON program has amassed files on antiwar protesters.

In the view of some civil libertarians, a form of martial law already exists in the U.S. and has been in place since shortly after the September 11 attacks when Bush issued Military Order Number One, which empowered him to detain any noncitizen as an international terrorist or enemy combatant. Today that order extends to U.S. citizens as well.

Farrell ends her article with the conclusion that while much speculation has been generated by KBR's contract to build huge detention centers within the U.S., "The truth is, we won't know the real purpose of these centers unless 'contingency plans are needed.' And by then, it will be too late."

UPDATE BY PETER DALE SCOTT

The contract of the Halliburton subsidiary KBR to build immigrant detention facilities is part of a longer-term Homeland Security plan titled ENDGAME, which sets as its goal the removal of "all removable aliens" and "potential terrorists." In the 1980s Richard Cheney and Donald Rumsfeld discussed similar emergency detention powers as part of a super-secret program of planning for what was euphemistically called "Continuity of Government" (COG) in the event of a nuclear disaster. At the time, Cheney was a Wyoming congressman, while Rumsfeld, who had been defense secretary under President Ford, was a businessman and CEO of the drug company G.D. Searle.

These men planned for suspension of the Constitution, not just after nuclear attack, but for any "national security emergency," which they defined in Executive Order 12656 of 1988 as: "Any occurrence, including natural disaster, military attack, technological or other emergency, that seriously degrades or seriously threatens the national security of the United States." Clearly September 11 would meet this definition, and did, for COG was instituted on that day. As the *Washington Post* later explained, the order "dispatched a shadow government of about 100 senior civilian managers to live and work secretly outside Washington, activating for the first time long-standing plans."

What these managers in this shadow government worked on has never been reported. But it is significant that the group that prepared ENDGAME was, as the Homeland Security document puts it, "chartered in September 2001." For ENDGAME's goal of a capacious detention capability is remarkably similar to Oliver North's controversial Rex-84 "readiness exercise" for COG in 1984. This called for the Federal Emergency Management Agency (FEMA) to round up and detain 400,000 imaginary "refugees," in the context of "uncontrolled population movements" over the Mexican border into the United States.

UPDATE BY MAUREEN FARRELL

When the story about Kellogg, Brown and Root's contract for emergency detention centers broke, immigration was not the hot button issue it is today. Given this, the language in Halliburton's press release, stating that the centers would be built in the event of an "emergency influx of immigrants into the U.S.," raised eyebrows, especially among those familiar with Rex-84 and other Reagan-era initiatives. FEMA's former plans 'for the detention of at least 21 million American Negroes in assembly centers or relocation camps' added to the distrust, and the second stated reason for the KBR contract, "to support the rapid development of new programs," sent imaginations reeling.

While few in the mainstream media made the connection between KBR's contract and previous programs, Fox News eventually addressed this issue, pooh-poohing concerns as the province of "conspiracy theories" and "unfounded" fears. My article attempted to sift through the speculation, focusing on verifiable information found in declassified and leaked documents which proved that, in addition to drawing up contingency plans for martial law, the government has conducted military readiness exercises designed to round up and detain both illegal aliens and U.S. citizens.

How concerned should Americans be? Recent reports are conflicting and confusing:

➤ In May, 2006, U.S. Immigration and Customs Enforcement (ICE) began "Operation Return to Sender," which involved catching illegal immigrants and deporting them. In June, however, President Bush vowed that there would soon be "new infrastructures" including detention centers designed to put an end to such "catch and release" practices.

➤ Though Bush said he was "working with Congress to increase the number of detention facilities along our borders," Rep. Bennie Thompson, ranking member of the House Homeland Security Committee, said he first learned about the KBR contract through newspaper reports.

➤ Fox News recently quoted Pepperdine University professor Doug Kmiec, who deemed detention camp concerns "more paranoia than reality" and added that KBR's contract is most likely "something related to (Hurricane) Katrina" or "a bird flu outbreak that could spur a mass quarantine of Americans." The president's stated desire for the U.S. military to take a more active role during natural disasters and to enforce quarantines in the event of a bird flu outbreak, however, have been roundly denounced.

Concern over an all-powerful federal government is not paranoia, but active citizenship. As Thomas Jefferson explained, "even under the best forms of government, those entrusted with power have, in time, and by slow operations, perverted it into tyranny." From John Adams's Alien and Sedition Acts to FDR's internment of Japanese Americans, the land of the free has held many contradictions and ironies. Interestingly enough, Halliburton was at the center of another historical controversy, when Lyndon Johnson's ties to a little-known company named Kellogg, Brown and Root caused a congressional commotion—particularly after the Halliburton subsidiary won enough wartime contracts to become one of the first protested symbols of the military-industrial complex. Back then they were known as the "Vietnam builders." The question, of course, is what they'll be known as next.

Additional links:

"Reagan Aides and the Secret Government," *Miami Herald*, July 5, 1987, http://fpiarticle.blogspot.com/2005/12/front-page-miami-herald-july-5-1987.html

"Foundations are in place for martial law in the US," July 27, 2002, *Sydney Morning Herald*, smh.com.au/articles/2002/07/27/ 1027497 418339.html

"Halliburton Deals Recall Vietnam-Era Controversy: Cheney's Ties to Company Reminiscent of LBJ's Relationships," NPR, Dec. 24, 2003, http://www.npr.org/templates/story/story.php?storyId=1569483

"Critics Fear Emergency Centers Could Be Used for Immigration Round-Ups," Fox News, June 7, 2006, http://www.foxnews.com/ story/0,2933,198456,00.html

"U.S. officials nab 2,100 illegal immigrants in 3 weeks," *USA Today*,

June 14, 2006, http://www.usatoday.com/news/nation/2006-06-14-immigration-arrests_x.htm

15

Chemical Industry Now EPA's Primary Research Partner

Sources:

Public Employees for Environmental Responsibility, October 5, 2005
Title: "Chemical Industry Is Now EPA's Main Research Partner"
Author: Jeff Ruch

Public Employees for Environmental Responsibility, October 6, 2005
Title: "EPA Becoming Arm of Corporate R&D"
Author: Jeff Ruch

Community Evaluator: Tim Ogburn
Student Researchers: Lani Ready and Peter McArthur

The U.S. Environmental Protection Agency (EPA) research program is increasingly relying on corporate joint ventures, according to agency documents obtained by Public Employees for Environmental Responsibility (PEER). The American Chemical Council (ACC) is now EPA's leading research partner and the EPA is diverting funds from basic health and environmental research towards research that addresses regulatory concerns of corporate funders.

Since the beginning of Bush's first term in office, there has been a significant increase in cooperative research and development agreements (CRADAs) with individual corporations or industry associations. During Bush's first four years EPA entered into fifty-seven corporate CRADAs, compared to thirty-four such agreements during Clinton's second term.

EPA scientists claim that corporations are influencing the agency's research agenda through financial inducements. One EPA scientist wrote, "Many of us in the labs feel like we work for contracts." In April 2005, EPA's Science Advisory Board warned that the agency was no longer funding credible public health research. It noted, for example, that the EPA was falling behind on issues such as intercontinental pollution transport and nanotechnology.

Furthermore, in April 2005, a study by the Government

Accountability Office concluded that EPA lacks safeguards to "evaluate or manage potential conflicts of interest" in corporate research agreements, as they are taking money from companies and corporations that they are supposed to be regulating.

According to Rebecca Rose, the Program Director of PEER, "Under its current leadership, EPA is becoming an arm of corporate R&D." She also notes that the number of corporate CRADAs under the Bush administration outnumbered those entered into with universities or local governments, adding, "Public health research needs should not have to depend upon corporate underwriting."

In October 2005 President Bush nominated George Gray to serve as the Assistant Administrator for the Environmental Protection Agency Office of Research and Development (ORD). At that time George Gray ran a Center for Risk Analysis at Harvard University where the majority of the funding came from corporate sources. Gray indicated upon nomination that he intends to continue and expand his solicitation of corporate research funds in his position with ORD.

PEER's Executive Director Jeff Ruch warns, "Injecting outside money into a public agency research program, especially when it is tied to particular projects, has a subtle but undeniable influence on not only what work gets done but also how that work is reported." He adds, "As what was one of the top public health research programs slides toward dysfunction, nothing about the background, attitude or philosophy of Mr. Gray suggests that he is even remotely the right person for this job."

In 2004 & 2005, EPA was plagued by reports of political suppression of scientific results on important health issues such as asbestos and mercury regulation (see *Censored 2005*, Story #3). In response ORD launched a public relations campaign, entitled "Science for You," using agency research funds to clean up its image.

Comments: George M. Gray was sworn in as the Assistant Administrator of Research and Development at EPA on November 1, 2005, with unanimous consent of the U.S. Senate.

UPDATE BY JEFF RUCH

This story illustrates how key environmental research is being diverted away from public health priorities in order to meet a corporate regulatory agenda. By enticing EPA into partnerships, entities such as the American Chemical Council (ACC), which is now EPA's leading research partner, can influence not only what EPA researches but how that research is conducted, as well.

For example, long-term health monitoring studies drop off EPA's list of priority topics because industry has no interest in funding such vital work—if anything, industry has an incentive to prevent such research from being conducted. By the same token, the industry push to allow human subject experiments to test tolerance to pesticides and other commercial poisons is precisely the type of research the industry desires to entice EPA into conducting, and thus legitimizing, despite an array of unresolved ethical problems.

A few updates since October 2005 worthy of note: a) A leading proponent of industry research partnerships, George Gray, has been confirmed as EPA Assistant Administrator for Research & Development. b) President Bush has proposed further cuts to EPA's already shrinking research budget. (see http://www.peer.org/news/news_id.php?row_id=661). This growing penury makes EPA even more interested in using corporate dollars to supplement its tattered research program. c) EPA is in the first weeks of its human testing program. A specially convened Human Subjects Review Board is now struggling to approve industry and agency studies in which people were not given informed consent or were given harmful doses of chemicals.

The EPA page of our website has several updates on this and related issues.

16

Ecuador and Mexico Defy U.S. on the International Criminal Court

Sources:

Agence France Press News (School of the Americas Watch), June 22, 2005
Title: "Ecuador Refuses to Sign ICC Immunity Deal for U.S. Citizens"
Author: Alexander Martinez

Inter Press Service, November 2, 2005
Title: "Mexico Defies Washington on the International Criminal Court"
Author: Katherine Stapp

Faculty Evaluator: Elizabeth Martinez, Ph.D.
Student Researchers: Jessica Rodas, David Abbott, and Charlene Jones

Ecuador and Mexico have refused to sign bilateral immunity agreements (BIA) with the U.S., in ratification of the International Criminal Court (ICC) treaty. Despite the Bush administration's threat to withhold economic aid, both countries confirmed allegiance to the ICC, the international body established to try individuals accused of war crimes and crimes against humanity.

On June 22, 2005 Ecuador's president, Alfredo Palacios, vocalized emphatic refusal to sign a BIA (also known as an Article 98 agreement to the Rome Statute of the ICC) in spite of Washington's threat to withhold $70 million a year in military aid.

Mexico, having signed the Rome Statute, which established the ICC in 2000, formally ratified the treaty on October 28, 2005, making it the 100th nation to join the ICC. As a consequence of ratifying the ICC without a U.S. immunity agreement, Mexico stands to lose millions of dollars in U.S. aid—including $11.5 million to fight drug trafficking.

On September 29, 2005 the U.S. State Department reported that it had secured 100 "immunity agreements," although less than a third have been ratified.

"Our ultimate goal is to conclude Article 98 agreements with every country in the world, regardless of whether they have signed or ratified the ICC, regardless of whether they intend to in the future," said John Bolton, former U.S. Undersecretary for Arms Control and current U.S. ambassador to the United Nations—and one of the ICC's staunchest opponents.

The U.S. effort to undermine the ICC was given teeth in 2002, when the U.S. Congress adopted the American Servicemembers' Protection Act (ASPA), which contains provisions restricting U.S. cooperation with the ICC by making U.S. support of UN peacekeeping missions largely contingent on achieving impunity for all U.S. personnel.

The ASPA prohibits U.S. military assistance to ICC member states that have not signed a BIA.

Legislation far more wide-reaching, however, was signed into law by President Bush on December 2004. The Nethercutt Amendment authorizes the loss of Economic Support Funds (ESF) to countries, including many key U.S. allies, that have not signed a BIA. Threatened under the Nethercutt Amendment are: funds for international security and counterterrorism efforts, peace process programs, antidrug-trafficking initiatives, truth and reconciliation commissions, wheelchair distribution, human rights programs, economic and democratic development, and HIV/Aids education, among others. The Nethercutt Amendment was readopted by the U.S. Congress in November 2005.[1]

In spite of severe U.S. pressure, fifty-three members of the ICC have refused to sign BIAs.

Katherine Stapp asserts that if Washington follows through on threats to slash aid to ICC member states, it risks further alienating key U.S. allies and drawing attention to its own increasingly shaky human rights record. "There will be a price to be paid by the U.S. government in terms of its credibility," Richard Dicker, director of Human Rights Watch's International Justice Program, told *IPS*.

But criticism of the administration's hard line has also come from unlikely quarters.

Testifying before Congress in March, Gen. Bantz J. Craddock, the commander of U.S. military forces in Latin America, complained that the sanctions had excluded Latin American officers from U.S. training programs and could allow China, which has been seeking military ties with Latin America, to fill the void.

"We now risk losing contact and interoperability with a generation of military classmates in many nations of the region, including several leading countries," Craddock told the Senate Armed Services Committee.

Experts say it is particularly notable that Mexico, which sells 88 percent of its exports in the U.S. market, is defying pressure from Washington.

"It's exactly because of the geographic and trade proximity between Mexico and the United States that Mexico's ratification takes on greater significance in terms of how isolated the U.S. government is in its attitude toward the ICC," Dicker told *IPS*.

Notes

1. "Overview of the United States' Opposition to the International Criminal Court," http://www.iccnow.org.

UPDATE BY KATHERINE STAPP

As noted by Amnesty International, the United States is the only nation in the world that is actively opposed to the International Criminal Court (ICC). However, more and more countries appear to be resisting pressure to exempt U.S. nationals from the court's jurisdiction. Since the time of my writing, the number of "bilateral immunity agreements," or BIAs, garnered by Washington has remained the same: 100, of which only twenty-one have been ratified by parliaments, while another eighteen are considered "executive agreements" that purportedly do not require ratification. Only thirteen states parties to the ICC (out of 100) have ratified BIAs with the United States, while eight others have reportedly entered into executive agreements. In the past two years, only four countries in Latin America and the Caribbean have signed BIAs, also known as Article 98 agreements.

Some key figures in the Bush administration have recently expressed doubts about the wisdom of withholding aid from friendly countries that refuse to sign. At a March 10 briefing, Secretary of State Condoleezza Rice likened the BIAs to "sort of the same as shooting ourselves in the foot . . . by having to put off aid to countries with which we have important counter-terrorism or counter-drug or in some cases, in some of our allies, it's even been cooperation in places like Afghanistan and Iraq."

Bantz Craddock, head of the U.S. Southern Command, remains a vocal critic of the American Servicemembers' Protection Act (ASPA) sanctions, noting in testimony before the House Armed Services Committee on March 16 that eleven Latin American nations have now been barred under ASPA from receiving International Military Education and Training funds. These include Brazil, Bolivia, Ecuador, and Mexico.

"Decreasing engagement opens the door for competing nations and outside political actors who may not share our democratic principles to increase interaction and influence within the region," he noted.

And in the 2006 Quadrennial Defense Review Report published on February 6, the Defense Department said it will consider whether ASPA restrictions on "foreign assistance programs pertaining to security and the war on terror necessitate adjustment as we continue to advance the aims of the ASPA."

Meanwhile, a May 11 poll by the University of Maryland's Program on International Policy Attitudes found that a bipartisan majority of the U.S. public (69 percent) believes that the U.S. should not be given special exceptions when it becomes a party to human rights treaties. 60 percent explicitly support U.S. participation in the ICC.

Mexico has stood firm in its refusal to sign a BIA, with the Mexican Parliament's Lower Chamber stating that immunity is not allowed under the Rome Statute that establishes the ICC. As a result, $3.6 million in military aid has been frozen, and further International Military Exchange Training aid cut to zero in the administration's proposed 2007 budget request. The country also stands to lose more than $11 million from the Economic Support Fund (ESF).

Other countries currently threatened with aid cuts include Bolivia, which could lose 96 percent of its U.S. military aid, and Kenya, which could lose $8 million in ESF aid.

More information can be found at:
Citizens for Global Solutions (http://www.globalsolutions.org/pro-grams/law_justice/icc/icc_home.html); Coalition for the International Criminal Court (http://www.iccnow.org/?mod=bia); The American Non-Governmental Organisations Coalition for the International Criminal Court (http://www.amicc.org/); Washington Working Group on the International Criminal Court (http://www.usaforicc.org/wicc/)

17

Iraq Reconstruction Promotes OPEC Agenda

Sources:
Harper's in coordination with *BBC Television Newsnight*, October 24, 2005
Title: "OPEC and the economic conquest of Iraq"
Author: Greg Palast

The Guardian, March 20, 2006
"Bush Didn't Bungle Iraq, You Fools: The Mission Was Indeed Accomplished"
Author: Greg Palast

Faculty Evaluator: David McCuan, Ph.D.
Student Researcher: Isaac Dolido

According to a report from journalist, Greg Palast, the U.S. invasion of Iraq was indeed about the oil. However, it wasn't to destroy OPEC, as claimed by neoconservatives in the administration, but to take part in it.

The U.S. strategic occupation of Iraq has been an effective means of acquiring access to the Organization of Petroleum Exporting Countries (OPEC). As long as the interim government adheres to the production caps set by the organization, the U.S. will ensure profits to the international oil companies (IOCs), the OPEC cartel, and Russia.

With the prolonged insurgency following the invasion, along with internal corruption and pipeline destruction, hard line neoconservative plans for a completely privatized Iraq were dashed. According to some administration insiders, the idea of a laissez-faire, free-market reconstruction of Iraq was never a serious consideration. One oil industry consultant to Iraq told Palast he was amused by "the obsession of neoconservative writers on ways to undermine OPEC."

In December 2003, says Palast, the State Department drafted a 323-page plan entitled "Options for Developing a Long Term Sustainable Iraqi Oil Industry." This plan directs the Iraqis to maintain an oil quota system that will enhance its relationship with OPEC. It describes several possible state-owned options that range from the Saudi Aramco model (in which the government owns the whole operation) to the Azerbaijan model (in which the system is almost entirely operated by the International Oil Companies).

Implementation of the plan was guided by a handful of oil industry consultants, promoting an OPEC-friendly policy but preferring the Azerbaijan model to the "self-financing" system of the Saudi Aramco, as it grants operation and control to the foreign oil companies (the 2003 report warns Iraqis against cutting into IOC profits). Once the contracts are granted, these companies then manage, fund, and equip crude extraction in exchange for a percentage of the sales. Given the way in which the interests of OPEC and those of the IOCs are so closely aligned, it is certainly understandable why smashing OPEC's oil cartel might not appeal to certain elements of the Bush administration.

According to the drafters and promoters of the plan, dismantling OPEC would be a catastrophe. The last thing they want is the privatization of Iraq's oil fields and the specter of competition maximizing production. Pumping more oil per day than the OPEC regulated quota of almost 4 million, would quickly bring down Iraq's economy and compromise the U.S. position in the global market.

Since the invasion of Iraq in 2003, profits have shot up for oil companies. In 2004, the major U.S. oil companies posted record or near record profits. In 2005 profits for the five largest oil companies increased to $113 billion. In February 2006, ConocoPhillips reported a doubling of its quarterly profits from the previous year, which itself had been a company record. Shell posted a record breaking $4.48 billion in fourth-quarter earnings—and in 2005, ExxonMobil reported the largest one-year operating profit of any corporation in U.S. history.

18

Physicist Concludes Official September 11 Explanation is Implausible

Sources:
Deseret Morning News, November 10, 2005
Title: "Y. Professor Thinks Bombs, Not Planes, Toppled WTC"
Author: Elaine Jarvik

Brigham Young University website, Winter 2005
Title: "Why Indeed Did the WTC Buildings Collapse?"
Author: Steven E. Jones

Deseret Morning News, January 26, 2006
Title: "BYU professor's group accuses U.S. officials of lying about 9/11"
Author: Elaine Jarvik

Faculty Evaluator: John Kramer, Ph.D.
Student Researchers: David Abbott and Courtney Wilcox

Research into the events of September 11 by Brigham Young University physics professor, Steven E. Jones, concludes that the official explanation for the collapse of the World Trade Center (WTC) buildings is implausible according to laws of physics. Jones is calling for an independent, international scientific investigation "guided not by politicized notions and constraints but rather by observations and calculations."

In debunking the official explanation of the collapse of the three WTC buildings, Jones cites the complete, rapid, and symmetrical collapse of the buildings; the horizontal explosions (squibs) evidenced in films of the collapses; the fact that the antenna dropped first in the North Tower, suggesting the use of explosives in the core columns; and the large pools of molten metal observed in the basement areas of both towers.

Jones also investigated the collapse of WTC 7, a forty-seven-story building that was not hit by planes, yet dropped in its own "footprint," in the same manner as a controlled demolition. WTC 7 housed the U.S. Secret Service, the Department of Defense, the Immigration and Naturalization Service, the U.S. Securities and Exchange Commission, the Mayor's Office of Emergency Management, the Internal Revenue Service Regional Council, and the Central Intelligence Agency. Many of the records from the Enron accounting scandal were destroyed when the building came down.

Jones claims that the National Institutes of Standards and Technology (NIST) ignored the physics and chemistry of what happened on September 11 and even manipulated its testing in order to get a computer-generated hypothesis that fit the end result of collapse, and did not even attempt to investigate the possibility of controlled demolition. He also questions the investigations conducted by FEMA and the 9/11 Commission.

Among the report's other findings:

➤ No steel-frame building, before or after the WTC buildings, has ever collapsed due to fire. But explosives can effectively sever steel columns.

➤ WTC 7, which was not hit by hijacked planes, collapsed in 6.6 seconds, just .6 of a second longer than it would take an object dropped from the roof to hit the ground. "Where is the delay that must be expected due to conservation of momentum, one of the foundational laws of physics?" Jones asks. "That is, as upper-falling floors strike lower floors—and intact steel support columns—the fall must be significantly impeded by the impacted mass . . . How do the upper floors fall so quickly, then, and still conserve momentum in the collapsing buildings?" The paradox, he says, "is easily resolved by the explosive demolition hypothesis, whereby explosives quickly removed lower-floor material, including steel support columns, and allow near free-fall-speed collapses." These observations were not analyzed by FEMA, NIST, or the 9/11 Commission.

➤ With non-explosive-caused collapse there would typically be a piling up of shattered concrete. But most of the material in the towers was converted to flour-like powder while the buildings were falling. "How can we understand this strange behavior, without explosives? Remarkable, amazing—and demanding scrutiny since the U.S. government-funded reports failed to analyze this phenomenon."

➤ Steel supports were "partly evaporated," but it would require temperatures near 5,000 degrees Fahrenheit to evaporate steel—and neither office materials nor diesel fuel can generate temperatures that hot. Fires caused by jet fuel from the hijacked planes lasted at most a few minutes, and office material fires would burn out within about twenty minutes in any given location.

➤ Molten metal found in the debris of the WTC may have been the result of a high-temperature reaction of a commonly used explosive such as thermite. Buildings not felled by explosives "have insufficient directed energy to result in melting of large quantities of metal," Jones says.

➤ Multiple loud explosions in rapid sequence were reported by numerous observers in and near the towers, and these explosions occurred far below the region where the planes struck.

In January 2006 Jones, along with a group calling themselves "Scholars for 9/11 Truth," called for an international investigation into the attacks and are going so far as to accuse the U.S. government of a massive cover-up.

"We believe that senior government officials have covered up crucial facts about what really happened on September 11," the group said in a statement. "We believe these events may have been orchestrated by the administration in order to manipulate the American people into supporting policies at home and abroad."

The group is headed by Jones and Jim Fetzer, University of Minnesota Duluth distinguished McKnight professor of philosophy, and is made up of fifty academicians and experts including Robert M. Bowman, former director of the U.S. "Star Wars" space defense program, and Morgan Reynolds, former chief economist for the Department of Labor in President George W. Bush's first term.

19

Destruction of Rainforests Worst Ever

Source:

The Independent, October 21, 2005
Title: "Revealed: the True Devastation of the Rainforest"
Author: Steve Connor

Faculty Evaluator: Myrna Goodman, Ph.D.
Student Researchers: Courtney Wilcox and Deanna Haddock

New developments in satellite imaging technology reveal that the Amazon rainforest is being destroyed twice as quickly as previously estimated due to the surreptitious practice of selective logging.

A survey published in the October 21 issue of the journal *Science* is based on images made possible by a new, ultra-high-resolution satellite-imaging technique developed by scientists affiliated with the Carnegie Institution and Stanford University.

"With this new technology, we are able to detect openings in the forest canopy down to just one or two individual trees," says Carnegie scientist Gregory Asner, lead author of the *Science* study and assistant professor of Geological and Environmental Sciences at Stanford University. "People have been monitoring large-scale deforestation in the Amazon with satellites for more than two decades, but selective logging has been mostly invisible until now." While clear-cuts and burn-offs are readily detectable by conventional satellite analysis, selective logging is masked by the Amazon's extremely dense forest canopy.

Stanford University's website reports that by late 2004, the Carnegie research team had refined its imaging technique into a sophisticated remote-sensing technology called the Carnegie Landsat Analysis System (CLAS), which processes data from three NASA satellites—Landsat 7, Terra and Earth Observing 1—through a powerful supercomputer equipped with new pattern-recognition approaches designed by Asner and his staff.[1]

"Each pixel of information obtained by the satellites contains detailed spectral data about the forest," Asner explains. "For example, the signals tell us how much green vegetation is in the canopy, how much dead material is on the forest floor and how much bare soil there is."

For the *Science* study, the researchers conducted their first basin-wide analysis of the Amazon from 1999 to 2002. The results of the four-year survey revealed a problem that is widespread and vastly underestimated, "We found much more selective logging than we or anyone else had expected—between 4,600 and 8,000 square miles every year of forest spread across five Brazilian states," Asner said.

Selective logging—the practice of removing one or two trees and leaving the rest intact— is often considered a sustainable alternative to clear-cutting. Left unregulated, however, the practice has proven to be extremely destructive.

A large mahogany tree can fetch hundreds of dollars at the sawmill, making it a tempting target in a country where one in five lives in poverty. "People go in and remove just the merchantable species from the forest," Asner says. "Mahogany is the one everybody knows about, but in the Amazon, there are at least thirty-five marketable hardwood species, and the damage that occurs from taking out just a few trees at a time is enormous. On average, for every tree removed, up to thirty more can be severely damaged by the timber harvesting operation itself. That's because when trees are cut down, the vines that connect them pull down the neighboring trees.

"Logged forests are areas of extraordinary damage. A tree crown can be twenty-five meters. When you knock down a tree it causes a lot of damage in the understory." Light penetrates to the understory and dries out the forest floor, making it much more susceptible to burning. "That's probably the biggest environmental concern," Asner explains. "But selective logging also involves the use of tractors and skidders that rip up the soil and the forest floor. Loggers also build makeshift dirt roads to get in, and study after study has shown that those frontier roads become larger and larger as more people move in, and that feeds the deforestation process. Think of logging as the first land-use change."

Another serious environmental concern is that while an estimated 400 million tons of carbon enter the atmosphere every year as a result of traditional deforestation in the Amazon, Asner and his colleagues estimate that an additional 100 million tons is produced by selective logging. "That means up to 25 percent more greenhouse gas is entering the atmosphere than was previously assumed," Asner explains, a finding that could alter climate change forecasts on a global scale.

Notes

1. Mark Shwartz, "Selective logging causes widespread destruction, study finds," Stanford University website, October 21, 2005.

20

Bottled Water: A Global Environmental Problem

Source:

OneWorld.net, February 5, 2006
Title: "Bottled Water: Nectar of the Frauds?"
Author: Abid Aslam

Faculty Evaluator: Liz Close, Ph.D.
Student Researchers: Heidi Miller and Sean Hurley

Consumers spend a collective $100 billion every year on bottled water in the belief—often mistaken—that it is better for us than what flows from our taps. Worldwide, bottled water consumption surged to 41 billion gallons in 2004, up 57 percent since 1999.

"Even in areas where tap water is safe to drink, demand for bottled water is increasing—producing unnecessary garbage and consuming vast quantities of energy," reports Earth Policy Institute researcher Emily Arnold. Although in much of the world, including Europe and the U.S., more regulations govern the quality of tap water than bottled water, bottled water can cost up to 10,000 times more. At up to $10 per gallon, bottled water costs more than gasoline in the United States.

"There is no question that clean, affordable drinking water is essential to the health of our global community," Arnold asserts, "But bottled water is not the answer in the developed world, nor does it solve problems for the 1.1 billion people who lack a secure water supply. Improving and expanding existing water treatment and sanitation systems is more likely to provide safe and sustainable sources of water over the long term." Members of the United Nations have agreed to halve the proportion of people who lack reliable and lasting access to safe drinking water by the year 2015. To meet this goal, they would have to double the $15 billion spent every year on water supply and sanitation. While this amount may seem large, it pales in comparison to the estimated $100 billion spent each year on bottled water.

Tap water comes to us through an energy-efficient infrastructure whereas bottled water is transported long distances—often across national borders—by boat, train, airplane, and truck. This involves burning massive quantities of fossil fuels.

For example, in 2004 alone a Helsinki company shipped 1.4 million bottles of Finnish tap water 2,700 miles to Saudi Arabia. And although 94 percent of the bottled water sold in the U.S. is produced domestically, many Americans import water shipped some 9,000 kilometers from Fiji and other faraway places to satisfy demand for what Arnold terms "chic and exotic bottled water."

More fossil fuels are used in packaging the water. Most water bottles are made with polyethylene terephthalate, a plastic derived from crude oil. "Making bottles to meet Americans' demand alone requires more than 1.5 million barrels of oil annually, enough to fuel some 100,000 U.S. cars for a year," Arnold notes.

Once it has been emptied, the bottle must be dumped. According to the Container Recycling Institute, 86 percent of plastic water bottles used in the United States become garbage or litter. Incinerating used bottles produces toxic byproducts such as chlorine gas and ash containing heavy metals tied to a host of human and animal health problems. Buried water bottles can take up to 1,000 years to biodegrade.

Worldwide, some 2.7 million tons of plastic are used to bottle water each year. Of the bottles deposited for recycling in 2004, the U.S. exported roughly 40 percent to destinations as far away as China, requiring yet more fossil fuel.

Meanwhile, communities where the water originates risk their sources running dry. More than fifty Indian villages have complained of water shortages after bottlers began extracting water for sale under the Coca-Cola Corporation's Dasani label. Similar problems have been reported in Texas and in the Great Lakes region of North America, where farmers, fishers, and others who depend on water for their livelihoods are suffering from concentrated water extraction as water tables drop quickly.

While Americans consume the most bottled water per capita, some of the fastest collective growth in consumption is in the giant populations of Mexico, India, and China. As a whole, India's consumption of bottled water increased threefold from 1999 to 2004, while China's more than doubled.

While private companies' profits rise from selling bottled water of questionable quality at more than $100 billion per year—more efficiently regulated, waste-free municipal systems could be implemented for distribution of safe drinking water for all the peoples of the world—at a small fraction of the price.

UPDATE BY ABID ASLAM

Consumer stories are a staple of the media diet. This article spawned coverage by numerous public broadcasters and appeared to do the rounds in cyberspace. Perhaps what seized imaginations was our affinity for the subject: apparently we and our planet's surface are made up mostly of water and without it, we would perish. In any case, most of the discussion of the issues raised by the source—a research paper from a Washington, D.C.–based environmental think tank—focused mainly on consumer elements (the price, taste, and consequences for human health of bottled and tap water), as I had anticipated when I decided to storify the Environmental Policy Institute (EPI) paper (in honesty, that is pretty much all I did, adding minimal context and background). However, a good deal of reader attention also focused on the environmental and regulatory aspects.

Further information on these can be obtained from the EPI, a host of environmental and consumer groups, and from the relevant government agencies: the U.S. Environmental Protection Agency for tap water and the U.S. Food and Drug Administration for bottled water.

Differences in the ways these regulators (indeed, regulators in general) operate and are structured and funded deserve a great deal more attention, as does the unequal protection of citizens that results.

Numerous other questions raised in the article deserve further examination. Would improved waste disposal and recycling address the researcher's concerns about resources being consumed to get rid of empty water bottles? If public water systems can deliver a more reliable product to more people at a lower cost, as the EPI paper says, then what are the obstacles to the necessary investment in the U.S. and in poor countries, and how can citizens here and there overcome those obstacles?

Some of these questions may strike general readers or certain media gatekeepers as esoteric. Then again, we all drink the stuff.

21

Gold Mining Company Threatens Ancient Andean Glaciers

Source:

CorpWatch.com, June 20, 2005
Title: "Barrick Gold Strikes Opposition in South"
Author: Glenn Walker

Inter Press Service, February 15, 2006
Title: "Chile: Yes, to Gold Mine But Don't Touch the Glaciers"
Author: Daniela Estrada

Faculty Evaluator: Andrew Roth, Ph.D.
Student Researcher: Michelle Salvail

Barrick Gold, a powerful multinational gold mining company, planned to melt three Andean glaciers in order to access gold deposits through open pit mining. The water from the glaciers would have been held for refreezing in the following winters. Opposition to the mine because of destruction to water sources for Andean farmers was widespread in Chile and the rest of the world. Barrick Gold's Pascua Lama project represents one of the largest foreign investments in Chile in recent years, totaling $1.5 billion. However, some 70,000 downstream farmers backed by international environmental organizations and activists around the world waged a campaign against the proposed mine.

In the fall of 2005, environmental activists dumped crushed ice outside the local headquarter of Barrick Gold in Santiago. Thousands had marched earlier in the year shouting slogans such as, "We are not a North American colony," and handing out nuggets of fool's gold emblazoned with the words *oro sucio*—"dirty gold."

In February 2006, Chile's Regional Environment Commission (COREMA) gave permission for Barrick Gold to begin the project, but did not approve the relocation of the three glaciers.

"The mine will cause severe damage to the local ecosystem because it will pollute the Huasco River as well as underground water sources," said Antonia Fortt, an environmental engineer with the Oceana Ecological Organization.

The Pascua Lama deposits are considered one of the world's largest untapped sources of gold ore, with a potential yield of 17.5 billion ounces of gold. Barrick's removal of the gold will employ cyanide leaching for on-site processing of the ore. Cyanide is a chemical compound that is extremely toxic to humans and other life forms. Environmentalists are worried that the cyanide will leach into the water systems and contaminate entire ecosystems downstream. Construction of the mine will begin in 2006 and begin full operations in 2009.

Barrick Gold also succeeded in convincing both the Chilean and Argentine governments to sign a binational mining treaty, which allows the unrestricted flow of machinery, ore, and personnel across the border. Lawsuits against the treaty are pending in Chilean courts.

Barrick Gold has been accused of burying fifty miners alive in Tanzania and blatantly disregarding environmental concerns in operations all over he world. George H. W. Bush, from 1995 to 1999, was the "Honorary Chairman" of Barrick's international Advisory Board.

Barrick Gold is the third largest gold mining company in the world, with a portfolio of twenty-seven mining operations in five continents. Gold sales in 2005 were $2.3 billion.

The company is based in Canada, but U.S. directors include: Donald Carty, CEO of AMR Corp and American Airlines, Dallas, Texas; J. Brett Harvey, CEO CONSOL Energy Inc., Venitia, Pennsylvania; Angus MacNaughton, President of Genstar Investment Inc., Danville, California; and Steven Shapiro, VP Burlington Resources, Inc., Houston,Texas.

22

Billions in Homeland Security Spending Undisclosed

Source:
Congressional Quarterly, June 22, 2005
Title: "Billions in States' Homeland Purchases Kept in the Dark"
Author: Eileen Sullivan

Faculty Evaluator: Noel Byrne, Ph.D.
Student Researchers: Monica Moura and Gary Phillips

More than $8 billion in Homeland Security funds has been doled out to states since the September 11, 2001 attacks, but the public has little chance of knowing how this money is being spent.

Of the thirty-four states that responded to *Congressional Quarterly*'s inquiries on Homeland Security spending, twelve have laws or policies that preclude public disclosure of details on Homeland Security purchases. Many states have adopted relevant nondisclosure clauses to the Freedom of Information Act (FOIA). The reason, state officials say, is that the information could be useful to terrorists.

Further hindering public demand for accountability, Department of Homeland Security (DHS) spokesperson Marc Short confirms, DHS will not release its records on state spending of funds.

"These non-disclosure policies are troubling," Steven Aftergood, director of the research organization Project on Government Secrecy, warns in an interview with *CQ*. "Accountability is the price we pay. We're giving away the ability to hold public officials accountable. More than we value public oversight, we fear a nebulous terrorist threat, and this is changing the character of American political life."

New York is one of many states that will disclose broad categories of purchases, such as personal protective gear, but will not specify type of equipment, which company makes it, how much it costs, or where it is going.

Roger Shatzkin, *CQ*'s interviewee on the subject of New Jersey's policy on Homeland Security spending disclosure, offered this example: "If there was a potential flaw in equipment, that could be exploited [by terrorists], so the state would not want that information to become public."

Aftergood counters that taxpayers have the right to know if law enforcement is using defective equipment: "One of the things that happens when you restrict information is that you reduce the motivation to fix problems and correct weaknesses."

Colorado's secrecy provision was enacted in 2003, but State Senator Bob Hagedorn says the law has been misinterpreted, authorizing automatic denial of access to any and all information regarding Homeland Security. Hagedorn told *CQ* that this broad application had never been his intention when sponsoring the bill. He warned against the shroud of secrecy as, in early 2005, state lawmakers discovered that Colorado did not have a Homeland Security plan, yet had spent $130 million in Homeland Security funds. "How the hell do you spend $130 million for homeland security when you don't have a damn plan?" Hagedorn asked. "At this point, the public still does not have an official answer to that question," he added.

CQ investigators confirm that federal lawmakers want to know more about how states are spending Homeland Security funds.

"There's a delicate balance that needs to be struck between ensuring our security and not advertising our vulnerabilities, but also ensuring how our security money is being spent," said a staff member for the House Homeland Security Committee who requested anonymity. "We're spending billions of dollars every year on grants to state and local governments . . . there should be some expectation [of] accountability."

23

U.S. Oil Targets Kyoto in Europe

Sources:
The Guardian, December 8, 2005
Title: "Oil Industry Targets EU Climate Policy"
Author: David Adam

The Independent, December 8, 2005
Title: "How America Plotted to Stop Kyoto Deal"
Author: Andrew Buncombe

Faculty Evaluator: Ervand Peterson, Ph.D.
Student Researcher: Christy Baird

Lobbyists funded by the U.S. oil industry have launched a campaign in Europe aimed at derailing efforts to tackle greenhouse gas pollution and climate change.

Documents obtained by Greenpeace reveal a systematic plan to persuade European business, politicians and the media that the European Union should abandon its commitments under the Kyoto protocol, the international agreement that aims to reduce emissions that lead to global warming.

The documents, an email and a PowerPoint presentation, describe efforts to establish a European coalition to "challenge the course of the EU's post-2012 agenda." They were written by Chris Horner, a Washington D.C. lawyer and senior fellow at the rightwing think tank the Competitive Enterprise Institute, which has received more than $1.3 million funding from the U.S. oil giant ExxonMobil. Horner also acts for the Cooler Heads Coalition, a group set up "to dispel the myth of global warming."

The PowerPoint document sets out plans to establish a group called the European Sound Climate Policy Coalition. It says: "In the U.S. an informal coalition has helped successfully to avert adoption of a Kyoto-style program. This model should be emulated, as appropriate, to guide similar efforts in Europe."

During the 1990s U.S. oil companies and other corporations funded a group called the Global Climate Coalition, which emphasized uncertainties in climate science and disputed the need to take action. It was disbanded when President Bush pulled the U.S. out of the Kyoto process. The group's website now says: "The industry voice on climate change has served its purpose by contributing to a new national approach to global warming."

Countries signed up to the Kyoto process have legal commitments to reduce greenhouse gas emissions. Oil and energy companies would be affected by these cuts because burning their products produces the most emissions.

The PowerPoint document written by Horner appears to be aimed at getting RWE, the German utility company, to join a European coalition of companies to act against Kyoto. Horner is convinced that, with Europe's weakening economy, companies are likely to be increasingly ill at ease with the costs of meeting Kyoto mandates and thus could be successfully influenced to pressure their government to reject Kyoto standards, as the U.S. government has. Horner's audiences have included several significant companies including Ford Europe, Lufthansa, and Exxon.

The document says: "The current political realities in Brussels open a window of opportunity to challenge the course of the EU's post-2012 agenda." It adds: "Brussels must openly acknowledge and address them willingly or through third party pressure."

It says industry associations are the "wrong way to do this" but suggests that a cross-industry coalition, of up to six companies, could "counter the commission's Kyoto agenda." Such a coalition are advised to steer debate by targeting journalists and bloggers, as well as attending environmental group meetings and events to "share information on opposing viewpoints and tactics."

24

Cheney's Halliburton Stock Rose Over 3,000 Percent Last Year

Sources:

Raw Story, October 2005
Title: "Cheney's Halliburton Stock Options Rose 3,281 Percent Last Year, Senator Finds"
Author: John Byrne

Senator Frank Lautenberg's website
Title: "Cheney's Halliburton Stock Options Soar to $9.2 Million"

Faculty Evaluator: Phil Beard, Ph.D.

Student Researchers: Matthew Beavers and Willie Martin

Vice President Dick Cheney's stock options in Halliburton rose from $241,498 in 2004 to over $8 million in 2005, an increase of more than 3,000 percent, as Halliburton continues to rake in billions of dollars from no-bid/no-audit government contracts.

An analysis released by Senator Frank Lautenberg (D-NJ) reveals that as Halliburton's fortunes rise, so do the Vice President's. Halliburton has already taken more than $10 billion from the Bush-Cheney administration for work in Iraq. They were also awarded many of the unaccountable post-Katrina government contracts, as off-shore subsidiaries of Halliburton quietly worked around U.S. sanctions to conduct very questionable business with Iran (See Story #2). "It is unseemly," notes Lautenberg, "for the Vice President to continue to benefit from this company at the same time his administration funnels billions of dollars to it."

According to the Vice President's Federal Financial Disclosure forms, he holds the following Halliburton stock options:

100,000 shares at $54.5000 (vested), expire December 3, 2007

33,333 shares at $28.1250 (vested), expire December 2, 2008

300,000 shares at $39.5000 (vested), expire December 2, 2009

The Vice President has attempted to fend off criticism by signing an agreement to donate the after-tax profits from these stock options to charities of his choice, and his lawyer has said he will not take any tax deduction for the donations. However, the Congressional Research Service (CRS) concluded in September 2003 that holding stock options while in elective office does constitute a "financial interest" regardless of whether the holder of the options will donate proceeds to charities. Valued at over $9 million, the Vice President could exercise his stock options for a substantial windfall, not only benefiting his designated charities, but also providing Halliburton with a tax deduction.

CRS also found that receiving deferred compensation is a financial interest. The Vice President continues to receive deferred salary from Halliburton. While in office, he has received the following salary payments from Halliburton:

Deferred salary paid by Halliburton to Vice President Cheney in 2001: $205,298

Deferred salary paid by Halliburton to Vice President Cheney in 2002: $162,392

Deferred salary paid by Halliburton to Vice President Cheney in 2003: $178,437

Deferred salary paid by Halliburton to Vice President Cheney in 2004: $194,852

(The CRS report can be downloaded at: http://lautenberg.senate.gov/Report.pdf)

These CRS findings contradict Vice President Cheney's puzzling view that he does not have a financial interest in Halliburton. On the September 14, 2003 edition of *Meet the Press* in response to questions regarding his relationship with Halliburton, where from 1995 to 2000 he was employed as CEO, Vice President Cheney said, "Since I left Halliburton to become George Bush's vice president, I've severed all my ties with the company, gotten rid of all my financial interest. I have no financial interest in Halliburton of any kind and haven't had, now, for over three years."

Comment: A similar undercovered story of conflicting interest and disaster profiteering by those in the top echelon of the U.S.

Government is of Defense Secretary Donald Rumsfeld's connections to Gilead Sciences, the biotech company that owns the rights to Tamiflu—the influenza remedy that is now the most-sought after drug in the world. This story was brought forward by *Fortune* senior writer, Nelson D. Schwartz, on October 31, 2005 in an article titled "Rumsfeld's growing stake in Tamiflu," and by F. William Engdahl for *GlobalResearch*, on October 30, 2005, in an article titled "Is avian flu another Pentagon hoax?"

Rumsfeld served as Gilead's chairman from 1997 until he joined the Bush administration in 2001, and he still holds a Gilead stake valued at between $5 million and $25 million, according to Federal Financial Disclosures filed by Rumsfeld.

The forms don't reveal the exact number of shares Rumsfeld owns, but whipped up fears of an avian flu pandemic and the ensuing scramble for Tamiflu sent Gilead's stock from $35 to $47 in 2005, making the Pentagon chief, already one of the wealthiest members of the Bush cabinet, at least $1 million richer.

What's more, the federal government is emerging as one of the world's biggest customers for Tamiflu. In July 2005, the Pentagon ordered $58 million worth of the treatment for U.S. troops around the world, and Congress is considering a multibillion dollar purchase. Roche expects 2005 sales for Tamiflu to total at about $1 billion, compared with $258 million in 2004.

UPDATE BY JOHN BYRNE

The media has routinely downplayed Cheney's involvement and financial investment in Halliburton, one of the largest U.S. defense contractors that received supersized no-bid contracts in Iraq. Ultimately, the importance of the story is that the Vice President of the U.S. is able to use his position of power to reap rewards for his former company in which he has a financial investment. Halliburton may also benefit from a chilling effect in which the Pentagon is more likely to favor Cheney's firm to seek favor with the White House.

Cheney continues to hold 433,333 Halliburton stock options, and receives a deferred salary of about $200,000 a year. According to Cheney's most recent tax returns, he held $2.5 million in retirement accounts, much of which likely came from his former defense firm.

Cheney recently filed disclosure reports that show he is valued at $94 million.

Senator Lautenberg's disclosure, brought forward by *Raw Story*, received no mainstream coverage. While the press has often noted that Cheney was formerly Halliburton's CEO, they routinely fail to mention how much money he accrued from the firm during his service there. They also fail to mention that he continues to receive a pension.

RawStory.com regularly reports on Halliburton and contracts awarded to the company.

SourceWatch.org also has a good library of resources on Halliburton and other defense contractors as well as the Vice President.

Another way to get involved is to contact your local senator or representatives about your concerns, and to ask them to push the Vice President to sell his stock options in Halliburton.

25

U.S. Military in Paraguay Threatens Region

Sources:

Upside Down World, October 5, 2005
Title: "Fears mount as U.S. opens new military installation in Paraguay"
Author: Benjamin Dangl

Foreign Policy in Focus, November 21, 2005
Title: "Dark Armies, Secret Bases, and Rummy, Oh My!"
Author: Conn Hallinan

International Relations Center, December 14, 2005
Title: "U.S. Military Moves in Paraguay Rattle Regional Relations"
Authors: Sam Logan and Matthew Flynn

Faculty Evaluator: Patricia Kim-Rajal, Ph.D.
Student Researchers: Nick Ramirez and Deyango Harris

Five hundred U.S. troops arrived in Paraguay with planes, weapons, and ammunition in July 2005, shortly after the Paraguayan Senate granted U.S. troops immunity from national and International Criminal Court (ICC) jurisdiction. Neighboring countries and human rights organizations are concerned that the massive air base at Mariscal Estigarribia, Paraguay is potential real estate for the U.S. military.

While U.S. and Paraguayan officials vehemently deny ambitions to establish a U.S. military base at Mariscal Estigarribia, the ICC immunity agreement and U.S. counterterrorism training exercises have increased suspicions that the U.S. is building a stronghold in a region that is strategic to resource and military interests.

The Mariscal Estigarribia air base is within 124 miles of Bolivia and Argentina, and 200 miles from Brazil, near the Triple Frontier where Brazil, Paraguay, and Argentina meet. Bolivia's natural gas reserves are the second largest in South America, while the Triple Frontier region is home to the Guarani Aquifer, one of the world's largest fresh water sources. (See Story #20.)

Not surprisingly, U.S. rhetoric is building about terrorist threats in the triborder region. Dangl reports claims by Defense officials that Hezbollah and Hamas, radical Islamic groups from the Middle East, receive significant funding from the Triple Frontier, and that growing unrest in this region could leave a political "black hole" that would erode other democratic efforts. Dangl notes that in spite of frequent attempts to link terror networks to the triborder area, there is little evidence of a connection.

The base's proximity to Bolivia may cause even more concern. Bolivia has a long history of popular protest against U.S. exploitation of its vast natural gas reserves. But the resulting election of leftist President Evo Morales, who on May 1, 2006 signed a decree nationalizing all of Bolivia's gas reserves, has certainly intensified hostilities with the U.S.[1]

When Secretary of Defense Donald Rumsfeld visited Paraguay in August of 2005, he told reporters that, "there certainly is evidence that both Cuba and Venezuela have been involved in the situation in Bolivia in unhelpful ways."

Military analysts from Uruguay and Bolivia maintain that the threat of terrorism is often used by the U.S. as an excuse for military intervention and the monopolization of natural resources.

A journalist writing for the Argentinian newspaper, *Clarin*, visited the base at Mariscal Estigarribia and reported it to be in perfect condition. Capable of handling large military planes, it is oversized for the Paraguayan air force, which only has a handful of small aircraft. The base is capable of housing 16,000 troops, has an enormous radar system, huge hangars, and an air traffic control tower. The airstrip itself is larger than the one at the international airport in Asuncion, Paraguay's capital. Near the base is a military camp that has recently grown in size.

Hallinan notes that Paraguay's neighbors are very skeptical of the situation, as there is a disturbing resemblance between U.S. denials about Mariscal Estigarribia and the disclaimers made by the Pentagon about Eloy Alfaro airbase in Manta, Ecuador. The U.S. claimed the Manta base was a "dirt strip" used for weather surveillance. When local journalists revealed its size, however, the U.S. admitted the base harbored thousands of mercenaries and hundreds of U.S. troops, and Washington had signed a ten-year basing agreement with Ecuador. (See Chapter 2, Story #17, for similarities between the Manta air base in Ecuador, and the current situation unfolding in Paraguay.)

As Paraguay breaks ranks with her neighbors by allowing the U.S. to carry out military operations in the heart of South America, Logan and Flynn report that nongovernmental organizations in Paraguay are protesting the new U.S. military presence in their country, warning that recent moves could be laying the foundation for increasing U.S. presence and influence over the entire region. Perhaps the strongest words come from the director of the Paraguayan human rights organization Peace and Justice Service, Orlando Castillo, who claims that the U.S. aspires to turn Paraguay into a "second Panama for its troops, and it is not far from achieving its objective to control the Southern Cone and extend the Colombian War."

Note

1. "Bolivian Gas War," http://www.Wikipedia.org, May 2006.

UPDATE BY BENJAMIN DANGL

The election of Evo Morales in Bolivia in December of 2005 brought more attention to the U.S. military presence in neighboring Paraguay. Since his election, Morales has nationalized the country's gas reserves and strengthened ties with Cuba and Venezuela to build a more sustainable economy. Such policies have not been warmly received in Washington. Responding to this progressive trend, on May 22, 2006 George Bush said he was "concerned about the erosion of democracy" in Venezuela and Bolivia.

Venezuelan President Hugo Chavez, himself a victim of a U.S.-backed coup, said Bush's comments mean, "He's already given the green light to start conspiring against the democratic government of Bolivia." U.S. troops stationed in Paraguay may be poised for such an intervention. However, human rights reports suggest the U.S. military presence has already resulted in bloodshed.

Paraguay is the fourth largest producer of soy in the world. As this industry expands, poor farmers are being forced off their lands. These farmers have organized protests, road blockades and land occupations against this displacement and have faced subsequent repression from military, police, and paramilitary forces.

Investigations by Servicio Paz y Justicia (Serpaj), a human rights group in Paraguay, report that the worst cases of repression against farmers took place in areas with the highest concentration of U.S. troops. This violence resulted in the deaths of forty-one farmers in three separate areas.

"The U.S. military is advising the Paraguayan police and military about how to deal with these farmer groups," Orlando Castillo of Serpaj told me over the phone. He explained that U.S. troops monitor farmers to find information about union organizations and leaders, then tell Paraguayan officials how to proceed. "The numbers from our study show what this U.S. presence is doing," Castillo said.

The U.S. government maintains the military exercises in Paraguay are humanitarian efforts. However, the deputy speaker of the Paraguayan parliament, Alejandro Velazquez Ugarte, said that of the thirteen exercises going on in the country, only two are of a civilian nature.

This presence is an example of the U.S. government's "counter-insurgency" effort in Latin America. Such meddling has a long, bloody history in the region. Currently, the justification is the threat of terrorism instead of communism. As Latin America shifts further away from Washington's interests, such militarization is only likely to increase.

Throughout these recent military operations, the U.S. corporate media, as well as Paraguayan media, have ignored the story. Soccer, not dead farmers or plans for a coup, has been the focus of most headlines.

For ongoing reports on the U.S. militarization of Paraguay and elsewhere visit www.UpsideDownWorld.org, a website on activism and politics in Latin America, and www.TowardFreedom.com. Benjamin Dangl's book, *The Price of Fire: Resource Wars and Social Movements in Bolivia* (forthcoming from AK Press, January 2007), includes further investigations into the U.S. military operations in Paraguay.

Ideas for action include organizing protests and writing letters to the U.S. embassy in Paraguay (www.asuncion.usembassy.gov). For more information on international solidarity, email Orlando Castillo at Serpaj in Paraguay: desmilitarizacion@serpajpy.org.py

UPDATE BY CONN HALLINAN

My article was written in late November 2005 during the run-up to the Bolivian elections. That campaign featured indigenous leader Evo Morales, a fierce critic of Washington's neoliberal, free trade policies that have impoverished tens of millions throughout Latin America. The Bush administration not only openly opposed Morales, it charged there was a growing "terrorism" problem in the region and began building up military forces in nearby Paraguay.

There have been a number of important developments since last fall. Morales won the election and nationalized Bolivia's petrochemical industry. In the past, such an action might have triggered a U.S.-sponsored coup, or at least a crippling economic embargo. Foreign oil and gas companies immediately tried to drive a wedge between Bolivia and other nations in the region by threatening to halt investments or pull out entirely. This included companies partially owned by Brazil and Argentina.

But Latin America is a very different place these days. Three days after the May 1, 2005 nationalization, Argentine President Nestor Kirchner, Brazilian President Lula De Silva, Venezuelan President Hugo Chavez, and Morales met in Puerto Iguazu and worked out an agreement to help Bolivia develop its resources while preserving regional harmony. As a result, it is now likely that foreign petrochemical companies will remain in Bolivia, although they will pay up to four times as much as they did under the old agreements. And if they leave, the Chinese and Russians are waiting in the wings.

The situation is still delicate. U.S. Defense Secretary Donald Rumsfeld recently compared Chavez to Adolph Hitler and linked him to Cuba's Fidel Castro and Morales. Aid is flowing to militaries in Colombia and Paraguay, and the White House continues to use private proxies to intervene in the Colombian civil war. While there is a growing solidarity among nations in the southern cone, some of their economies are delicate.

Ecuador is presently wracked by demonstrations demanding the expulsion of foreign oil companies and an end to free trade talks with

the U.S. This is an ongoing story. While the alternative media continues to cover these developments, the mainstream media has largely
ignored them.

A note on reading the mainstream: the *Financial Times* recently
highlighted a Latinobarometro poll indicating that most countries in
South America were rejecting "democracy" as a form of government.
But since free markets and neoliberalism were sold as "democracy"—economic policies that most South Americans have overwhelmingly rejected—did the poll measure an embrace of
authoritarianism or a rejection of failed economic policies? Tread
carefully.

To stay informed of developments in this area visit websites of
School of the Americas Watch (http://www.soaw.org/new/) and
Global Exchange (http://www.globalexchange.org/) or contact Conn
Hallinan at connm@ucsc.edu

CENSORED 2007 HONORABLE MENTIONS

Deregulation Champion Named Chair of FERC

Source:
Common Dreams, July 2, 2005
Title: "Energy Adviser Who Solicited Enron to Help Write Nat'l Energy Policy to Be
Named Chair of FERC"
Author: Jason Leopold

The Bush administration announced on June 29, 2005 that Joseph
Kelliher, a staunch supporter of the free-market principles of deregulation, would be named to chair the Federal Energy Regulatory
Commission (FERC). This news was a welcome surprise to many
industry lobbyists and energy executives who know Kelliher and have
a cozy relationship with him. A FERC chairperson's primary responsibility is to protect consumers from the manipulative tactics of the
energy industry. In 2003, after a legal battle, the White House was
forced to release several hundred pages of task force-related documents that showed the extent to which Kelliher went to solicit key
players in the industry to help write the National Energy Policy.

IMF Measures Lead to Economic Collapse in Iraq

Sources:
World Socialist Web Site, February 21, 2006
Title: "IMF Measures Wreak Havoc On Iraqi People"
Author: James Cogan

The Progressive, January 3, 2006
Title: "IMF Occupies Iraq, Riots Follow"
Author: Matthew Rothschild

Large scale rioting broke out in Iraq in December as a result of IMF insistence on lifting fuel subsidies and privatizing state-owned companies in exchange for loans. The immediate impact of IMF measures was a 500 percent rise in the cost of petrol, diesel, cooking gas, and kerosene. The broader impact is soaring inflation on all consumer goods. The main cause of Iraq's budgetary crisis is the collapse of oil exports. Oil production has dropped 50 percent since the U.S. occupation. Iraq must now import at world market prices. Riots erupted in Iraq as a result of the IMF-induced economic collapse two months prior to the February bombing of the Shiite mosque.

Thousands Killed by Death Squads in Iraq

Sources:
GreenLeft, March 15, 2006
Title: "IRAQ: Thousands killed by government death squads"
Author: Doug Lorimer

Truthout, March 3, 2006
Title: "Negroponte's Serious Setback"
Author: Dahr Jamail

More than 7,000 people have been killed by Iraqi interior ministry death squads in recent months, many showing signs of torture. John Negroponte was the U.S. ambassador in Iraq from June 2004–April 2005—precisely the time Pentagon chiefs were considering the "Salvador option," the proposal to organize death squads from within U.S.-recruited Iraqi security forces, to target Sunni resistance and their sympathizers. (Negroponte was an interesting choice as ambassador to Iraq. While U.S. ambassador to Honduras 1981–1985, he oversaw CIA recruitment of the infamous death squads from within the Honduran military. Resulting civilian deaths soared into the tens of thousands.)

EPA Library Axed

Source:
PEER website, February 2, 2006
Title: "Bush Axing Libraries While Pushing for More Research"

Under Bush's proposed budget, the EPA is slated to shut down its network of libraries that serve its own scientists as well as the public. EPA's scientists use the libraries to research questions such as the safety of chemicals and the environmental effects of new technologies. EPA enforcement staff use the libraries to obtain technical information to support pollution prosecutions and to track the business histories of regulated industries. "How are EPA scientists supposed to engage in cutting edge research when they cannot find what the agency has already done?" asked PEER Executive Director Jeff Ruch.

Peruvians Violated by Pipeline: Ruptured Pipeline in Peru Poisons Indigenous Communities

Sources:
IPS, March 2, 2006
Title: "Rights of Isolated Indigenous Communities Violated by Amazon Pipeline"
Author: Ángel Páez

IPS, March 2, 2006
Title: "Bank Rejects Rapid Review of Controversial Pipeline"
Author: Emad Mekay

A $1.6 billion pipeline stretching from the Amazon Jungle to the Peruvian coastline is devastating indigenous communities. Financed by various foreign investors, including Hunt Oil from Texas, shoddy construction has resulted in four ruptures, leaking gas into water resources. Contagious disease from foreign employees of gas companies is spreading into the indigenous population, including influenza, diarrhea, and syphilis.

Pentagon's Database on Children

Source:
Vermont Guardian, January 17, 2006
Title: "Mining for Kids: Children Can't 'Opt Out' of Pentagon Recruitment Database"
Author: Kathryn Casa

A $70.5 million database of over 30 million children and young adults is being used by the Pentagon for recruiting purposes. Parents cannot remove their children's names from the database. The No Child Left Behind Act requires schools to report data of children in secondary schools to military recruiters. The Pentagon purchases information supplied by private corporations, including General Motors and Hooked on Phonics.

Dismantling the VA Healthcare System

Sources:
Military.com, September 29, 2005
Title: "Dismantling VA"
Author: Larry Scott

The Bush administration has recently stepped up efforts to dismantle the Veterans' Administration health care system by privatizing its functions. Funds are now being used from the VA budget to study the outsourcing of healthcare workers' jobs.

Shoshone vs. U.S.

Sources:
The New Standard, March 6, 2006
Title: "Western Shoshone Struggle Earns World Recognition"
Author: Michelle Chen

Oxfam America, Spring 2006
Title: "United Nations Intervenes on Behalf of Native American Tribe," *Freedom Socialist*, December 2005 / January 2006

Title: "No to radioactive garbage on Native land!"
Author: Jonathon Hurd

The UN High Commission on Human Rights sternly rebuked the

U.S. government for civil and human rights violations against the Western Shoshone Nation. In the first UN decision to specifically target U.S. policy toward Native Americans, the U.S. government was urged to halt any plans to appropriate Western Shoshone territory for private development or environmentally destructive government projects. The disputed territory is not only viewed as prime real estate for the mining industry and geothermal energy development, but is also the site of over 1,000 nuclear bomb tests. It also contains Yucca Mountain, where the DoE intends to build the highly controversial nuclear waste repository.

Power Plants Go Unregulated

Sources:
Common Dreams, September 13, 2005
Title: "Senate Vote Leaves Women and Children at Risk of Mercury Poisoning"
Authors: Sierra Club

BushGreenWatch.org, September 16, 2005
Title: "Six Senate Democrats Vote to Retain Bush Mercury Rule"

In March 2005 the EPA took power plants off the list of sources of toxic pollutants, and instead has created a pollution trading scheme. A resolution challenging the EPA's cutback of Clean Air Act requirements to reduce mercury emissions failed in the Senate this September, leaving an estimated one in six women at risk of passing mercury poisoning on to their newborn children. Despite the Senate vote against the resolution, many states continue to lead the way with plans to crack down on mercury pollution from coal-fired power plants.

War Profiteering Defense Contractors

Sources:
OneWorld U.S., August 31, 2005
Title: "Report Scores Runaway CEO Pay, Alleges War Profiteering"
Author: Abid Aslam

The Boston Globe, August 30, 2005
Title: "U.S.: CEOs with Defense Firms Double Salaries Since 9/11"
Author: Bryan Bender

CEOs in the U.S. defense industry have seen a 200 percent pay increase since September 11, 2001—as compared to an average 7 percent increase for all CEOs—equal to 431 times what the average worker earns. This data is revealed in a report by the Institute for Policy Studies and United for a Fair Economy.

Selling the Amazon

Source:
AlterNet, January 17, 2006
Title: "Selling the Amazon for a Handful of Beads"
Author: Kelly Hearn

Declassified contracts reveal that sixteen multinational oil companies use the Ecuadorian military like a private army. Occidental Oil built a military base for Ecuadorian troops near a Quichua Indian community. Indigenous communities are being intimated, and have signed over land and future rights to sue in exchange for plates and cups, soccer balls, and modest allotments of food and medicine.

Red Cross's Deadly Silence

Source:
Left Turn Magazine No.16, May/June 2005
Title: "Protecting Torture: The Red Cross' Deadly Silence"
Author: Rafeef Ziadah

The International Committee of the Red Cross (ICRC) confidentiality policy gives detaining powers legitimacy in Abu Ghraib, Guantanamo Bay's Camp X-Ray, and many Israeli detention centers. The policy, in effect, allows ICRC to politely ask torturers to stop torturing, while promising not to tell the rest of the world. While ICRC is maintaining "good working relations with authorities," prisoners continue to be tortured.

World Health Organization Allows Genetic Engineering of Smallpox

Source:

Third World Resurgence No. 176, April 2005
Title: "NGOs urge WHO to reject genetic engineering of smallpox"

OrganicConsumers.org, April 4, 2005
Title: "International Campaign to Stop Genetic Engineering of Smallpox Virus"

Despite the eradication of smallpox, strands still exist in two laboratories in the U.S. and Russia. Research is being done to develop even more deadly versions of the smallpox virus. The Department of Homeland Security claims they are experimenting with the virus in order to facilitate the development of vaccines to combat the possible use of smallpox in a terrorist attack. Despite criticism that accidental release of the virus could threaten millions of lives, the World Health Organization has approved the genetic modification of the deadly smallpox virus and continuing research.

THIS MODERN WORLD

by TOM TOMORROW

They prefer to discuss the war in abstract terms.

I'M SO PROUD OF THE NOBLE SACRIFICES OUR VALIANT TROOPS HAVE MADE BRINGING THE BLESSINGS OF LIBERTY AND FREEDOM TO THE OPPRESSED PEOPLES OF IRAQ.

IT WARMS MY HEART TO THINK OF IT, IN A GENERAL AND NON-SPECIFIC KIND OF WAY.

They're most comfortable with symbolic gestures of support.

THE NUMEROUS RIBBON MAGNETS ON MY CAR CLEARLY DEMONSTRATE THE STEADFAST DEPTH OF *MY* RESOLVE!

AND THEY WON'T EVEN DAMAGE THE *PAINT!*

They'd rather not follow the news from Iraq *too* closely.

DICK CHENEY SAYS THE INSURGENCY IS IN ITS *FINAL THROES!* CONDI RICE AGREES THAT IT'S *LOSING STEAM!*

THAT'S ALL *I* NEED TO KNOW! VICTORY MUST BE RIGHT AROUND THE *CORNER!*

They definitely don't want to think about the body bags being unloaded under cover of darkness.

AHEM! IF YOU DON'T MIND, THEY'RE CALLED "TRANSPORT TUBES" THESE DAYS!

"BODY BAG" IS *SUCH* AN UNCOUTH TERM!

And they *really* resent being confronted with the actual faces of the fallen.

CINDY SHEEHAN'S SON WOULD *NOT* HAVE WANTED HER TO BE SUCH A TRAITOROUS AMERICA-HATING @#&$%*!!

HE *WOULD*, HOWEVER, HAVE WANTED *US* TO *DENOUNCE* HIS MOTHER AS VITRIOLICALLY AS *POSSIBLE!*

I'M *SURE* OF IT!

They know what they want to believe--and they're not going to let *REALITY* get in the way.

AFTER ALL--EVERYTHING WOULD BE *JUST FINE*--

--IF EVERYONE WOULD JUST *PRETEND THAT THINGS ARE FINE!*

THERE'S A LIGHT AT THE END OF THE TUNNEL-- I JUST *KNOW* THERE IS!

CLAP HARDER, EVERYONE! CLAP *HARDER!*

CHAPTER 2

Censored Déjà Vu
What Happened to Previous Censored Stories

by Peter Phillips, Kate Sims, Tricia Boreta, and the Project Censored writing team

Censored #1 2006
Bush Administration moves to eliminate open government

At the end of 2004, the mainstream media ignored a congressional report on secrecy in the George W. Bush administration. According to the report, the cumulative effect of the Bush administration's efforts to maintain secrecy has been an unparalleled assault on those laws that have made our government relatively open and accountable. The report revealed that laws were rewritten and practices changed to reduce public and congressional scrutiny of executive activities. The administration has obtained unique authority to conduct government operations in secret, with little or no judicial oversight. Since 2001, the use of national security classifications has accelerated, the presumption of disclosure has been eliminated, and automatic declassifications are increasingly postponed or avoided.

Original source: Lightfoot, Karen, "New Report Details Bush Administration Secrecy," Press Release from the Office of Henry Waxman, *Common Dreams*, September 14, 2004; United States House of Representatives Committee on Government Reform—Minority Staff Special Investigations Division: Report, "Secrecy in the Bush Administration," September 14, 2004.

UPDATE BY CHARLENE JONES

Efforts by the Bush administration to operate in secret have accelerated since publication of the Waxman report in 2004. Senator Patrick Leahy (D-Vt.) calls it "the first White House in modern times that is openly hostile to the public's right to know." Federal departments are classifying documents at the rate of 125 a minute, using new loosely defined security designations. According to the federal Information Security Oversight Office, officials classified 15.6 million documents in 2004, nearly twice those in 2001. Meanwhile the declassification of material slowed to only 28 million pages, down from 204 million in 1997. Intelligence agencies have also removed thousands of historical documents that had been available for years. Since 1999 a secret program at the National Archives has restored classified status to more than 55,000 previously declassified pages. The program began during the Bill Clinton Administration, but according to the *New York Times*, gathered speed under President George W. Bush.

Since September 11, according to the Reporters Committee for Freedom of the Press, the government has taken an "astonishing amount of information away from the American people." Thomas Kean, chairman of the 9/11 Commission, was quoted in the *New York Times* saying, "You'd just be amazed at the kind of information that's classified—everyday information, things we all know from the newspaper." And, according to the *Boston Globe*, documents not vital enough for the "classified" designation are given pseudo-classifications such as "For Official Use Only" and "Sensitive But Unclassified."

The 2005 Secrecy Report Card from OpenTheGovernment.org found that:

➤ Government concealment is costing taxpayers more money. Costs of classifying documents rose from $4.7 billion in 2001 to $7.2 billion in 2005 (not including CIA classification activities).

➤ Between 2001 and 2005, officials invoked the "State secrets privilege" (to keep federal court hearings and documents from the public) thirty-three times more often than officials did during height of the Cold War.

➤ FOIA requests have quadrupled since 2000 to more than 4 million (according to the Coalition of Journalists for Open Government, FOIA denials increased 22 percent in the same time period).

➤ Between 2001 and 2005, nearly two-thirds of 7,045 federal advisory committee meetings were closed to the public and secrecy orders were issued on 124 patents.

In December 2005, President Bush issued an executive order said to help process the backlog of FOIA requests by appointing a chief

FOIA officer in all federal agencies. FOIA officers are already in place, however, and the executive order did nothing to rescind impediments put in place during his first administration.

In 2004 and again in 2005, Rep. Waxman proposed sweeping "Restore Open Government" acts to restore public access to presidential records, prohibit secret advisory committees, promote timely declassification of government documents, and improve the operations of FOIA.

Neither bill was debated on the floor of the House, nor did they receive attention in the news. Both bills were cleared from the books at the end of their congressional session.

On June 24, 2005, the Senate approved less comprehensive bills introduced by John Cornyn (R-Tex.) and Patrick Leahy (D-Vt.) that address FOIA reform and protection specifically. These bills would strengthen FOIA and close loopholes, set up a commission to oversee FOIA processing, and mandate that legislation making government information exempt from FOIA provide an explanation for the exemption within the text of the bill. As of March 2006, one bill (S. 394) had been sent to the Senate Judiciary Committee, another (S. 589) was awaiting debate on the Senate floor, and the last (S. 1181) had passed the Senate and been sent to the House.

On April 26, 2006, the House Government Reform Committee approved the Executive Branch Reform Act of 2006 to end secret meetings between lobbyists, contractors and executive branch officials, provide protection to national security whistleblowers, and end the use of pseudoclassifications (as mentioned above).

Update Sources: *New York Times*. "U.S. reclassified many documents in secret review," February 21, 2006; *Roanoke Times*. "The White House's maestro of secrets," February 17, 2006; "Home Front Confidential," Reporters Committee for Freedom of the Press, September 2005; *Atlantic Journal Constitution*. "Study: Feds' secrecy grown gets costlier; Critics say loss of access hurts public," September 4, 2005; *Atlantic Journal Constitution*. "Study: Feds' secrecy has spread under Bush," November 23, 2005; "Executive Order to 'Improve' Freedom of Information Act," OMB Watch, 2005; "The Card Memo," Coalition of Journalists for Open Government, 2005; *New York Times*, "Since 2001, sharp increase in the number of documents classified by the government," July 3, 2005; *Boston Globe*. "In terror war's name, public loses information," April 24, 2005; *U.S. Fed News*. "Committee approves bill to end secret contacts between lobbyists and executive branch officials," April 6, 2006; *States News Service*. "Senate Approves Cornyn-Leahy FOIA Reform," June 24, 2005; *States News Service*. "Statement of Patrick Leahy on sunshine week 2006 and assault on public's right to know," March 15, 2006; Mendoza, Martha. "Federal agencies fall far short of the requirements of the Freedom of Information Act," *Associated Press Worldstream*, March 17, 2006.

For more information:
www.democrats.reform.house.gov
www.ombwatch.org
http://www.cjog.net

Censored #2 2006
Media Coverage Fails on Iraq

Part 1: Update on Coverage of War Crimes in Iraq

Between 2003 and 2005, the United States conducted two major sieges against the Iraq city of Fallujah. The first resulted in a defeat for Coalition forces. The second (November 8, 2004) generated widespread charges of human rights violations. Non Governmental Organizations (NGOs) around the world claimed U.S. forces broke many international laws with impunity. Iraqi civilians were denied access to food supplies and doctors were not allowed to help the wounded. Meanwhile, the U.S. media applauded the invasion as a major success with minimal casualties. Embedded reporters were denied entry to the destroyed areas and provided little coverage of the carnage or illegal use of weapons.

Original Sources: Trotochaud, Mary and Rick McDowell. "The Invasion of Fallujah: A Study in the Subversion of Truth," *Peacework*, December 2004–January 2005; Walsh, David. "U.S. Media Applauds Destruction of Fallujah," *World Socialist Web Site*, November 17, 2004; Jamail, Dahr. "Fallujah Refugees Tell of Life and Death in the Kill Zone," *The NewStandard*, December 3, 2004.

UPDATE

Media coverage of the Iraq invasion showed no improvement throughout 2005 and 2006. According to journalist Dahr Jamail, criticism from human rights groups and other NGOs has had no impact on U.S. military policies. The use of illegal weapons like depleted uranium, cluster bombs, and fuel/air bombs may have actually increased since the attack on Fallujah in 2004. The military also admitted to using white phosphorous during and after the siege of Fallujah. White phosphorous may be used as smoke screens or for marking targets, but it is illegal when used for an offensive attack, especially if civilians may be in the designated areas. According to RAI television in Italy, dead women and children were found in Fallujah after the invasion with deep burns on their bodies caused by white phosphorus. Plus, officers from the second Infantry Fire Support Element admitted using white phosphorus as a weapon while in Iraq.

Update Sources: Wilson, Jamie. *Guardian* (Manchester), November 16, 2005.
Email update: Dahr Jamail

Part 2: Civilian Death Toll is Ignored
In October 2004 a well-established British medical journal, *The Lancet*, published a study claiming that nearly 100,000 civilians had died in Iraq since the invasion began. Researchers undertook a national survey of Iraq to estimate mortality rates before the invasion and after the invasion. Research results showed that, after the invasion in early 2003, the leading cause of death for Iraqi civilians was military violence.

Original Sources: Les Roberts et al, "Mortality Before and After the 2003 Invasion of Iraq," *The Lancet*, October 29, 2004; Horton, Richard. "The War in Iraq: Civilian Casualties, Political Responsibilities," *The Lancet*, October 29, 2004; Guterman, Lila. "Lost Count," *The Chronicle of Higher Education*, February 4, 2005; Hollar, Julie. "CNN to Al Jazeera: Why Report Civilian Deaths?" *FAIR*, April 15, 2004.

UPDATE
While the figures produced by Dr. Les Roberts and his colleagues have become widely accepted throughout Europe, the *Lancet* article did receive some criticism after its publication, mostly from the U.S. press.

What was not noted in the U.S. mainstream is that Roberts used nearly identical sampling techniques to study mortality in the Congo,

Bosnia, and Rwanda—and that U.S. and British officials quoted these findings without question in speeches condemning those killings. According to Roberts, "Tony Blair and Colin Powell have quoted those results time and time again without any question as to the precision or validity."

In December 2005, George W. Bush declared that the Iraqi civilian death toll was around 30,000, most likely based on estimates from the Iraq Body Count website. However the researchers at Iraq Body Count remind people that they only count deaths reported and confirmed in the media. One researcher said, "We've always maintained that the actual count must be much higher."

There have been no other surveys done in Iraq to measure an up-to-date civilian death toll. Journalist Dahr Jamail asserts that at this point (the middle of 2006) there have probably been many more than 100,000 civilians killed in Iraq and maintains that, even at the time of its publication, the *Lancet* figure was low, for two reasons:

In order not to skew the survey, the researchers erred on the conservative side. They omitted areas of major combat operations, like Fallujah and Najaf, eliminating thousands of deaths.

The baseline for this survey (to which new figures are compared) was the last two years of the sanctions, when the death rate was already much higher than normal.

Jamail concludes that one would have to double the *Lancet*'s initial figure to even approach an accurate estimate of the post-invasion civilian death toll.

Update Sources: Ruder, Eric. "How a study of Iraqi casualties was dismissed: The true toll of the U.S. war," *Socialist Worker*, November 11, 2005, http://www.socialistworker.org/2005-2/565/565_05_TrueToll.shtml.
Email Update: Dr. Les Roberts
Email Update: Dahr Jamail

Censored # 3 2006
Another Year of Distorted Election Coverage

Story number three in Censored 2006 was about the uncovered controversy surrounding the presidential election of 2004. The unusual discrepancy between election results and exit polls brought up the question of whether exit poll data was a reliable predictor of actual vote count. Almost two years later factors such as the purge of black voters, the million missing ballots cast but not counted, and the malfunctioning voting machines all point to the possibility of fraud and corruption.

Original Sources: Freeman, Steve and Josh Mitteldorf. "A Corrupted Election," *In These Times*, February 15, 2005; Palast, Greg and Rev. Jesse Jackson. "Jim Crow Returns To The Voting Booth," *Seattle Post-Intelligencer*, January 26, 2005; Fitrakis, Bob and Harvey Wasserman. "How a Republican Election Supervisor Manipulated the 2004 Central Ohio Vote," *www.freepress.org*, November 23, 2004.

UPDATE BY KRISTINE MEDEIROS

In 2005, Rep. John Conyers asked the Government Accountability Office (GAO) to examine the allegations of election fraud and corruption in the 2004 election. In September 2005 the GAO concluded that, while there is no evidence that the election was rigged, the U.S. election system has a number of serious weaknesses. It found that electronic voting systems "have caused local problems in federal elections resulting in the loss of votes or miscounts of votes."

One of the major concerns with electronic voting systems, the GAO reports, is that they can be hacked because of inadequate security systems. The report cited a number of examples. On Diebold's Accu-Vote-TS, the voter may touch the screen for one candidate and the vote will be recorded and counted for another. In Florida, security reviews showed that someone with access to an optical scan system can falsify election results without any record of the deed. Other computer security experts (in a test environment) used smart cards and memory cards to improperly access administrator functions, vote multiple times, change vote totals, and produce false elections reports. "It is incumbent upon Congress," concluded Rep. Conyers, "to respond to this problem and to enact much needed reforms such as a voter verified paper audit trail that protects all Americans' rights to vote."

In the 2000 election 2 million African-Americans' votes were not cast and Kerry vowed to the NAACP that it would not happen again. But nearly 3 million votes were cast and not counted in the 2004 election. Journalist Greg Palast predicted what happened in 2004, and he is predicting it for the 2006 and 2008 elections. Behind the 2000 felon purge lists and behind the 2004 caging lists were databases from the same companies that now have homeland security contracts.

Palast claims that there is a pattern to the manipulation of national elections. This includes "spoiling" ballots (such as the hanging chads), rejecting "provisional ballots," voters finding themselves at the "wrong" precinct or wrongly "scrubbed" from voter rolls, "caging" lists used to challenge voters with "suspect" addresses, not counting absentee ballots, and delayed registrations. Many of these were tactics used during the "Jim Crow" era following the Civil War. They are also tactics that the U.S. has chastised dictatorships and rogue nations for using.

Meanwhile, for 2006 and 2008, the GOP is pushing new voter ID requirements that, if passed, could quadruple the number of voters turned away from the polls for "wrong" ID (like a missing middle initial on your voter registration).

To learn more about Palast's forecasts for the 2006 and 2008 elections, read "Armed Madhouse" by Greg Palast (gregpalast.com). For more information about the controversy over the 2004 presidential election, read "Was the 2004 Election Stolen?" by Robert Kennedy Jr. in the June 1, 2006 edition of *Rolling Stone* magazine and "Was the 2004 Election Stolen? NO" by Fahad Manjoo on Salon.com, June 6, 2006.

Update Sources: Bleifuss, Joel. "Ghosts in the Voting Machines," *In These Times*, December 29, 2005; Palast, Greg, "How They Stole Ohio and the GOP 4-step Recipe to 'Blackwell' the USA in 2008, Abracadabra: Three million votes vanish," *Buzzflash*, June 2, 2006; Palast, Greg. *Armed Madhouse*, Dutton Adult 2006; Kennedy, Robert Jr., "Was the 2004 Election Stolen?" *Rolling Stone*, June 1, 2006; Manjoo, Fahad. "Was the 2004 Election Stolen? NO" *Salon.com*, June 6, 2006

Censored #4 2006
Surveillance Society Quietly Moves In

On December 13, 2003 President Bush signed the Intelligence Authorization Act, further eroding civil liberties threatened by the Patriot Act. The law increased funding for intelligence agencies and allowed the FBI access, without judicial review, to records of those suspected of criminal activity. It also widely broadened the definition of surveillable financial institutions, making personal consumer data readily available.

Despite a huge amount of controversy, government tracking and data-mining programs are still in operation. The Pentagon's Total Information Awareness is still in operation despite denial of funding. The MATRIX database was shut down on April 15, 2005, but then reintegrated into other programs. According to the *Capitol Hill Blue*, "The super-secret National Security Agency, under an executive order signed by President Bush not long after September 11, 2001, began monitoring phone conversations and emails of American citizens even though the agency's charter limits their activities to overseas communications."

Original Sources: Swartz, Nikki. "PATRIOT Act's Reach Expanded Despite Part Being Struck Down," *Information Management Journal*, March/April 2004; Miranda, Anna Samson. "Grave New World," *LiP Magazine*, Winter 2004; Hampton, Teresa and Doug Thompson. "Where Big Brother Snoops on Americans 24/7," *Capitol Hill Blue*, June 7, 2004.

UPDATE

In December 2005, the *New York Times* admitted to sitting on the information about the executive order (published by the *Capitol Hill Blue*) for over a year. The *New York Times* had delayed the publication at the request of the White House, under the pretense that releasing such information would jeopardize investigations and alert terrorists to their supervision. Project Censored, which had been criticized for citing the *Capitol Hill Blue* article, was exonerated.

On March 9, 2006, President Bush made many of the Patriot Act provisions permanent. According to the *Baltimore Sun*, despite a year of wrangling, the final version of the measure imposed no meaningful restraints on the vast power Congress granted the government to spy on its own citizens. In some ways, the new law is worse. Not even the secret seizure of library, medical, and business records without probable cause was adequately addressed, though American communities found that provision so offensive that nearly 400 so far have registered formal protests.

Senators demanding greater privacy protections gained traction late last year when it was revealed that the Bush administration has been secretly wiretapping Americans for years without any sort of court approval. In the end, though, nearly all settled for minor concessions from President Bush that leave the worst features of the Patriot Act intact.

In response, says the *Baltimore Sun*, Senate Judiciary Committee Chairman Arlen Specter offered new legislation that would demand evidence of a link to a foreign power before library, business, and medical records could be obtained, eliminate a one-year period before gag orders on requests for such records could be challenged in court, and require that the target of a "sneak and peek" search warrant be notified within seven days of its execution. But this bill is not expected to pass unless the atmosphere in the Senate changes.

The two most important components of the supposedly defunct Total Information Awareness (TIA) program have been renamed and moved to the National Security Agency (NSA). The Pentagon's Counterintelligence Field Activity Office (CIFA) is utilizing the fact-gathering Threat And Local Observation Notice (TALON) program to collect information about "suspicious incidents" and compile dossiers on anti-war meetings, Halliburton protests, and counter-recruitment movements on school campuses. Along with a push to increase CIFA's investigatory capabilities, the Pentagon is supporting legislation to create an exception to the Privacy Act for intelligence agencies, abling them to share information from their spying and data mining programs.

New surveillance and data mining programs are surfacing, from the Department of Homeland Security's ADVISE to the CIA's National Clandestine Service. The government is handing out subpoenas to rummage through search engine data. All in all, this was a frightening year for civil liberties.

Update Sources: *Baltimore Sun.* "Not-so-patriotic act," March 13, 2006; Cockburn, Alexander and Jeffrey St. Clair. "*The New York Times* and The NSA's Illegal Spying Operation: Time Delayed Journalism," *CounterPunch*, December 17, 2005; Gregory, Anthony. "Bush's Secret Surveillance State," *The Future of Freedom Foundation*, December 26, 2005; Babington, Charles. "Congress Renews Patriot Act," *Washington Post*, March 9, 2006; Leopold. Jason. "Bush-NSA Spying in Defiance of Court, Congress," *truthout*, December 29, 2005; Leopold, Jason. "The

NSA Spy Engine—Echelon," *truthout,* January 9, 2006; Bleifuss, Joel. "FBI, DoD, NSA: All Spying on You," *In These Times,* January 28, 2006; Isikoff, Michael. "The Other Big Brother," *Newsweek,* January 30, 2006; Perry, Nat. "Bush's Mysterious New Programs," *ConsortiumNews,* February 21, 2006; Harris, Shane. "TIA Lives On," *National Journal,* February 23, 2006; Pincus, Walter. "Senate Panel Blocks Eavesdropping Probe," *Washington Post,* March 8, 2006,

Censored #5 2006
U.S. Uses Tsunami to Military Advantage in Southeast Asia

After 2004's devastating tsunami, U.S. military activity increased in the region. While supplying aid, the U.S. simultaneously pushed its military agenda forward. Containing China's economic and military power is the primary reason for expanding a military presence. Shortly after the tsunami, the U.S. revived the Utapao military base in Thailand that was used during the Vietnam War. The U.S. reactivated its military cooperation agreements with Thailand and the Visiting Forces Agreement (VFA) with the Philippines. The Bush administration revived its hope of establishing closer ties to the Indonesian military.

Original Sources: Bedi, Rahul. "U.S. turns tsunami into military strategy," *Jane's Foreign Report (Jane's Defence),* February 15, 2005; Bedi, Rahul. "U.S. has used tsunami to boost aims in stricken area," *Irish Times,* February 8, 2005; Lobe, Jim. "Bush Uses Tsunami Aid to Regain Foothold in Indonesia," *Inter Press Service,* January, 18 2005.

UPDATE

As Southeast Asia is deeply affected by the devastation of the tsunami, the Bush administration continues its agenda of militarizing the region. However, virtually all the military alliances established shortly after the tsunami are strained, and efforts to forge stronger military alliances are facing growing opposition.

The Visiting Forces Agreement, which was reactivated by the U.S. with the Philippines, is facing opposition and possible nullification by the Philippine Congress after four U.S. Marines were accused of raping a Filipino woman in November 2005. The resolution calling for an end to the agreement resulted in threats from a U.S. embassy official, who told a senior official of the Philippine Foreign Affairs Department that if the resolution passed, military aid and other financial support from the U.S. would be cut.

The U.S. continues to strengthen military ties with Indonesia despite concerns over human rights abuses by Jakarta forces. The U.S. State Department announced the resumption of military grants through Foreign Military Financing (FMF), allowing Indonesia to purchase lethal weaponry. In its desire for increased military interaction with Indonesia, the U.S. Defense Department has been pushing for weapons sales restrictions enacted by Congress to be loosened. The East Timor and Indonesian Action Network says that Secretary of State Condoleezza Rice is undermining the message Congress sent to the Indonesian government about improving its human rights protections and accountability.

The resumption of FMF is the most significant agreement yet between the U.S. and Indonesian military since the reactivation of the International Military Education and Training and nonlethal Foreign Military Sales shortly after the tsunami. The Minister Counselor for Political Affairs at the Indonesian embassy in Washington said that if restricted by the U.S., Indonesia will modernize its military with the help of other countries, including China. The U.S. State Department also said that the resumption of FMF is in the interest of national security. U.S. military aid to Indonesia now outstrips medical or social aid.

The U.S. Air Force is one step closer to establishing a base in India. On November 7, 2005, over 250 aircrew and 15 F-16 fighters were sent from Japan for a twelve-day joint Air Force exercise while 70,000 protestors rallied outside the gates.

According to a statement made by the U.S. Embassy, the years 2002–2005 were the most active in military operations between India and the U.S. in the past forty years. Not only India's strategic location but its growth as an economic power may make the prospects of having bases more sought-after to counterbalance China's influence. Leftist parties in India state that the exercise was part of a U.S. military strategy to establish bases in the region.

Update Sources: AFX-Asia. "U.S. to resume military aid for Indonesia," *AFX News Limited*, November 23, 2005; *Indo-Asian News Service*. "U.S.

conduct major air force exercise amidst protests," November 7, 2005; *Xinhua News Agency*. "U.S. unhappy with Philippine move to abrogate visiting forces agreement," January 25, 2006; Global News Wire–Asia Africa Intelligence. "U.S. military wants more interaction with Indonesia," *Financial Times Information*, November 22, 2005; Persek, William Jr., "Surprise, India will pull ahead," *International Herald Tribune*, January 31, 2006; Global News Wire–Asia Africa Intelligence. "VFA Termination on hold as U.S. softens on custody," February 10, 2006; Quismundo, Tarra V., "When does the counting start? Debate Rages," *Philippine Daily Inquirer*, May 12, 2006.

Censored #6 2006
The Real Oil for Food Scam

In the late fall of 2004, a small group of U.S. senators, hardcore supporters of the war in Iraq, launched a crusade to "expose" the Oil-for-Food program implemented by the United Nations as the "greatest scandal in the history of the UN." But former UN Inspector Scott Ritter called the attack nothing more than a hypocritical charade to shift attention away from the quagmire in Iraq, and legitimize the invasion by using Iraqi corruption, and not the missing weapons of mass destruction, as the excuse.

Original Sources: Gordon, Joy. "The U.N. is Us: Exposing Saddam Hussein's silent partner," *Harper's Magazine*, December 2004; Ritter, Scott. "The Oil for Food 'Scandal' is a Cynical Smokescreen," *Independent* (London), December 12, 2004.

UPDATE BY SARAH RANDLE

In 2005 and 2006, there was additional coverage of the U.S. role regarding the kickbacks and smuggling in the Oil for Food Program, but in the end the issue was characterized as a failure of the UN. The Independent Inquiry Committee into the United Nations Oil-for-Food Programme (the Volcker Report) took a closer look at the scandal. The report, released in 2006, lays little blame at the feet of the secretary general; most of it is reserved for the members of the Security Council, noting their failure to provide clear directives and guidelines for the program. This is not, however, how it has been portrayed by Republican-leaning news sources.

Update Sources: Urquhart, Brian. "The Oil for Food Program: Who is Guilty?" *New York Review of Books*, February 9, 2006.

Censored #7 2006
Journalists Face Unprecedented Dangers to Life and Livelihood

In last year's story, the International Federation of Journalists reported that 2004 was the deadliest twelve month span ever documented—129 media workers were killed, and forty-nine of these deaths occurred in Iraq. Heightened risks for non-embedded reporters were noted as U.S. military-involved killings were on the rise.

Original Sources: Weissman, Steve. "Dead Messengers: How the U.S. Military Threatens Journalists," *truthout*, Feb. 2, 2005, http://www.truthout.org/docs_2005/022405A.shtml; Jamail, Dahr. "Media Repression in 'Liberated' Land," *InterPress Service*, November 18, 2004, http://www.ipsnews.net/interna.asp?idnews=26333.

UPDATE BY LESLEY AMBERGER

Kidnappers in Iraq, political assassins in Beirut, and hit men in the Philippines made murder the leading cause of work-related deaths among journalists worldwide in 2005.

International Federation of Journalists (IFJ) Secretary General Aidan White described 2005 as "a year of unspeakable violence against media." The IFJ reported record numbers of media professionals killed in 2005. A total of 150 media workers were killed, including eighty-nine "killed in the line of duty, singled out for their professional work." This surpasses the IFJ reported deaths in 2004. At least sixty-one deaths of media workers in 2005 resulted from accidents, including the forty-eight Iranian media workers who were killed in a December 6 military aircraft crash in Tehran.

A total of thirty-eight deliberate killings occurred in the Middle East, all but three in Iraq, making the Middle East the most dangerous place for journalists last year. In addition to the thirty-five targeted killings in Iraq, the U.S. military forces were involved in another five deaths, bringing the number of military-involved killings of journalists to eighteen since the 2003 invasion.

The IFJ numbers differ from those of other media organizations such as the Committee to Protect Journalists (CPJ) and Reporters Without Borders because they include support staff such as drivers and translators with journalists.

Analyses from all three media organizations display a long-term trend. Journalist murders often remain unsolved and unpunished. About 90 percent of recorded killings were not appropriately investigated and occurred with impunity. Less than 15 percent of journalist murders since 1992 have resulted in the capture and prosecution of those who ordered the murders.

CPJ Executive Director Ann Cooper says, "the war in Iraq might lead one to think that reporters are losing their lives on the battlefield. But the fact is that three out of four journalists killed around the world are singled out for murder, and their killers are rarely brought to justice. It's a terrible indictment of governments that let warlords and criminals dictate the news their citizens can see and hear."

Update Source: Committee to Protect Journalists. "From Iraq to Philippines, Murder is top cause of journalist deaths in '05," *Special Report 2006*, January 3, 2006, http://www.cpj.org/Briefings/2006/ killed_05/killed_release_03jan05.html

Censored #8 2006
Iraqi Farmers Threatened By Bremmer's Mandates

Before he left his position, Paul Bremmer, the leader of the Coalition Provisional Authority, issued exactly 100 orders that remade Iraq's economy in the image of the U.S. Economy Plan. One of these orders, "Order 81," allows foreign corporations to patent seeds and force local farmers to purchase them for their crops. Initially, farmers will see an increase in production levels and be all too willing to abandon their old ways in favor of the new technologies. But then they will be locked in, having to pay a license fee for each variety.

Original Sources: Focus on the Global South and GRAIN staff. "Iraq's new Patent Law: a declaration of war against farmers," *Grain.org*, October 2004; Palast, Greg. "Adventure Capitalism," *TomPaine.com*, October 26, 2004; Smith, Jeremy. "U.S. Seeking to Totally Re-engineer Iraqi traditional farming system into a U.S. style corporate agribusiness," *The Ecologist*, February 4, 2005.

UPDATE BY LINDSAY SAN MARTIN

The privatization of Iraq's domestic market economy translates into large profits for Western multinational companies. To circumvent international opposition and dispute, the United States set out to ensure that the New Iraqi Government would "not press for full sovereignty." According to Meacher, Bremmer's new Transitional Administrative Law (TAL) effectively gives the Kurds, the most pro-American section of the population, a veto over the new constitution because the TAL itself states that it can only be amended by a 75 percent vote in parliament. Since the Kurds hold more than 25 percent of the seats in parliament, the possibility of a veto of the New Constitution was improbable. Voters approved the new Constitution in October 2005, with provinces dominated by Kurds and Shi'ite Arabs overwhelming approving it and upholding Bremmer's 100 orders. This paves the way for foreign corporations, many of whom were unable to do business in Iraq during Saddam Hussein's regime, to profit off of Iraq's newly structured domestic market economy.

Update Sources: Juhasz, Antonia. "Bush's Economic Invasion of Iraq," *Los Angeles Times*, August 14, 2005; Meacher, Michael. "My Sadness at the Privatisation of Iraq" *Times* (London). August 12, 2005; Hassan, Ghalli. "Iraq's New Constitution," *OnlineJournal*, September 21, 2005.

Censored #9 2006
Iran's New Oil Trade System Challenges U.S. Currency

Iran was scheduled to announce the opening of a new oil exchange (or bourse) in March of 2006. This new oil exchange would be euro-dominated and could be seen as a threat to the U.S. dollar, which has held global dominance as a world currency reserve. The U.S. would be particularly threatened by the influence a new oil exchange could have on China, impacting its trade agreements with Iran and a possible delinking of the dollar-yuan arrangement with the U.S.

Original Source: Clark, William. "Iran Next U.S. Target?" *GlobalResearch.ca*, October 27, 2005.

UPDATE BY ZOE HUFFMAN
On March 20, 2006, the Iranian Oil Bourse was scheduled to begin operating. It was still on track in February. Then, sometime in March, it was announced that the bourse had been postponed. And, in June, the Iranian Minister of Finance announced that they had not yet decided whether the bourse would be in euros or U.S. dollars. Throughout all of this, mainstream media continued to center on Iran's nuclear proliferation and U.S. efforts to seek sanctions and possible military actions through the oversight of the UN Security Council. The bourse is still on the platform but there is no timeline for its opening. Middle East observers find this suspicious but there are no reports at this time of backroom deals.

The issue is a two-pronged problem. On one hand, there could be an economic threat to the dominance of the dollar in the global exchange of oil. On the other, the nuclear proliferation of Iran convolutes the "what-ifs" of an oil exchange in euros. In the corporate media, the exchange has been virtually ignored or merely a side note to the nuclear proliferation case. This all ties into whether or not the U.S. will take military action against Iran. Any military action in Iran has been predicted to fail, and could hinder talks with Iran.

In talks, the Russians have stood by the side of Iran and the need for a nuclear energy source. China has been aloof, and yet has been opposed to Chapter 7 in UN Security Council talks. There is doubt as to whether or not actions are being enforced due to nuclear proliferation or the oil exchange. It could possibly be a combination of both.

Update Sources: Update from author William Clark; Daly, John C.K., "UPI Intelligence Watch," *UPI*, February 6, 2006; *Deutsche Presse-Agentur.* "Iran still insisting on Persian Gulf oil bourse," April 1, 2006; *Middle East Financial News Wire.* "Iranian bourse deadline," May 20, 2006.

Censored #10 2006
Mountaintop Removal Threatens Ecosystem and Economy

Mountaintop Removal (MTR) is the practice of blowing the tops off of mountains, and in some cases taking out entire ranges, to get at the coal near the surface. MTR has polluted more than 1,200 miles of streams and watersheds in the United States. Clean water for the entire Appalachian region is in danger of being lost forever to the practice. MTR fills valleys with vegetation, rock, and earth called "overburden," which is dumped and compacted in the valley below. The area is then planted with inexpensive, nonnative plants in order to comply with environmental laws that require mining companies to restore affected areas to "a level or gently rolling configuration." The result is a flat, barren plateau that will not support the region's unique diversity of life.

Original Source: Conner, John. "See you in the Mountains: Katuah Earth First! Confronts Mountaintop Removal," *Earthfirst!* November/December 2004.

UPDATE BY DAVID ABBOTT

The practice of MTR is spreading so fast that an accurate accounting of the affected area is not available, but at least 400,000 acres in Tennessee, Kentucky, Virginia, and West Virginia have been destroyed by the practice. If it continues unabated, by 2012 a section of the Appalachians the size of Rhode Island will have been flattened in order to get a few feet of coal.

A loophole in regulation allows mining companies to dump mountaintop waste into seasonal streambeds—what the coal industry describes as "dry hollows." Slurry waste—a byproduct of the mining process—is seeping into wells and water supplies while schools and communities are covered in toxic soot. Opponents of MTR have attempted to get the U.S. Office of Surface Mining (OSM) to enforce a buffer zone prohibiting mining activity within 100 feet of a stream and to get the Army Corp of Engineers to regulate streambed fill. But occasional court victories by advocacy groups are usually set aside on appeal, and local protests are largely ignored or suppressed.

Despite pressure from consumer rights groups, mining regulations continue to be relaxed. When mining companies are fined, they often find legal loopholes that allow them to avoid payment and environmental cleanup. One popular method coal companies use to avoid responsibility is to set up a "subsidiary" in a specific area. Then, when they violate the law, and are charged and fined, the "subsidiary" declares bankruptcy, leaving the mess behind and shielding the real culprits from punishment.

In 2003, Florida-based National Coal Company (NCC) began MTR operations at Zeb Mountain in the Appalachians of Tennessee. NCC moved in after a smaller coal company was unable to recover financially from the violations and fines accumulated while operating the mine. In August 2004, Knoxville author Chris Irwin and fellow Earthfirst! activists Debbie Shumate and Amanda Womac went to NCC's office in West Knoxville to discuss with NCC executives the logic of destroying Zeb Mountain. Their presence was peaceful and they left after failing to gain an audience with any NCC staff members. However, Irwin and Womac quickly received temporary restraining orders issued by NCC citing "rowdy protest . . . use of bludgeons . . . and blocking of traffic." Soon after, Irwin, Womac and others found themselves named in a lawsuit. The protesters' lawyer maintained that the lawsuit, considered a Strategic Lawsuit Against Public Participation (SLAPP), was filed in retaliation for (and to silence) criticism from the protesters about NCC's use of MTR in Tennessee.

Ignoring the intimidation, the activists continued organizing to halt the use of MTR, and in 2006, after almost two years, the coal company dismissed the lawsuit.

Recent books by Erik Reece of the University of Kentucky and Penny Loeb, a former editor of *U.S. News and World Report* (who wrote about MTR in 1997) examine the practice from beginning to end. Another recent book entitled "Missing Mountains," edited by Bobbie Ann Mason, is a collection of essays, fiction, and poetry by thirty-five Appalachian authors who are against the MTR practice. In-depth articles in *National Geographic, Harper's,* and even the *New York Times* and the *Washington Post* are bringing the issues to a larger audience, but with an industry-friendly government in control of environmental and safety regulations, it remains to be seen if reporting will have any real effect.

Update Sources: Mitchell, John G., "When Mountains Move," *National Geographic,* March 2006; Reece, Erik. "Moving Mountains," *Grist.org,* 16 February 2006, http://www.truthout.org/issues_06/ 021706EC.shtml; Kentucky Coal Council & Kentucky Coal Association. "Expanded Online Kentucky Coal Facts," 2005, http://www.coaleducation.org/Ky_Coal_Facts/index.htm; Lydersen, Kari. "Resisting Mountaintop Removal in Tennessee," *The New*

Standard., November 21, 2005, http://www.alternet.org/enviro-health/28489/; Slavin, Peter. "The Coal Mine Next Door," *The American School Board Journal*, March 2006, http://www.asbj.com/current/coverstory.html; Hawthorne, Michael. "EPA chief turns coal lobbyist: Mercury foe now represents a top polluter," *Chicago Tribune*, February 9, 2006; Ivins, Molly. "SLAPP," http://www.alternet.org/story/24293/.

Censored #11 2006
Mandatory Mental Screening Program Usurps Parental Rights

Story # 11 from the 2006 book concentrated on President Bush's New Freedom Commission on Mental Health and its efforts to promote mental health screening programs in public schools throughout the U.S. According to the Center for Disease Control, youth suicides in the U.S. have declined 25 percent in the last ten years, yet the President's Commission insists there is a child suicide epidemic and suggests that public schools are in a "key position" to carry out the screening of America's students and school employees. In 2004 and 2005, Congress and the President appropriated over $900 million for the implementation of a new mental screening system. TMAP, the Texas Medication Algorithm Project, is a program designed to advise physicians regarding drug prescription. Critics of TMAP point out the project's inclination to promote newer, more expensive drugs than those already established, and the redirection of ever increasing profits to the pharmaceutical industry.

Original Sources: Lenzer, Jeanne. "Bush Plans To Screen Whole U.S. Population For Mental Illness," *Asheville Global Report*, British Medical Journal, no. 284, June 24-30, 2004, http://www.agrnews .org/issues/284/#2; Paul, Ron. "Forcing Kids Into a Mental Health Ghetto," *Truth News*, September 13,2004, http://www.truthnews.net/world/2004090078.htm.

UPDATE BY LAUREN POWELL

After simplifying his Parental Consent Act of 2005 (H.R. 181) for fiscal year 2006, Representative Ron Paul (R-TX) was again unsuccessful in passing legislation. Paul's bill would have prohibited federal spending on "universal or mandatory" mental health screening programs. The bill would have also halted federal funding to education institutions that interpret a parent's refusal to allow the screening of their child as abuse or education neglect. Paul's bill was voted down 97–304.

Surveys such as TeenScreen have accelerated over the past two years. Used by school officials to evaluate depression, suicidal tendencies, and other mental illnesses, about one in six of the students screened for mental disorders are referred for treatment and medication. Says Phyllis Schlafly, "If this is a preview of what would happen when 52 million public school students are screened, it would mean hanging a libelous label on 17 million American children and putting 8 million children into the hands of the psychiatric/pharmaceutical industry. " Despite a lack of verification that TeenScreen is effective in the prevention of suicide and depression, it utilizes passive consent—parental consent forms that need to be signed if the parent does *not* want their child to participate.

Survey screening programs are already prompting legal action by parents. In 2005, one family brought suit against an Indiana school district after discovering that their "happy, normal" daughter had been "TeenScreened" without their consent, and diagnosed with obsessive compulsive and social anxiety disorder. In another case, Fields v. Palmdale School District, the Court declared that school power supersedes parental authority at the "threshold of the school door." Ignoring parental concern with a sex survey given to first, third, and fifth graders, the Court ruled in favor of proposed mental health screening through the public school system.

In 2005, the Center for Public Integrity found that, since 1998, the pharmaceutical industry spent more than $800 million in lobbying and campaign donations, $10 million to 527 organizations and tax-exempt political committees. Among the top recipients were George W. Bush and members of influential drug industry committees. The drug industry's lobbying efforts are exceeded only by the insurance industry. One third of lobbyists are former federal government employees from both the House and Senate.

Update Sources: Ismail, M. Asif. "Drug Lobby Second to None: How the Pharmaceutical Industry Gets it's Way in Washington," www.publicintegrity.org, July 7, 2005; Hasslberger, Sepp. "Psychiatric Drugs: TeenScreen Draws Criticism, Legal Challenge," www.nemediaexplorer.org, June 17, 2005; Barlas, Stephen. "Anti-Screen Legislation Returns to Congress," www.psychiatrictimes.com, June 1, 2005; Barlas, Stephen. "House Follows Bush's Request on Mental Health Budgets," www.psychiatrictimes.com, September 1, 2005; Schlafly, Phyllis. "Activist Courts Protect Mental Health Screening of Children in Public Schools," Copley News Service, November 15, 2005; Pringle, Evelyn. "TeenScreen: The Lawsuits Begin," www.counterpunch.org, June 13, 2005; Texas Department of State Health Services, "TMAP-A Collaborative Effort," www.dshs.state.tx.us/mhprograms/TMAPover.shtm; "TeenScreen: A Front Group for the Psycho-Pharmaceutical Industrial Complex," www.psychsearch.net/teenscreen.html.

Additional information: www.teenscreen.org and www.open secrets.org

Censored #12 2006
Military in Iraq Contracts Human Rights Violators

Story #12 of the 2006 edition was about the U.S. government contracting private corporations to recruit, hire, and train civilians to go overseas and perform tasks traditionally fulfilled by military personnel. With the discovery of detainee abuse at Abu Ghraib in Iraq, the subject was raised of nonmilitary contractors committing illegal war crimes overseas and evading U.S. military law due to their status as private contractor/civilian.

Original Sources: Yeoman, Barry. "Dirty Warriors: How South African Hitmen, Serbian paramilitaries, and other human rights violators became guns for hire for military contractors in Iraq," *Mother Jones*, November/December 2004; Chatterjee, Pratap. "Intelligence, Inc." *www.corpwatch.org*, March 7, 2005; Groner, Jonathan. "Untested Law Key in Iraqi Abuse Scandal," *www.law.com*, May 11, 2004.

UPDATE BY KATHRYN ALBERGATE

After the events of 2004, military investigations into prisoner abuse revealed what the mainstream media have not: the abusers at Abu Ghraib were not only military personnel, but privately contracted civilians, doing the duties that they were not necessarily qualified to perform. In a 2006 update, author Pratap Chatterjee said that much of the problem with private contractors "isn't their policies but the lack of training and oversight."

The most recent report from a 2005 Pentagon investigation states that during the eighteen months examined, no private contractor was disciplined or charged with any criminal offense in relation to their work in Iraq. However, seven U.S. military soldiers were convicted for their role in the detainee abuse at Abu Ghraib.

The two private contracting corporations that were most often named in connection with the abuse scandals are CACI International Inc. and Titan Corporation.

MEJA (Military Extraterritorial Jurisdiction Act) of 2000 permits prosecution in U.S. federal courts of Defense Department contractors who commit crimes while working with the military outside the United States. However this law has some unfortunate limitations. It applies only to crimes carrying a minimum one-year sentence and only to contractors hired under the Department of Defense. In recent years, many private contractors have been hired through the Department of the Interior, to which MEJA does not apply. As of 2006, no private contractors have been prosecuted for detainee abuse at Abu Ghraib. According to journalist David Phinney, efforts to hold private contract employees accountable is likely to fall short in light of "a U.S. administration that critics say has repeatedly redefined torture in its 'war on terror' and in the war on Iraq." In the first week of January 2006 President George Bush signed a bill outlawing the torture of detainees, but reserved the right to bypass the law at his discretion.

In September 2005, CACI's contract with the U.S. army was not renewed. Lockheed Martin has become one of the biggest recruiters to date of private interrogators. In June 2005, its subsidiary Sytex advertised eleven job openings for new interrogators in Iraq and in July the company sought twenty-three interrogators for Afghanistan. Ads on several websites for current and former military personnel offered a $70,000 to $90,000 salary, plus a $2,000 sign-up bonus from Lockheed Martin. Not only is Lockheed Martin supplying the U.S. military with interrogators, but with information and transportation. According to author Pratap Chatterjee, "Lockeed Martin won't speak to anyone about their interrogation contracts. I imagine they would say they are completely opposed to torture, though. Even CACI would say that." In an update, Mr. Chatterjee revealed that the Democrats have a new set of regulations proposing to stop war profiteering.

Update Sources: Chatterjee, Pratap. "Meet the New Interrogators: Lockheed Martin," *CorpWatch.org*, November 4, 2005; Human Rights Watch. "Q&A: Private Military Contractors and the Law," October 21, 2004, http://hrw.org/english/docs/2004/05/05/iraq8547_txt.htm; McCarthy, Ellen. "CACI Plans to Drop Interrogation Work," *Post-Newsweek Business Information*, Inc. Newsbytes, September 15, 2005; Phinney, David. "Prison Interrogation For Profit," *CorpWatch.org*, September 15, 2004; Savage, Charlie. "Bush Could Bypass New Torture Ban," *Boston Globe*, January 4, 2006; Spiegel, Peter. "Iraq: No Contractors Facing Abu Ghraib Abuse Charges," *Financial Times*, August 9, 2005.

Censored #14 2006
Corporations Win Big on Tort Reform, Justice Suffers

On February 18, 2005, President Bush signed the Class Action Fairness Act (CAFA) into law. CAFA was decried by citizens' and lawyers' groups for limiting peoples' access to the courts, weakening the constitutional right to trial by jury, consumer and worker protections, and denying due process in civil cases to all but the wealthiest in our society. CAFA was just one example of the attack the Bush administration is carrying out against access to the courts, decreasing liability for corporations that cause harm to individuals and society as a whole. A study done in 2003 showed that there was no correlation and in fact the number of litigations decided in U.S. federal courts is down 79 percent since 1985. After the passing of CAFA, the insurance industry made record profits in a year that should have been a catastrophe due to natural disasters such as Katrina.

Original Sources: Court, Jamie. "Supremes Limit Punitive Damages," *Dollars and Sense*, March/April 2004, http://www.dollarsandsense.org/0304court.html;Goodman, Amy et al. "Tort reform: The Big Payoff for Corporations, Curbing the lawsuits that hold them accountable," *Democracy Now!* February 4, 2005, http://www.democracynow.org/article.pl?sid=05/02/04/1537236.

UPDATE BY DAVID ABBOTT
A tort is "a wrongful act, damage, or injury done willfully, negligently, or in circumstances involving strict liability, but not involving breach

of contract, for which a civil suit can be brought." Proponents of changes in the U.S. legal system have tried to associate tort litigation with a host of ills, from driving doctors out of business to closing municipal swimming pools, increased insurance costs to the rising cost of healthcare.

CAFA may not have had the effect that corporate America intended, but it has been seen as a wedge issue that the Republicans can use against the Democrats to push through the real agenda, which is Medical Malpractice tort reform. CAFA passed in the Senate on a vote of 72-26. In 2004, it was blocked by a filibuster in which the vote was 59-39. Although the law was not changed to any significant degree, eighteen senators changed their vote. Apparently, Democrats were scared of being branded as "soft on tort." The costs of blocking a relatively innocuous law and being branded a "tort reform opponent" were too high. CAFA was easy to support in the end because it was harmless. But it is only the first and least objectionable item on Bush's tort reform agenda. The next issue to be raised will be national medical malpractice reform. In this area, the reforms that were floated by the President during his campaign were far from harmless. CAFA is just a small piece of a larger effort to block plaintiffs' access to the courts, and to shield certain corporations from litigation.

During his six years in office, Bush has endorsed measures that would shield certain corporations from lawsuits. Several of the proposals resulted from Hurricane Katrina and the looming threat of a bird flu pandemic and include the Help Efficient, Accessible, Low Cost, Timely Health Care Act of 2003 (HEALTH). HEALTH caps some pain-and-suffering jury awards at $250,000 and provides a sliding scale for lawyers' fees. Also passed in 2005, the Protection of Lawful Commerce in Arms Act provides gun makers immunity, in most cases, from lawsuits holding them responsible for gun violence. The Asbestos Trust Fund bill, sponsored by U.S. Sen. Orrin Hatch, R-Utah, would create a fund to reimburse those suffering from exposure to asbestos and halt litigation. Lawyers and organized labor oppose the move, saying the fund would not have enough money.

It seems that Senate Democrats chose not to pick a fight on CAFA in order to save their strength for the next, more significant tort reform fight. Now Republicans may cite CAFA's "success" or its bipartisan support as a reason to push for further, much more destructive "reform."

Update Sources: Chimerine, Lawrence and Ross Eisenbre. "The frivolous case for tort law change: Opponents of the legal system exaggerate its costs, ignore its benefits," *Economic Policy Institute*, May 17, 2005, http://www.epi.org/content.cfm/bp157; Newsbatch. "What are the latest developments regarding tort reform?" June 2006, http://www.newsbatch.com/tort.htm; Sebok, Anthony J., "The Class Action Fairness Act of 2005: A reasonable law, but one that should not be a wedge for wide tort reform," February 21, 2005, http://writ.news.findlaw.com/sebok/20050221.html

Censored #17 2006
U.S. Uses South American Military Bases to Expand Control of the Region

According to the 2006 story, Eloy Alfaro Air Base in Manta, Ecuador, is the center of a controversy that includes U.S. efforts to counter insurgencies in Colombia and aims to block mass emigration from Ecuador to the U.S. A ten-year lease agreement in 1999 between Ecuador and the U.S. limits the activities at the base to counternarcotics surveillance flights. However, the U.S. abuses the lease agreement by contracting private corporations to conduct the fumigation of coca crops (along with a host of other military operations). Critics say that the U.S. is using Manta as a foundation to tighten control over the entire region. The FBI are militarizing the Ecuadorian police, providing military tactics and "antiterrorist" training. The Bush administration says that they are mixing military and police roles to "govern its counter-terror efforts in the hemisphere."

Original Sources: Flynn, Michael. "What's the Deal at Manta," *Bulletin of the Atomic Scientists*, January/February 2005; Isacson, Adam, Lisa Haugaard and Joy Olso, "Creeping Militarization in the Americas," *NACLA Report on the Americas*, November/December 2004; Sharma, Sohan and Surinder Kumar. "Colombia- A Shill (proxy) Country For U.S. Intervention In Venezuela," *Z Magazine*, December 29, 2004.

UPDATE BY NICK RAMIREZ AND LAUREN POWELL
Ecuador is in the middle of Colombia's ongoing civil war and U.S. involvement in that civil war. Manta serves as a staging area where

thousands of U.S. mercenaries, contracted through private corporations, have clashed with Colombian insurgents. Companies working at the base include Military Professional Resources Inc., Virginia Electronics, DynCorp, and Lockheed Martin. Many employ retired military personnel.

In 2005, as U.S. officials denied their intentions to expand a military presence in Manta, the U.S. spent $80 million in construction projects that include the expansion of Manta's runway, hangers, and dormitories. Local observers say that the number of U.S. servicemen exceed the 300 cap, with as many as 450 either stationed at Manta or booked in hotels. Locals call violations of the lease agreement (which has displaced some 15,000 residents) unconstitutional.

In 2005, when Ecuador refused to grant U.S. military personnel immunity through the ICC, the U.S. suspended both military training and aid. As a result, Ecuador may lose up to $7 million in aid (see Chapter One, Story #16).

In November 2005, the El Universo news station in Ecuador reported that twenty-eight missiles from Bolivia had been transported to the U.S. military in Manta. However, Chancellor Francisco Carrion denied that any missiles had arrived in Manta. Deputy Foreign Minister, Diego Ribadeneira, maintains that the Manta base agreement does not allow the U.S. to have missiles in Manta, as its only objective is to curb narcotics trafficking.

Ribadeneira further stated that he does not think that the Manta airbase agreement will be renewed in 2009 because of the domestic tension it has created.

Update Sources: *El Universo.* "Misiles bolivianos llevados a base militar de EE.UU. en Ecuador," November 26, 2005; *El Universo.* "Carrion: Misiles no han llegado a base de Manta," November 29, 2005; Hallinan, Conn. "Dark Armies, Secret Bases, and Rummy, Oh My!" Foreign Policy in Focus, November 21, 2005; "Washington to cut Latin American aid," *UPI*, November 23, 2005; Diehl, Jackson, "A losing Latin Policy, Are We About to Punish Democratic Allies?" *Washington Post*, March 10, 2006; "U.S. Security Forces Work Alongside Ecuador Airmen," FDCH Regulatory Intelligence Database, July 25, 2005; Desjarlais, Master Sgt. Orville F. Jr., "Airmen Support Counterdrug Mission in Manta," *Air Force Print News*, July 26, 2005; Reichard, Lawrence and Anthony Kolenic. "Manta: Transforming

Ecuador Into Another Cambodia, Another Colombia," Council on Hemispheric Affairs, May 27, 2004; *BBC*. "Ecuadorian Foreign Minister Opposes agreement on U.S. base," February 11, 2006; *BBC*. "Official says Ecuador unlikely to renew U.S. air base agreement," February 10, 2006; Council on Hemispheric Affairs. "Manta Transforming Ecuador into another Cambodia, another Colombia," http://www.coha.org/NEW_PRESS_RELEASES/New_Press_Releases _2004/04.24_Manta.htm.

Censored #18 2006
Little Known Stock Fraud Could Weaken U.S. Economy

Story #18 of 2006 reported an increasingly common trend in investment that allows certain firms to cash in big—but puts smaller investors and entrepreneurs in danger. Called "short selling," it involves an investor getting "borrowed" stock from a broker to sell at a high value. In this reversal of the classic "buy low/sell high" model, the stock must *drop* in value for the investor to make money. Once the stock has dropped, the investor buys it at the lower value and pockets the difference. The law is that the investor *must* buy the stock back within a given time period. So if the stock price stays the same or increases, the investor must buy the stock back at the higher rate—and lose money.

Normal "short selling," while controversial, is legal in the U.S.— not so for "naked short selling." In this case, the investor borrows the stock to sell but then never buys it back. This causes an artificial devaluing of the stock that is not representative of the health of a company. Worse, some hedge fund firms have hired analyst companies to do research into companies and then release artificial negative findings to the public. This drives the value of a company's stock down and ensures a profit for the hedge funds.

The government does little to regulate this practice or the large hedge fund companies that profit from it. Critics charge that it harms small, start-up companies that are not yet able to rebound from an artificial devaluing of their stock.

Original Sources: Hendricks, David. "Naked Short Selling Is A plague For Businesses And Investors," *San Antonio Express-News*, March 2, 2005; Thiel, Karl. "Who's behind Naked Shorting?"

TheMotleyFool.com, March 30, 2005; Patch, Dave. "SEC's Donaldson Addresses Liquidity Fraud," Financial Wire Stockgate Today Series, September 20, 2004; "Dateline NBC Cancelled and Attorney Accuses DTCC of Cheap Thuggery" April 7, 2005.

UPDATE BY JOE BUTWILL

Since 2005, naked short selling has begun to get more mainstream coverage.

On March 26, 2006, *60 Minutes* aired a news piece entitled "Betting On A Fall" which focused on a legal dispute between a pharmaceutical company and a hedge fund firm. The pharmaceutical company accused the hedge fund of hiring a stock analyst to release an artificial negative report to devalue its stock. Its accusations were supported by former hedge fund employees. After the report was released, the pharmaceutical company's stock began to slide—by 50 percent in six months. The pharmaceutical company subsequently had two disappointing earning reports, but it claims that the hedge fund and the analyst company created this decline in earnings with their initial report. The hedge fund company claims that it did nothing wrong and that the analysts released an honest and objective report. Meanwhile, the analyst company is fighting a lawsuit by another company that directly parallels the pharmaceutical company's case.

As the last two years have been a "bear market," interest in hedge funds has grown. In a "bear market," hedge funds use short selling along with traditional methods to allow investors to create quicker revenue. Biotech companies are turning to hedge funds to create capitol for research. Universities large and small are investing their endowment money in hedge funds.

Unfortunately, these unsophisticated investors may be ignorant to the risks. Biotech startups may be devaluing their own stock to make quick cash. People who donate money to the universities are concerned that the money they are giving for education is going to be lost due to bad management of the investments.

In recent months, another glaring problem with hedge funds has come forward—money laundering. Since hedge fund regulations are so minimal it is difficult to track the flow of money, who it is coming from and where it is going. Some are concerned that drug dealers, terrorists, and other criminal enterprises are able to launder their money with relative ease. The SEC and the treasury commission cannot decide who should take responsibility for this issue, and, with a lack of an actual crisis, no urgency has been placed on addressing this problem.

Update Sources: *60 Minutes.* "Betting On A Fall," CBS Broadcasting Inc., March 26, 2006; Thornton, Emily and Arlene Weintraub, with Susan Zegel. "Biotech's Boon Or Bane? Hedge funds are providing financing where VCs won't. But there are strings attached" *Businessweek*, April 10 2006; Hovanesian, Mara Der and Dawn Kopecki. "Where's The Heat On Hedge Funds?" *Businessweek*, June 19,2006; Tergesen, Anne and Roben Farzad. "Big Risk On Campus," *Businessweek*, May 15, 2006.

Censored #19 2006
Child Wards of the State Used in AIDS Experiments

Story #19 of 2006 was about an allegation that AIDS drugs were tested on young orphans at New York's Incarnation Children's Center (ICC), an orphanage. The testing sponsor, pharmaceutical company GlaxoSmithKline, was partially funded by divisions of the National Institute of Health. Without parents to give consent, this vulnerable population of children as young as 3 months old, under control of the state, were exposed to dangerous side effects of experimental drug regimens. The center is run by Columbia University's Presbyterian Hospital, and the trials were conducted by Columbia University Medical Center doctors. The *Observer* investigation that revealed Glaxo sponsored at least four trials since 1995 using the population of predominately Hispanic and African American children at Incarnation. The trials were part of a broader series of HIV and AIDS drug trials that were conducted on orphaned children in at least seven states.

Original Sources: Barnett, Antony. "GlaxoSmithKline Allegedly Used Children as Laboratory Animals" *UK Observer*, April 4, 2004; Goodman, Amy. "Guinea Pig Kids: How New York City is Using Children to Test Experimental AIDS Drugs" *Democracy Now!* December 2004.

UPDATE BY ANDREW SLOAN
In May of 2006 AIDS researcher Liam Scheff revealed to Project

Censored that he was one of the original investigators into the ICC scandal. Scheff claims that the "GlaxoSmithKline Allegedly Used Children as Laboratory Animals" article in the *London Observer* was deliberately edited by staff to cut all citations and references to him as the original investigator.

Scheff's piece entitled, "The House That AIDS Built," was published January 2004 on AltHeal's web site, three months before the *London Observer's* piece. He spoke of his tours through ICC, and included transcripts of interviews with a legal guardian of two children held at ICC, and another interview with the medical director of ICC, Dr. Katherine Painter.

Scheff noted that these were not new drugs being tested, but modifications of classic AIDS drugs like AZT and Nevirapine, both of which have dangerous, if not lethal, side effects. A few of the studies conducted at ICC include a study of Lopinavir/Ritonavir on infants with HIV.

Last year Project Censored did not thoroughly cover the cases of the children being used for testing. As children of the state, this vulnerable population of orphans have little say about the regimens they are given. Because each state leans towards administering drugs as the best treatment for children tested to be HIV-positive, or children born to HIV-positive mothers, regulations are enforced to ensure strict adherence.

Clinical trials sponsored by the National Institute of Health are not limited to New York or the Incarnation Children's Center (ICC). They are conducted in participating hospitals around the world. An AP article in May 2005 reported clinical trials on children in seven states and over four dozen different studies. ClinicalTrials.gov, a service of the NIH, lists 957 studies as having locations in forty-two U.S. states, 332 studies outside of the U.S., and fifty-six without location data. This amounts to 1,345 trials being carried out on children around the world.

GlaxoSmithKline is not the only pharmaceutical company sponsoring these trials and providing experimental drugs. There is also Pfizer, Genentech, Chiron/Biocine, BristolMeyersSquibb, Boeringer-Ingelheim, Abbott Laboratories, and others.

Another issue Scheff brought to light is the procedures used to administer drugs to children who resist the treatment. As Katherine Painter, medical director of ICC explained, "For some cases, it's better administered through a gastric tube." A gastric tube is stuck straight into the stomach through the skin and abdominal wall musculature. Another way is to use a Nasogastric tube that goes through the nose.

In many states, if a parent notices that their child is healthier off the drugs than on them, and decides not to give the child the prescribed drugs, child services can come to take the child away. Each state has different regulations, but there continues to be a significant population of orphaned children subjected to such experimentation.

An additional finding by the AP study was that, for the orphans with HIV, "overall mortality while receiving the study drug was significantly higher in the daily [dose] group." Doctors, therefore, are faced with a serious conflict of interests. In 2002, the *New England Journal of Medicine* began to allow doctors writing drug review articles to receive up to $10,000 a year from a drug company in consulting and speaking fees. "If a doctor is doing that kind of business with four or five companies," says Dr. Sidney Wolfe on an ABC interview, "he or she can get as much as $40,000 or $50,000 in a year and not violate the New England Journal of Medicine policy."

Scheff has published his work in the *New York Press*, *Crux Magazine*, *Hustler*, AltHeal, Indymedia, and helped with a documentary called "Guinea Pig Kids" that aired on BBC.

Update Sources: Scott, Janny and Leslie Kaufman. "Belated Charge Ignites Furor Over AIDS Drug Trial," *New York Times*, July 17, 2005; Solomon, John. "Researchers Tested Drugs on Foster Kids," *Associated Press*, May 4, 2005; Jennings, Peter and John McKenzie. "New England Journal of Medicine relaxes conflict-of-interest rules for authors of drug review articles," *ABC News: World News Tonight*, June 12, 2002; Scheff, Liam. "The House That AIDS Built," *AltHeal.org*, January 2004.

Censored #20 2006
American Indians Sue for Resources; Compensation Provided to Others

Since 1887 the U.S. government has been legally obligated to manage thousands of Native American land-based trusts or Individual Indian Money accounts accumulated from leases and royalty payments for oil, timber, and minerals taken from tribal lands. Since 1887 the government has failed miserably as a diligent trustee by allowing an accounting fiasco of epic proportions, which cost Native Americans billions of dollars in lost royalties. After the 1994 American Indian Trust Reform Act failed to exact any reconciliation from the Department of Interior, the largest class action lawsuit ever filed against the federal government was initiated in 1996 on behalf of some 500,000 Native Americans. Cobell v. Norton seeks to force the government to complete an historical accounting of revenues generated for more than 100 years by leases on American Indian land held in trust and make payment.

Original Sources: Awehali, Brian. "Trust Us, We're the Government: How to Make $137 Billion of Indian Money Disappear," *LiP*, Winter 2004; Wagner, Angie. "Despite Wealth of Resources, Many Tribes Still Live in Poverty," *News from Indian Country*, March 8, 2004.

UPDATE BY CHARLENE JONES

In 2005, Elouise Cobell, lead plaintiff in the suit against the Department of Interior, defended a $27.5 billion proposal to settle as a bargain for taxpayers and asked the House Resources Committee to demand that federal officials cooperate. She charged that decades of fund mismanagement had lost hundreds of millions of dollars and indicated that the current offer forgave the Interior for many missed trust fund payments dating back to the 19th century. According to Cobell, totals owed would far exceed any cited in recent corporate fraud scandals, and are estimated to be $176 billion.

The Bush administration persists in its position that the Native Americans' claims are unreasonable, refusing to offer a full explanation of accounting or settlement figures. U.S. District Judge Royce C. Lamberth, overseeing the case since the 1990s, has been severely critical of the government's delays, according to *The Washington Post*. He emphasized that the Interior's negligence cannot be absolved and cited malfeasance in the management of the Individual Indian Money accounts. Lamberth, according to *Indian Country Today*, disapproves of the Interior's failure to identify how much money tribes are owed, expressing his exasperation for obstructionism by government officials. Consequently, the Justice Department, in an extraordinary move in the summer of 2005, asked for Lamberth's removal from the ten-year-old case, arguing the judge has lost impartiality. The request is expected to be heard by the U.S. Court of Appeals. Plaintiffs plan to fight any attempt to remove Lamberth from presiding over continued litigation.

Despite such impediments, according to *Mother Jones*, Cobell v. Norton has sustained victories in court and revealed evidence of government abandonment of factual accounting, chronic incompetence, and giveaway contracts of Native American resources to energy and mineral industries. The suit persists and the wait for acceptable settlement legislation from Congress lengthens.

Update Sources: *Nieman Watchdog*, "D.C. lawyer again blasts Interior over handling of Indian trust," January 25, 2006; *Washington Post*, "Straight Shooter to Some, Loose Cannon to Others," September 15, 2005; *Indian Country Today*. "If Indian Trust case goes bad, fire the judge!" September 22, 2005; *Mother Jones*, "Accounting Coup," September/October 2005; *News From Indian Country*. "Appeals court: Indian money accounting would be impossible."

For more information:
http://www.indiantrust.com
http://resourcescommittee.house.gov/issues/naia/trustfund101.htm

Censored #25 2006
Homeland Security Was Designed to Fail

The Department of Homeland Security was touted as the Bush administration's domestic answer to terrorism, and yet it has never been given adequate funding or treated as a priority. At the time of the department's inception, preparing for war in Iraq seemed to be the president's primary focus. Consolidating twenty-two agencies into one cumbersome bureaucracy was a monumental task that many experienced government employees believed would not succeed. Staffing it with political appointees rather than experts and allowing special interests to dictate policy further set it up for failure.

Original Sources: Brzezinski, Mathew. "Red Alert," *Mother Jones*, September/October 2004; Brzezinski, Mathew "Fortress America: On the Front Lines of Homeland Security: an interview with Mathew Brzezinski," *NPR*, September 24, 2004.

UPDATE BY SANDY MURPHY

Soon after *Censored 2006* was released, Susan B. Glasser and Michael Grunwald of *The Washington Post* published an in-depth report, "Department's Mission Was Undermined From Start." The Glasser/Grunwald article talks about Tom Ridge's frustration as DHS Secretary and the constant Whitehouse dismissals of his requests.

Secretary Ridge found that what he thought was the key reason for his new department's existence—a comprehensive intelligence center to track terrorists in order to prevent another September 11–type attack—was not part of the plan. One of his top advisers said, "It was as if the White House created us and then set out to marginalize us." Tom Ridge resigned shortly after Bush was reelected.

Glasser and Grunwald noted that the department's response to Hurricane Katrina, its first major challenge, "exposed a troubled organization where preparedness was more slogan than mission." The largest natural disaster in the history of the United States put a media spotlight on FEMA and the Department of Homeland Security's inability to do its job. Concerns were raised over whether the department could be effective in a terrorist attack if it could not even handle a hurricane that came with advance warning.

During the hearings held after the disastrous response to Hurricane Katrina, former FEMA director Michael Brown complained of a lack of support from the White House. "There was a cultural clash which didn't recognize the absolute inherent science of preparing for disaster . . . and the policies and decisions implemented by the DHS put FEMA on a path to failure," he said.

According to Frank Rich of the *New York Times*, President Bush accepted no responsibility for the mishandling of Katrina's aftermath until "after America's highest-rated TV news anchor, Brian Williams, started talking about Katrina the way Walter Cronkite once did about Vietnam." According to the commission set up to investigate the disaster, even now there has been little progress toward repairing the ailing DHS due to "inconsistent executive commitment."

Following Katrina, the DHS was unable to replace the affected area's emergency communication system because of the $150 million cost, so it is being done piecemeal. But money did not seem to be an issue when no-bid reconstruction contracts were handed out.

Karl Rove was put in charge of the reconstruction effort in New Orleans and, as expected, loyalty was rewarded far more than expertise. Frank Rich says the list of recipients included the Fluor Corporation, a major donor to the Republican Party, and to a client of former FEMA director, Joe Allbaugh. Among the organizations to which FEMA's website suggests that donations go is Pat Robertson's Operation Blessing, even though, according to I.R.S. documents, half of the money Operation Blessing receives goes to Robertson's Christian Broadcasting Network. Like Michael Brown, the two top deputies still at FEMA are experts in public relations, not disaster preparedness or relief.

Attention paid to the inadequacies of the DHS and FEMA following Katrina has done little to change presidential policies. President Bush's 2006 budget requested close to $22 billion for the Department of Homeland Security, along with $11 billion for domestic security programs outside the DHS. By contrast, the budget requested an *increase* of $28.5 billion for military spending, bringing the total budget to $440 billion—not including additional money earmarked for Iraq and Afghanistan.

Update Sources: Sanger, David E., "Bush Budget Plan for $2.77 Trillion Stresses Security," *New York Times,* February 7, 2006; Glasser, Susan B. and Michael Grunwald. "Department's Mission Was Undermined From Start," *Washington Post,* December 22, 2005; Congressional website, http://thomas.loc.gov/; Brown, Michael. "Live From..." *CNN,* February 10, 2006, Transcript 021002CN.V85; Rich, Frank, "Message: I Care About the Black Folks," *New York Times,* September 18, 2005; Warrick, Joby. "Crisis Communications Remain Flawed; Despite Promises to fix Systems, First Responders Were Still Isolated After Katrina," *Washington Post.* December 10, 2005.

For more information:
http://www.fcc.gov/homeland/
http://www.ojp.usdoj.gov/nij/topics/commtech/radiospectrum/welcome.html

CHAPTER 3

Thirty Years of Censored News

by Peter Phillips, Charlene Jones, Sandy Murphy, Carl Jensen and Project Censored

INTRODUCTION: A CENSORED EPIPHANY

by Carl Jensen, Ph.D.

1976 is well remembered as the year the United States celebrated its Bicentennial, North and South Vietnam were reunited as one nation, and Democrat Jimmy Carter defeated incumbent President Gerald Ford.

1976 is less well known as the year a trifecta of events would occur that would have a positive impact on the public's right to know for years to come.

Mother Jones was founded in San Francisco by Adam Hochschild, Richard Parker, and Paul Jacobs and would achieve national distinction for its investigative stories that are underreported by the major news media.

Project Censored was founded at Sonoma State University, in Rohnert Park, California, and would become the longest running national news media research project in the country.

The Body Shop, an international purveyor of herbal cosmetics, was founded in Brighton, England, by Anita Roddick, who would become a major financial supporter of Project Censored and many human rights organizations.

It was during the summer of 1976 that I sensed I was onto something significant in the area of news media analysis. In previous classes, my students and I had produced two cablevision programs— one titled "A Decade of Conspiracy: From Dallas to Watergate," and another titled "CENSORED: The Great American Media Mystery." Both were three hour-long programs that were cablecast to local communities in Northern California.

The 1975 JFK project revealed that the public would change its mind if it were given sufficient information about a problem. The changing public attitude about the Iraq War is a good current example.

The 1976 "Censored" project revealed that there are important news stories that are not reported by the mainstream media. It featured the potential hazards of the Pacific Gas & Electric nuclear power plant in Eureka, California, and should have served as an early warning as to what happened at Three Mile Island, Pennsylvania, on March 28, 1979.

At the same time, the failure of the mainstream media to cover the Watergate burglary continued to mystify me. It happened in June 1972 but it didn't become a major media story until early 1973. In the interim, Richard Nixon was re-elected by a massive landslide vote, just five months after the biggest political crime of our time. It was obvious that the mass media hadn't fulfilled their primary responsibility to inform the public. In this case, they hadn't pursued before the election the Watergate story that was initially broken by Woodward & Bernstein at the *Washington Post*. Pre-election knowledge of Watergate would have been very important for the American public.

Walter Cronkite, the "most trusted man in America," tried to produce the smoking gun before the election. He had scheduled an unprecedented two-part CBS evening network news segment to air the Watergate charges. But, after the first segment aired, a call was made from the White House to Bill Paley, chairman of CBS at the time. As a consequence, the second segment was reduced and toned down. That unpublicized call provided a documented example of censorship exercised by the administration over a major television news network.

I started comparing the news in the alternative press to that in the establishment press, and found a major difference in the kinds of material they covered.

As a result, instead of merely accepting the conventional wisdom that the mass media were the valuable watchdogs they were supposed to be, I focused on the failure of the media to fully inform the public.

But how could I explore that issue, involve students, and get the public to become aware of the problem? Suddenly, one afternoon, as I was sitting at my desk in my den at home, I had an epiphany.

"Sandra!" I yelled to my wife. "Have I got an idea!"

She came running into the den.

"It's called Project Censored!" And I explained how I was going to have students find censored news stories, write them up, submit them to a national panel of judges, and then announce the "Top Ten Censored Stories" of the year. Sandra, bless her, was impressed. And that was the genesis of Project Censored.

I spent the next five weeks working up the concept, the format, the class syllabus, the resources, the logo, the stationery, the pamphlets, and all the rest that went into the development of Project Censored. Much of that has endured these thirty years.

I realized from the beginning that it would be difficult to attract national attention to the project if I didn't have some prominent media personalities involved. So I developed the idea of using well-known individuals as judges to give the project added exposure and credibility.

The first year I had a hard sell to persuade major media figures to participate as judges. After all, it was a new media effort conducted by some unknown assistant professor of sociology at some unknown college called Sonoma State located somewhere out there in northern California.

One of the people I invited to participate was investigative journalist I. F. Stone. I didn't hear back from him for some time. Then, one night at about 10 p.m., I got a call from him at home. He said he appreciated the invitation but he couldn't accept. Sensing my disappointment, he explained that to truly evaluate the twenty-five censored nominations, he would personally have to research each of the stories individually himself and that just wasn't possible.

It was this kind of attention to detail that made I. F. Stone such a respected journalist. I told him I understood and he encouraged me to pursue the effort, saying, "This project is one of the most significant media research projects being undertaken in the country."

With I. F. Stone's blessing, I knew I was on the right track.

I was naively anxious to have a politically balanced panel of judges to ward off criticism that this was just another left-wing media group and so I was very pleased when President Gerald Ford's former press secretary, Ron Nessen, agreed to be a judge.

However, after receiving preliminary information about the project, Nessen wrote me saying he must decline since he disagreed with the premise of the project and felt it would be extremely misleading to the public. I called him and explained the premise. We were simply trying to expose stories that the major news media had overlooked or under covered. He acknowledged that it sounded worthwhile and again agreed to be a judge, so I sent him a copy of the twenty-five nominations for top ten censored stories. Again, I received a letter from him declining to serve as a judge. Here is how he explained his position:

"I was wrong in my original belief that you were trying to find stories censored by various levels of government officials.

"But now I see that you are pursuing a different idea with which I also disagree.

"For the most part the stories nominated as "best censored" raise the question of why allegations published in *Mother Jones, New Times, The Progressive, Rolling Stone,* and Ralph Nader were not picked up by the *New York Times* and Walter Cronkite.

"The project suggests that there is some kind of conspiracy by the 'establishment' press to surpress (sic) certain allegations by the 'advocacy' press. What nonsense! Maybe the allegations weren't picked up because they're not true."

Incidentally, Ron Nessen was appointed to succeed Gerald F. terHorst as President Ford's press secretary after terHorst resigned in protest over Ford's pardon of Richard Nixon. That didn't seem to bother Nessen.

Another conservative I persuaded to be a judge was the late Edward Teller, former director of the Lawrence Livermore National Laboratory and a senior fellow at the Hoover Institution at Stanford University. Known as the "Father of the Hydrogen Bomb," his conservative credentials were impeccable. After he agreed to serve on the panel, I sent him the synopses of the top twenty-five censored stories. One afternoon, shortly after, I received a call in my office at the University.

"Is this Carl Jensen?"

"Yes," I replied, wondering whose gruff, angry voice it was.

"I cannot participate in your research project!"

"Who is calling please?" I asked.

"This is Edward Teller. I would never associate myself with this left-wing project. Please remove my name from your list."

With that he abruptly hung up. With no great sorrow, I removed his name from the list of judges. With that kind of attitude, he wouldn't have been much of an impartial judge anyway.

Despite my repeated efforts over the years, the only "pure" conservative I was able to persuade to be a judge was James J. Kilpatrick, a national columnist with the Universal Press Syndicate, who served in 1980. He refused to participate more than once however.

Nonetheless, I got what I felt was a very impressive panel of judges to participate in the first year of Project Censored. They were Ben Bagdikian, journalist, educator, and author of *Media Monopoly*; Noam Chomsky, social critic and professor at Massachusetts Institute of Technology; Robert Cirino, educator and author of *Power to Persuade* and *We're Being More Than Entertained*; Nicholas Johnson, chair of the National Citizen's Committee for Broadcasting and former member of the Federal Communications Commission; Victor Marchetti, former official of the CIA, author and lecturer; Jack Nelson, professor of Social Education at the Graduate School of education, at Rutgers University; Jerry terHorst, syndicated columnist with the *Detroit News* and *Universal Press Syndicate*; and Sheila Rabb Weidenfeld, talk show host and former press secretary to First Lady Betty Ford.

One day, in 1979, I picked up the ringing phone in my office at the university, and before I could speak, I was challenged with, "Are you the guy that does the censored stories stuff?"

"Yes, I am," I replied.

"Well. You should do a story about me."

"Why would that be?" I asked.

"Cause I'm the most censored guy in America."

"And you would be?"

"Larry Flynt! The publisher of *Hustler*."

I knew who Larry Flynt was. We had a brief interesting discussion of censorship. We agreed on the dangers of censorship for a free society and we disagreed about the limits of censorship. Flynt was opposed to censorship of any kind. I felt censorship was acceptable in some instances, such as military censorship during time of war and child pornography.

Nonetheless, I agreed to monitor *Hustler* for some of its investigative stories about issues not covered by the mainstream media. I also discovered that other similar magazines, *Playboy* and *Penthouse*, most notably, also ran some good investigative articles. Some of my male students were delighted when I added them to our research list.

In 1982, I received a phone call from an attorney in Los Angeles.

"Hello," I said.

"Is this Carl Jensen, the director of Project Censored?"

"Yes, it is."

"Are you looking into a story about Synanon?"

"Yes, I am."

"I would like to suggest that you are making a mistake by investigating Synanon."

I was surprised at the tenor of the conversation. The voice which originally sounded merely business-like, now had more of a threatening feel to it.

"I don't understand what you're saying."

"I think you understand exactly what I'm saying," the caller said firmly. "If you know what's good for your health, you'll stop investigating Synanon."

By now, I did understand fully what the caller was saying. And I was damned angry.

"Who the hell are you and what makes you think you can threaten me like that?"

"I am an attorney for Synanon and you will regret it if you don't get off Synanon's case."

With that, the caller hung up. I also hung up and, I must admit, I was shaking a bit. I remembered full well how Synanon admitted placing a deadly rattlesnake in the mailbox of another critic of Synanon.

I told my "censored" class about the phone call and assured them that we wouldn't be dropping the Synanon story from our list of nominations for "best censored stories of 1982." As it turned out, the Synanon story was the thirteenth censored story of that year.

In the mid-eighties, I received a letter, post-marked from Phoenix, Arizona, that threatened to kill me and "other left-wing pigs" like me. I had received a number of threats over the years that I simply ignored because they didn't seem authentic. But there was something about the tone of this one that bothered me.

So what could I do but turn to my "friends" at the FBI. As soon as I mentioned Phoenix, I had their attention. An FBI agent came out to our home right away and picked up the letter. A few months later it was returned covered with fingerprinting dust. It turned out that an identical letter had been sent from Phoenix to the White House.

Because of such threats, I made an unsuccessful effort to keep our home address and phone number secret. I still receive phone calls warning me about apocalyptic events the media aren't reporting.

Not all correspondence was threatening. In the early 1980s I got a call from an attorney down in Los Angeles. He said he was representing a client who preferred to remain anonymous at this time. Then he came right to the point. His client was interested in buying Project Censored. I explained that Project Censored was an academic research project and it wasn't for sale. I added that we appreciated the interest. He was disappointed and said his client would also be disappointed. I later learned his anonymous client was the Bhagwan Shree Rajneesh, famous for his 1993 Rolls Royces and his controversial ashram up in Oregon.

I never did discover why the Bagwan wanted to own Project Censored.

By 1979, I realized we weren't getting much media coverage. After all we were criticizing the media and then asking them to publicize our criticism. Nevertheless, I naively expected them to act more professional. In any case, to make it easier for the press to cover the story, I decided to hold a press conference in San Francisco, the largest nearby media center.

I reserved a large conference room at the old San Francisco Library and sent invitations to nearly a hundred Bay Area media outlets. On the appointed day, all the students in the class and I took off for our press conference in the City some fifty miles south of the University. We were prepared to proudly announce the ten best censored news stories of 1978 to the assembled media representatives.

Only two media representatives showed up. One was the photographer and the other was the writer for a publication called *Feed/Back: The California Journalism Review* published at San Francisco State University. They took a photo of the rows of empty chairs reserved for the press with the Sonoma State students seated at the head table patiently waiting for the media.

Feed/Back later published the story and photos about the irony of the San Francisco press conference about media censorship that was censored by the media. My students told me that experience was the most persuasive example I could have given them illustrating media censorship.

The annual Junk Food News (JFN) effort evolved from criticism of Project Censored by news editors and directors that the real issue isn't censorship, but rather a difference of opinion as to what information is important to publish or broadcast.

Editors often pointed out there is a finite amount of time and space for news delivery—about twenty-three minutes for a half-hour network television evening news program—and that it's their responsibility to determine which stories are most critical for the public to know. The critics said I wasn't exploring media censorship but rather I was just another frustrated academic criticizing editorial news judgment.

This appeared to be a legitimate criticism, so I decided to monitor the stories that editors and news directors consider to be worthy enough to fill their valuable news time and space.

In the course of this research, I didn't find an abundance of hard-hitting investigative journalism. Quite the contrary. Indeed, what I did find is the journalistic phenomenon I call "Junk Food News," which, in essence, represents the flip side of the Top Twenty-five Censored Stories announced annually by Project Censored.

In 1877, John B. Bogart, an editor with the *New York Sun*, offered a definition of news that has not only endured into the twenty-first century but, indeed, seems to have become even more descriptive of news in recent years.

Bogart wrote, "When a dog bites a man, that is not news, because it happens so often. But if a man bites a dog it's news."

His definition implied the need for a sensationalistic aspect for an event to become news. It's an ingredient that now appears to be endemic in the press. "Man bites dog" is the classic example of Junk Food News.

One of the ongoing problems we have with Project Censored is funding. In the early days, I kept writing unsuccessful grant proposals to the point where I was spending most of my time writing proposals. Since this didn't make sense to me, I quit writing the proposals and concentrated on Project Censored and my classes. At the time, I was supporting Project Censored out of my own pocket with an occasional contribution from people who liked what we were doing.

Then in 1989, I got a call from a person I had never met. He asked how I was doing with the Project and whether I could use any money. That person was Marty Teitel and he happened to be the executive director of the C.S. Fund, a private foundation in Freestone,

California, that makes grants. The C.S. Fund support enabled us to hire, for the first time, students to help with the project.

A few years later, I received a fax from an Anita Roddick, of The Body Shop, also asking if we could use some money. The only body shop I was acquainted with was the Body Shop on Santa Monica Boulevard down in Los Angeles, a somewhat sleazy health club. But, as it turned out, Anita Roddick was not with the L.A. Health Club. She was the founder and president of The Body Shop, a beauty and bath shop, headquartered in England. She was one of the world's leading entrepreneurs with shops throughout the world. She also was a leading social activist and business ethicist.

When I faxed Ms. Roddick back thanking her for her interest and proposed financial support, I received a fax immediately back, asking, "How much and where should I send it?" And the Body Shop became a major donor for many years.

Nonetheless, funding remains a constant problem, and Peter Phillips spends more time seeking financial support than he should. We're still looking for a foundation or an "angel" who believes in the public's right to know as much as we do.

1989 also marked the publication of the first Censored Yearbook. It was a modest, self-published spiral bound book but sales showed there was a substantial interest in an annual book. Thanks to Dan Simon, the publisher of Seven Stories Press, who strongly believes in the public's right to know, it is now an award-winning annual book published by Seven Stories Press in New York. Over the years, we've had a series of distinguished media critics write the introduction for the book including Hugh Downs, Jessica Mitford, Walter Cronkite, Michael Crichton, Jim Hightower, Danny Schechter, Gary Webb, Mumia Abu-Jamal, Noam Chomsky, Robert W. McChesney, Amy Goodman, Greg Palast, and Norman Solomon.

A question I am often asked is whether it would make any difference in our society if people were better informed about the kinds of stories Project Censored exposes. Obviously I believe that it would make a difference, and the example I give concerns a story about hunger.

Hunger in Africa was consistently nominated as a censored subject during the early 1980s. When I would ask journalists why they did not cover the tragedy unfolding there, they would say, "It is not news," or, "Everyone already knows about starving Africans," or "Nothing can be done about it anyway."

Early in 1984, an ABC-TV News correspondent in Rome came upon information that led him to believe that millions of lives were being threatened by drought and famine in Africa. He asked the home office in New York for permission to take his crew to Africa to get the story. After all they already were in Rome.

The answer from ABC-TV in New York was "No."

Later, a BBC television crew, traveling through Ethiopia, captured the stark reality of children starving to death. The visual images were televised throughout the world. And the world responded with "We Are the World." Overnight, the BBC story sparked a world-wide reaction with Live Aid that reportedly saved the lives of seven million Ethiopians.

Indeed, the media can make a difference.

There's an ironic twist to this story. I subsequently discovered who it was at ABC that refused to let the network's TV crew go to Africa in 1984. One might suspect that such a person would be reprimanded and criticized for his decision, yet this was not the case. The person who said "No" to the ABC-TV crew in Rome was Rick Kaplan. Rather than being reprimanded, Kaplan was rewarded with promotions to executive producer of Ted Koppel's *Nightline*, then *PrimeTime Live*, and ABC's *World News Tonight*. He then went on to become president of CNN and subsequently, MSNBC.

Equally ironic, in mid-1986, it was the same Rick Kaplan who killed a two-part *Nightline* series on Project Censored which was going to explore whether the news media ever overlook, under-cover, or censor important stories.

Not all major media personalities reject press criticism. Hugh Downs, a longtime moderator of ABC's *20/20* news magazine with Barbara Walters and a strong Project Censored fan recently wrote me about the state of the press. He said, in part:

"On my own nefarious career, now mothballed in favor of what I laughingly call my retirement, I have mixed feelings about biting the hand that fed me for decades, but the fact is that mainstream journalism has struck out when it comes to informing the people about what is really going on."

He also noted that we "now have a leader who claims to be above the law and can censor and spy and assume more and more power, without having to account for such behavior."

That, of course, is why we need Project Censored now more than ever.

National columnist Molly Ivins specifically wrote about the need for Project Censored in a column published on September 22, 2005, where she said, in part:

> What we need in this country—along with a disaster relief agency—is a Media Accountability Day. One precious day out of the entire year when everyone in the news media stops reporting on what's wrong with everyone else and devotes a complete twenty-four-hour news cycle to looking at our own failures. How's that for a great idea? ...Happily, the perfect news peg, as we say in the biz, for Media Accountability Day already exists—it's Project Censored's annual release of the ten biggest stories ignored or undercovered by mainstream media. Project Censored is based at Sonoma State University, with both faculty and students involved in its preparation.

After thirty years, Project Censored is well prepared for Media Accountability Day. Now, where are the media?

Carl Jensen, Ph.D., is a professor emeritus of communication studies at Sonoma State University and founder of Project Censored. He is the author of *Censored Yearbooks* (1989–1996), *20 Years of Censored News*, *Stories the Changed America: Muckrakers of the 20th Century*, and editor of *The Millennium* by Upton Sinclair.

PROJECT CENSORED #1 STORIES FROM 1976 TO 2005

2005
Wealth Inequality in Twenty-First Century Threatens Economy and Democracy

Wealth inequality has so sharply increased that one percent of the U.S. population now owns about a third of the riches in the country. Global economic analysis groups warn that further increase in such imbalances in the U.S. and throughout the world will have catastrophic effects if left unchecked.

Original Sources: *Multinational Monitor* 24, no. 5, May 2003; Wolff, Edward, "The Wealth Divide: interview with Edward Wolff," by Robert Weissman, *BuzzFlash,* March 26 and 29, 2004; Johnston, David Cay, "A Buzzflash Interview: with David Cay Johnston, Parts I & II." *BuzzFlash*; Vidal, John, "Every third person will be a slum dweller within 30 years, UN agency warns," *The Guardian* (London), October 4, 2003; Weissman, Robert, "Grotesque Inequality," *Multinational Monitor*, July/August 2003.

UPDATE BY ALEXANDRIA GREY AND KRISTEN MCCARTY

Domestic: The wealth and inequality gap between the rich and poor in the United States continues to increase dramatically. Tax income of the top one percent of the population increased 129 percent between 1979 and 2003, while income of the poorest fifth of the population rose by four percent, or only $600, according to the Center on Budget and Policy Priorities. Data also indicate capital income from interest, dividends, rents and capital gains that is subject to taxation has become more concentrated among the top one percent. Extending reduced tax rates on capital gains and dividend income is likely to be even more regressive than in the past. The further up the wealth scale one goes, the more income comes from investments. Under the Bush tax cuts, according to the *New York Times,* this income enjoys about the lowest rate in the tax code. The Congressional Budget Office reports show the income gap widening with a long-term trend of increasing income inequality, according to the Center on Budget and Policy Priorities.

The current U.S. poverty line is widely regarded as far too low for a family to survive on in most parts of the country, according to *Dollars & Sense*. The threshold concept was devised more than forty years ago, and since then the Census Bureau has recalculated the original equation to formulate levels and account for inflation. Antipoverty advocates point out, however, the Census Bureau has not considered changes in family expenditures on food and necessities such as childcare, healthcare, transportation and utilities over several decades. In addition, federal poverty figures make no adjustment for regional differences in cost. If calculations were reformulated, there would be a significant increase in the number of people living below the country's official poverty line.

Global: The inequality gap between the world's wealthiest and poorest populations is growing. According to the *Human Development Report 2005*, the richest fifty individuals in the world have a greater total income than the poorest 416 million people. Five percent of the world's income is distributed among 40 percent of the world's population, while the richest 10 percent of the world's population receive 54 percent of the global income. If the current trend of global inequality continues, the world's population will see catastrophic effects. According to the United Nations, as reported in *The Guardian*, analysts predict by 2030 more than 56 percent of the population in developing countries will live in slums. Over the next thirty years 2 billion more people will move to urban areas and 70 percent of these will be added to the 920 million already living in slums.

Update Sources: Jeremy Seabrook, "Comments & Analysis: Powder Keg in the Slums" *The Guardian*, Sept. 1, 2004; Jens Martens, "A Compendium of Inequality, The Human Development Report 2005," Global Policy Forum, http://hbr.undp.org/reports/global/2005/; Editorial Desk, "New Hope for the Fabulously Wealthy," *New York Times*, June 7, 2005; Isaac Shapiro and Joel Friedman, "New, Unnoticed CBO Data Shows Capital has Become Much More Concentrated at the Top," Center on Budget and Policy Priorities, Jan. 29, 2006; Isaac Shapiro and Joel Friedman, "New CBO Data Indicate Growth in Long-Term Income Inequality Continues," Center on Budget and Policy Priorities, January 29, 2006.

Ellen Frank, "Dear Dr. Dollar: Can You Explain How Poverty is Defined in Government Statistics? Is This a Realistic Definition?" *Dollars and Sense*, January/February 2006.

For more information

http://www.pbs.org/now/politics/income.html
http://www.cbpp.org
http://www.powerpac.org
http://www.globalpolicy.org

2004
The Neoconservative Plan for Global Dominance

U.S. foreign policy strategies charted by neoconservatives for thirty years called for regime change in Iraq as early as 1989. These strategists played important roles in the Defense Departments of Gerald Ford, Ronald Reagan and George H.W. Bush, and today occupy key posts in the White House, Pentagon and State Department. Following the Cold War, they produced the Defense Planning Guidance Report, advocating U.S. military dominance around the globe and the Project for the New American Century (PNAC) which seeks U.S. military supremacy and control of global economic markets.

Original Sources: *The Sunday Herald*, September 15, 2002,"Bush Planned Iraq 'Regime Change' Before Becoming President," by Neil Mackay. *Harper's Magazine*, October 2002, "Dick Cheney's Song of America," by David Armstrong. *Mother Jones*, March 2003,"The 30 Year Itch," by Robert Dreyfuss. *Pilger.com*, December 12, 2002, "Hidden Agendas," by John Pilger. *Random Lengths News*, October 4, 2002, "Iraq Attack-The Aims and Origins of Bush's Plans," by Paul Rosenberg. Corporate Media Partial Coverage: *Atlantic Journal Constitution*, 9/29/02, "The President's Real Goal in Iraq," by Jay Bookman.

UPDATE BY PETER PHILLIPS AND MIKE FANNING
Since its founding, the PNAC has attracted numerous others who have signed policy letters or participated in the group. Within the PNAC, eight have been affiliated with the number one defense contractor Lockheed-Martin, and seven were associated with the number three defense contractor Northrop Grumman.

In September 2000, PNAC produced a seventy-six-page report entitled *Rebuilding America's Defenses: Strategy, Forces and Resources for a New Century*. The report was similar to the *Defense Policy Guidance* document written by Lewis Libby and Paul Wolfowitz in 1992. This is not surprising in that Libby and Wolfowitz were participants in the production of the 2000 PNAC report. Steven Cambone, Doc Zakheim, Mark Lagan, and David Epstein were also heavily involved.

Corporate media in the U.S. never did report on the level of influence of the PNAC and the number of members who were appointed to high positions in the George W. Bush administration. Positions held by PNAC founders in the Bush administration include: Elliot Abrams, National Security Council; Richard Cheney, Vice-President; Paula Dobriansky, Department of State, Under Secretary of Global Affairs; Aaron Friedberg, Vice President's Deputy National Security Advisor; Francis Fukuyama, President's Council on Bioethics; Zalmay Khalilzad, U.S. Ambassador to Afghanistan; Lewis Libby; Chief of Staff for the Vice President; Peter Rodman, DOD, Assistant Secretary of Defense for International Security; Henry S. Rowen, Defense Policy Board, Commission On Intelligence Capabilities of U.S. regarding Weapons of Mass Destruction; Donald Rumsfeld, Secretary of Defense; Vin Weber, National Commission Public Service; Paul Wolfowitz, Department Secretary Of Defense, President of the World Bank. (See Chapter 10 for more extensive analysis of the PNAC).

PNAC has remained active in its pursuit of its goals of expanding the U.S. military's role of global dominance. They sent a letter to Congress in January of 2005 calling for further increase of U.S. ground forces worldwide.

In an apparent attempt to downplay the importance of the PNAC the *Washington Post* presented a narrow listing and analysis of the key members in a March 2005 review and in June of 2006 the *Post* wrote that PNAC's doors may be closing soon. Nonetheless, for an organization as historically powerful and influential as the PNAC, corporate media's failure to cover their goals and power is tantamount to gross pandering to the political elite.

Update Sources: Nace, Ted. *Gangs of America*, San Francisco: Berrett-Koehler Publishers Inc., 2003; The Project for a New American Century, *Rebuilding America's Defenses, Project for a New American Century: Strategy, Forces and Resources for a New Century*, September 2000 (www.newamericancentury.org); Neal, Terry. "Valcans' Vindication?" *Washington Post*, March 14, 2005; Kamen, Al, "In the Loop," *Washington Post*, June 12, 2006.

2003
FCC Moves to Privatize Airwaves

After President Bush took office, the Federal Communications Commission (FCC) was asked to allow broadcasters to lease frequencies they use under their licenses and lay groundwork for full privatization of airwaves. The FCC administers the broadcast spectrum on behalf of the American people by licensing broadcasters to use for free, but not own, radio or TV frequencies. It is led by a chairman who has dismissed this historic FCC mandate and threatens to end media regulation.

Original Sources: Rifkin, Jeremy. "Mayday, mayday: Global media giants are lobbying for the most sinister privatisation of all: the airwaves," *London Guardian,* April 28, 2001; Koerner, Brendan I. "Losing Signal," *Mother Jones,* September/October 2001; Kidd, Dorothy. "Legal Project to Challenge Media Monopoly," *Media File,* May/June 2001.

UPDATE BY BENJAMIN REILLY

Since the story was featured as number one in the 2003 collection, results by the FCC to privatize the airwaves have been mixed. FCC rules governing media ownership began to be refashioned in 2001, according to the *San Antonio Current,* when President George W. Bush appointed Michael Powell as FCC chairman and the commission undertook its legal requirement to review media ownership rules. With lobbying pressure from corporate media, Powell lifted the ownership ban. Initially refusing to hold public hearings on the issue, Powell finally relented and held one. Twelve more were sponsored by two commissioners who opposed the rule changes, Michael Copps and Jonathan Adelstein. The Center for Public Integrity, as cited by the *Current,* revealed Powell and FCC staffers held seventy-one closed door meetings, sixty-six of them with CEOs and lobbyists, and five with public interest groups between September 2002 and April 2003. Powell's rule changes passed in June, 2003, lifting a cross-ownership ban, making it easier for television companies to buy more stations and ending prohibition on newspaper companies buying broadcasters in large U.S. markets.

However, in 2004 the Third U.S. Circuit Court ruled in a lawsuit between the Prometheus Radio Project (a movement organized by pirate radio enthusiasts) and the FCC, in favor of Prometheus. The FCC's moves to deregulate were called "arbitrary and capricious," and the rule changes were sent back for better justification. "Basically this slows down the corporations' plan to merge at will," said Prometheus' Pete Tridish, as quoted in *The Philadelphia Weekly*. "I just hope the FCC realizes that they really did ignore the public and its concerns when it drew up all these plans."

Following Powell's resignation from the FCC in 2005, President Bush nominated Kevin J. Martin, a Republican member of the FCC since 2001, as the new chairman. At first appearance, according to the *Salt Lake City Weekly*, Martin's appointment seemed an improvement with Martin indicating an importance to maintaining localism. *The Washington Post*, however, later reported the new chairman pushed decisions that made the country's largest phone companies even bigger, and plans to advance a deregulatory agenda including the re-writing of ownership rules. Major FCC actions in 2005 included approving SBC Communications Inc.'s purchase of AT&T Corp., Verizon Communications Inc's acquisition of MCI Inc. and Sprint Corp's merger with Nextel Communications Inc.

If Prometheus Radio Project versus FCC shows anything, conglomerates and the FCC will have to be more creative to pass further privatization proposals. Yet Martin may be more successful by avoiding Powell's strategy of broad policy restructure and tackling one rule at a time, starting with the one that may face the least resistance, cross-ownership. While the appeals court rejected Powell's efforts to ease limits and faulted the FCC's rulemaking methods, according to *The Boston Herald*, it had no issue with removing the cross-ownership prohibitions specifically.

Update Sources: Sorg, Lisa. "A Confluence of Dunces; Lobbyists and a Stacked FCC Make the Rules," *San Antonio Current*, January 21, 2004; Valania, Jonathan. "Clearing the Airwaves; Local Activists Win a Surprising Victory Over the FCC's Lax Ownership Rules," *Philadelphia Weekly*, July 7-July 13, 2004; Alterman, Eric. "Meet the new FCC Boss; Bush's new FCC Chairman Looks a lot Like his old FCC Chairman," *Salt Lake City Weekly*, March 31, 2005; Mohammed, Arshad. "Agenda at FCC Depends on Powers of Persuasion, Martin's Negotiating Skills Face Tests in Coming Year," *Washington Post*, December 23, 2005; Gatlin, Greg. "FCC Chairman Puts Metro Media Ownership in Cross Hairs,"

Boston Herald, March 23, 2006; http://money.cnn.com/2005/
01/21/news/newsmakers/powell_resigning/; http://www.freepress
.org/departments/display/16/2003/121/1/17.

2002

Project Censored moved our yearly cycle forward by six months in
2002. Historically our release dates had been late Spring. By moving
our cycle forward our book release now comes out in time for the academic Fall semester. We advanced the year on the title of our annual
book to reflect the year of release as the approaching year instead of
the previous year. There is not a Censored 2002 yearbook, but rather
a Censored 2003 that was released in August of 2002.

2001

World Bank and Multinational Corporations Seek to Privatize Water

Assisted by the World Bank, multinational corporations seek control
of world water systems and supplies as more than one billion people
lack access to fresh drinking water. If current trends persist, by 2025
the demand for fresh water is expected to rise by 56 percent more
than the amount of water that is currently available.

Original Sources: Barlow, Maude. "The Global Water Crisis and the
Commodification of the World's Water Supply," *International Forum
on Globalization: Special Report,* June 1999 from PRIME July 10,
2000; Shultz, Jim. "Just Add Water," *THIS,* July/August 2000;
Shultz, Jim. "Water Fallout: Bolivians Battle Globalization," *In These
Times,* May 15, 2000; Shiva, Vandana. "Monsanto's Billion-Dollar
Water Monopoly Plans," *Canadian Dimension,* February, 2000;
Shultz, Jim. "Water Fallout," *Canadian Dimension,* February, 2000;
Zoll, Daniel. "Trouble on Tap," *San Francisco Bay Guardian,* May 31,
2000; Chatterjee, Pratap. "The Earth Wrecker," *San Francisco Bay
Guardian,* May 31, 2000.

UPDATE BY ASHLI CASSARA

World Bank and multinational corporations are continuing their
efforts to privatize our water globally. The World Bank has been using
its financial power to encourage governments to privatize public ser-

vices including water distribution. Corporations like Bechtel and Metito are stepping into lucrative deals arranged by the World Bank.

It is currently estimated that 1.1 billion people worldwide do not have access to fresh drinking water. There are also another 2.6 billion people who are lacking minimal sanitation. Third world country governments are often failing to protect water and allow private corporations to take scarce water resources.

The Singapore government recently allowed the Singapore Utilities International to align with Metito. This alliance hopes to supply clean water throughout the Middle East. The CEO of Metito said, "The Middle East is on the verge of a wave of privatizations of government utilities. With the World Bank and the World Trade Organization putting pressure on governments in the region to liberalize and open the next stage, transmission and distribution, to private sector involvement, Metito is strongly positioned to enter this new market for the region and benefit the consumers. By teaming with Singapore Utilities International we added internal intelligence vital to clean water supply for the Middle East region."

A similar merger took place in Cochabamba, Bolivia when Bechtel took over their municipal water system. Local community members resisted the 200 percent increase in water rates and took to the streets. Bechtel was ultimately forced to leave the country. Bechtel filed a law suit against the people of one of poorest nations in the world, but bad press and continued resistance lead to their dropping the suit in January of 2006. The joint statement released pertaining to Bechtel's lawsuit read: "The Government of Bolivia and the international shareholders of Aguas del Tunari declare that the concession was terminated only because of the civil unrest and the state of emergency in Cochabamba and not because of any act done or not done by the international shareholders of Aguas del Tunari." Bechtel and an Italian company were the largest individual shareholders, each owning 27.5 percent of the consortium while the Bolivian government owned only 20 percent.

The World Water Forum was founded in 1996 and is made up of 300 non-governmental organizations from forty countries. The latest World Water Forum, held in March 2006, declined to include access to water as a basic human right.

The 2004 trading results and balance sheets for the world's major water multinational companies showed a strong asset base and massive profits. Water is now a huge profitable commodity with some of the largest multinational corporations leading the way to privatization.

Update Sources: McCarthy, Michael, ed., "Water Crisis is now one of the Greatest causes of Mass Suffering," *Global News Wire—Europe Intelligence Wire,* March 22, 2006; *European Information Service.* "4th World Water Forum Opens in Mexico," March 20, 2006; Elias, Paul. "Engineering Giant Bechtel drops $25 million Bolivian Water Claim," *Associated Press Worldstream,* January 20, 2006; *al-Bawaba.* "Metito alliance with Singapore Government Body SUI to further develop clean water supply in the GCC," Comtex News Network, December 20, 2006; Safo, Amos. "Barons Make Huge Profits on the back of Poor Countries," *Global News Wire - Asia Africa Intelligence Wire,* December 12, 2005; Cevallos, Diego. "Global: Forum Declines to term Access to Water a Basic Right," *Inter Press Service,* March 22, 2006.

2000
Multinational Corporations Profit From International Brutality

In the name of commerce, multinational corporations often argue their presence and investment will improve human rights through "constructive engagement" with repressive governments. However, companies engage in business ventures in countries known for major human rights violations and have funded the suppression of media and political opposition.

Original Source: Bray, John. "Petroleum and Human Rights: The New Frontiers of Debate," *Oil and Gas Journal,* November 1, 1999; Chatterjee, Pratap. "Meet Enron, Bush's Biggest Contributor," *The Progressive,* September 2000; Tuodolo, Felix. "Nigerian Military Opens Fire on Youths After Shell Oil Spill," *EarthFirst!,* September/October 2000; *Houston Chronicle,* January 28 & November 18, 2000; Hirsh, Michael and Kenneth Klee. "Ubiquity and its Burdens," *Newsweek,* January 31, 2000; *The Washington Post,* July 27, 2000.

UPDATE BY: KATIE O'CONNELL AND JOE BUTWILL
The U.S. government has continued to support corporations that are

doing business in countries where human rights abuses take place. Corporations once claimed that their presence and investment would improve human rights, also known as "constructive engagement." Changes in corporate practices are occurring after increasing international pressures and a growing number of lawsuits that are raising the question of corporate accountability for actions committed at foreign installations. The George W. Bush administration has defended some companies charged with human rights abuses, particularly those in the energy sector.

In a new report, "World: The Scariest Predators in the Corporate Jungle," by Thalif Deen, Deen reports that the world's oil, gas and mining industries account for nearly two-thirds of all violations of human rights, environmental laws and international labor standards. According to a soon-to-be-released United Nations study, "The extractive industries—oil, gas and mining—also account for most allegations of the worst abuses, up to and including complicity in crimes against humanity." A more detailed study is expected to be released later this year. These are typically for acts committed by public and private security forces protecting company assets and property; large-scale corruption, violations of labor rights, and a broad array of abuses in relation to local communities, especially the indigenous peoples.

Kathryn Mulvey of Corporate Accountability International said that human rights abuses by extractive industries are among "the most concentrated, visible and urgent to address."

In an attempt to address human rights abuses the U.N. passed the U.N. Global Compact. In this, companies would have an even playing field eliminating bribes and other incentive programs that companies use to gain an unfair advantage over other competitors. The Compact would also have at its core standards for human rights, labor standards, the environment and anticorruption. Seventy countries and 2000 companies have signed on with the Compact.

Some countries are also standing up, such as India did to Coca-Cola by shutting down a bottling plant that was polluting a local water supply. Continued vigilance will be needed if we are to see an end to foreign human rights abuses by U.S. companies.

Update Sources: Forero, Juan. "Rights Groups Overseas Fight US

Concerns in US Courts," *New York Times*, June 26, 2003; Nussbaum, David. "World in Focus: Costs of Corruption," *The Advertiser*, January 28, 2006; Raeves, D. "Everything Gets Worse With Coca-Cola," *Inter-Press Service*, August 21, http://ipsnews.net/news.asp?idnews=29973; Deen, Thalif. "World: The Scariest Predators in the Corporate Jungle," *Inter-Press Service*, May 23, 2006, http://www.ipsnews.net/news.asp?idnews=33262.

1999
Secret International Trade Agreement Undermines the Sovereignty of Nations

The Multilateral Agreement on Investment (MAI) would establish vast protections for foreign investment that threaten national sovereignty by giving corporations near equal rights to nations. MAI could thrust the world economy closer to a system where international corporate capital holds free reign over democratic values and socioeconomic needs of people.

Original Sources: Bleifuss, Joel. "Building the Global Economy," *In These Times*, January 11, 1998; Dixon, Bill. "MAI Ties," *Democratic Left*, Spring 1998; Kothari, Miloon and Tara Krause. "Human Rights or Corporate Rights?" *Tribune Des Driots Humains*, Denver Post, August 2, 1998; *Charleston Gazette*, September 7, 1998; *San Francisco Chronicle*, April 10, 1998; *Washington Times*, March 21, 1998.

UPDATE BY WALT DONALDSON AND LAUREN POWELL
There is little doubt now that the Multilateral Agreement on Investment (MAI) would have had a detrimental effect on trade and the national sovereignty of third world countries. In mid-1998, due to an inability to resolve issues such as exemptions for cultural industries and a proposal to allow European Union members to give each other preferential treatment, France, Canada and Australia withdrew from the MAI. After three years of underreported operation starting in 1995, the Organization for Economic Cooperation and Development (OECD), which directed the MAI negotiations, formally suspended the bilateral investment treaty. Though MAI talks ceased, officials from the twenty-nine participating countries agreed that discussions were still necessary to protect overseas investment.

Smaller alternative trade agreements now exist as offshoots of the World Trade Organization (WTO) in place of the MAI. The North American Free Trade Agreement (NAFTA), the General Agreement of Tariffs and Trade (GATT), the Free Trade Area of the Americas (FTAA) and the Central American Free Trade Agreement (CAFTA) accomplish similar business goals. According to the *Washington Post*, most controversial is a misinterpreted legal clause included in CAFTA, NAFTA and other bilateral investment treaties. Designed to safeguard foreign investors from unfair treatment by a participant state, "investor-state arbitration" provisions give foreign business rights over local citizen interest. Both CAFTA and NAFTA license multinational corporations the right to sue a national government for monetary damages if it believes the actions of the participant government to be discriminatory, violate international law or expropriate the company's investment. The court that oversees such disputes consists of three private international arbitrators chosen by the parties concerned. Mistreated citizens do not hold position in such cases, thus critics of these treaties argue that the terms defy state and national sovereignty.

The resulting factor is that exploitative corporations are protected from foreign governments, and those governments are apt to put corporate interest above their own citizens. Keith Slack, an extractive industries expert for Oxfam America stated that investor protection clauses "essentially restrict the ability of governments to impose public interest or environmental regulations of corporate operations." According to the United Nations, by 1999, 82 percent of people living in mineral and energy exporting countries earned less that $1 per day; a 21 percent increase from 1981.

Update Sources: Eviatar, Daphne. "A Toxic Trade-off," *Washington Post*, August 14, 2005; Office of the United States Trade Representative, http://www.ustr.gov/Trade_Agreements/Regional/FTAA/Section_Index. html.

1998
Clinton Administration Aggressively Promotes U.S. Arms Sales Worldwide

During the Clinton administration the United States became the world's leading arms merchant. U.S. weapons are used in almost every global conflict, taking a devastating toll on civilians, military personnel and the economies of developing nations.

Original Sources: Lumpe, Lora. "Costly Giveaways," *The Bulletin of Atomic Scientists,* October 1996; Honey, Martha. "Guns 'R' US," *In These Times,* August 1, 1997.

UPDATE BY MIKE OLIVERA AND JOE BUTWILL

Since the original story was published, U.S. arms sales have soared. In a U.S. Arms Sales Report given to Congress by Richard F. Grimmett, a specialist in national defense foreign affairs, U.S. sales of arms between 1997–2000 and 2001–2004 increased up to three times in Africa alone.

In 1999 when the U.S. passed the Code of Conduct on Arms Transfers act of 1999, Congress was trying to prohibit arms sales to countries that do not promote democracy, human rights, or are actively involved in armed aggression. The code, however, allowed for presidential exceptions and required two-thirds of Congress to vote to overrule these exceptions.

The growing availability of small arms has been a major factor in the increasing number of conflicts worldwide, and it hinders smooth rebuilding and development after a conflict has ended. It is estimated that there are around half a billion military small arms around the world. 300,000 to 500,000 people around the world are killed by them each year. Small arms, which include grenades, handguns, mortars, and landmines, are the main cause of civilian casualties.

The U.S. has been sending foreign nations increased arms and aid for the "War on Terror." terror is the newly justifiable reason for sending, selling or trading aid to regions and countries known to violate human rights. Since September 11, the George W. Bush administration has made the distribution of security assistance a centerpiece of the "War on Terrorism." In its haste to gain the cooperation of regimes of geostrategic significance to the "War on Terrorism," the administration is disregarding normative restrictions on U.S. aid to human rights abusers. The Federation of American Scientists highlights this tradeoff by juxtaposing data on increases in military aid to the administration's allies in its global war on terror with excerpts from the State Department's recently released reports on human rights. Countries like Uzbekistan, Nepal and Indonesia listed by the State Department as having poor human right records still receive U.S. arms.

Update Sources: http://www.globalissues.org/Geopolitics/Arms Control.asp; Federation of American Scientists: Grimmett, Richard, U.S. Arms Sales Agreements with and Deliveries to Major Clients, 1996-2004, http://www.fas.org; December 19, 2005 The War and Terrorism and Human rights, http://fas.org/terrorism/at/docs/Aid& Humanrights.html.

1997
Risking The World: Nuclear Proliferation In Space

Virtually no media attention was paid to the launch of NASA's Cassini probe which carried seventy-two pounds of plutonium-238. Press coverage was devoted to the failed Russian space probe that crashed into the South Pacific with its payload of 200 grams of the same substance.

Original Sources: Grossman, Karl. "Risking the World: Nuclear Proliferation in Space," *Covert Action Quarterly*, Summer 1996; Grossman, Karl. "Don't send plutonium into space," *Progressive Media Project*, May 1996.

UPDATE BY ERIN ROEHM AND SANDY MURPHY

Karl Grossman reasoned in 1996, "You don't have to be a rocket scientist to know that what goes up sometimes comes down—and sometimes on people's heads." In the past the old duck and cover drill was thought to be a worthwhile exercise; now we are left to wonder where we can duck to avoid radiation. The threat lies not only with the falling debris, but the invisible force of radiation that nuclear materials can bring. Often the public is unaware the risk is there.

The fear of worldwide radiation exposure continued with the launch of the New Horizons mission to Pluto on January 16, 2006. Like Cassini, it used plutonium to generate electricity for instruments on board, though the new mission had only one-third the amount, as reported by CBS and several other news sources. Two Mars Rovers launched in the interim used the radioactive fuel as well, in much smaller quantities. Though NASA's Environmental

Impact Statements assured containment procedures were planned along with application of the latest technology regarding the care and handling of the plutonium, opponents argue tampering with the balance of radiation on the Earth could have catastrophic consequences. The reality is that nuclear radiation poses a risk to human beings and it is unknown exactly how high this risk is, especially under such variable circumstances.

In a review of the original Project Censored article, Grossman credits much of the public opposition and action to the stir the original Censored article caused. A 2006 CBS news report noted that hundreds of protesters chanted anti-nuclear slogans before NASA launched the Cassini spacecraft to Saturn, but only thirty anti-nuclear protesters showed up for the New Horizons' launch to Pluto. "Folks tend to forget," said protest organizer Maria Telesca of the Global Network Against Weapons & Nuclear Power in Space. The decline in protesters could be due to the lack of coverage on the current launch.

Lockheed Martin's Titan IV rocket, the one used for Cassini, continued to be used until 2005 despite three mishaps. One, in 1998, involved the rocket going out of control and exploding after taking off from Cape Canaveral, Florida, according to the Caltech/JPL Mars Society webpage on the Titan rocket.

Opponents of the use of plutonium argue that solar energy would be as effective. The European Space Agency (ESA) sent up the International Rosetta Mission in March, 2004, which is using lighter, more efficient solar cells than were available in the past. Rosetta is on a deep space mission that will last over ten years and plans to land on a comet in 2014, according to the ESA website. However, the distance from the Sun must be taken into account when considering solar power. Rosetta will be between 1 and 3 AU (astronomical units) from the Sun, according to the Jet Propulsion Lab. The *Encyclopedia Britannica* lists Earth as 1 AU from the Sun, with Saturn at 9.539 AU, and Pluto at 39.785 AU. Astronomy Professor Kevin McLin of Sonoma State University explains it this way, "The intensity of the sunlight drops as the square of the distance. That means by the time a spacecraft is at the orbit of Saturn (about ten times the Earth-Sun distance) the solar radiance is only one percent what it is at the Earth. As a result, solar panels would have to be 100 times bigger for the same power." NASA has used solar cells on several closer missions.

Though the New Horizons launch went off with out a hitch, nuclear fuel has been used on spacecraft and satellites since 1964, with several accidents, as Karl Grossman stated in his article. The limited media coverage and the spins put on the Horizon launch prove that the media play a large role and have a great responsibility to educate the world.

Update Sources: Associated Press, "Plutonium-Fueled Probe Set to Launch," CBSNews.com, January 16, 2006; Ulrich, Dr. Peter B., ed., "Final Environmental Impact Statement for the Cassini Mission," *National Aeronautics and Space Agency,* June 1995; Mars Society of Greater Los Angeles, "Titan: the ICBM and the Launch Vehicle," Caltech/JPL, http://meridiani2.usc.edu/launch/titan.html; European Space Agency, Science and Technology; Rosetta Mission page, http://sci.esa.int/science-e/www/area/index.cfm?fareaid=13, last updated February 15, 2005; Hagen, Regina. "Nuclear Powered Space Missions—Past and Future," http://www.space4peace.org/ianus/npsm2.htm , November 8, 1998; *Encyclopedia Britannica,* "The Solar System," Vol. 27, 1985; Halvorson, Todd. "Safety Officials Relieved at Launch," *Florida Today,* January 20, 2006; http://www.space4peace.org/articles/pluto-kuiper/safety_officials_relieved.htm.

1996
Telecommunications Deregulation: Closing Up America's "Marketplace of Ideas."

The Telecommunications Deregulation Act moved through Congress under the guise of "encouraging competition," but created huge concentrations of media power. It eliminated anti-trust regulations, dismantled limitations on the number of radio stations owned by a company, and lifted the FCC ban on joint ownership of a broadcast radio or TV license in the same market—allowing one company total control over the three primary community sources of news.

Original Sources: *Consumer Project on Technology.* "Federal Telecommunications Legislation: Impact on Media Concentration," July 14, 1995; Nader, Ralph, James Love, and Andrew Saindon. *TAP-INFO,* an Internet Newsletter.

UPDATE BY VANESSA BONAVENTURE

Deregulation advocates said less telecommunication regulation was vital to competitiveness, but opponents feared monopolization and a breakdown in consumer rights. Intended to stimulate investment, competition and advance the information superhighway, the 1996 Telecommunications Act helped the nation's broadcast networks accomplish what some critics had predicted: industry monopolization. According to the media reform group Freepress.org, since 1996 broadcast, television, telephone and computer industries have used an open door to unprecedented control over media content and the national delivery system. By replacing regulatory mandates with free-market policies, big media has threatened America's "marketplace of ideas," and not delivered on promises of more competition, diversity, lower prices and jobs, according to Common Cause, a public interest advocacy organization.

"The Telecommunications Act was covered (rather extensively) as a business story, not a public story," wrote media critic Robert McChesney in *Corporate Media and the Threat to Democracy*, "largely reflecting the priorities of special interests—local phone companies, long-distance providers, and cable and broadcast corporations. Special interests managed to prevail in a big way, benefiting from the legislative process and from a largely uninformed American public."

The act prompted a wave of media mergers, reducing the number of diverse voices in radio and television, and driving out local businesses unable to compete with large corporations. As a result, local TV stations, increasingly owned by out-of-town corporations, have been forced to produce less local programming or none at all, according to Freepress.org. Because the law extended the terms of Federal Communications Commission licenses, it became more difficult for broadcast licenses to be revoked so companies are less accountable to consumers.

In 2002 Consumer's Union Director Gene Kimmelman contended, in the *New York Times*, that any greater consolidation would be harmful to the public, but given the media conglomeration since the 1990s, "we may have lost all the diversity on the airwaves already." The FCC, led by Michael Powell, attempted in 2003 to further relax or eliminate industry ownership restrictions and extend the reach of companies by passing rules that allowed one company to own three TV stations, eight radio stations and a newspaper in a single market. They would also have allowed TV networks to own stations that reach up to 45 percent of the national market. The new rules were met with public outcry, congressional resistance and a federal court ruling that overturned most changes.

Powell, who set an agenda for consolidation and deregulation policies, stepped down as FCC chairman in 2005. However, Telecom mergers continue and are driven to maximize profit while the smaller voices of localism and diversity are lost. As quoted by Freepress.org, Clear Channel CEO Lowry Mays said it best, "We're not in the business of providing news and information. We're not in the business of providing well-researched music. We're simply in the business of selling our customers products."

According to the *New York Times*, conditions were set under Powell at the FCC, giving the next chairman the opportunity to rewrite rules governing the industry. A very small number of very large corporations now straddle broadcast, cable networks and the Internet. The implications of further media business deregulation and dissolution of public interest obligations are clear: the marketplace of ideas may be closing up shop.

Update Sources: McChesney, Robert W., *Corporate Media and the Threat to Democracy*, New York: Seven Stories Press, 1997; Schwartz, John. "The Nation; Bigger is Always Way Better," *New York Times*, February 24, 2002; Goodale, Gloria. "Now for a Word from our Sponsors," *Christian Science Monitor*, August 27, 2004; Labaton, Stephen. "Reshaping Telecommunications: The Regulators," *New York Times*, February 15, 2005; "The Fallout from the Telecommunications Act of 1996: *Common Cause*. "Unintended Consequences and Lessons Learned," May 9, 2005.

For more information

http://www.pbs.org/newshour/media/conglomeration
http://www.freepress.net/issues/consolidation
http://www.freepress.net/rules/page.phP.n=fcc
http://www.freepress.net/issues/ownership

1995
The Deadly Secrets of the Occupational Safety Agency

After the National Institute for Occupational Safety and Health (NIOSH) revealed 240,450 American workers had been exposed to hazardous materials, the Reagan Administration refused to fund a $4 million notification program and opposed legislation requiring it to do so.

Original Sources: Lurie, Peter, Sidney Wolfe, and Susan Goodwin. "Unfinished Business: Occupational Safety Agency Keeps 170,000 Exposed Workers in the Dark About Risks Incurred on Job," *Health Letter*, March 1994.

UPDATE BY LAUREN POWELL AND JENNA GOLL

NIOSH receives a yearly average of 450 requests to assess hazardous occupational environments, yet according to a 2004 article in *USA Today*, less than two percent of commercially used chemicals have been tested for cancer causing components. In 1998, the *Houston Chronicle* reported that the Occupational Safety and Health Administration (OSHA) had strengthened standards for only twenty-six of approximately 650,000 chemicals and chemical mixtures exposed to U.S. workers.

Industry-backed institutes fund the majority of hazardous material research. The process is slow, often resulting in years of delay to prevent illness and notify affected workers. As a result, workers have come to serve as 'canaries', or uninformed test subjects for the investigation of human chemical carcinogens in the environment. Peter Infante, former director of OSHA's Office of Standards Review noted in a 1995 article that twenty-one of twenty-two chemicals classified as lung carcinogens were first identified through studies of workers.

As for the early 1980s NIOSH study of high-risk exposure, the NIOSH website confirms that though field guidelines, sampling methodology, and analysis of management interview responses have been published, the bulk of the data remains unpublished. The National Occupations Exposure Survey (NOES) database has not been updated since July 1, 1990.

Update Sources: "National Occupational Exposure Survey," NIOSH, www.cdc.gov/noes. Morris, Jim. "In strictest confidence; The chemical industry's secrets; Rules for hazardous chemicals evolve slowly; Industry challenges frustrate regulation," *Houston Chronicle*, September 27, 1998; Armour, Stephanie. "Is work giving you cancer?" *USA Today*, February 2, 2004; Weiss, Rick. "Change at CDC draws protest," *Washington Post*, August 31, 2004.

1994
The United States Is Killing Its Young

The U.S. homicide rate for young people ages fifteen to twenty-four is five times greater than its nearest competitor and nine out of ten young people murdered in industrialized countries are slain in the U.S. Since the 1970s, while other industrialized nations were bringing children out of poverty, the U.S. slipped backward, with a current rate more than double that of any other major industrialized nation.

Original Sources: Reaves, Gayle. "U.N. Says US Dangerous for Children," *Dallas Morning News*, September 25, 1993; *USA Today*. "Report: 12 Million Kids Go Hungry in USA," June 16, 1993.

UPDATE BY ASHLEY RICE-KIENER

In 1994 Project Censored highlighted the alarming statistics of youth homicide in the United States. The Centers for Disease Control, and Prevention reported in 1997 the United States had the highest rates of childhood homicide, suicide and firearms-related deaths of any of the world's richest nations, according to *The Washington Post*. Fortunately, youth homicides have decreased since the late 1990s.

In 2001 the *Seattle Times* reported the CDC found total gun deaths dropped more than one-fourth during the mid 1990s to the lowest level since 1966. According to FBI reports and the National Crime Victimization Survey cited by the *Irish Times*, youth homicides decreased by 68 percent between 1993 and 1999, and overall youth crime in 1998 was at its lowest rate in twenty-five years.

There were about 3,800 juveniles arrested for homicides in 1993, according to FBI reports cited by the *Milwaukee Journal Sentinel*. In 1999 that number dropped to about 1,400. The Justice Department and National Center for Education Statistics data reveal serious violent crimes in schools declined by 34 percent during that period, also cited by the *Milwaukee Journal Sentinel*, and students carrying weapons to schools declined by 30 percent. In 2000 there were only sixteen school-associated homicides, meaning that in a school population of 52 million students there was less than a one in 3 million chance of being killed in one of America's schools.

Regardless of statistics, many parents and students fear the possibility of a shooting occurring at school and children killing children remains a disturbing issue. This fear has grown excessively because of "saturation coverage of school shootings" by the media, according to the Justice Policy Institute and the Children's Law Center as reported by the *Pittsburgh Post-Gazette*. A study conducted in 2000 made three recommendations regarding students, schools and violence: the media should avoid phrases such as "another in a series of school shootings" and focus on declining school violence; schools should implement more programs that promote peace and nonviolent behavior; and the gun industry should be regulated.

Many feel gun violence in schools has been inspired by violent video games. The 1999 Columbine school shooters in Littleton, Colorado made the computer, internet and video games scapegoats for youth violence. However, in 2000, *The New York Times* conducted a study and found in only six of 100 shooting cases did the killers have a known interest in violent games," as reported by the *Milwaukee Journal Sentinel*.

Lastly, more than ten years ago the United States signed the United Nations Convention on the Rights of the Child with the intent to consider ratification but has not done so. The CRC calls for protecting children and providing them "the full range of human rights," and was ratified more quickly and by more governments (except Somalia and the U.S.) than any other human rights instrument, according to the Child Rights Campaign and Child Rights Information Network. The United States must ratify the CRC to more fully protect its children and youth.

Update Sources: Havemann, Judith. "For Children, An Epidemic of Homicide; US Leads Rich Nations in Violence Against Youth," *Washington Post*, February 7, 1997; Elizabeth, Jane. "Violence in Schools Decreasing, but Fears Increasing," *Pittsburgh Post-Gazette*, April 6, 2000; Schiraldi, Vincent. "Coumbine's Image Lasts, but Youth Violence Declines," *Milwaukee Journal Sentinel*, March 14, 2001; McClaim, Erin. "US Gun Deaths Show Big Decline in Mid-

1990s," *Seattle Times*, April 13, 2001; Smythe, Patrick. "Disgruntled Law Student Kills Three in US School," *Irish Times*, Jan. 17, 2002; http://www.childrightscampaign.org; http://www.crin.org.

1993
The Great Media Sell-Out to Reaganism

The Reagan Administration ushered in the era of giant, monopolistic media empires as the three big networks, ABC, CBS and NBC were acquired by corporations that might have been deemed unqualified under earlier Federal Communications Commission (FCC) standards. In return, big media dispensed relentlessly positive news about Reaganism and the great "trickle-down" dream.

Original Source: Bagdikian, Ben H., "Journalism of Joy," *Mother Jones*, May/June 1992.

1990
Global Media Lords Threaten Open Marketplace of Ideas

A handful of mammoth companies, driven by profits, have begun to dominate the world's mass media. They predict by the 1990s, five to ten corporate giants will control most of the world's important newspapers, magazines, books, broadcast stations, movies, recordings and videos.

Original Source: Bagdikian, Ben. "Lords of the Global Village," *The Nation*, June 12, 1989.

1988
The Information Monopoly

The rapid centralization of media ownership raises critical questions about the public's access to diversity of opinion. Prevailing corporate concern with the bottom line and traditional publisher avoidance of controversy fosters widespread self-censorship among writers, journalists, editors and news directors.

Original Sources: Bagdikian, Ben. "The 26 Corporations That Own

Our Media," *EXTRA!*, June 1987; Bagdikian, Ben. "The Media Brokers," *Multinational Monitor*, September 1987; Lamb, Lynette. "Censorship in Publishing," *UTNE Reader*, January/February 1988; Bagdikian, Ben. *The Media Monopoly*, Boston: Beacon Press, 1983.

UPDATE EDITED BY LAUREN POWELL
Student researchers: Amanda Halpin and Julee Melhus

The number one stories of 1988, 1990, and 1993 addressed media consolidation and centralization, citing the work of Ben Bagdikian, author of several editions of *The Media Monopoly*. In 1982 Bagdikian found that fifty corporations controlled more than half of the media industry. By his second edition in 1986, the number had decreased to twenty-six. In 1989, the top five media conglomerates were: Time Warner Inc. of the U.S., Bertelsmann AG of Germany, News Corporation Ltd. of Australia, Hatchette S.A. of France and Capital Cities/ABC Inc. of the U.S.

Critics stress media consolidation leaves power over public opinion in the hands of a few large media corporations. Commenting on the homogenization of news, Nicholas Johnson, former member of the Federal Communications Commission and author of *How to Talk Back to Your Television Set*, told Multinationalmonitor.org, "When you're talking about what the American people as a whole have learned from all the available information when they vote or make a consumer choice or express an opinion on an issue, the range is pretty narrow." When the public is given a limited spectrum, information is tapered to the exclusive big business agenda. With shareholders as the ultimate priority, goals of media companies are disconnected from news and information production, and journalistic integrity is undermined.

In 1995 Disney bought Capital Cities/ABC and Time Warner merged with Turner Broadcasting to make up the top two media companies. By 1996, as predicted by Bagdikian, twenty-six major media corporations had dwindled to ten. Today five conglomerates own 90 percent of the media industry: Time Warner (CNN and AOL), Disney (ABC), News Corporation (Fox News), Bertelsmann (Random House), and Viacom (formerly CBS), largely as result of the Telecommunications Act of 1996.

The Telecommunications Act lifted significant regulations on media ownership under the pretense of spurring competition. Instead, extensive consolidation among media companies resulted. According to Common Cause, a public interest advocacy group, deregulation activities included: elimination of the forty station national ownership cap on commercial radio which spawned a frenzy of mergers—$700 million worth in the first week after the Act was passed; lifting rules on rates for non-basic cable; permitting the FCC to relax bans on broadcast-cable cross-ownership; increasing from 25 to 35 percent of television households in the national audience a single company may access; abolishing the cap on television stations a single company may own, and repealing laws that prevented broadcast networks from owning cable.

Supporters of the Telecom Act predicted the increase of 1.5 million jobs in the industry and an economic explosion of $2 trillion. Contrary to predictions, by 2003 industry market value had diminished by $2 trillion along with the liquidation of half a million telecom jobs, according to Common Cause. Rather than promoting competition, the result was massive consolidation, a decrease in local news and cable, and an increase in price. Consumers were the ultimate victims, and media conglomerates the victorious profiteers.

The Act was covered in mainstream media, but as a business story rather than a policy story. The public was uninformed of the social impact of the Act, thus public debate on the issue did not exist. In 2006, one decade after the Telecommunications Act, reform to the legislation is happening once more. Similarly, telecommunication activity in Congress is being kept out of mainstream news, with a few exceptions concerning recent coverage of Network Neutrality. (See Chapter One, Story #1; see Chapter 6 for more information on this year's legislation.)

Update Sources: Wexler, Celia Viggo, Mary Boyle and Matt Shaffer. "The Fallout From the Telecommunications Act of 1996," *Common Cause*, May 9, 2005; *The Museum of Broadcast Communications*. "US Policy: Telecommunications Act of 1996;" Stoll, Michael. "Bagdikian: A New Political Twist to the Old Media Monopoly," *Gradethenews.org*, May 21, 2004; Johnson, Nicholas. "An Interview with Nicholas Johnson," *Multinationalmonitor.org*, 1995.

1992
CBS and NBC Spiked Footage of Iraq Bombing Carnage

CBS and NBC refused to broadcast uncensored footage taken deep inside Iraq at the height of the air war. The footage, from two producers whose earlier work had earned NBC seven Emmy awards, contradicted U.S. claims that civilian damage from the American-led bombing campaign was light.

Original Source: Bernstein, Dennis and Sasha Futran. "Sights Unseen," *San Francisco Bay Guardian*, March 20, 1991.

UPDATE BY STACY WILLIAMS AND SARAH RANDLE

The air war in Iraq today continues with substantial under-reporting of civilian casualties (see Chapter One, Story #10). In Dahr Jamail's piece on the Missing Air War in Iraq, he shows that the U.S. military has kept reporters off air bases and aircraft carriers, with the exception of a few helicopter rides over Iraq. According to the LexisNexis media database, the phrase "air war" appeared in the New York Times in reference to the current U.S. military effort in Iraq (as of early December 2005) not once. The same can be said for both the *Washington Post* and *Time Magazine* for the year 2005.

The U.S. Air Force has claimed that "nearly 70 percent of all munitions used by the air component since the start of the operation have been precision-guided," and "every possible precaution is taken to protect innocent Iraqi civilians, friendly coalition forces, facilities and infrastructure." Yet a study by the Lancet British Medical Journal released in 2004 found that an estimated 85 percent of over 100,000 violent deaths in Iraq were generated by coalition air strikes. Seymour Hersh in the *New Yorker*, states that to date there have been no significant U.S. studies on civilian deaths in Iraq but that Iraqi medical personnel, working in areas where U.S. military operations continue, report that they feel the "vast majority" of civilian deaths are the result of actions by the occupation forces.

U.S. military forces in both Baghdad and Washington do not provide press with daily accounts of missions the Air Force, Navy and Marine units fly or of the tonnage they drop, as was routine in the Vietnam War. Although, when referring to battlefield success in Fallujah, a press release for the third Marine Aircraft Wing stated:

"Since the beginning of the war, the third wing has dropped more than five hundred thousand tons of ordnance, this number is likely to be much higher by the end of operations." In the battle for Fallujah more that seven hundred Americans were killed or wounded; U.S. officials did not release estimates of civilian dead, but press reports at the time told of women and children killed in the bombardments.

Update Sources: *TomDispath.com*, "Tomgram: Dahr Jamail on the Missing Air War in Iraq," January 2006, http://www.tomdispatch.com/index.mhtml?pid=42286; Hersh, Seymour M., "Up in the Air," *The New Yorker*, November 28, 2005, http://www.newyorker.com/printables/fact/051205fa_fact; Roberts, Les et al. "Mortality Before and after the 2003 Invasion of Iraq," *The Lancet*, October 29, 2004.

1991
The Gulf War: Truth Was the First Casualty

Scant media attention was given to the U.S. ambassador telling Saddam Hussein the U. S. had "no position" concerning Iraq's border dispute with Kuwait. Meanwhile, the White House lobbying Congress not to apply sanctions against Iraq just days before the invasion of Kuwait. Buried, too, was President Bush's rejection of Iraq's offer to pull out of Kuwait and release all hostages.

Sources: Hertsgaard, Mark. "The First Casualty," *Image Magazine*, October 14, 1990; Gersh, Debra. "Storytelling from the Persian Gulf," *Editor & Publisher*, October 20, 1990; Moore, Mike. "Imperial Thoughts," *The Quill*, October 1990; McBrien, John. "Saddam Was Bush-Whacked On Invasion," *The Spotlight*, October 8, 1990.

UPDATE BY CHARLENE JONES AND SHAUNA KING

The media and the American public paid little attention to the behavior of the George H. W. Bush's Administration and events leading up to Iraq's invasion of Kuwait. Coverage picked up, however, when congressional hearings in 1991 lead to accusations by prominent senators that former ambassador to Iraq April Glaspie had mislead Congress about the U.S. stance with Saddam Hussein just days before he invaded Kuwait. According to *The San Francisco Chronicle*, Glaspie's appearance before the Senate Foreign Relations Committee and the House Foreign Affairs Committee presented a U.S. ambassador who repeatedly warned Hussein against using force to settle his border dispute with Kuwait. In contrast, said the legislators, were cables showing her taking a conciliatory tone with Saddam, and that nowhere did she deliver that kind of warning she described in her testimony. Although Glaspie told Congress that the Iraqi version of her conversation with Saddam was fabrication, with few exceptions her cables paralleled the Arabic transcript available to reporters by the Iraqi Foreign Ministry after the invasion.

The 1992 presidential campaign also centered media and public attention on the former Bush administration's relationship with Saddam. According to *The Washington Post, Providence Journal* and *USA Today*, in the 1980s, Bush approved billions in loan guarantees and export licenses for items with possible nuclear applications Bush himself signed a secret directive promoting more U.S. trade with Iraq. The White House blocked the U.S. Commerce Department effort to stop the flow of U.S. technology to Iraq and opposed congressional sanctions against Iraq. Both former presidential candidate Ross Perot and former Senator Al Gore challenged Bush to release documents related to Iraq, including the personal message he sent to Saddam through Glaspie only days before the Iraqi invasion of Kuwait. Gore described the Bush administration actions a "cover-up that is significantly larger than the Watergate cover-up."

Many, including the *New York Times* and *The Washington Post*, suggested Bush's "non-position" gave Hussein the impression the United States would turn a blind eye to what he planned to do to his neighbors. *The Australian* newspaper, in its review of the documentary film "The Trial of Saddam Hussein, the Trial You'll Never See," called the 1990 invasion of Kuwait an example of U.S. collusion with Saddam.

In defending his actions, former President Bush cited national honor and denied he gave a "green light" to Hussein, according to the *San Antonio Express-News,* as did Tariq Aziz, Iraq's deputy prime minister at the time, who said neither he nor Saddam Hussein thought Ambassador Glaspie acquiesced to Iraq's plans to invade. However, former *Newsweek* and *Associated Press* reporter Robert Parry castigated both the Reagan and George H. W. Bush administrations for various propaganda campaigns to build support for their foreign policy in his book "Fooling America." He also blamed the press for its failures to ask hard questions after Iraq invaded Kuwait and allowing its integrity to be stolen.

Update Sources: Parry, Robert R., "Fooling America, How Washington Insiders Twist the Truth and Manufacture the Conventional Wisdom," 1992; Dickinson, Brian. "The high price of America's cozying up to Saddam Hussein," *Providence Journal*, October 25, 1992; Sciolino, Elaine. "US envoy allegedly misled Congress on warning Saddam/Secret cab show friendly tone, senators say," *San Francisco Chronicle*, July 13, 1991; Lewis, Anthony. "Nodding to Bullies," *New York Times*, August 28, 1992; Hoagland, Jim. "Hiding behind Glaspie; The character deficit in this case belongs to George Bush," *Washington Post*, October 21, 1992; Gelb, Leslie H., "A Bush Green Light to Iraq?" *New York Times*, October 22, 1992; *San Antonio Express-News*. "Iraqi says Glaspie didn't give go ahead," November 27, 1992; AFP. "Film exposes US links with Saddam in days of infamy," *Australian*, October 27, 2004.

1989
George Bush's Dirty Big Secrets

If the establishment press had reported on Bush background stories with the same intensity as the alternative media, it might have made a difference in the 1988 presidential election. The president of the Association of Alternative Newsweeklies claimed that if the average American voter had read the alternative press coverage of the 1988 election, Bush would not have been president.

Original Sources: Meeker, Richard. "George Bush's Dirty Secrets," *San Francisco Bay Guardian*, November 2, 1988. *EXTRA!*, "The GOP-Nazi Connection," September/October 1988.

UPDATE BY DANA DANYANOVITCH AND SARAH RANDLE

The 1988 presidential election may have had a different outcome for George H. W. Bush if we knew of the more recent finding behind his Zapata Corp. CIA connection, his possible role in the Bay of Pig's Invasion in 1961, the Bush/Bin Laden family ties, and the other various exposed secrets. Bush may have been involved with the CIA long before he was chosen as CIA director in 1976 by President Gerald Ford. He was involved with the CIA in the 1960s through the Bush family company, Zapata Offshore, which was an oil exploration company. Zapata is a holding company for the Omega Protein Corporation, a marine protein business that processes the Atlantic menhaden into industrial oils. The extent of Bush's involvement in the CIA during the 1960s is unknown. However, when Bush became Vice President in 1981, the Securities and Exchange Commission destroyed Zapata's filing records during the last six years of Bush's involvement in the company.

Adam Trueblood of the *Oregon Herald* affirms that Bush played a role in the supervision of the Castro insurgency and takeover in Cuba. Bush may also have had a role in the Bay of Pigs invasion in 1961, which was a U.S. funded plan to overthrow the government of Fidel Castro.

Kevin Phillips shows in *American Dynasty*, these connections would help explain why Bush's years as president and vice president involved counter-insurgencies, illegal arms deals, secret military build-ups, and scandals like Iran-Contra and many cover-ups.

The last two generations of the Bush family members have developed personal, business, and financial relationships with the rulers of Saudi Arabia and the entire Persian Gulf. It's hard to discern where Bush policies end and personal relationships begin. One of the most important connections is that with the Bin Laden family. When Bush was CIA director he enlisted Texas businessman James Bath as a CIA aide. Bath had just become a representative for two wealthy Saudi families, one being the Bin Ladens. Once Bush left the CIA he received help from Bath to start up a petroleum and energy business called Arbusto, funded mostly by Saudi money, some of which was Bin Laden capital. In the 1990s the Bush family and the Bin Laden family crossed again when they were both financially involved with the Carlyle Group, a private equity investment firm. Bush was Senior Advisor to the Carlyle Asia Advisory Board until October 2003. During that time the Bin Laden family were minor investors until after September 11, 2001 when the family sold its $2.02 million investment back to the firm.

The American public knows little about the hidden CIA side of George H. W. Bush and the corporate media like to keep their distance.

Update Sources: Trueblood, Adam. "Poppy's Crime Spree." April 2005, http://www.oregonherald.com/n/trueblood/Poppy's%20Crime.html. Phillips, Kevin. "American Dynasty: Aristocracy, Fortune, and the Politics of Deceit in the House of Bush," 2004. http://www.american-dynasty.net/Harvard.htm; http://en.wikipedia.org/wiki/Carlyle_group; http://en.wikipedia.org/wiki/Zapata_Oil.

1987
Criticizing the President's Policies Can Be Dangerous

Political opponents of the Reagan administration's Central American policies became the targets of mysterious break-ins, IRS audits, FBI questioning and physical surveillance.

Original Sources: Chase, Sylvia. "Heat on the Left: TARGET 4," Producers Jonathan Dann and Angus Mackenzie of the Center for Investigative Reporting, *KRON-TV*, February 18-20, 1987; Roland, Neil. "Nicaragua Visitors: US Harasses Us," *San Francisco Examiner, UPI*, February 19, 1987; Hinckle, Warren. "Info-Thieves Hit the Women's Building," *San Francisco Examiner*, March 13, 1987.

UPDATE BY LINDSEY BABB AND SARAH RANDLE

The accusations of the IRS, the FBI and other government agencies spying on Americans were met with public outrage. Former FBI employee Frank Varelli affirmed the invasion of privacy in 1987. Varelli reported that he was instructed to provide reports on the CIS-PES, the Committee in Solidarity with the People of El Salvador. He also stated the FBI led him to believe the CISPES was a radical terrorist organization, when in reality he found it to be a peaceful, non-violent organization devoted to changing the policies of the United States towards Central America.

The Foreign Intelligence Surveillance Court was supposed to oversee and supply a court order for any and all electronic surveillance for intelligence purposes within the U.S. The Reagan administration directly violated the Foreign Intelligence Surveillance Act by 'spying' on American citizens without probable cause authorized by the FISA court. The policies of FISA were changed in 1990, with the presidency of George H.W. Bush, when a bill was passed requiring the president to inform the FISA court of any covert actions taken with forty-eight hours.

Today, the threat of invasion of privacy is not over. The George W. Bush administration has been using the National Security Agency to run millions of emails and phone call through their computers, searching for specific keywords, phrases and patterns. These policies put forth by the Bush administration today mirror those of the Reagan presidency not long ago.

Update Sources: "The Hunt for Red Menace." http://www.thirdworld traveler.com/FBI/Hunt_Red_Menace.html. Glide, Kyle. "President should not take over US." 2005. Google News. Weinberger, Caspar. "Reagan's Defense Secretary was caught up with Iran-Contra affair," *San Francisco Chronicle*, 1987.

1986
Fiercest Aerial War in America Is Unreported in U.S. Press

The people of El Salvador were victims of the most intense saturation bombing ever conducted in the Americas with U.S. supplied bombs and missions often directed by U.S. military leaders. More than one-fifth of the Salvadoran population of 5 million became refugees—a higher percentage than South Vietnam at the height of the Vietnam War.

Original Sources: Cockburn, Alexander. "Remember El Salvador?" *The Nation*, June 1, 1985; Hughes, Patrick M. "Letter from Patrick M. Hughes, Director," *Refugee Legal Services*, Laredo, Texas, January 24, 1986.

UPDATE BY SARAH SHORT

The Salvadorean civil war from 1980 to 1992 was marked by controversy regarding minimally-publicized aid given by the United States government. The United States, throughout the course of the war, provided over $1 billion dollars in military and $4.5 billion dollars in economic aid, advisors, and training. Almost one quarter of the aid went directly to the Salvadorean air force

The Salvadorean Air Force, the Fuerza Aerea Salvadorean (FAS), initially was comprised of fewer than a thousand men divided into a paratroop battalion, a security force, an antiaircraft unit, and four flying squadrons. Then, with aid from the U.S., the FAS was modernized and increased with the goal of building a powerful helicopter force capable of lifting infantry for offensive tactics and providing gunship support. In 1982 alone, the U.S. military assistance and sales program was $82,501,000. The FAS, with U.S. intervention, became the largest air force in Central America. From 1981 to 1986, the FAS bombed villages that allegedly supported the rebels, leading to high civilian casualties.

The end of the war came in 1992 with the signing of peace accords between the government and the rebel alliance, the Marxist Farabundo Martí National Liberation Front (FMLN). A compromise solution disarmed the FMLN forces, made the FMLN a legal political party, and granted amnesty to FMLN members. More than half of the army was demobilized, and most of the paramilitary security forces were disbanded. Former FMLN members joined a new national police force, and the United Nations and Organization of American States observers stayed in El Salvador to aid in completing the disarmament and holding free and fair elections.

Update Sources: Corum, Sr. James S. "The Air War in El Salvador," *Aerospace PowerJournal,* Summer 1998; Dyer, Gwyenne, "El Salvador Guerillas Shift to Economic Targets," *Toronto Star,* February 27, 1986; Evans, Ernest. "El Salvador's Lessons for Future US Interventions," *World Affairs,* Summer 1997.

1985
The Well-Publicized Soviet Military Build-Up Scare Was a Lie

U.S. military leaders lied about the Soviet arms build-up and falsified information to inflate Soviet military expenditures. By instilling fear in the American public, they hoped to capture a higher military budget.

Original Sources: "Taking Stock: The US Military Build-up." *Defense Monitor* XII, no. 4, 1984; Gregory, William H., "Soviet Defense Spending," *Aviation Week & Space Technology,* February 13, 1984.

UPDATE BY DANIELLE SPRIDGEN

In May of 1992 the United States found out that their government had lied about the strength of the Soviet military in order to increase the U.S. military budget. Caspar W. Weinberger, Ronald Reagan's Secretary of Defense, requested $20.5 billion dollars annually for Reagan's "Star Wars" program for fiscal years 1985–1989, more than 43 percent higher than the military budget during the Vietnam War. Congress cut each request and in the end appropriated $14.68 billion. To justify expanded military funding the Department of Defense ignored a CIA report on the stagnation of Soviet spending for military from 1977–1983. During Reagan's two terms in office, military spending increased the national debt by triple what it was before.

By the end of the Cold War in 1990, military spending in Russia had decreased dramatically. Russia had a defense budget in 1989 of approximately 155 billion rubles (somewhere around $39 million USD). In 1995, Russia's defense budget was cut to 78.9 trillion rubles (about $19 million USD) while in comparison, the United States' defense budget was $249 billion.

According to The Center for Defense Information, the requested budget amount in 2005 was $400.1 billion. This figure does not even take into consideration the Afghanistan and Iraq wars. The total budget requested for fiscal year 2006 is $419.3 billion (also not including the Afghanistan and Iraqi wars). Weapons of Mass Destruction and a war on terror is the latest DOD propaganda ploy to increase the budget for the military.

Update Sources: Ronald Reagan's Military Buildup www.u-s-history.com/ pages/h1957.html. Russian Military Budget news directed by John Pike www.globalsecurity.org/military/world/russia/mo-budget.htm. Center for Defense Information.

1984
Israel: Merchant of Death in Central America

President Reagan's policy objectives in Central America circumvent congressional objections with quiet help from Israel. The fifth biggest exporter of arms in the world, Israel is the largest supplier of weapons to Latin America and a major source of training in intelligence and counter-insurgency techniques.

Original Sources: Lusane, Clarence. "Israeli Arms in Central America," *Covert Action Information Bulletin*, Winter 1984; Gelb,

Leslie H., "Israel Stepping Up Arms Sales to Central America," *New York Times*, December 17, 1982.

UPDATE BY SANDY MURPHY

In 1984 the U.S. State Department denied having plans to give money to Israel for covert operations in Central America. According to the *New York Times*, the denial was triggered by a story in the Israeli newspaper *Haaretz* claiming the U.S. suggested that Israel channel American aid to Central American anti-communist forces, and the aid would be outside the U.S. government budget. However, when the Iran-Contra scandal broke in 1986, Israel proved to be the middleman in the secret U.S. scheme to fund Nicaraguan Contra rebels by selling arms to Iran. The Israeli intermediary in the arms sales, Amiram Nir, was sought for questioning, but Israel insisted he be granted immunity. Nir was killed in a small plane crash in Mexico in 1988 during the time Oliver North was on trial. North had suggested it was Nir's idea to divert funds from the arms sales to Nicaraguan rebels, which Israel denied.

The Israeli connection to the Iran-Contra scandal was rarely mentioned in U.S. newspapers, other than a few opinion columns. The only television newscasts mentioning it were ABC's *World News Tonight* and *The MacNeil-Lehrer News Hour* on PBS.

By 2003 Israel had become the world's third largest weapons exporter, and continues to sell to Latin America and the rest of the globe, according to the *Jerusalem Post*. The country has about 600 private companies that specialize in Third World arms sales. Even when laws are broken—two planeloads of weapons from Tel Aviv made it into Rwanda during the genocide despite an Israeli ban on selling to civil war-torn countries—no one was charged with a crime.

According to the *Jerusalem Post*, the Israeli government sold munitions to South Africa during apartheid, to dictator Augusto Pinochet's Chile, and to China after the Tiananmen Square incident when other countries refused because of human rights issues. More recently *Flight International* reported tension between Hugo Chavez and the Bush administration has meant Israeli, rather than U.S. companies, will handle Venezuela's military upgrades.

At least twice, the United States insisted Israeli-Chinese weapons deals be rescinded so China would not have access to sensitive U.S.

technology. Israel continues to receive $2-3 billion in military aid from the U.S. government each year, making it easier for them to compete against American weapons dealers, and, in some cases, with American technology. Israeli Defense Minister Shaul Mofaz signed an agreement in 2005 that gave the U.S. veto power over where Israel sells its arms in exchange for the U.S. removal of all the restrictions that had been imposed over defense trade with China.

Update Sources: AP, "Israeli Latin Role is Denied by U.S.," *New York Times*, April 22, 1984; AP, "Man Killed in Mexican Crash Is Indeed Iran-Contra Figure," *New York Times*, December 3, 1988; O'Sullivan, Arieh. "Arming the Chinese Dragon," *The Jerusalem Post*, September 4, 1998; Schechter, Erik. "Trigger Happy," *The Jerusalem Post*, Oct. 24, 2003; Trimble. "Aiming south," *Flight International*, April 19, 2005; O'Sullivan, Arieh. "Yaron: Fence to be completed by end of year," *The Jerusalem Post*, September 15, 2005.

1983
Fraudulent Testing Provides an Illusion of Safety

The former president of the largest testing lab in the country, which conducted about one-third of the toxicity and cancer testing of chemicals in America, was indicted for allegedly fraudulent tests. A major investigation of testing laboratories, standard-setting boards, and regulatory agencies that oversee the science of testing for safety, revealed that much of the research aimed at ensuring a safer world is either fraudulent or useless.

Original Sources: Miller, Judith and Mark Miller. "Testing Fraud," *Focus/Midwest*, September 1982; "The Dowie, Mark, Douglas Foster, Carolyn Marshall, David Weir, and Jonathan King. "Illusion of Safety," *Mother Jones* and the Center for Investigative Reporting, 1982.

UPDATE BY CAROLYN ROJAS
In the wake of the Industrial Bio-Test scandals, the Food and Drug Administration (FDA) finalized the Good Laboratory Practices regulations. These were followed by guidelines for pesticide toxicology studies established by the Environmental Protection Agency (EPA). Unfortunately, the laws and guidelines in place to ensure healthy liv-

ing situations for Americans are still ignored by many companies. Private laboratories continue to be caught falsifying test results for everything from water supplies and petroleum products to pesticide residue and superfund sites.

American Environmental Laboratories had its water-testing certification revoked in 1996 after it was discovered that water deemed "safe for drinking" by the company had been tainted with raw sewage, according to the *Boston Business Journal*. The Massachusetts Department of Environmental Protection conducted a review that revoked the company's water-testing certificate.

In 1997 Hess Environmental Laboratories pled guilty to numerous counts including falsification of claims and violations of the Clean Water Act, as reported by the EPA. Hess admitted to cheating hundreds of customers, including numerous municipalities, environmental consulting firms, schools, Wal-Mart and Kraft Foods, by falsifying or never performing tests.

Uncovering one of the largest cases of lab fraud in 1998, EPA officials confiscated laboratory documents and computers from Intertek Testing Services in Richardson, Texas. Intertek was hired to test abandoned hazardous waste locations designated as Superfund sites across the country, according to *Chemist Magazine*. In 2000, thirteen employees of Intertek were indicted for falsifying test results from thousands of Superfund sites. It is estimated more than 59,000 projects and 250,000 separate tests worth more than $35 million were affected by work conducted by Intertek labs operating in Texas. Those named in the case ranged from a former vice president, to bench-level lab analysts. Intertek, with a worldwide network of 280 labs, was also under investigation at two other locations, New Jersey and Puerto Rico.

In 2001 the former president of Caleb Brett USA., a subsidiary of Intertek Testing Services, pled guilty to obstruction of justice for conspiring to mislead EPA investigators about falsifying chemical analysis of millions of gallons of reformulated gasoline. According to the EPA, approximately 200 to 300 million gallons of the fake reformulated gasoline were distributed in New York, New Jersey and Connecticut.

More recently in 2006, a former owner of Quality Water Systems, a Montana wastewater management company, pled guilty to providing false information to environmental regulators in

Idaho and Montana, according to the U.S. Attorney's Office District of Idaho.

Update Sources: Benavides, Lisa. "State Shuts Lab for Faulty Water Tests," *Boston Business Journal,* October 18, 1996; Environmental Protection Agency, "Pennsylvania Laboratory Admits Fraud," *Environmental Protection Agency Press Release,* November 14, 1997; Environmental Protection Agency, "Crackdown Continues on False Lab Reports Scheme," *Environmental Protection Agency Press Release,* Nov. 29, 2001; Novak, Roger A., "The Long Arm of the Lab Laws," *Chemist,* November, 2001; Margasak, Larry. "Private Labs Fake Environmental Tests," *Associated Press,* Jan. 22, 2003; McNeil, Jean. "Montana Man Admits Falsifying Wastewater Tests," *United States Attorney's Office District of Idaho Press Release,* January 31, 2006.

1982
The Real Story Behind Our Economic Crisis

A UCLA professor, testifying before the California legislature, stated the basic causes of the economic crisis are monopolies, militarism and multi-nationalization. Compounded with the lack of a competitive economy, these are the root of the worst economic crisis since the Great Depression.

Original Source: *Village Voice,* January 1981, testimony by UCLA Professor Maurice Zeitlin, California Senate Committee on Industrial Relations, December 9, 1980.

UPDATE BY THERESA PETRELLESE AND LINDSEY BRANDON
Since Maurice Zeitlin's 1981 warning about monopoly, militarism and multinationalism causing economic crisis, wealth inequality continues to grow in the United States and corporate America continues to spread across the globe.

A report by the Institute for Policy Studies cited by globalissues.org, noted U.S. corporations lead the 200 top corporations worldwide with eighty-two, a whopping 41 percent of the total. Global 500 companies generate 25 percent of the gross world output, according to Endgame Research and Training. Transnational corporations are growing 8 to 10 percent per year, while the world economy is advancing by only two or three percent. This means that increased concentration of wealth and power is occurring in the top corporations of the world

Endgame's collected data also points out that Fortune 500 companies are responsible for 42 percent of the U.S. gross national product. An astonishing two percent of the nation's corporations control 75 percent of business in the country. The top 500 industrial corporations, which represent only one tenth of one percent of corporations, control over two-thirds of business resources, employ two-thirds of industrial workers, account for 60 percent of sales, and collect more than 70 percent of the profits.

As American corporate wealth continues to grow, the ownership of America's corporate assets have also become significantly more concentrated.

In 2001, ten percent of the U.S. population held 71 percent of the wealth, and of that ten percent the top one percent controlled 38 percent of the total wealth, according to United for a Fair Economy.

In addition, the unequal distribution of wealth has contributed to a sharp increase in the number of billionaires at both a national and global level. According to *Forbes Magazine,* cited by Alternet.org, there were 374 billionaires in the United States in 2004. The average net worth of individuals on the Forbes list reached $2.8 billion in 2004, up from an average of $400 million in the early 1980s.

The numbers worldwide are even more startling. *The Irish Times* reported, "the world's richest 500 individuals have a combined income greater than that of the poorest 416 million people. Some 2.5 billion people living on less than $2 per day make up 40 percent of the world's population but account for 5 percent of global income. In contrast, the richest ten percent account for 54 percent of it."

According to the Economic Policy Institute, U.S. corporate profits are up and wages of average Americans are down. More and more people are deeper in debt, poverty is on the rise, and job creation has not kept pace with population growth. Zeitlin's warnings about economic crisis are still applicable as corporate control concentrates and vast inequality in distribution of wealth rises.

Update Sources: Leondar-Wright, Betsy. "More Billionaires, More Bankruptcies," United for a Fair Economy, December 15, 1999; Shah, Anup. "Corporate Power Facts and Stats," http://www.globalissues.org, May 15, 2001; Draffan, George. "Facts on the Concentration of Wealth," http://www.endgame.org/primer-wealth.html; Editorial. "Worlds Apart in Wealth and Income," *Irish Times*, September 8, 2005; Collins, Chuck and Felice Yeskel. "Billionaires R Us," http://www.alternet.org, October 24, 2005; Mishel, Lawrence and Ross Eisenbrey. "What's Wrong with the Economy," *Economic Policy Institute*, December 21, 2005; Council on International and Public Affairs, "Too Much, A Commentary on Excess and Inequality," February 6, 2006.

1981
Distorted Reports of the El Salvador Crisis

U.S. media coverage of the civil war in El Salvador was dangerously misleading. Supporting a misguided U.S. foreign policy, it perpetuated a position that current government of the Central American country is a "moderate" junta, struggling to maintain order in the face of extremist minorities.

Original Sources: Connor, James L., "El Salvador's Agony and US Policies," *America*, April 26, 1980; "El Wipfler, William L., "Salvador: Reform as Cover for Repression," *Christianity and Crisis*, May 12, 1980; Nelson, Anne. "The Continuing Calamity of El Salvador," *Inquiry*, May 5, 1980; Nelson, Anne. "Central American Powder Keg," *Inquiry*, November 10, 1980; Lernoux, Penny. "El Salvador's Christian Democrat Junta," *The Nation*, December 13, 1980; Petras, James. "The Junta's War Against the People," *The Nation*, December 20, 1980.

UPDATE BY AUDRA ANDERSON AND SANDY MURPHY

In a 2001 *Washington Post* editorial, U.S. Representative Joe Moakley reminded readers of the truth about El Salvador's civil war stating, "Peace was achieved in El Salvador only when Congress finally cut off military aid to that government, whose brutal military was infamous for its propensity to murder and oppress its civilian population. For more than a decade, the Reagan-Bush policy allowed the civil war to rage with our military aid flowing in to the tune of $6 billion."

Ronald Reagan's death in 2004 stirred up memories, and *The Washington Post* reported reactions from Central Americans. While ultra-right conservatives thought highly of him, others remembered him as "an anti-communist zealot, whose obsession blinded him to the human rights abuses of those he supported with funding and CIA training." Reporters Mary Jordan and Kevin Sullivan wrote that Gerson Martinez, a former rebel leader in El Salvador, said the U.S. - backed wars under Reagan created a massive wave of refugees who fled to the United States. Martinez called that migration "the daughter of Reagan's policies." Martinez also called the rampant street gangs in his country "the grandchildren" of policies under Reagan because they were created by refugees who had joined gangs in the U.S. and brought that culture back to El Salvador. It is now a critical security issue in El Salvador.

The corporate media in general has failed to address claims that since the signing of the Peace Accords that ended the war in El Salvador, the U.S. has abandoned that country. El Salvador is still recovering from the effects of their civil war. Michael Ring, director of U.S. -El Salvador Sister Cities, states, "On the plus side . . . the great majority of accords have been followed." However, he adds a string of serious problems. Unemployment is extremely high and the largest source of income comes from Salvadorans working in the U.S. and sending money home. Violent crime, exacerbated by poverty and the availability of guns, caused rates of death higher than during some years of the war. Small farmers are being bankrupted by global trade rules, and basic services are being privatized. Environmental disasters, such as flooding, are worse due to deforestation. PBS observes that "El Salvador has the highest level of environmental damage in the Americas . . . and some experts fear that at the current rate of destruction, the country will run out of drinking water in less than fifteen years."

The U.S. returned to El Salvador in 2000 to establish an anti-drug trafficking military base at the international airport in Comalapa. The Farabundo Marti National Liberation Front (FMLN) opposed the action, fearing more U.S. intervention in the country's internal affairs.

A 2004 report for PBS's Frontline World observed the continuing political divide in El Salvador. The National Republican Alliance (ARENA) party formed by Roberto D'Aubuisson, the late death squad leader, continues to control the presidency. Members of the George W. Bush administration made their concerns known to the people of El Salvador during its 2004 presidential election, warning that relations with the U.S. could change detrimentally should the opposition party, FMLN, win.

Frontline World's reporter Joe Rubin noted that the ARENA government passed "an almost blanket amnesty" for war criminals, but some have been prosecuted in the U.S. A federal judge in Fresno, California ruled against former security chief Alvaro Saravia for helping to organize the murder of Archbishop Romero, and was ordered to pay $10 million to his family. Saravia went into hiding shortly before the trial began.

Update Sources: Jordan, Mary and Kevin Sullivan."In Central America, Reagan Remains A Polarizing Figure," *Washington Post,* June 10, 2004; Moakley, Joe. "What Really Happened in El Salvador," *Washington Post,* February 12, 2001; Cassidy, Esther, Deborah Shaffer, Rob Kuhns and Bill Kavanagh. "Enemies of War," *Public Broadcasting Service,* circa 1998, http://www.pbs.org/itvs/enemiesofwar/ story.html; Ring, Michael. "Enemies of War- El Salvador Today: The Hope and the Challenge," http://www.pbs.org/itvs/enemiesofwar/per- spectives3.html; Lanchin, Mike. "El Salvador's Suffering Lingers On," *BBC News,* 2004; Rubin, Joe. "El Salvador: Payback," *PBS Frontline World,* October 12, 2004.

1980
The Corporate Crime of the Century

Corporate America "dumps" dangerous chemicals, toxic pesticides and defective medical drugs and devices that have been restricted or banned in the U.S. on less wary Third World countries. *Every* pesticide banned or restricted in this country has been exported elsewhere.

Original Source: Dowie, Mark, Barbara Ehrenriech, Stephen Minken, Mark Shapiro, Terry Jacobs and David Weir. "The Corporate Crime of the Century," *Mother Jones,* November 1979.

UPDATE BY DAVID ABBOTT AND CRYSTAL BLACKFORD

In November 1979, *Mother Jones* devoted nearly an entire issue to the exporting of banned or substandard products into overseas markets, a practice known as "dumping." On January 15, 1981, Jimmy Carter signed an executive order creating a uniform notification system for the export of hazardous or domestically restricted products. The order was short-lived, as Ronald Reagan almost immediately overturned it saying the controls were, "unduly burdensome for

U.S. industry, and would threaten U.S. jobs." The Consumer Product Safety Commission (CPSC) changed the way federal laws were interpreted under Reagan, and even voted to allow the export of fabrics that failed U.S. flammability standards. The agency never formally changed its policy against exporting other unsafe products but issued a press release in 1984 saying it reserved the right to make exceptions. Since then, exceptions have totaled hundreds of shipments, which are almost never turned away because there is often no legal basis for refusing them in the countries to which they are shipped.

The *Mother Jones* articles pointed out that dumping is not exclusive to the U.S. Many other countries—most notably Germany—do the same thing, but "American business leaders, who tout themselves as the most ethical businesspeople in the world, should lead the way in ending dumping worldwide," adding that "they are actually poisoning the very markets they seek to develop."

In April 1994, the Clinton administration enacted tighter export policy controls on pesticides which required that foreign governments be notified of the shipment of U.S.-banned pesticides, but the policy had little effect on the practice. The *Boston Globe* ran a three-part series beginning on July 11, 1994, entitled "Foul Trade: Using U.S. Exports can be Risky," which documented the manner in which U.S. companies take advantage of weaker laws in third-world countries by exporting goods, drugs, and pesticides that are illegal in the U.S.

Dumping of substandard and dangerous products by U.S. manufacturers disappeared from the press until November 2004 when ConsumerReports.org ran an article entitled, "Rejected by U.S., Unsafe Goods go Abroad" which puts the number of documented illegal exports between 1994-2004 above 900. Consumer Reports also notes that since 1990, the CPCS has cited more than 22,000 products for safety violations and it is not known how many of those products were exported.

But the practice was so obscure that the current and former heads of the CPSC claim to know little about it. Ann Brown, commission chairwoman from 1994-2001, says she didn't focus on the issue but added, "Anything that is not good enough for the U.S. should not be sent abroad." Hal Stratton, the current chairman, asked, "Has this happened since I've been around? I don't know of any countries or consumers who have complained about that. I think it is a serious issue. I think it's something we probably need to look at."

Among the goods that have been illegally exported are:

▶ Wellmax extension cords were shipped to Panama in 2001 after nearly a million of them were recalled in the U.S. because their undersized wires could overheat and cause a fire. The CPSC notified Panamanian officials about the danger but had no authority to stop their exportation. In July 2004 we found some of the defective cords for sale over the Internet, for "export only," by Wellmax, an importer in Santa Fe Springs, California.

▶ Balloon-tongue "Zapper" toys were exported to the Dominican Republic in 2001, after 835,000 distributed by eight toy companies in the U.S. were recalled because children could inhale the balloons or choke. In August 2004 we found them still being sold in a party-goods store in Santiago, Dominican Republic.

▶ More than 500 flammable girls' and women's chenille sweaters were shipped to Israel and Japan in 1999. They failed U.S. flamma-bility standards and would burn faster than newspaper if ignited, according to a CPSC recall notice. (The company, BCBG Max Azria, was fined for trying to sell some of the recalled sweaters to employ-ees at its company store in California.)

Update Sources: *ConsumerReports.org*, "Rejected by US, Unsafe Goods go Abroad," November 2004. http://www.consumerreports. org/cro/personal-finance/dangerous-products-unsafe-goods-go-abroad-1104/index.htm.

1979
The Dangers of Nuclear Power Plants

The Union of Concerned Scientists released a report citing the fail-ure of the Nuclear Regulatory Commission to inspect nuclear power plants. Contrary to the common perception that the nuclear industry is closely regulated, UCS found only 1 to 5 percent of safety-related nuclear power plant activities are inspected.

Original Source: Union of Concerned Scientists. "Scientists' Group Judges Federal Nuclear Safety Inspection Effort," November 26, 1978.

UPDATE BY MARIAH MORRIS

According to Cleveland's *Plain Dealer*, in 1998 the nuclear energy industry went to Congress to complain that the Nuclear Regulatory Commission was being too harsh, tedious, and inconsistent during plant inspections. That same year, New Mexico Senator Pete Domenici, chairman of the subcommittee that oversaw the NRC's budget, told the agency to back off or the budget for plant inspections would be cut by 40 percent. The focus then changed to cost-benefit effectiveness and preventing known hazards.

Recent reports have cited many existing plants for repeated federal violations, unmonitored groundwater contamination, and incomplete plant inspections. As Congress gives more inspection responsibilities to the plants themselves, the Nuclear Regulatory Commission (NRC) stands accused of "becoming a lapdog for the nuclear power industry," says Senator Harry Reid of Nevada, as quoted by the *Plain Dealer* in 2002.

In 2006 the *New York Times* reported that Indian Point 2, a nuclear plant in New York, leaked a radioactive form of hydrogen called tritium into surrounding groundwater. Researchers say the chemical will inevitably reach the Hudson River, though they believe the amount is not a health risk. The Braidwood Generating Station, a nuclear plant in Illinois also contaminated a nearby family's well with tritium, making it unsafe to use.

The *Plain Dealer* followed one story for several years. They revealed that new management at Davis-Besse nuclear plant in Ohio discovered a large rust hole in the reactor's lid in 2002. After ignoring cracks in the nozzles for five years the plant was shut down. Until this discovery Davis-Besse had received top ratings from the NRC.

In 2001 the *Times-Picayune* quoted Vice President Dick Cheney saying, "If you want to do something about carbon dioxide emissions, then you ought to build nuclear plants." Although Cheney has not addressed the inevitable increase of radioactive waste in his energy plan, he has proposed that 1,300–1,900 new generating plants be built across the nation.

No Nukes says that radioactive isotopes in nuclear waste such as Plutonium-239, which is deadly to humans, can take a quarter to half a million years to decay and become "harmless."

Congress voted in 2002 in favor of allowing the U.S. Department of Energy to move ahead with its plan to bury over 70,000 tons of high-level radioactive waste in Yucca Mountain, reported the *Sacramento Bee*. The site lies ninety miles outside of Las Vegas, Nevada and seventeen miles from the border of the Death Valley National Park in California. Barbara Boxer, a U.S. senator who voted against the approval said, "If the groundwater is contaminated, that will be the demise of the park and the surrounding community." Nevada has already filed suit against the project, alleging that the Energy Department altered scientific standards for evaluating Yucca's geological merits. Seven billion dollars has already been invested in the project.

Update Sources: Koff, Stephen. "Cracks appear in NRC's new rules; Critics say safety assumptions by self-policing nuclear industry don't pass acid test," *Plain Dealer*, September 22, 2002; Wald, Matthew L., "A Leak at Indian Point Prompts Monitoring," *New York Times*, March 5, 2006; Mangels, John and John Funk. "Nuclear plant ruling attacked; Cost swayed NRC in Davis-Besse case, watchdogs declare," *Plain Dealer*, October 4, 2002; Editorial, "Davis-Besse's legal fall-out," *Plain Dealer*, January 24, 2006; Darce, Keith. "Are We Changing Our Nuclear Reactions?" *Times-Picayune* (New Orleans), April 29, 2001; Gyorgy, Anna and friends. *No Nukes: Everyone's Guide to Nuclear Power*. Boston, MA: South End Press, 1979; Gordon, Greg. "Senate approves Yucca dump site," *Sacramento Bee*, July 10, 2002.

1978
The Myth of Black Progress

Most of the indices of Black poverty, illegitimacy, unemployment and drug abuse show worsening conditions. Even those considered successful are losing ground compared to their white counterparts.

Original Source: Dreyfuss, Joel. "Black Progress Myth and Ghetto Reality," *The Progressive*, November 1977.

UPDATE BY SANDRA MOORE

The poverty and unemployment that lead to the urban riots of the 1960s and grew worse through the complacency of the '70s continued to stifle the progress of blacks into the '80s. A 1991 *Newsweek* article entitled, "A Crisis of Shattered Dreams," stated that during the

'80s "the seeming indifference of the Reagan administration sent a signal that whites didn't need to feel guilty about black concerns anymore."

Newsweek noted that by the early 1990s one quarter of all African American men were in jail, on probation, or on parole. Sixty percent of all black children were born to mothers without husbands. According to the *Herald Sun* in 1992, more than 40 percent of all black children lived below the poverty line, compared to about 16 percent of white children. Thirty percent of all AIDS cases and almost half of America's murder victims were black.

The 1990s also brought blacks more opportunities for socioeconomic mobility than at any time in the history of the United States. A 2003 editorial in *Business Week* noted that poverty was substantially reduced and millions of black people rose into the middle class. Through the '90s and into the twenty-first century there has been a large reduction in the percentage of black families living below the poverty line. The numbers have decreased from 31 percent in 1992, where it had hovered since the 1960s, to 21 percent in 2001. However, the economic gap between blacks and whites had failed to close during this same period.

According to *Business Week*, from the general prosperity of the 1990s emerged a vibrant and successful black middle class, who began to experience increased life expectancy, wages, homeownership and greater wealth. Currently, even though there are more black executives and managers in Corporate America than before, they still earn much less than their white counterparts. The magazine noted that "the relative earnings of black women have actually worsened. In 2001, the average net worth of black families was 16 percent that of white families, down from 22 percent in 1992."

Mortimer B. Zuckerman of *U.S. News & World Report* wrote, "Slavery was America's defining historical challenge. Today it is race." This country's inability to combat racism and its effects is the greatest obstacle to black progress.

Zuckerman went on to note that blacks are also lagging behind in education and no successful remedy has been found to narrow the gap that exists in academic achievement between whites and blacks. He quotes Abigail and Stephen Thernstrom, authors of the book, *No Excuses: Closing the Racial Gap in Learning*, "this is now probably the greatest civil rights issue facing our country." This issue must be resolved before blacks can make any substantial long-lasting progress.

Update Sources: Whitaker, Mark, et al., "A Crisis of Shattered Dreams," *Newsweek,* May 6, 1991; Rucci, M., "The Great White Lie," *Herald Sun,* May 16, 1992; Editorial. "Black Progress: Two ways to look at it," *Business Week,* July 14, 2003; Zuckerman, Mortimer B., "A Hard Look at What Works," *U.S. News & World Report,* November 24, 2003.

1977
Jimmy Carter and the Trilateral Commission

Members of the Trilateral Commission (TLC) had agreed on Carter's potential as president as far back as 1970. Vice President Walter Mondale and many members of Carter's administration were also drawn from TLC's membership rolls.

Original Sources: Crozier, Michael, Samuel P. Huntington, and Joji Watanuki. "Report on the Governability of Democracies to the Trilateral Commission," *The Crisis of Democracy,* New York University Press, 1975. Minter, William. "From the Folks Who Brought Us Light at the End of the Tunnel," *Seven Days,* February 14, 1977; Chomsky, Noam. "Trilateral RX for Crisis: Governability Yes, Democracy No," *Seven Days; The Review of the News,* August 18, 1976. Smith, Gar. *The Berkeley Barb,* July 30, 1976; Allen, Gary, *Jimmy Carter/Jimmy Carter,* Seal Beach, California: '76 Press; Allen, Gary. "Carter Brings Forth a Cabinet," *American Opinion,* February 1976; Latham, Aaron. "Carter's Little Kissingers," *New York Times,* December 13, 1976.

UPDATE BY MALIA LYTLE
The Trilateral Commission (TLC) remains fully active and has grown since its creation in 1973 by David Rockefeller. It began as a way to centralize authoritative ideas about problems in the world, and to promote the globalization of economies. The TLC included business and governmental elites from United States, Europe, and the Far East. According to the commission's website, it has grown to an average of 350 people, now including citizens from the Pacific Asian region. Eighty-seven members are from the United States.

Its members are elite leaders in business, media, academia, public service, labor unions, and other non-governmental organizations. They come from countries around the world. Biannual meetings are held to discuss global policy issues. Members chosen from the media include the leaders of top corporations such as CBS, NBC, ABC, *The Washington Post*, and *The Wall Street Journal*. Other corporate leaders include those from Exxon, Mobil, and Shell oil companies. TLC is funded by corporations and foundations, as well as individuals.

The TLC continues to dominate the leadership of the U.S. government. A recent list of members shows the president of the World Bank, Paul Wolfowitz; Vice President of the United States Richard Cheney; and Paula J. Dobriansky, the U.S. Under Secretary of State for Global Affairs, as former members. To keep its "unofficial" character, when a member takes a position in the executive branch of the U.S. government, they give up their official TLC membership. Not only was Jimmy Carter a member before he became president, but so were George H. W. Bush, Bill Clinton, and George W. Bush. Ronald Reagan prided himself in not taking part in "secret societies," however, a majority of his campaign team were members and Rockefeller was one of his major supporters.

In 1996 the *Pittsburgh Post-Gazette* quoted co-founder David Rockefeller: "It [TLC] is well-known, but little understood." That could be because TLC sessions are closed to the media. Because it is a private organization with members selected by its executive branch based on recommendations from TLC members, there is no opportunity for any public representation to vote in members, question agreements, or demand knowledge.

A TLC publication released in early 2003, before the attack on Iraq, informs its members of the need for cooperation when dealing with terrorism. From an article titled, "Addressing the New International Terrorism: Prevention, Intervention, and Multilateral Cooperation," Joseph S. Nye Jr. confronts attitudes concerning support for going to war. "Different perceptions are natural . . . but if the divergence becomes too great, it can have dangerous effects. . . . American irritation with its allies could reinforce unilateralist responses to problems that would benefit from more cooperative approaches. Over time, such friction could spill over into other areas such as trade and the movement of people."

Update Sources: Roddy, Dennis B., "Trilateral Commission: Club, Not

Cabal," *Pittsburgh Post-Gazette*, April 28, 1996; Nye, Joseph S. Jr., "A North American Perspective," in "Addressing the New International Terrorism: Prevention, Intervention and Multilateral Cooperation," http://www.trilateral.org/projwork/tfrsums/tfr56.htm, 2003.

CHAPTER 4

Junk Food News and News Abuse

by Katherine Albergate, Lesley Amberger, Lindsay San Martin, and Kate Sims

One early criticism of Project Censored was from editors and publishers claiming that what the project refers to as *censorship* is simply a disagreement with the decisions they make regarding what is or is not newsworthy. During the first published volume of Censored research in 1993, founder Carl Jensen addressed this complaint and discussed the reasoning behind his creation of the Junk Food News chapter:

> "Many news professionals have said that the issue isn't so much censorship (or self-censorship) per se, as it is a difference of opinion about precisely what information is important to publish or broadcast. They also point out that there is finite amount of time and space for news delivery—about twenty-three minutes for a half hour network television evening news program—and that it's their responsibility to determine which stories are most critical for the public to know.
>
> This struck me as a legitimate argument, so I decided to review the stories that editors and news directors consider to be most worthy of filling their valuable time and space. However, in the course of this research project, I did not find an abundance of hard hitting investigative journalism. Quite the contrary. Indeed, what did become evident was a journalistic phenomenon I call Junk Food News (JFN), which, in essence, represents the flip side of the "Best Censored Stories." The typical JFN diet consists of sensationalized, personalized and homogenized trivia. . . . The problem is not the lack of time and space for news, but the quality of the news selected to fill that time and space. We're suffering from news inflation-there seems to be more of it than ever before, but it isn't worth as much as it used to be.
>
> News should be nutritious for society. We need more

steak and less sizzle from the press. The news should warn us about those things that make our society ill, whether economically, politically, or physically. And there is such news out there, as Project Censored has revealed time and again."
—Carl Jensen, *Censored 1993*

Carl's words become more relevant with each passing year, as celebrity baby booms eclipse increasing infant mortality and the homes of the wealthy overshadow the growing rate of homelessness in America. As the available entertainment becomes increasingly titillating, real news (about the government, economy, foreign policy, etc.) appears increasingly less so. And the corporate executives that run the newsrooms of today know on which side their bread is buttered.

This year's Junk Food News list is packed with entertainment goodies and celebrity tidbits so fattening that they may only be safely read on a treadmill at the gym. Here is the 2007 edition of the high calorie journalism we call Junk Food News:

1. Angelina Jolie and Brad Pitt get together
2. Nick Lachey and Jessica Simpson break-up
3. *American Idol* hits an all time high
4. The Runaway Bride that didn't
5. Martha Stewart is back in town
6. *Brokeback Mountain* breaks through
7. Britney Spears (it just wouldn't be a list without her)
8. Myspace infiltrates our space
9. Steroids in Baseball get pumped up
10. *The DaVinci Code* ad nauseum

1. On March 20 of 2006, newspapers and television news programs were abuzz with speculation that Brad Pitt and Angelina Jolie *might* have gotten married at George Clooney's villa on the coast of Italy. It turned out not to be true, but the very possibility made our hearts flutter in anticipation, didn't it?

Of course, it was not the biggest story of the day on March twentieth (the third anniversary of the U.S. invasion of Iraq), but it did beat out an avalanche of interesting tidbits that were readily available on any newswire. You weren't nearly as likely to hear about an Iraqi Police Report charging U.S. troops with the deaths of local, non-combatant civilians (sound familiar?). You also weren't as likely to hear about a new study by glaciologists warning that the world's mountain glaciers are melting at a faster rate than at any time in the past 150 years.

On the plus side, the Archbishop of Canterbury picked that day to announce that he does not believe creationism should be taught in schools and he called upon U.S. fundamentalists to discontinue their campaign to force the issue in public classrooms. It was big news in Europe, but there was not a peep in the U.S.

Sources: *UPI Wire,* "No Italian Wedding For Brad Pitt, Angelina Jolie," March 20, 2006; *MSNBC,* "Clooney Says no Pitt-Jolie Wedding at his Villa," March 21, 2006; Schofield, Matthew. "Iraqi Police Report Details Civilians' Deaths at Hands of U.S. Troops," *Knight Ridder Newswire,* March 20, 2006; Connor, Steve. "Chilling Proof That Glacier Meltdown is Getting Faster," *Independent* (London), March 20, 2006; Bates, Stephen. "Archbishop: Stop Teaching Creationism," *Guardian* (Manchester), March 21, 2006.

2. As Jessica Simpson and Nick Lachey quickly transformed from the "Newlyweds" to newly divorced, their spot on Project Censored's Junk Food News list jumped from number 5 in 2006 to number 2 in our 2007 edition. Nick and Jessica's divorce, on December 16, 2005, was announced by The Associated Press, the Los Angeles City News Service, The Times Union of New York, and *The Seattle Times.* On that same day the vote for a new parliament was being held in Iraq. Nick and Jessica's uncoupling probably garnered more airtime than every other divorce combined—but hey, does anybody know how Iraq's election turned out?

Sources: *The Associated Press State and Local Wire Entertainment News, Los Angeles,* "Jessica Simpson Files for Divorce from Nick Lachey," December 16, 2005; Pierce, Meredith. "Jessica Simpson Files for Divorce," *City News Service, Los Angeles,* December 16, 2005; *New York Times* "Iraq Votes for a Third Time," December 17, 2005.

3. On the evening of January 17, 2006, FOX launched a two-hour season premiere to kick off the fifth season of *American Idol.* The most-watched television network program drew 35.5 million viewers—the best opening and audience for any non-sports program in the 2005-2006 television season. That very same week, Pakistani jeweler Shah Zaman lost two sons and one daughter in a U.S. air strike near his home in a poor region of the Northwest Frontier Province. A total of eighteen citizens died in the attack (none of them related to al-Qaeda or insurgent organizations), prompting Pakistan to file a formal protest with the Americans. Thousands marched in protests chanting anti-American slogans.

The FOX network is able to correctly tabulate the amount of votes needed to end someone's career on a karaoke television show, but the most sophisticated military that has ever existed still cannot differentiate innocent villagers from its latest military adversary.

Sources: Burke, Jason and Imtiaz Gul. "The Drone, the CIA and a Botched Attempt to Kill Bin Laden's Deputy," *Observer*, January 15, 2006; *BBC News* "Pakistan warns U.S. over air strike," January 17, 2006; Linzer, Dafna and Griff Witte. "U.S. air strike targets Al Qaeda Zawahiri," *Washington Post*, January 14, 2006; Dehnart, Andy, "What a long strange 'Idol' season it's been," *MSNBC*, May 4, 2006.

4. Number four on this year's Junk Food list is the saga of Jennifer Wilbanks, "The Runaway Bride" from Georgia. At first, the situation seemed like a serious news story of a woman gone missing, possibly abducted by kidnappers. But just as her fiancée and family members had convinced police to embark on an extensive 'woman' hunt, the erstwhile bride-to-be showed up with a common case of "cold feet". Dubbed "The Runaway Bride," mainstream media quickly adopted the ridiculous story as their front-page pet, as police investigated the criminal status of Wilbank's runaway stunt and morning talk shows hosted in-depth exposés of her wedding melodrama. On May 26, 2005, The Runaway Bride was indicted in court. On that same day there was a manhunt underway for Jordanian exile al-Zarqawi. Who was found first?

Sources: Huff, Richard. "Errant bride says 'I will' to Couric," *Daily News* (New York), June 14, 2005; Kranes, Marsha. "Jilter Faces Jail—Flee-Ancee Indicted for Lying to GA. Cops," *New York Post*, May 26, 2005; Rothwell, Nicolas. "Zarqawi most wanted, dead or alive," *Australian*, May 26, 2005.

5. According to the American Journalism Review, in March of 2005, coverage of Martha Stewart's legal woes had exceeded coverage of the crisis in Darfur by at least five times. On August 3, 2005, a week before she was due to complete her five months of house arrest, the media announced that Martha's sentence was to be extended by three extra weeks. While it wasn't the biggest story of the day (it lost out to Iraq and the celebrity steroid abuse scandal), media speculation over what violation could have engendered such a penalty sucked up enough airtime to squeeze out other news. Martha's minor sentence adjustment was more vital to the American public than a report that Chevron had paid Nigerian troops to kill outspoken critics—or that space shuttle astronauts were reporting they had witnessed "widespread environmental destruction on Earth" while in space. Both stories were available on the newswires that day, but went ignored by the corporate press.

Sources: Ricchiardi, Sherry. "Déjà Vu," *AJR*, February/March 2005; Usborne, David. "America's Domestic Goddess Breaks Terms of Her House Arrest," *Independent* (London), August 5, 2005; Baker, David R. "Chevron Paid Nigerian Troops After Alleged Killing," *San Francisco Chronicle*, August 4, 2005; Franks, Jeff. "Shuttle Commander Sees Wide Environmental Damage," Reuters, Thursday, August 4, 2005.

6. When Ang Lee's *Brokeback Mountain* was released in theaters in December 2005, viewers were enthralled or outraged by the story of unrequited love between two gay cowboys. And the press offered countless articles on the subject. During the "Oscar buzz" of March 2006 there were 680 *Brokeback Mountain* articles published nationally over a one-month period. During the same month, international protests marked the build up to the third anniversary of the U.S. invasion in Iraq and President Bush's budget proposal announced a slash in funding for almost every social program within the federal government. While FOX's Bill O'Reilly criticized movies like *Brokeback Mountain*, lamenting their corrosive influence on the values of American society, he apparently took no issue with Bush's budget plan targeting programs in education, the arts, social security, health care, housing subsidies, and drug-free schools.

Sources: Mathews, Jack. "Festival's Oscar-worthy turns bring quality back to box office," *Daily News* (New York), September 20, 2005; Goldstein, Patrick. "Films caught in political cross-fire," *Los Angeles Times*, January 31, 2006; Council For a Livable World. "Key numbers in latest Bush budget request," February 14, 2006; Rich, Frank. "Bush of a Thousand Days," *New York Times*, April 30, 2006.

7. On February 7, 2006, photos were published of pop sensation Britney Spears operating a motorized vehicle without a seatbelt, her infant son seated on her lap. While America worried over baby Sean Preston's future with a mommy like Brit, the President's new budget requested nearly $1 billion in cuts to education. Defense budget spending in 2007 would rise another seven percent to $440 billion dollars while child-survival and health programs would be cut by 20 percent. The budget also requested that funding for the Corporation for Public Broadcasting be slashed by $53.5 million in 2007 and $50 million more in 2008. Rep. Ed Markey, D-Mass. remarked, "Oscar the Grouch has been friendlier to the Sesame Street characters than President Bush, who has chosen to make huge cuts to children's television programming. The public broadcasting system represents the last stronghold of quality child-oriented programming—we owe this to America's children." The general public will probably not learn about this until it is too late, but we will almost certainly hear every detail of Ms. Spears parenting foibles.

Sources: Lobe, Jim. "Guns Over Butter, Abroad and at Home," *Common Dreams News Center, Inter Press Service*, February 7, 2006; Trescott, Jacqueline. "Small gains for cultural programs in Bush budget plan," *Washington Post*, February 7, 2006; Klein, Rick. "GOP takes aim at PBS funding," *Boston Globe*, June 08, 2006; *MSNBC*, Scarborough Country. "Britney Spears' latest parenting mishap," February 7, 2006; *Reuters*. "Bush Seeks to Slash Public Broadcast Funds," February 7, 2006.

8. "My myspace" has become a popular catch-phrase on campuses, in clubs, and at home. The new online social forum has given voice to thousands of underground bands, filmmakers, and countless adolescents with teenage angst. Myspace has taken blogging and chatting to a new level, giving users a whole page to display their "unique" qualities.

Throughout 2005 and 2006, Myspace.com enjoyed a plethora of media headlines ranging from a Connecticut teacher being suspended for chatting with his students on Myspace, to Rupert Murdoch's purchase of Intermix (the Myspace parent company) on July 19, 2005. In January 2006, while millions of Myspacers were watching David Lehre's new short film, *Myspace: The Movie*, the *Christian Science Monitor* released an article about the government's development of a massive computer system that can collect huge amounts of data on Internet users. Meanwhile, on the same day, Myspace reported that site registration had reached 58 million. Did these users know that there could possibly be a huge file locked away in some government office tracing every download, blog, and site they visit? Maybe Myspace.com should add a feature for concerned users entitled "MyGovernmentSpace," for people who want to know what information is being compiled in their government folder.

Sources: Comp, Nathan. "Myspace Milestones," *Wisconsin State Journal*, March 28, 2006; Griffiths, Katherine. "News Corp pays $580M to expand on the internet," *Independent* (London), July 19,

2005; Clayton, Mark. "US Plans Massive Data Sweep," *Christian Science Monitor*, February 9, 2006.

9. In early March 2006, the U.S. media was abuzz with the next exposé on the steroids in baseball saga. On March 8, 2006, *San Francisco Chronicle* reporter Lance Williams appeared on the CBS *Early Show*. While he discussed the physical transformation and alleged steroid use by Giants superstar Barry Bonds, another case was brewing in Barry and Lance's hometown. That very same day, San Francisco supervisors passed a motion seeking the impeachment of President Bush. They claimed he failed to carry out his responsibilities by leading the country into war in Iraq and eroding civil liberties, among other indiscretions. The ruling also called for the impeachment of Vice President Dick Cheney. Supervisor Chris Daly said the measure was especially critical in light of the federal government's insufficient response to hurricane Katrina and revelations about a domestic wiretapping program.

Sources: Kirkpatrick, David D. "Call for censure is rallying cry to Bush's Base." *New York Times*, March 16, 2006; *CBS News*. "Book: Barry Bonds A Steroids User," March 7, 2006; Epstein, Edward and Charlie Goodyear. "San Francisco Supervisors Ask Lawmakers to Impeach Bush," *San Francisco Chronicle*, March 1, 2006.

10. Wrapping up the Junk Food News list for 2007 is the *well*-promoted novel, and America's favorite controversy du jour, *The Da Vinci Code*. The buzz surrounding the novel and motion picture can be traced in mainstream media throughout the U.S. from April of 2005 through at least June of 2006—more than one year of continuous commentary on the celebrated *Da Vinci Code*. On September 8, 2005, MSNBC ran a Stone Phillips' special entitled "Secrets behind *The Da Vinci Code*," which took the audience on a dramatic journey through the controversy and religious scandal that has gripped the imagination of the U.S. public. During this same week, in early September of 2005, Hurricane Katrina had struck New Orleans, devastating the lives of millions. Although both the *Da Vinci Code* and Hurricane Katrina were highly publicized in the American media, the country's citizens might have benefited more from a revelation of the secrets behind FEMA and the controversies surrounding the failure of support for the hurricane victims than from the minutiae behind a second-rate piece of literature and a less-than-impressive summer blockbuster.

Sources: Philips, Stone. "Secrets Behind the Da Vince Code," *MSNBC Dateline Special*, September 8, 2005; Bandow, Doug. "Serious mess of Bush's making," *Australian*, September 5, 2005; Kirkpatrick, David D. and Scott Shane. "Ex-FEMA Chief Tells of Frustration and Chaos," *New York Times*, September 15, 2005.

News Abuse

A few years ago, Project Censored researchers began to notice news stories that can not appropriately be called "Junk Food" but that eventually take on the role of Junk Food News (repetitive, salacious reporting taking the place of actual, informative news). Initially these stories expose an event worthy of coverage. But, in the end the story overwhelms headlines, primetime segments, and internet news sites, skewing the essential facts of the story and overemphasizing its importance. While coverage of these stories inundates the public with redundant information and useless trivia, unwritten news stories go unheard for lack of space.

Here are the top five News Abuse stories as voted on by the Project Censored community:

1. Natalie Holloway
2. Bird Flu
3. Finger in Wendy's Chili Bowl
4. Dick Cheney Shoots Friend
5. Katrina Criminals in Superdome

1. By June 2005, everyone had heard the story of Natalie Holloway, the eighteen-year-old from Alabama who disappeared on May 30, the last night of her vacation in Aruba. What you probably did not hear about was what happened in Ciudad Juarez, Mexico, three days before the date of Natalie's disappearance. Tens of thousands of people marched through the border city to demand that authorities do more to stop a wave of violence that has left perhaps thousands of cases of murdered and missing women unsolved and unpunished. Most of the protesters were young students, Natalie's age, who were given the day off to attend the state legislators' organized march. They came to protest a series of bizarre incidents in which young women, all maquiladora factory workers, were sexually assaulted, asphyxiated, and dumped in the desert. As of May 30, 2005, the day when coverage of Natalie's disappearance began, federal investigators said that at least 350 women have been killed in Ciudad Juarez since 1993. Estimates throughout the entire region put the number closer to 1,500. For over a decade, independent journalists have tried, unsuccessfully, to get the story major coverage on U.S. television.

Sources: AP *International News*. "Thousands of people march against disappearance, killings in Mexican Border City," May 27, 2005; Espinosa, Maria Cecilia. "Latin America: The Shame of Murdered, Raped, and Ignored Women," *IPS-Inter Press Service*, November 11, 2004; "Thousand of people march against disappearance, killings in Mexican border city," *Associated Press International News*, May 27, 2005.

2. Like the terror alert updates in 2002, forewarnings of avian flu pervaded the twenty-four hour news channels throughout 2005. The specter of a world wide influenza pandemic is nothing to be taken lightly and news editors were warranted in their decision to cover such a possibility. But most U.S. coverage of the avian flu focused on the potential for genetic mutations that would make it more deadly, and comparisons to the 1918 influenza pandemic that took some 500,000 lives (despite the fact that the Avian Flu has, as of 2006, caused less than 125 deaths worldwide).

In 2005, the fact that a U.S. company had developed a vaccine for the avian flu, and its stock price was increasing, received some scant coverage in the press. Yet, though the information was readily available, no one in the mainstream mentioned that Defense Secretary Donald Rumsfeld was chairman of the board of Tamiflu's parent company (Gilead Sciences) until he became Defense Secretary in 2001—and that he is still a major stockholder. Since Rumsfeld became Defense Secretary, Gilead's stock price has gone from around $7 per share to slightly above $50 a share in 2006. In October 2005, as Tamiflu was becoming the hottest drug in the world market, the Pentagon announced it had stockpiled quantities of Tamiflu for members of the military.

Sources: McKay, Betsy. "Avian virus caused the 1918 pandemic, new studies show," *Wall Street Journal*, October 6, 2005; Siegel, Marc. "Bird flu and Chicken Littles; The science may not support public health officials' dire predictions," *Los Angeles Times*, April 6, 2006; Schwartz, Nelson D., "Rumsfeld's growing stake in Tamiflu," *CNN*, October 31, 20005; Engdahl, F. William. "Is Avian Flu another Pentagon Hoax?" *GlobalResearch.ca*, October 30,2005.

3. On March 22, 2005, thirty-nine-year-old Anna Ayala claimed that she had found a human fingertip in her bowl of chili. Officially announced on March 23, 2005, the story of the Wendy's chili finger debacle instantly became national news. Not only was it heavily covered in mainstream media across the West Coast, it was also covered in mainstream newspapers on the East Coast and in the Midwest for five days straight. Though equally unappetizing, what you were less likely to hear about was that during the same month the U.S. government had begun approving the shipment of previously unapproved (and untested) genetically modified corn to super markets across the country. Although a finger in a chili bowl is certainly disgusting, one would think the prospect of the government foisting untested pseudo-corn onto unsuspecting U.S. consumers would make news on a larger scale.

Sources: Murphy, Dave. "Santa Clara County; Was Finger Cooked Along with Chili? Officials Say It May Have Been Later in the Process," *San Francisco Chronicle Final Edition, Bay Area*, March 26, 2005; Ching, Lim Li. "Contamination by Experimental Genetically Engineered Crops Should Not be 'Found Acceptable'," *CommonDreams.org*, March 23, 2005; Bay City News. "Couple pleads Guilty In Chili finger scam," *CBS5*, September 9, 2005.

4. "The shot heard 'round the world" took on a whole new meaning when Vice President Dick Cheney wounded fellow hunter Harry Whittington. Cheney maintained that he had accidentally sprayed his friend with pellets from behind as he, Cheney, was aiming at a quail. From February 13-17, ABC, CBS, and NBC were consumed with the story, running it as the lead every day except for Thursday of that week. News stations managed to rack up fifty-nine minutes of "Cheney sticking to his guns." While the hunting accident gave rise to a short, vicious round of Cheney-bashing, none of it amounted to anything substantive or far-reaching. Most criticism focused on Cheney's inclination to pass the blame and "control the intelligence," as if this was somehow an unusual occurrence in the vice-presidential office. Only the Guardian of London examined Cheney's behavior following the incident in the context of the extraordinary (and unique) secrecy powers bestowed upon him in 2003. In the U.S., the opportunity to investigate and perhaps question the vice-president's behavior throughout his tenure was not taken, and it quickly passed. The following week, true to mainstream news tradition, the story died as quickly as it had arisen. A LexisNexis search of the months following the accident found it difficult even to determine how Mr. Whittington was recuperating from his so-famously inflicted wounds.

Sources: Blumenthal, Sidney. "Cheney has a vice-like grip: Bush has granted his deputy the greatest expansion of powers in US history," *Guardian* (London), March 3, 2006; VandeHei, Jim and Sylvia Moreno. "White House Deferred to Cheney on Shooting; In a Break With Policy, Hunting Accident Was Not Disclosed for 14 Hours," *Washington Post*, February 14, 2006; Oldenburg, Ann. "It's open season on Dick Cheney," *USA TODAY*, February 14, 2006.

5. Hurricane Katrina was one of the worst natural disasters in history to hit the United States. In New Orleans alone, the event gave rise to a host of stories. The people who fled, the people who couldn't flee, the warnings that had been given, the failure of FEMA, the rebuilding contracts so quickly granted and so slowly acted upon, the workers who were abused and, finally, the canals that broke. On August 29, 2005 the Industrial Canal in the heart of New Orleans was breached and over three meters of water flooded the Ninth Ward, the poorest neighborhood in the city. FEMA was slow in providing aide and many sought shelter in the Superdome and Civic Center. As might be expected, the unstable and devastating circumstances brought out both the best and the worst in people.

Most people worked together to better an untenable situation, sharing food and blankets and caring for each other's young and elderly. But it seems the only information getting through to network and cable news programs was that a violent mob rule had overtaken the Superdome. Reports of rapes, assault, murder, and looting plastered headlines everywhere. ABC, CBS, and NBC covered 263 minutes of Hurricane Katrina the week that the first levee broke. The overwhelmingly black population was often portrayed as amoral and vicious rather than as an uprooted community struggling with the many challenges (including crime) that would likely arise in the aftermath of one of the worst floods in American history. Although some coverage revealed the social injustices occurring in urban areas, more often than not, it painted criminals and non-criminals alike with the same brush.

Sources: Schleifstein, Mark. "Flooding will only get worse," *Times-Picayune* (New Orleans), August 31, 2005; Thevenot, Brian, Keith Spera, and Doug MacCash. "Old West has nothing on Katrina aftermath; Death, violence, lawlessness put cities under martial law," *Times-Picayune* (New Orleans); August 31, 2005; Torpy, Bill. "HURRICANE KATRINA: Cities dread influx of the poor, black," *Atlanta Journal-Constitution*, September 4, 2005; Zizek, Slavoj. "The Subject Supposed to Loot and Rape: Reality and fantasy in New Orleans," *In These Times*, October, 2005.

THIS MODERN WORLD

by TOM TOMORROW

THIS WEEK: THE BUSH ADMINISTRATION'S COURAGEOUS AND NEVER-ENDING...

G.W.O.T.*

***GLOBAL WAR ON TRUTH**

THEY UNDERSTAND THAT TRUTH IS THE *ENEMY*--AND THAT IT WILL *DESTROY* THEM IF GIVEN THE CHANCE!

FORTUNATELY, THE INSURGENCY IS IN ITS *LAST THROES!*

BUNCHA *DEAD ENDERS!*

WHO EVEN *READS* NEWSPAPERS ANY MORE, ANYWAY?

THE ATTORNEY GENERAL SAYS THEY HAVE THE POWER TO IMPRISON *JOURNALISTS* WHO TELL TOO *MUCH* TRUTH!

ABU GHRAIB--SECRET PRISONS-- WARRANTLESS WIRETAPS--TORTURE--

--THESE STORIES SERVE ONLY TO PROVIDE AID AND COMFORT TO THE *ENEMIES*--

--OF THIS *ADMINI-STRATION!*

IN AN EFFORT TO *CONTAIN* THE TRUTH, THEY'VE BEEN MONITORING REPORTERS' *PHONE RECORDS*-- MUCH TO THE AMUSEMENT OF CONSERVATIVES EVERYWHERE!

HA, HA! YOU KNOW WHAT'S FUNNIER THAN *UNCONSTITUTIONAL GOVERNMENT SURVEILLANCE?*

UNCONSTITUTIONAL GOVERNMENT SURVEILLANCE OF THE *BIASED LIBERAL MEDIA!*

STOP! YOU'RE *KILLING* ME!

OF COURSE, MANY ORDINARY AMERICANS ARE DOING *THEIR* PART FOR THE WAR ON TRUTH AS WELL!

MURTHA SAYS IRAQI CIVILIANS WERE *MASSACRED* BY U.S. MARINES!

THAT'S *SHOCKING!* THAT HE WOULD SAY THAT, I MEAN.

WE'D BETTER START *SLIMING* HIM *IMMEDIATELY!*

WITH ANY LUCK, OUR CHILDREN WILL INHERIT A NATION *UNTHREATENED* BY THE INSIDIOUS MENACE OF THE *UNFILTERED TRUTH!*

COMING UP NEXT--OUR CORRESPONDENT *KAREN RYAN* VISITS *ANOTHER* FRESHLY PAINTED SCHOOL IN IRAQ!

AND MORE GOOD NEWS-- *MOST* OF OUR TROOPS WERE *NOT* KILLED IN ROADSIDE AMBUSHES YESTERDAY!

FIRST THESE MESSAGES!

TOM TOMORROW©2006... www.thismodernworld.com

CHAPTER 5

The Ongoing Contest
Media Reform and Democracy

Bailey Malone, Kristine Medeiros, Jessica Rodas, and Andrew Roth,
Sonoma State University*

Democratic media reform is an ongoing contest. Within that contest, power is not distributed equally. For example, the corporate media do not cover the media reform movement. Yet, despite existing power inequalities, there is much to be gained when independent media producers, educators, community members and others organize to advocate for media reform.

An informed and active public is essential for self-government. A truly democratic press contributes to self-government by informing and empowering all members of society. The United States' Constitution acknowledges freedom of the press as a core principle of democracy, and the Supreme Court has effectively affirmed this value in numerous decisions. However, as media reform advocates have consistently shown, an oligopolist corporate version of a "free" press fails to fulfill citizens' needs, sometimes dramatically thwarting democracy. As Robert McChesney, founder of Free Press (freepress.net), and others argue, "Without a viable press system, our ability to create a just, humane, and viable society is sharply limited, if not made impossible."[1]

Thus, a burgeoning popular movement—with participants spanning the spectrum of political perspectives—aims to establish a workable media system that will function as an alternative to the existing corporate model. Broadly speaking, the media reform movement addresses the related issues of media ownership, independent media, and democratic governance. The May 2005 National Conference for Media Reform in St. Louis served as a galvanizing occasion for many in the media reform movement.[2]

In this chapter, we ask: What has happened since the 2005 media reform conference? What gains have been made in the fight for more independent, democratic media? And, what challenges to that goal remain? Of course, complete answers to these broad questions go beyond the scope of a single chapter. Here we focus on four topics:

> ➤ municipalities' struggles for free or low-cost wireless internet access (Wi-Fi),
> ➤ independent newsweeklies' opposition to their increasing consolidation,
> ➤ Spanish-language journalists' use of print and radio news to mobilize activism, and
> ➤ progressive television programming to inform and engage the public regarding civil liberties and the environment.

These four topics span a range of media distribution formats, from print to broadcast to Internet. As we see it, two important themes connect these topics. First, each shows the importance of independent media that serve local communities and their needs, while linking these to broader publics and their concerns. A second theme that unites the four cases we discuss involves political organization: Each exemplifies the tangible payoffs of continued, expanding organization.

THE STRUGGLE FOR MUNICIPAL WI-FI

As an alternative to the services offered by the cable-telephone duopoly that controls 98 percent of the broadband market, municipalities are increasingly offering their residents free or low-cost wireless Internet (Wi-Fi).[3] Ultimately at stake is Internet neutrality, with ownership by a handful of corporations threatening free and unfettered access for all people. To provide universal and affordable use, municipalities place nodes on city-owned structures like traffic signals and streetlights. These nodes broadcast an interconnecting broadband signal, creating a wireless mesh network, or cloud, of Internet access.

Municipal Wi-Fi is an increasingly relevant option in a country that has fallen from fourth to sixteenth in broadband penetration since 2001.[4] Sixty percent of households in the U.S. do not have a broadband connection.[5] When it is available, broadband has been called the "slowest, most expensive, least reliable broadband in the world."[6] The number of broadband subscriptions plunges inrural, minority, low income, undereducated or senior citizen households.[7] Free Press founder Robert McChesney calls opposition to municipal Wi-Fi "the death knell for rural areas, for poor communities."

Currently fourteen states have laws either restricting or banning municipalities from operating their own high-speed networks.[8] In 2005 Wi-Fi restrictions passed in five states, while eight such bills were defeated with the help of media democracy activists.[9] McChesney is confident about beating opponents of municipal Wi-Fi in the state legislature. He believes that "we'll continue to win whenever we organize, because their position is simply unsupportable." Currently pending in Congressional committees is competing legislation that would either protect municipalities or prevent them from providing such services. Senators John McCain (R-AZ) and Frank Lautenberg (D-NJ) introduced the Community Broadband Act of 2005 "to preserve and protect the ability of local governments to provide broadband capability and services." Representative Pete Sessions (R-TX)—a former SBC executive—introduced the Preserving Innovation in Telecom Act of 2005 "to prohibit municipal governments from offering telecommunications, information, or cable services except to remedy market failures by private enterprises to provide such a service."[10] Senator John Ensign's (R-NV) re-write of the 1996 Telecommunications Act requires municipalities "to permit non government entities to bid to provide such service—preference is given to non government entities." McChesney asserts that "the telecommunication monopolists are trying to make it, if not illegal, then virtually impossible for communities to set up competing Internet service provisions."

In June 2005 the Supreme Court ruled in favor of cable companies in Brand X v. FCC, allowing them to monopolize broadband lines and close their use to independent Internet Service Providers (ISPs). With the physical infrastructure of the Internet under private control, cable companies could seek to filter content or manipulate access speed. The Court affirmed a disputed 2002 FCC ruling that cable lines would be classified as an unregulated "information" service rather than a regulated "telecommunication" service.[11] The FCC also claims that 38 million Americans have a "high-speed" subscription (only 200 kbps according to their definition), which is actually five times slower then standard DSL, ten times slower then cable, and twenty-five times slower then the normal connection in Japan.[12] The Japanese are also unleashing a connection 500 times faster than the FCC's definition of high-speed.[13] The Japanese government encourages community Internet projects, granting municipalities subsidies covering one-third of the cost of each program.[14] Americans also pay ten to twenty-five times more per megabit for their connections then in Japan.[15]

Despite pressure from corporations and government representatives sympathetic to special interests, municipal Wi-Fi continues to expand. As of April 2006 there were fifty-eight regional or citywide Wi-Fi networks, thirty-two city "hot zones," and sixty-nine planned deployments.[16] By 2010, areas covered by municipal Wi-Fi will have grown from 1,500 square miles in 2005 to 126,000,[17] with the U.S. estimated to spend $700 million in the next three years alone.[18]

In October 2005, Philadelphia awarded a contract to Earthlink to provide low cost Wi-Fi at around $20.00 per month, service to low-income users at less than $10 per month, and free service at twenty-two locations.[19] Their plan includes a Digital Inclusion Fund to provide computers and training to children and low-income users, and to share 5 percent of revenue with the city.[20] Esme Vos, founder of Muniwireless,[21] laments, "Philadelphia started out ambitious and in the end just became average. Its network is run by Earthlink. Where is Wireless Philadelphia, the nonprofit, in all of this?"

A telecommunications bill passed in Pennsylvania in December 2004[22] dubbed the Verizon bill, prevents municipalities from providing broadband services, with an exception for Philadelphia included at the last minute. Proponents of such legislation operate under the supposition that the lack of "advantages that local governments supposedly have, rather than their own short-term profit objectives, are responsible for the failure of the established providers to make the investments" that communities require.[23] This is so despite the fact that corporations receive public subsidies, tax breaks, and incentives to assuage their broadband efforts. Verizon received subsidies from Pennsylvania ten times the cost of the Philadelphia program.[24] Comcast received a $30 million grant to build their headquarters in the state.[25] These are the same corporations that employ expensive lobbies and run active campaigns, coercing politicians and citizens voting on legislation and referendums to prohibit municipal Wi-Fi.[26]

In April 2006, San Francisco also awarded a contract to Earthlink—partnering with Google, Motorola and Tropos Network—to deploy free Wi-Fi at 300 kbps and offer premium service at around $20.00 per month.[27] The ISP was granted long term rights for ten years, with two four-year renewal options,[28] "locking San Francisco into that model despite changing technology," according to Sascha Meinrath, co-founder of the Champaign-Urbana Community Wireless Network. There are other concerns in the Earthlink/Google proposal, including the lack of a Digital Inclusion Fund, right to privacy considerations, and a connection speed slower then half the competing bids.[29] Google will offer free Wi-Fi service, allowing users to sign in at a portal page that allows advertising to be matched with their location and tracked within a few hundred feet.[30] Google retains the data for 180 days before deleting it, prompting privacy concerns following a federal subpoena for user search records in 2005.[31]

There are other options. In March 2006, St. Cloud, Florida, a suburb of Orlando with population 28,000, deployed the country's first free municipal Wi-Fi.[32] The Champaign-Urbana Community Wireless Network (CUWiN) uses free, automated software to turn old desktop computers into Wi-Fi hotspots—decentralized, non-proprietary local area networks (LANs).

Broadband technologies are "bringing about a paradigm shift in how we are living our lives."[33] In the effort to retain affordable, unfettered access to the Internet, the U.S. government can protect the rights of municipalities to deploy wireless networks. The outcome of competing federal legislation will determine whether net neutrality will be protected or destroyed.

ALTERNATIVE WEEKLIES FIGHT TO SURVIVE

In November 2005 the federal government approved a merger between New Times and Village Voice Media, which allows for the creation of a seventeen paper alternative weekly chain. This legislation increases the likelihood that all alternative weeklies will eventually be consolidated. Smaller, alternative newspapers are afraid because the combined New Times and Village Voice will reach 22 to 25 percent of the total circulation of the 126 members that make up the Association of Alternative Newsweeklies. According to a draft merger agreement obtained by the *San Francisco Bay Guardian*, four of the nine members of the board are not experienced journalists but investment bankers or venture capitalists. The company—now known as New Times Media—has planned to use a national advertising outlet to sells advertising space for its weeklies in San Francisco, New York, Los Angeles, Seattle, and Phoenix.

The merger was completed on January 31, 2006, sparking fears in California's alternative weeklies because four of the biggest markets are in California: San Francisco, the East Bay, Los Angeles and Orange County. Only months after the merger these preliminary fears appear to be justified as the new power chain tries to eliminate competitive alternative weeklies in California's markets, to the detriment of both readers and advertisers. The *San Francisco Bay Guardian* has now filed a suit against *San Francisco Weekly*, the *East Bay Express*, and New Times Newspapers, the Phoenix-based chain that owns the two local weeklies. The suit charges that the nation's largest alternative newsweekly chain has illegally sold advertising below cost in an effort to put the *Bay Guardian* out of business. Neither the Justice Department nor the Attorney General's Office has made an effort to help the alternative weeklies. For these reasons, the *Bay Guardian* filed a private lawsuit and is taking matters into their own hands.

There are more alternative weeklies in California than any other state (twenty-three all together) from the *Chico News and Review* in the North to the *San Diego Reader* in the south. These California newspapers pride themselves on exercising their First Amendment rights and reporting stories and viewpoints that daily, corporate newspapers do not cover. As Bruce Brugmann, editor of the *San Francisco Bay Guardian*, argues, independent newsweeklies have a duty to their communities and they aim to be model newspapers, willing to fight the competition of the local monopoly papers. The *Bay Guardian* was founded in 1966 and has become an important part of politics and culture in California. One of the only competitors that the New Times conglomerate has not yet knocked out, Brugmann and the *Bay Guardian* refuse to be pushed out of business without a fight. Brugmann states: "We don't dislike competition. We thrive on it. But we believe that competitors should play fair and New Times like many big corporate chains is breaking the law and using its considerable national resources in an effort to destroy a locally owned competition so it will have the San Francisco market to itself."[34]

The threat of consolidation is serious because it appears that New Times is intentionally targeting liberal cities and newspapers. The *Village Voice* is a perfect example of a paper that had the reputation of having a staff of liberal writers, which was seen as a major flaw by many. Executive editor for New Times Mike Lacey has been quoted as saying, "I wish there were more conservative writers at the papers. There aren't. There isn't anything imposed about the editorial viewpoint from Phoenix."[35] The new operators of New Times, CEO Jim Larkin and Mike Lacey, fired many longtime liberal journalists after the merger, creating a chilly work environment at *Village Voice*. Columnist Cynthia Cotts described the merger as "a hostile takeover by a company whose media purchases produced a signature bloodbath."[36]

A bloodbath it has been, but the *San Francisco Bay Guardian* is fighting to survive. After years of warning against the dangers of anti-competitive behavior, Brugmann and the *Bay Guardian* are now taking legal action to show that a locally owned independent business can challenge chain domination in news media. The *Bay Guardian* hopes that the suit will put a stop to predatory pricing and illegal advertising practices. Robert McChesney agrees that the power chains need to stop trying to stronghold alternative weeklies, "As a society it is something we should discourage, or make extremely difficult to do. As a society we have come up with policies to promote diverse voices, giving them new tools so they can be successful. In the short term that means preventing mergers whenever possible, or slowing down the rate. In the long term we just have to come up with a much more enlightened policy about media ownership in a digital age, and a series of policies that make it easier, not more difficult to start new media."

The *San Francisco Bay Guardian* reports that in three to five years New Times chain might be sold to an even bigger company such as Viacom (which owns dozens of television and radio stations, book publishers, film studios, and cable networks including MTV), Google, or Gannet which publishes *USA Today*, also known as a notoriously bottom line driven newspaper. It is true that Gannet has experimented with its own weekly newspapers, "known in the alternative weekly world as 'faux alts' for their lack of political edge and progressive value."[37] Many newspapers such as the *Bay Guardian* believe that if the New Times chain is sold to any of these companies then independent newsweeklies will not survive, because the people who work for Gannet and corporations similar to it do not have either

238 | CENSORED 2007

an understanding of journalism's core principles or the necessary reporting experience.

The mission of the alternative press, Brugmann says, is to be alternative to and competitive with local and mainstream press. This goal can only be reached when the newspapers are independent and can criticize and talk about issues freely from different viewpoints. For Brugmann and others, the threat of conglomeration impinges negatively on First Amendment rights, local communities, and community-based media. If the *Bay Guardian* succeeds in its struggle for continued independence, they will win more than money. They will prove that with strength, determination, and ambition, independent media can compete with and outperform their corporate counterparts.

VOCES UNIDAS! (UNITED VOICES)

The most problematic aspect of the Spanish-language system of communications in the U.S. is low circulation. The remedy to this problem is to attract new audiences for Spanish-language media. Ultimately, progressive media must expand their audiences to reach various ethnic groups and cultures, promoting community-based leadership and support for positive social change. Non-English media offer accurate, comprehensive, and educational information in Spanish and other languages to help meet the demands and interests of diverse communities. In Santa Rosa, California, the independent newspaper *La Voz* and the radio station KBBF are embracing these challenges to effectively reach large segments of Sonoma County's sizable Latino community.

A leading newspaper in San Francisco's North Bay region, the bilingual *La Voz* is now in the fifth year of publishing. According to Timothy Morse, *La Voz's* publisher, "We have enjoyed the challenges of creating a new type of publication. Our unique format reflects our changing demographics more accurately than any other print media on the street today." The purpose of *La Voz* newspaper is not only to inform but also engage the public in activities that enrich individuals and groups. As a bilingual newspaper its mission is simple: Open quality communication channeling between cultures with accurate information that educates and informs the public for the common good of all.

Currently, *La Voz* serves five counties, with 70 percent of its distribution centered in Sonoma County. An internal audit revealed a readership of 80,000, based on publication of 30,000 newspapers. *La Voz* has strategically placed the newspaper in street racks or stands, "where cultures cross paths," according to Morse. Their independent audit shows an average pick ratio of over 90 percent. This is a figure that other publications only wish for, and it indicates that English readers are an increasing audience segment.

La Voz actively collaborates with other organizations aligned with its mission. Working with the Sonoma County Office of Education is an important effort toward that end. The Sonoma County Office of Education subscribes to approximately 7000 newspapers for use in the classroom and sent home for use by parents, siblings and other family members. "We wholeheartedly support their programs and look forward to reporting the unfolding results in the short and long term future," Morse says. Similar partnerships are developing in the four additional counties that *La Voz* currently serves.

Thirty-five years ago, Santa Rosa, California's KBBF (89.1 FM) became the first community-based, non-commercial Spanish language station in the country.[38] This project was developed with the joint effort of the Latino community, the local organizations, professionals, and students of Sonoma State University, all of whom recognized the needs to reach the region's Spanish-speaking immigrants and to build an educational and cultural bridge between the Latino and Anglo communities. In May 1973, the Bilingual Broadcasting Foundation (KBBF's parent company) Incorporated obtained a license for the first public and noncommercial, bilingual radio station in the United States.

KBBF has become an essential broadcast outlet for Spanish speakers in California. From its beginning, the station has broadcast in Spanish and English, twenty-four hours a day, 365 days a year, reaching eighteen northern California counties. KBBF's programs consistently provide information and opinion to thousands of people who are not adequately served by English-only broadcasts.

In Fall 2005, activists prompted the constitution of an entirely new board of directors, "determined to return the station to its original mission of serving the regions' Spanish-speaking farmworkers and immigrant families."[39] According to the board's new secretary, Evelina Molina, the changes are a return to the station's original mission. Over the years, KBBF "started becoming controlled by different interests . . . It stopped being what it was born to be," with programming "specially geared to farmworkers." Guided by a new board of directors, KBBF now plays an even more important political role in the communities it serves.

This was clearly evident in Spring 2006. As hundreds of thousands of people across the country publicly protested against anti-immigrant legislation proposed in Congress, KBBF served as a catalyst in coordinating one of the largest protest marches in Sonoma County in recent decades. On March 31, 2006 (César Chávez Day), between 3,700 and 5,000 people gathered to protest against the Border Protection, Antiterrorism, and Illegal Immigration Control Act of 2005. KBBF's daily morning program, "Hour of the Farmworker"—co-hosted by Salvador Mendoza, a former vineyard worker, and Jose Gonzalez, a former machinist—played a pivotal role in informing people about both the legislation and the opportunity to demonstrate public opposition to it. "KBBF was enormously important in getting the word out," according to Richard Coshnear, a Santa Rosa immigration lawyer.[40] As others at the protest noted, it was workers—the primary audience of Mendoza and Gonzalez's show—that led the way at César Chávez Day march.

Journalists at Spanish-language media such as *La Voz* and KBBF reach Latino and Hispanic communities, providing crucial news and informed opinion. Community members turn to these papers and broadcasts with confidence in media that speak their language and reflect their culture.

"BETTER HUMAN DRAMAS": TELEVISION TO REACH AND ACTIVATE

Corporate journalism treats elites as both "the sources and subjects of most political stories,"[41] primarily because, for most journalists, "'news' is about what those in power say and do."[42] An exclusive focus on the actions and beliefs of powerful elites limits the content of news coverage and the scope of political debate. Nowhere has this been more obvious than in the case of televised news and public affairs programming. For example, David Croteau and William Hoynes showed how programs such as ABC's *Nightline* and PBS's

Newshour foster the illusions of balance among interviewed news sources and, correspondingly, of rigorous debate among those sources.43 Croteau and Hoynes concluded that "media limit political debate by the narrow range of stories they address and, even more importantly, by the limited range of voices and perspectives regularly featured as part of their coverage."44 By contrast, journalism in a democratic society should promote diverse discussion and debate.

Two new television programs succeed in this aim and serve as a model for meaningful reform of television news and public affairs programming. *Sierra Club Chronicles* and *The ACLU Freedom Files* premiered in early 2006. Produced by filmmaker Robert Greenwald—the director of *Wal-Mart: The High Cost of Low Price* and *Outfoxed*—and supported by the Sierra Club and the American Civil Liberties Union, these two programs provide a "stage" for telling stories that the corporate media have ignored or misrepresented. From that stage, they authorize people whom the corporate media seldom treat as newsworthy to present their experiences and perspectives. As Anthony Romero, executive director of the ACLU, has noted, "The free exchange of ideas is premised on as many voices speaking out as possible." Each episode of *Chronicles* and *Freedom Files* provides just this. *Freedom Files* features real clients and the attorneys who represent them, and an early episode of *Chronicles* gave voice to iron workers and paramedics who suffered health problems after exposure to foul air at the site of the World Trade Center after September 11. *Chronicles* and *Freedom Files* model what is possible when journalism expands the narrow range of sources that corporate media conventionally employ.

Positioning people typically ignored by corporate media as newsworthy sources of information and opinion leads to coverage of stories disregarded by corporate media. *Chronicles* and *Freedom Files* aim to explore "how people are affected by policy." Greenwald sees film as an ideal medium for countering the simple-minded view of policy articulated by most corporate news. According to him, the progressive world-view is "more nuanced, more complex. . . . Film is a great medium for this kind of storytelling." Thus, for example, the issues that *Freedom Files* addresses—including free speech, freedom of religion, and gender bias—cannot be fully appreciated in abstract terms; *Freedom Files* shows the "very real human faces to these issues." The programs' thirty-minute format permits depth of coverage and dramatic storytelling, including interviews, documentary, comedy, drama, music and animation, which would not be possible within the constraints of the corporate model of news and public affairs programming.

If episodes of *Chronicles* and *Freedom Files* draw on a true diversity of sources, to tell stories that the corporate media either ignore or misrepresent, they also stand apart in one further way. The two programs focus, in Greenwald's words, on "problems with solutions." The programs reject a "sky-is-falling" perspective, in favor of emphasizing how "with community involvement, something can be done." Anyone who has ever felt hopeless and helpless after viewing the corporate media's version of the evening news will appreciate the difference. Each segment of *Chronicles* and *Freedom Files* aims to "reach and activate" the audience. "We did not want it to be like homework or spinach, because nobody likes either one," Greenwald notes. Instead, these programs show that true political participation goes "beyond the simple level of who we're going to choose to be our political leaders." Greenwald understands this as part of his responsibility as a progressive filmmaker: Given the subject matter, it is easy to produce messages that are "emotional, strong, and that depress people." But, he insists, "It is completely irresponsible, both creatively and politically, to explore these subjects and to not consciously include alternatives and opportunities to be actively involved."

Sierra Club Chronicles and *ACLU Freedom Files* are broadcast to approximately twenty-six million U.S. homes via LinkTV, a noncommercial, independent network available through DirecTV and Dish satellite services. Though the Sierra Club, the ACLU and Greenwald sought to partner with LinkTV because of its strong penetration in traditional "red" (Republican-voting) states, they also targeted the internet and other distribution possibilities as critical: "The radical change in the distribution possibilities have put us at an extraordinary golden age of opportunity," Greenwald observes. Taking advantage of this opportunity, the *Chronicles* and *Freedom Files* websites feature full-length episodes for viewing or downloading and step-by-step guidelines for organizing home and community screenings and discussion of episodes.

"We need to be forward looking now," Greenwald says, because we are "looking at the most profound revolution since the printing press." Giving voice to issues and perspectives marginalized from public debate by the corporate news media, *Sierra Club Chronicles* and

ACLU Freedom Files represent two pioneering steps forward in this media revolution.

CONCLUSIONS

In the contest for media reform, independent media and democratic self-government join, hand in hand. Each of the cases in this chapter—Wi-Fi access, independent newsweeklies, Spanish-language media, and progressive television—are sites where the ongoing contest between independent media and their corporate counterparts take place. These cases show what is possible when people organize for media reform; they also give some indication of what is at risk, in the absence of such organizing.

Independent media serve local communities, reaching audiences that their corporate counterparts do not address, to treat issues that the corporate media ignore or misrepresent. But the importance of independent media extends beyond this crucial point, to at least three deeper levels. First, independent media treat ordinary people as important sources of news and information, as is clear in the case of *Sierra Club Chronicles* and *ACLU Freedom Files*. Second, they involve people from diverse backgrounds as journalists. Recall Mendoza and Gonzalez's *Hour of the Farmworker* program on KBBF. Third, independent media engage their audiences as agents, who are capable of participating, powerfully and effectively, in the political process, as the contests to protect newsweeklies' independence and establish Internet neutrality show.

Access to quality media is crucial to democratic-self-government. When "access" is understood to mean not only the right to consume but also the opportunity to produce media, all members of society become empowered and we take a step closer to McChesney's vision of a just, humane, and truly viable society.

Andrew Roth is an Assistant Professor of Sociology at Sonoma State University and Associate Director of Project Censored. Bailey Malone, Kristine Medeiros, and Jessica Rodas are undergraduate research interns with Project Censored.

* Authors are listed alphabetically; all shared equally in the authorship of this chapter. We are grateful to Bruce Brugmann, Robert Greenwald, Sascha Meinrath, Robert McChesney, Timothy Morse, and Esme Vos, each of whom responded generously to our requests for interviews.

Notes

1. McChesney, Robert and John Podesta, "Let There Be Wi-Fi," *Washington Monthly*, January/February 2006, http://www.washingtonmonthly.com/features/2006/0601. podesta.html; Turner, S. Derek, "Broadband Reality Check," *Free Press*, August 2005, http://www.freepress.net/docs/broadband_report.pdf.

2. For firsthand accounts of the conference, see Brown, Sandy, Joni Wallent, Kristine Snyder, Luke Judd, Christopher Cox, Jacob Rich, Lori Rouse, Mark Thompson, Sean Arlt, Brittney Roeland, and Britt Walters, "Media Democracy in Action: Update on Media Reform Conference and Media Activist Groups Nationwide," pp 263–280 in *Censored 2006*, New York: Seven Stories Press, 2005.

3. McChesney, Robert and John Podesta, "Let There Be Wi-Fi," *Washington Monthly*, January/February 2006, http://www.washingtonmonthly.com/features/2006/0601.podesta. html.

4. Ibid.

5. Aaron, Craig and Ben Scott, "United States of Broadband," www.Tompaine.com, July 11, 2005, http://www.tompaine.com/articles/2005/07/11/the_united_states_of_broadband.php.

6. McChesney, Robert and John Podesta, "Let There Be Wi-Fi," *Washington Monthly*, January/February 2006, http://www.washingtonmonthly.com/features/2006/0601.podesta. html.

7. Fox, Susannah, "Digital Divisions," Pew Internet & American Life Project, October 5, 2005, http://www.pewinternet.org/PPF/r/165/report_display.asp ; Public Knowledge; "Principles for an Open Broadband Future," Public Knowledge, July 6, 2005, http://www.publicknowledge.org/content/papers/open-broadband-future.

8. McChesney, Robert and John Podesta, "Let There Be Wi-Fi," *Washington Monthly*, January/February 2006, http://www.washingtonmonthly.com/features/2006/0601.podesta. html.

9. Ibid.

10. Szczepanczyk, Mitchell, "Community Internet Under Attack," *Z Magazine*, September 2005, http://zmagsite.zmag.org.

11. Center for Digital Democracy, "Brand X: Plan B," Center for Digital Democracy, July 13, 2005, http://www.democraticmedia.org.

12. Aaron, Craig and Ben Scott, "United States of Broadband," www.Tompaine.com, July 11, 2005, http://www.tompaine.com/articles/2005/07/11/the_united_states_of_broadband.php.

13. McChesney, Robert and John Podesta, "Let There Be Wi-Fi," *Washington Monthly*, January/February 2006, http://www.washingtonmonthly.com/features/2006/0601.podesta. html.

14. Ibid.

15. Turner, S. Derek, "Broadband Reality Check," *Free Press*, August 2005, http://www.freepress. net/docs/broadband_report.pdf.

16. Muniwireless, "Muniwireless April 2006 Summary of City and County Projects," Muniwireless, April 25, 2006, http://muniwireless.com/municipal/reports/1163/.

17. ABI Research, "Metro Wi-Fi Coverage to top 126,000 Square Miles by 2010, Says ABI Research," ABI Research, March 15, 2006, http://www.abiresearch.com.

18. Muniwireless, "Muniwireless market sizing report now available," Muniwireless, September 26, 2005, http://muniwireless.com/municipal/reports/841/.

19. Media Alliance, "Where do the SF wireless proposals stand on digital inclusion?" Media Alliance, March 14, 2006, http://www.media-alliance.org.

20. Ibid.

21. Muniwireless, "Muniwireless April 2006 Summary of City and County Projects," Muniwireless, April 25, 2006, http://muniwireless.com/municipal/reports/1163/.

22. McChesney, Robert and John Podesta, "Let There Be Wi-Fi," *Washington Monthly*, January/February 2006, http://www.washingtonmonthly.com/features/2006/0601.podesta. html.

23. Baller, Jim, "Jim Baller's Initial Reaction to Senator Ensign's Municipal Networks Provision," The Baller Herbst Law Group, July 29, 2005, http://www.baller.com.

24. McChesney, Robert and John Podesta, "Let There Be Wi-Fi," *Washington Monthly*, January/February 2006, http://www.washingtonmonthly.com/features/2006/0601.podesta. html.
25. Ibid.
26. Szczepanczyk, Mitchell, "Community Internet Under Attack," *Z Magazine*, September 2, 2005, http://zmagsite.zmag.org.
27. Media Alliance, "Where do the SF wireless proposals stand on digital inclusion?" Media Alliance, March 14, 2006, http://www.media-alliance.org.
28. Ibid.
29. Media Alliance, "Google Wi-Fi Bid Lacking in Privacy, Speed, Digital Divide Elements," Media Alliance, April 6, 2006, http://www.media-alliance.org.
30. Kopytoff, Verne, "Wi-Fi plan stirs Big Brother concerns." *San Francisco Chronicle*, April 8, 2006, C1.
31. Ibid.
32. Baltuch, Jonathan,"St. Cloud, Florida citywide Wi-Fi update," Muniwireless, March 21, 2006, http://muniwireless.com/municipal/1109/.
33. Public Knowledge, "Principles for an Open Broadband Future," Public Knowledge, July 6, 2005, http://www.publicknowledge.org/content/papers/open-broadband-future.
34. Redmond, Tim, "Bay Guardian Sues New Times Chain for Predatory Pricing," *San Francisco Bay Guardian*, October 20, 2004.
35. Kurtz, Howard, "The Village Voice's No-Alternative News: Corporate Takeover," *Washington Post*, October 24, 2005.
36. Ibid.
37. Morgan, Fiona, "Will Merger Take the Alt out of Weeklies?" *The Independent Weekly*, September 14, 2005, http://www.indyweek.gyrobase.com.
38. Robinson, Bruce, "Voice of the Worker: Bilingual KBBF-FM Returns to Its Roots," Metroactive.com, March 8, 2006, http://www.metroactive.com/bohemian/03.08.06/kbbf-0610.html.
39. Ibid.
40. Hay, Jeremy, "Organizing: Network of Latino Radio, Churches, Union Helped Fuel Rally," *Santa Rosa Press-Democrat*, April 1, 2006.
41. Entman, Robert M. and David L. Paletz, "Media and the Conservative Myth." *Journal of Communication*, 30 (4): 154-165, 1980.
42. Croteau, David and William Hoynes, *By Invitation Only: How the Media Limit Political Debate*, Monroe, ME: Common Courage, 1994.
43. Ibid.
44. Ibid.

THIS MODERN WORLD

by TOM TOMORROW

PORTER GOSS'S HANDPICKED THIRD IN COMMAND AT THE CIA IS UNDER INVESTIGATION BY THE **FBI** FOR HIS ROLE IN THE **DUKE CUNNINGHAM** SCANDAL...HE IS SAID TO HAVE FREQUENTED POKER PARTIES AT THE **WATERGATE** AT WHICH CROOKED CONGRESSMEN WERE SUPPLIED WITH BOTH **BRIBES** AND **PROSTITUTES**...

GOSS IS RUMORED TO HAVE ATTENDED THESE PARTIES AS WELL--BUT WHEN **HE** RESIGNS ABRUPTLY ON A FRIDAY AFTERNOON, WITH NO EXPLANATION **GIVEN**--

--THE NEWS MEDIA BLAME IT ON A **BUREAUCRATIC TURF WAR**--AND LEAVE IT AT **THAT??**

GOOD **GRIEF!**

DON'T WORRY, CHARLIE BROWN! THE MAINSTREAM MEDIA WILL REDEEM THEMSELVES--I **KNOW** THEY WILL! THEY'LL ASK TOUGH QUESTIONS AND PUBLISH HARD-HITTING STORIES--AND THE BLATANT HYPOCRISY AND CORRUPTION OF REPUBLICANS WILL BE **EXPOSED** ONCE AND FOR **ALL!**

REALLY?

NAH.

AND YET, I FALL FOR IT EVERY TIME.

HOPE SPRINGS ETERNAL, CHARLIE BROWN.

...WITH APOLOGIES TO THE LATE, GREAT CHARLES M. SCHULZ...

CHAPTER 6

Corporate Media Today

by Ben Frymer, Nick Ramirez, David Abbott, Lauren Powell and Joe
Butwill

INTRODUCTION

by Joe Butwill

2006 marked the ten-year anniversary of the Telecommunications Act,
which represented a major step toward the deregulation of media ownership rules. Several factors have come together to impact media concentration in the U.S., and the culmination of events does not bode well
for the free press. Kevin Martin was appointed to replace Michael
Powell as chair of the Federal Communications Commission (FCC) by
George W. Bush on March 8, 2005, after having served on the commission since July 2001. Martin has wasted no time pushing for further
deregulation of the communications industry. The youthful chairman
is a long-time Bush loyalist, who shares the administration's belief in
the ideology of free markets. In addition, Congress is moving forward
with an update to the Telecommunications Act sponsored by the
Chairman of the House Commerce and Energy Commission
Representative Joe Barton, R-TX, who is leading the charge to deregulate the communications industry in order to "promote growth." With
Republicans in control of the House of Representatives, the Senate, the
White House, the Supreme Court, and now the leadership of the FCC,
much of what they hope to achieve will pass into law with minimal
interference from the courts.

MARTIN ON DEREGULATION

by Nick Ramirez

In a speech to the Newspaper Association of America on April 4, 2006,
Martin proposed the elimination of the 1975 newspaper/broadcasting

cross-ownership ban, which, if lifted, would allow newspapers to buy broadcasting stations in the same markets as their print media. According to Martin, major newspaper corporations are struggling because, "Much has changed since the days of disco and leisure suits, including the media marketplace." With the expansion of the Internet, and an increase in the number of television and radio stations over the past thirty years, metropolitan newspapers can no longer compete; they are losing stock values and readership is dwindling. Martin blamed the decline on the cross-ownership ban, and the fact that, "[The] public has not been convinced of the need for change," and he went on to encourage newspapers to help disseminate information about the supposed benefits of media consolidation. "We can't take on this process alone," he said. "Your job is to educate the public about the changes in the media landscape."

Controversy surrounds the issue of the number of media outlets a single news corporation will be able to own in a local area if the ban is lifted. Contrary to Martin's comments, large newspaper corporations already have sizable ownership of broadcasting stations and Web sites: Gannett owns twenty television stations, the *New York Times* owns nine television stations and thirty-five websites, the *Washington Post* owns six television stations, and the Tribune Company owns twenty-eight television stations and more than fifty websites. If the cross-ownership ban is lifted it will further deregulate the industry, allowing newspaper giants to be more heavily concentrated in both print and broadcast media within the same cities of their publications. Gannet owns more than 100 news publications, and for each one it can have broadcasting stations in the same city. FCC Commissioner Michael Copps voiced opposition to media consolidation and the lifting of the ban. "The issue is whether a few large conglomerates will be granted content control," he said at a discussion held at Old Dominion University, organized by Free Press. "Will we still be able to get local news and clashing views?"

Martin also hopes to hasten the speed with which phone companies can enter the television provider market. Phone companies, including Verizon Communications and AT&T, have spent $60 million on lobbying the federal government to speed up the process of acquiring franchise agreements. In order to be established in an area, cable companies need to negotiate franchising agreements with local officials. AT&T and Verizon are pushing to require application approval within thirty days, which would allow them to bypass many of the hurdles cable companies have to clear. In Congress, a House bill which is being proposed will create a national franchise, where phone companies could sidestep local officials altogether. Texas, Virginia, and Indiana have already passed laws allowing phone companies to speed up the process.

Proposals to eradicate the newspaper/broadcasting cross-ownership ban have been debated and repeatedly defeated in the FCC since 1996. When the Commission voted to lift the ban in 2003, the Third Circuit Court overturned that order, stating that the ban was in the public's interest. The key players behind the current Congressional update of the 1996 Telecommunications Act are Barton, Representative Fred Upton, R-MI and Senator Ted Stevens, R-AK. Barton was a staunch supporter of former FCC Chairman Michael Powell and his efforts toward deregulation. Upton has chaired the Commerce Telecommunications and the Internet Subcommittee for the past four years. He said that the revision must replace "wrong-headed government regulation," advocating an open market for new technologies. Stevens is Senate president pro-tempore and chairman of the Commerce Committee. He is catering to the needs of his largely rural state which relies primarily on traditional wired telephone services. He's not gung-ho about a congressional deadline for the transition to digital TV, or implementing new technologies that will uproot wired telephone services and pose a threat to the universal service fund his state receives. Other lawmakers involved in the revision include Representatives Rick Boucher, D-VA, John Dingell, D-MI, Edward Markey, D-MA, Charles (Chip) Pickering, R-MS, James Sensenbrenner, R-WI, and Cliff Stearns, R-FL, as well as Senators Conrad Burns, R-MT, Byron Dorgan, D-ND, Daniel Inouye, D-HI, John McCain, R-AZ, John (Jay) Rockefeller, D-WV.

Sources: Chairman Martin's Remarks Before the Newspaper Association of America 2006Annual Convention, www.fcc.gov, April 4, 2006; Hatch, David and Molly M. Peterson. "Key Members of Congress," *National Journal's Insider Update*, www.njtelecomupdate.com/tb-FNLKIII3345608805.html; Nicholson, David. Critics of Big Media Press FCC for Action, March 31, 2006, http://www.freepress.net/news/14718.

TELECOMMUNICATIONS REFORM AND THE PUSH TO DEREGULATE THE INTERNET

by Lauren Powell

The escalation of Internet access since the Telecommunications Act of 1996 has not been accompanied by corresponding legislation. The Act underestimated the socioeconomic impact of Internet usage, thus failed to create legislation to regulate broadband ownership and distribution.

Congress also failed to assign the FCC direct authoritative statute concerning Internet law. In effect, the entirety of the Internet was paid loose attention by the 1996 Act. According to the Museum of Broadcast Communications, the only Internet-focused section was the Communications Decency Act, which criminalized the transmission of indecent material to minors over computer networks. With telecommunications reform in Congress once more, precise regulatory Internet legislation and implementation is pivotal to maintain indiscriminate access as it stands.

Central to recent legislative controversy is "network neutrality" or "common carriage," a concept fundamental to the Internet, which enforces operation under egalitarian access. Both Internet Service Providers (ISPs) and users are entitled to equal speed and content. The notion envisions non-discriminatory competition and innovation among providers and consumers. Regardless of the connection being made—from a corporate website or from a startup—Internet speed is to remain consistent and content unrestricted. Congress, heavily lobbied by Telecom companies, will stifle this democratic process if no amendments are made to recent pending legislation.

In June of 2006, the full House of Representatives passed Joe Barton's Communications, Opportunity, Promotion, and Enhancement Act of 2006 (H.R.5252, The COPE Act). This legislation is a telecommunications reform bill with insufficient net neutrality language. The bill falls short of protecting an open Internet and allows broadband providers—primarily phone companies—to charge Internet content and service providers for use of their fiber optic lines. The bill may allow phone companies to create a two-tiered system in the form of a priority-speed tier for commercial providers able to pay premiums, and a less-efficient tier for independent providers unable to pay. Phone companies pledge that there is no plan to discriminate against those who don't pay, yet there is no denial that some will have faster service than others. Broadband providers see tiering as fair—they provide the fiber optic "pipes"— thus they should be able to charge what they want.

The COPE Act denies the FCC regulatory authority by only allowing case-by-case investigation on net neutrality violations. The FCC may impose fines up to $500,000, but may not compose broader rules. The bill also removes the requirement for phone companies to obtain permission from prospective communities seeking service. This strategy is aimed to allow national franchising rather than local by replacing the authority of more than 30,000 local franchisers with a national system overseen by the FCC. Barton's supporters argue that competition will be promoted by allowing phone companies to package services competitive to cable-packaged video, voice, and Internet. Phone companies predict cheaper rates and developmental incentive for Internet services. Yet opponents insist that national franchising will further stratify the already anti-competitive duopoly of phone and cable companies.

Advocates for the COPE Act, including phone companies like AT&T and BellSouth, claim that net neutrality need not be an issue in the telecommunications reform. They argue that the Internet has not been regulated thus far, and insist that regulation will hinder competition. Critics argue that a lack of regulation, as proven by effects of the 1996 Act (see the chapter three updates for the number one stories of 1988, 1990, and 1993, directly leads to consolidation, monopolization and higher prices.

The opposing criticism revolves around the reality that phone companies are increasing their involvement in the content industry. Critics argue that protective legislation in necessary to prevent such companies from favoring their own business and squashing non-commercial sites.

Though the *Los Angeles Times* and *Washington Post* covered net neutrality, the issue was covered as mid-C section business news rather than front page press explanatory of the huge social impact of telecommunications reform, media consolidation, and democratic media. The *New York Times* covered the COPE Act similarly in the business section, along with a few editorials, yet addressed the issue's entirety only the day after passage. The *New York Times* gave little press to the extensive Congressional debate and intense lobbying to shape telecommunications reform prior to its passing. Without consumer knowledge of telecommunication reform, and without information given early enough for consumers to act, the industry is likely to revel in consolidation mayhem. Without the enforcement of net neutrality, doors are opened to Internet taxes and exclusive revenue generation for big phone companies. The new era of Internet access may be run on "pay as you search" or "pay as you post" rules instead of competition amongst innovators. The spectrum of searchable information may also be abridged to benefit those who can afford superior service.

For updates on further decisions, see www.freepress.net/netfreedom and www.freepress. net/congress. See Chapter One story #1 for more background information on Internet regulation including *National Cable & Telecommunications Association vs. Brand X Internet Services.*

Ben Frymer is an Assistant professor of Sociology in the Hutchins School of Liberal Studies at Sonoma State University. Nick Ramirez, David Abbott, Lauren Powell, and Joe Butwill are undergraduate research interns with Project Censored.

Sources: Declan, McCullagh and Anne Broache. "Republicans Defeat Net Neutrality Proposal," *Cnet*, April 6, 2006; Clark, Drew. "Wyden Offers 'Net Neutrality' Bill," *Technology Daily*, March 2, 2006; Wellings, Frannie. "Telcom Bills Moving in Both Houses of Congress," *Free Press*, May 10, 2006; Granelli, James S. "Phone, Cable May Charge Dot-Coms That Want to Race Along the Internet," *Los Angeles Times*, April 9, 2006; Surowiecki, James. "Net Losses," *The New Yorker*, March 20, 2006; Puzzanghera, Jim. "Panel Vote Shows Rift Over Net Neutrality," *Los Angeles Times*, April 27, 2006; Legum, Judd, and Nico Pitney, Payson Schwin, Faiz Shakir, and Amanda Tekel. "The End of the Internet As We Know It?" Center for American Progress, April 12, 2006; Teal, Kelly M. "Net Neutrality Gets New Support from House Judiciary, Senate," *Phone+*, May 19, 2006; Bernier, Paula and Kelly M. Teal. "Telecom Act Hits 10-Year Mark," *Xchange*, Febuary 1, 2006; Labaton, Stephen. "House Backs Telecom Bill Favoring Phone Companies," *New York Times*, June 9, 2006; Abate, Tom. "Telecom Reform Moves Forward; House Panel Ok's Measure Favored by Phone Companies," *San Francisco Chronicle*, April 6, 2006.

NEWS MEDIA OWNERSHIP EMPIRES

NEWS CORPORATION

TELEVISION

FOX Broadcasting Company: Indiana: WTVW-TV/FOX 7 Evansville, WFFT-TV/FOX 55 Ft. Wayne, WXIN-TV/FOX 59 Indianapolis, WSJV-TV/FOX 28 South Bend, WFXW-TV/FOX 38 Terre Haute, IN. Kentucky: WDKY-TV/FOX 56 Lexington, WDRB-TV/FOX 41 Louisville. Maryland: WBFF-TV/FOX 45 Baltimore. Michigan: WFQX-TV/FOX 33/45 Traverse City, WSMH-TV/FOX 66 Flint, WXMI-TV/FOX 17 Grand Rapids, WSYM-TV/FOX 47 Lansing, WMQF-TV/Channel 19 Marquette, WJBK-TV/FOX 2 Detroit. Ohio: WXIX-TV/FOX 19 Cincinnati, WJW-TV/FOX 8 Cleveland, WTTE-TV/FOX 28 Columbus, WRGT-TV/FOX 45 Dayton, WOHL-TV/FOX 25 Lima, WUPW-TV/FOX 36 Toledo, WYFX-TV/FOX 17/62 Youngstown. Pennsylvania: WFXP-TV/FOX 66 Erie, WWCP-TV/FOX 8 Johnstown-Altoona, WTXF-TV/FOX 29 Philadelphia, WPGH-TV/FOX 53 Pittsburgh, FOX 56 WOLF/FOX 56 Wilkes-Barre, WPMT-TV/FOX 43 Harrisburg. Virginia: WAHU-LPTV/ Channel 27 Charlottesville, WVBT-TV/FOX 43 Norfolk, WRLH-TV/FOX 35 Richmond, WFXR/WJPR-TV/FOX 21/27 Roanoke/Lynchburg. Washington D.C.: WTTG-TV/FOX 5. West Virginia: WVFX-TV/FOX 46 Clarksburg, WVAH-TV/FOX 11 Charleston. Connecticut: WTIC-TV/FOX 61 Hartford. Maine: WPFO-TV Channel 23 Portland. Massachusetts: WFXT-TV/FOX 25 Boston. New York: WXXA-TV/FOX 23 Albany, WYDC-TV/FOX 48 Elmira, WUTV-TV/FOX 29 Buffalo, WNYW-TV/FOX 5 New York, WUHF-TV/FOX 31 Rochester, WFXV-TV/FOX 33 Utica, WSYT-TV/FOX 68 Syracuse, WICZ-TV/FOX 40 Binghamton, WNYF FOX 28, Watertown. Rhode Island: WNAC-TV/FOX 64 Providence. Vermont: WFFF-TV/FOX 44 Burlington. Alabama: WBRC-TV/FOX 6 Birmingham, WZDX-TV/FOX 54 Huntsville, WALA-TV/FOX 10 Mobile, WCOV-TV/FOX 20 Montgomery, WDFX-TV/FOX 34 Dothan. Florida: WFTX-TV/FOX 4 Ft. Myers, WAWS-TV/FOX 30 Jacksonville, WOFL-TV/FOX 35 Orlando, WSVN-TV/FOX 7 Miami, WOGX-TV/FOX 51 Gainesville, WPGX-TV/FOX 28 Panama City, WTLH-TV/FOX 49 Tallahassee, WTVT-TV/FOX 13 Tampa, WFLX-TV/FOX 29 West Palm Beach, Georgia: WFXL-TV/FOX 31 Albany, WAGA-TV/FOX 5 Atlanta, WFXG-TV/FOX 54 Augusta, WXTX-TV/FOX 54 Columbus, WGXA-TV/FOX 24 Macon, WTGS-TV/FOX 28 Savannah. Mississippi: WXXV-TV/FOX 25 Biloxi, WUFX/FOX 35 Jackson, WLOV-TV/FOX 27 Columbus-Tupelo. North Carolina: WCCB-TV/FOX 18 Charlotte, WGHP-TV/FOX 8 Greensboro, WFXI-TV/FOX 8/14 Greenville-N. Bern, WRAZ-TV/FOX 50 Raleigh, WSFX-TV/FOX 26 Wilmington. South Carolina: WTAT-TV/FOX 24 Charleston, WACH-TV/FOX 57 Columbia, WHNS-TV/FOX 21 Greenville-Spart, WFXB-TV/FOX 43 Florence/Myrtle Beach. Tennessee: WDSI-TV/FOX 61 Chattanooga, WEMT-TV/FOX 39 Tri-

Cities, WTNZ-TV/FOX 43 Knoxville, WHBQ-TV/FOX 13 Memphis, WZTV-TV/FOX 17 Nashville. Arkansas: KPBI-TV/FOX 46 Ft. Smith, KLRT-TV/FOX 16 Little Rock. Illinois: WYZZ-TV/FOX 43 Peoria, WFLD-TV/FOX 32 Chicago, WQRF-TV/FOX 39 Rockford, WRSP-TV/FOX 55/27 Springfield. Iowa: KFXA-TV/FOX 28/40 Cedar Rapids, KLJB-TV/FOX 18 Davenport, KDSM-TV/FOX 17 Des Moines, KYOU-TV/FOX 15 Ottumwa. Kansas: KTMJ FOX 6,KSAS-TV/FOX 24 Wichita-Huchinson. Louisiana: WNTZ-TV/FOX 48 Alexandria, WGMB-TV/FOX 44 Baton Rouge, KADN-TV/FOX 15 Lafayette, KVHP-TV/FOX 29 Lake Charles, WVUE-TV/FOX 8 New Orleans, KMSS-TV/FOX 33 Shreveport, KARD-TV/FOX 14 Monroe. Minnesota: KQDS-TV/FOX 21 Duluth, KMSP-TV/FOX 9 Minneapolis, KXLT-TV/FOX 47 Rochester. Missouri: KBSI-TV/FOX 23 Paducah (KY), WDAF-TV/FOX 4 Kansas City, KTVI-TV/FOX 2 St. Louis, KQFX-TV/FOX 11 Columbia-Jefferson City, KSFX-TV/FOX 27 Springfield, KFJX-TV / Channel 14 Joplin. Nebraska: KPTM-TV/FOX 42 Omaha, KTVG-TV/FOX 17 Lincoln-Grand Isld., KPTH-TV/FOX 44 Sioux City, KIIT-TV/ FOX 11 North Platte. North Dakota: KVRR-TV/FOX 15 Fargo. Oklahoma: KOKH-TV/FOX 25 Oklahoma City, KOKI-TV/FOX 23 Tulsa. South Dakota: KEVN-TV/FOX 7 Rapid City, KTTW-TV/FOX 17 Sioux Falls. Texas: KXVA-TV/FOX 15 Abilene, KCIT-TV/FOX 14 Amarillo, KTBC-TV/FOX 7 Austin, KUIL TV FOX 64 Beaumont, KDF-TV/FOX 47 Corpus Christi, KDFW-TV/FOX 4 Dallas, KFOX-TV/FOX 14 El Paso, KRIV-TV/FOX 26 Houston, KJTV-TV/FOX 34 Lubbock, XHRIO-TV / Channel 2 McAllen, KPEJ-TV/FOX 24 Odessa, KIDY-TV/FOX 6 San Angelo, KABB-TV/FOX 29 San Antonio, KFXK-TV/FOX 51/30 Tyler, KVCT-TV/FOX 19 Victoria, KWKT-TV/FOX 28/44 Waco, KJTL-TV/FOX 18 Wichita Falls. Wisconsin: WLUK-TV/FOX 11 Green Bay, WEUX-WLAX-TV/FOX 25/48 LaCrosse, WMSN-TV/FOX 47 Madison, WITI-TV/FOX 6 Milwaukee, WFXS-TV/FOX 55 Wasau. Arizona: KSAZ-TV Phoenix, KMSB-TV/FOX 11 Tucson, KECY-TV Yuma. Colorado: KXRM-TV/FOX 21 Colorado Springs, KDVR-TV Denver, KFQX-TV Grand Junction. Idaho: KTRV-TV/FOX 12 Boise, KXTF-TV Twin Falls, KFXP-TV/FOX 31 Idaho Falls. Montana: KBTZ-TV/FOX 24 Butte, KLMN-TV/FOX 26 Great Falls. New Mexico: KASA-TV/FOX 2 Albuquerque. Utah: KSTU-TV/FOX 13 Salt Lake City. Wyoming: KFNB Casper-Riverton, KLWY-TV/FOX 27 Cheyenne. California: KBFX-LP/FOX 58 Bakersfield, KCVU-TV/FOX 30 Chico, KBVU-TV/FOX 29 Eureka, KMPH-TV/FOX 26 Fresno, KTTV FOX 11 Los Angeles, KTVU-TV/FOX 2 San Francisco, KDFX-TV/FOX 11 Palm Springs, KTXL-TV/FOX 40 Sacramento, KCBA-TV/FOX 35 Monterey, XETV-TV/FOX 6 San Diego, KKFX-TV/FOX 24 Santa Barbara. Nevada: KVVU-TV/FOX 5 Las Vegas, KRXI-TV/FOX 11 Reno. Oregon: KFXO-TV/FOX 39 Bend, KLSR-TV/FOX 34 Eugene, KMVU-TV/FOX 26 Medford, KPTV/FOX12 Portland. Washington: KCPQTV/FOX 13 Seattle, KAYU-TV Spokane, KFFX-TV Tri Cities, KCYU-TV/FOX 68 Yakima. Alaska: KTBY-TV/FOX 4 Anchorage, KFXF-TV/FOX 7 Fairbanks. Hawaii: KHON-TV/FOX 2 Honolulu

BSkyB-FOXTEL, Fox Movie Channel, Fox News Channel, Fox Sports

Arizona, Fox Sports Bay Area (with Rainbow Media Holdings), Fox Sports Chicago (with Rainbow Media Holdings), Fox Sports Detroit, Fox Sports Intermountain West, Fox Sports Midwest, Fox Sports Net, Fox Sports New England (with Rainbow Media), Fox Sports New York (with Rainbow Media), Fox Sports Northwest, Fox Sports Ohio (with Rainbow Media), Fox Sports Pittsburgh, Fox Sports Rocky Mountain, Fox Sports South, Fox Sports Southeast, Fox Sports West, Fox Sports West #2, FX, National Geographic Channel, SKYPerfecTV, SPEED Channel, STAR, and Stream

FILM

20th Century Fox, 20th Century Fox Espanol, Fox Searchlight Pictures, and Fox Television Studios. 20th Century Fox Home Entertainment, 20th Century Fox international, 20th Century Fox Television, Blue Sky Studios, Fox Searchlight Pictures, Fox Studious Australia, Fox Studios Baja, Fox Studios LA, Fox Television

MAGAZINES

donna hay, InsideOut, SmartSource, TV Guide, The Weekly Standard, Big League, News America Marketing

BOOKS

HarperCollins Publishers: Access Travel, Amistad Press, Avon, Branded Books Program, Cliff Street Books, The Ecco Press, Eos, HarperAudio, HarperBusiness, HarperCollins, HarperCollins General Book Group, HarperEntertainment, HarperInformation, HarperResource, HarperSanFrancisco, HarperTorch, Morrow/Avon, Perennial, Regan Books, Quill, William Morrow, William Morrow Cookbooks, and Zondervan. **HarperCollins Children's Book Group**: Greenwillow Books, HarperFestival, HarperTrophy, Joanna Cotler Books, and Laura Geringer Books. Greenwillow Books, HarperFestival, HarperTrophy, Joanna Cotler Books, and Laura Geringer Books

NEWSPAPERS

United States: *New York Post.* **United Kingdom:** *News of the World, News International, Sun, Sunday* (London) *Times,* and *The* (London) *Times.* **Australia:** *Advertiser, Australian, Courier-Mail, Daily Telegraph, Fiji Times, Gold Coast Bulletin, Herald Sun, Mercury, Newsphotos, Newspix, Newstext, NT News, Post-Courier, Sunday Herald Sun, Sunday Mail, Sunday Tasmanian, Sunday Telegraph, Sunday Territorian, Sunday Times,* and *Weekly Times*

AOL TIME WARNER INC.

AMERICA ONLINE

AOL Instant Messenger, ICQ, AOLbyPhone, AOL Call Alert, AOL CityGuide, AOL Europe, AOL Latino, AOL Wireless, AOL Voicemail, CompuServe Interactive Services, ICQ, inStore, KOL, Mirabilis, MapQuest, Moviefone, AOL Music Now, Netscape, Nullsoft, RED, SingingFish, Tegic

Communications, Truveo, Weblogs, Wildseed, Winamp, Xdrive

TIME WARNER CABLE

Roadrunner/Roadrunner—Business Class digital phone; Urban Cableworks of Philadelphia, Texas and Kansas City Cable Partners, L.P.; Capital News 9-Albany, Albany, NY; MetroSports, Kansas City, MO; News 8-Austin, Austin, TX; News 10 Now-Syracuse, Syracuse, NY; News 14, Carolina-Charlotte, Charlotte, NC; News 14 Carolina-Raleigh, Raleigh, NC; NY1 News, New York, NY; R News, Rochester, NY; Sportsnet NY (part ownership)

HOME BOX OFFICE

Cinemax, Picturehouse, HBO Independent Productions, HBO Multiplexes, HBO on Demand, HBO HD, Cinemax HD, HBO Video, HBO Domestic and International Program Distribution, WBTV Latin America. Joint ventures: HBO Asia, HBO Brazil, HBO Czech, HBO Hungary, HBO India, HBO Ole, HBO Poland, HBO Romania, HBO Siberia, E! Latin America Channel

TURNER BROADCASTER SYSTEM

Adult Swim, Atlanta Braves, Boomerang, Cartoon Network, Cartoon Network Asia Pacific, Cartoon Network Europe, Cartoon Network Lain America, Cartoon Network Studios, CNN/U.S., CNN Airport Network, CNN en Espana, CNN en Espanol Radio, CNN Headline News, CNN Headline News in Asia Pacific, CNN Headline News in Latin America, CNN International, CNN Mobile, CNNMoney.com, CNN Newsource, CNN Pipeline, CNN.com, CNNRadio, CNNStudentNews.com, CNN to Go, NASCAR.com, GameTap, PGA.com, TBS, TCM Asia Pacific, TCM Classic Hollywood in Latin America, TCM Europe, TNT HD, TNT Latin America, Turner Classic Movies, Turner Network Television, Turner South, TCM & Cartoon Network Asia Pacific, Williams St. Studio. Joint ventures: BOING, Cartoon Network Japan, CNN+, CETV, CNNj, CNN Turk, CNN-IBN, CNN.de (German), CNN.co.jp (Japanese), Court TV, NBC/Turner, NASCAR Races, n-tv, WTBS, Zee/Turner

NEW LINE CINEMA

Picturehouse, New Line Distribution, New Line Home Entertainment, New Line International Releasing, New Line Merchandizing/Licensing, New Line Music, New Line New Media, New Line Television, New Line Theatricals. Subsidiary: Fine Line Features

WARNER BROTHERS ENTERTAINMENT

Castle Rock Entertainment, Dark Castle Entertainment, Warner Brothers Pictures, Warner Brothers Television, The WB Television Network Kid's WB, Warner Home Video, Warner Brothers Consumer Products, TelePictures Productions, Warner Independent Pictures, Warner Brothers Interactive Entertainment, Warner Brothers Games, Warner Brothers International Cinemas, Warner Brother's Online, DC Comics, MAD Magazine, Warner

Brothers Animation, Hanna-Barbera, Looney Tones

TIME INCORPORATED

25 Beautiful Gardens; 25 Beautiful Homes; 25 Beautiful Kitchens; 4X4; Aeroplane; All You; Amateur Gardening; Amateur Photographer; Ambientes; Angler's Mail; Audi Magazine; Baby Talk; Balance; Bird Keeper; BMX Business News; Bride To Be; Bulfinch Press; Business 2.0; Cage & Aviary Birds; Caravan; Center Street; Chat; Chilango; Classic Boat; Coastal Living; Cooking Light; Cottage Living; Country Homes & Interiors; Country Life; Cycle Sport; Cycling Weekly; Decanter; English Women's Weekly; Entertainment Weekly; Essence; Essentials; European Boat Builder; Eventing; EXP; Expansion; Family Circle (U.K.); Field & Stream; Fortune; Fortune Asia; Fortune Europe; FSB: Fortune Small Business; Golf.com; Golf Magazine; Golf Monthly; Guitar; Hair; Health; Hi-Fi News; Homes & Gardens; Horse; Horse & Hound; IPC; Ideal Home; In Style; In Style (Australia); In Style (U.K.)' International Boat Industry; Land Rover World; Life; Life and Style; Little, Brown and Company Adult Trade Books; Little, Brown and Company Books for Young Readers; Livingetc; Loaded; Manufactura, MBR-Mountain Bike Rider; MiniWorld; Mizz; Model Collector; Money; Motor Boat & Yachting; Motor Boats Monthly; Motor Caravan; MotorBoating; NME; Now; Nuts; Obras; Outdoor Life; Parenting; Park Home & Holiday; People; People en Espanol; Pick Me Up; Popular Science; Practical Boat Owner; Practical Parenting; Prediction; Progressive Farmer; Quad Off-Road Magazine; Quien; Quo; Racecar Engineering; Real Simple; Ride BMX; Rugby World; Salt Water Sportsman, Ships Monthly; Shoot Monthly; Shooting Times; Ski; Skiing; Soaplife; Southern Accents; Southern Living; Sporting Gun; Sports Illustrated; Sports Illustrated for Kids; Stamp Magazine; Sunset; Sunset Books; SuperBike; Targeted Media, Inc.; *Teen People; The Field; The Golf+; The Railway Magazine; The Shooting Gazette; This Old House; This Old House Ventures; Time; Time Asia; Time Atlantic; Time Canada; Time For Kids; Time Pacific;* Time Inc. Strategic Communications; Time Warner Audio Books; Time Warner Book Group U.K.; Time Warner Book Group Distribution Services; *TransWorld Business; TransWorld Motocross; TransWorld Skateboarding; TransWorld Snowboarding; TransWorld Surf; TV & Satellite Week; TV Easy; TV Times; Uncut; VolksWorld; Vuelo; Wallpaper;* Warner Books; Warner Faith; *Web User; Wedding; What Camera; What Digital Camera; What's on TV; Who; Woman; Woman & Home; Woman's Own; Woman's Weekly; Women & Golf; World Soccer; Yachting; Yachting Monthly; Yachting World; Yachts.* Joint ventures: Advantages, S.A., BOOKSPAN, *Elle,* European Magazines Unlimited, *Marie Claire (U.K.), Quo*

TIME WARNER INVESTMENTS

Arroyo Video Solutions, BigBand Networks, BroadLogic, Entropic Communications, Exent, GoldPocket, Glu Mobile, MediaVast, N2 Broadband, PlanetOut, Si TV, Skypilot Networks, SkyStream Networks, SmartBargains, Vindigo, Visible World, Waterfront Media

GANNETT

REGIONAL NEWSPAPERS

Norwich Bulletin (CT) The News Journal (DE) The Daily Times (MD) Asbury Park Press (NJ) Courier News at Bridgewater (NJ) Courier-Post at Cherry Hill (NJ) Hone News Tribune at East Brunswick (NJ) Daily Record at Morristown (NJ) The Daily Journal at Vineland (NJ) Press & Sun-Bulletin at Binghamton (NY) Star-Gazette at Elmira (NY) Poughkeepsie Journal (NY) Rochester Democrat and Chronicle (NY) Observer-Dispatch at Utica (NY) The Journal News at Westchester County (NY) The Burlington Free Press (VT) Montgomery Advertiser (AL) The Baxter Bulletin (AR) Florida Today at Brevard County (FL) The News-Press at Fort Myers (FL) Pensacola News Journal (FL) Tallahassee Democrat (FL) The Courier-Journal (KY) The Town Talk at Alexandria (LA) The Daily Advertiser at Lafayette (LA) The News-Star at Monroe (LA) Daily World at Opelousas (LA) The Times at Shreveport (LA) The Clarion-Ledger at Jackson (MS) Hattiesburg American (MS) Asheville Citizen-Times (NC) Muskogee Phoenix (OK) The Greenville News (SC) The Leaf-Chronicle at Clarksville (TN) The Jackson Sun (TN) The Daily News Journal at Murfreesboro (TN) The Tennessean at Nashville (TN) The Daily News Leader (VA) The Herald-Dispatch (WV) Rockford Register Star (IL) The Indianapolis Star (IN) Journal and Courier at Lafayette (IN) Chronicle-Tribune at Marion (IN) The Star Press at Muncie (IN) Palladium-Item at Richmond (IN) The Des Moines Register (IW) Iowa City Press-Citizen (IW) Battle Creek Enquirer (MI) Detroit Free Press (MI) Lansing State Journal (MI) Livingston County Daily Press & Argus (MI) Times Herald at Port Huron (MI) St. Cloud Times (MN) Springfield News-Leader (MO) Telegraph-Forum at Bucyrus (OH) Chillicothe Gazette (OH) The Cincinnati Enquirer (OH) Coshocton Tribune (OH) The News-Messenger at Fremont (OH) Lancaster Eagle-Gazette (OH) News Journal at Mansfield (OH) The Marion Star (OH) The Advocate at Newark (OH) News Herald at Port Clinton (OH) Times Recorder at Zanesville (OH) Argus Leader (SD) The Post-Crescent at Appleton (WS) The Reporter at Fond du Lac (WS) Green Bay Press-Gazette (WS) Herald Times Reporter at Manitowoc (WS) Marshfield News-Herald (WS) Oshkosh Northwestern (WS) The Sheboygan Press (WS) Stevens Point Journal (WS) Wausau Daily Herald (WS) The Daily Tribune at Wisconsin Rapids (WS) The Arizona Republic (AZ) Tucson Citizen (AZ) The Desert Sun at Palm Springs (CA) The Salinas Californian (CA) Tulare Advance-Register (CA) Visalia Times-Delta (CA) Fort Collins Coloradoan (CO) The Honolulu Advertiser (HI) Great Falls Tribune (MT) Reno Gazette Journal (NV) Statesman Journal (OR) The Spectrum (UT) Pacific Daily News (Guam); Army Times Publishing, *Company Army Times, Armed Forces Journal, Navy Times, Marine Corps Times, Air Force Times, Federal Times, Defense News, Military Market, Military City, Gannett Offset, USA Today, USA Today Weekend,* Newsquest Media Group

TV STATIONS

KPNX-TV (Phoenix, AZ) KTHV-TV (Little Rock, AK) KXTV-TV (Sacramento-Stockton-Modesto, CA) KUSA-TV (Denver, Co) WUSA-TV (District of Columbia) WTLV-TV (Jacksonville, FL) WJXX-TV (Jacksonville, FL) WTSP-

TV (Tampa-St. Petersburg, FL) WXIA-TV (Atlanta, GA) WMAZ-TV (Macon, GA) WLBZ-TV (Bangor, ME) WCSH-TV (Portland, ME) WZZM-TV (Grand Rapids, MI) KARE-TV (Minneapolis-St. Paul, MN) KSDK-TV (St. Louis, MO) WGRZ-TV (Buffalo, NY) WFMY-TV (Greensboro, NC) WKYC-TV (Cleveland, OH) WLTX-TV (Columbia, SC) WBIR-TV (Knoxville, TN)

AFFILIATED COMPANIES & SUBSIDIARIES

Captivate Network Clipper Magazine, Gannett Media Technologies International, Hawaii.com, Nursing Spectrum Point Roll, Inc.101, Inc. Partnerships: Career Builder.com, ShopLocal.com, Topix.net

NEW YORK TIMES

PUBLICATIONS

The Boston Globe Telegram and Gazette

REGIONAL NEWSPAPERS

Sarasota Herald-Tribune (FL) The Press Democrat (CA) The Ledger (FL) Star-News (NC) Herald-Journal (SC) Star-Banner (FL) The Gainesville Sun (FL) The Tuscaloosa News (AL) TimesDaily (AL) The Gadsden Times (AL) Times-News (NC) The Courier (LA) The Dispatch (NC) Daily Comet (LA) Petaluma Argus-Courier (CA)

TV STATIONS

4 CBS affiliated stations (WREG-Memphis, TN; WTKR-Norfolk, VA; WHNT-Huntsville, AK; KFSM-Ft. Smith, AK); *2 NBC affiliated stations* (KFOR-Oklahoma City, OK; WHO-Des Moines, IW); *2 ABC affiliated stations* (WNEP-Wilkes-Barre/Scranton, PN; WQAD- Monline, IL); *1 UPN* (Oklahoma City, OK)

OTHER INVESTMENTS

About, Inc. and approximately 35 other websites Investments in: Discovery Times Channel—50% Donohue Malbaie Inc.—49% Madison Paper Industries—40% Metro Boston—49% New England Sports Ventures, LLC—17%

WASHINGTON POST OWNERSHIP

PUBLICATIONS

The Gazette Newspapers (MA) *The Herald* (WA), *Newsweek*

TV STATIONS

2 NBC affiliates (WDIV-Detroit; KPRC-Houston, TX); *2 ABC affiliates* (WPLG-Miami-Ft. Lauderdale, FL; KSAT-San Antonio, TX); *1 CBS affiliate* (WKMG-Orlando, FL); *1 independent* (WJXT-Jacksonville, FL)

CABLE SYSTEMS

CableOne Kaplan, Inc. Washington. Newsweek Interactive PostNewsweek Tech Media Group Owns interests in: Los Angles Times-Washington Post News Service BrassRing, Inc.

KNIGHT-RIDDER OWNERSHIP
(KNIGHT RIDDER WAS BOUGHT BY THE MCCLATCHY COMPANY ON JUNE 27, 2006.)

REGIONAL NEWSPAPERS

American News (SD) Akron Beacon Journal (OH) Belleville News-Democrat (IL) The Bellingham Herald (WA) Sun Herald (MS) The Idaho Statesman (ID) Bradenton Herald (FL) The Charlotte Observer (NC) The Observer (SC) The State Columbus (SC) Ledger-Enquirer (GA) Contra Costa Times (CA) News Tribune (MN) The News-Sentinel (IN) Fort Worth Star-Telegram (TX) Grand Forks Herald (ND) The Kansas City Star (KS) Lexington Herald-Leader (KY) The Macon Telegraph (GA) The Miami Herald (FL) el Nuevo Herald (FL) Herald The Herald (CA) The Sun News (SC) The Olathe News (KS) The Olympian (WA) Philadelphia Daily News (PH) The Philadelphia Inquirer (PH) St. Paul Pioneer Press (MN) San Jose Mercury News (CA) The Tribune (CA) Centre Daily Times (PA) The Wichita Eagle (KS) The Times Leader (PA) Farm Forum (SD) Highland News Leader (IL) The Journal-Messenger (IL) The Legal Reporter (IL) O'Fallon Progress (IL) Pinckneyville Democrat (IL) Command Post (IL) Sparta News-Plaindealer (IL) Alameda Journal (CA) Berkeley Voice (CA) The Journal (CA) The Montclarion (CA) The Piedmonter (CA) The Pine Journal (MN) Budgeteer News (MN) The Daily Telegram (WS) Lake County News-Chronicle (MN) The Argyle American (TX) Colleyville Courier (TX) Diario La Estrella (TX) The Messenger (TX) Grapevine Courier (TX) The Haslet Harbinger (TX) Justin Journal (TX) The Keller Citizen (TX) Mansfield News-Mirror (TX) The Ponder Pilot (TX) The Roanoke Register (TX) Southlake Journal (TX) The Trophy Club Times (TX) Westlake First News (TX) Agweek (ND) The Star-Herald (MO) The Democrat-Missourian (MO) Lee's Summit Journal (MO) Florida Keys Keynoter (FL) The Reporter (FL) The Valley Adviser (CA) The Horry County Gazette (SC) Art Museum Area (PH) Home News (PH) Bridesburg Star (PH) Fishtown Star (PH) Girard Home News (PH) Three Star (PH) North Star (PH) Northeast Times (PH) Port Richmond Star (PH) The Cambrian (CA) Central Coast Sun Bulletin (CA) The Abington Journal (PA) The Sunday Dispatch (PH) Burlingame Daily News (CA) East Bay Daily News (CA) Los Gatos Daily News (CA) Palo Alto Daily News (CA) Redwood City Daily New (CA) San Mateo Daily News (CA) Almaden Resident (CA) Campbell Reporter (CA) Cupertino Courier (CA) Los Gatos Weekly-Times (CA) Rose Garden Resident (CA) Saratoga News (CA) Sunnyvale Sun (CA) Willow Glen Resident (CA)

INVESTMENTS

Newspapers: 75% of Fort Wayne Newspapers Agency; 49.5% of the voting common stock and 65% of the nonvoting common stock of Seattle Times Company; **Newsprint:** 33.3%, with Cox Enterprises and Media General, Inc., of SP Newsprint Co.; 13.5% of Ponderay Newsprint Company; **Electronic Media:** 33.3%, with Tribune Company and Gannett Co., Inc., of CareerBuilder, LLC; 20.2%, with Gannett Co., Inc., The McClatchy Company, Tribune Company, The Washington Post Company and A. H. Belo Corporation, of Classified Ventures, LLC; 23.6% of Tribe Networks, Inc.;

One-third ownership, with Gannett Co., Inc. and Tribune Company, of CrossMedia Services, Inc.; **Other:** 50%, with Tribune Company, of Knight Ridder/Tribune Information Services, Inc.; 50%, with Tribune Company, of Newscom LLC; 25%, with The New York Times Company, Advance Publications, Inc., and Dow Jones & Co., Inc., of Media Consortium LLC; 28.9% of the voting stock of Newspapers First

OTHER

Knight-Ridder Shared Services, Knight-Ridder/Tribune Information Services, Knight-Ridder Washington Bureau

TRIBUNE COMPANY

REGIONAL NEWSPAPERS

Chicago Tribune (IL) Newsday (NY) Los Angles Times (CA) The Sun (MD) South Florida Sun-Sentinel (FL) Orlando Sentinel (FL) The Hartford Courant (CT) The Morning Call (PA) Daily Press (VA) The Advocate (CT) Greenwich Times (CT)

TELEVISION STATIONS

(Superstation WGN), *19 WB affiliated:* (WPIX-TY - New York, NY) (KTLA - Los Angles, CA) WGN-TV - Chicago, IL) (WHPL-TV - Philadelphia) (WLVI - Boston) (KDAF-TV, Dallas) (WBDC-TV, Washington D.C.) (WATL-TV, Atlanta) (KHWB-TV, Huston) (KTWB-TV, Seattle) (WBZL-TV, South Florida) (KWGN-TV, Denver) (KPLR-TV, St. Louis) (KWBP-TV, Portland) (WTTV-TV, Indianapolis) (KSWB-TV, San Diego) (WTXX-TV, Hartford) (WNOL-TV, New Orleans) (WEWB-TV, Albony) *6 FOX affiliated:* (KCPQ-TV, Seattle) (KTXL-TV, Sacramento) (WXIN-TV, Indianapolis) (WTIC-TV, Hartford) (WXMI-TV, Grand Rapids) (WPMT-TV, Harrisburg) *1 ABC affiliated:* (WGNO-TV, New Orleans) *other:* (CLTV Chicagoland Television 24-Hour News)

SPANISH LANGUAGE NEWSPAPERS

Hoy and *El Sentinel*

RADIO

WGN-AM, Chicago

WEBSITES

CareerBuilder.com, Apartments.com, cars.com, NewHomeNetwork.com, Homescape.com, CalenderLive.com, MetroMix.com, Showtime Interactive, SouthFlorida.com, Ctnow.com, MergeDigital.com, 7cities.com, Chicagosports.com

PARTNERS AND SUBSIDIES

Tribune Media Services, TMS Entertainment Products, TMS Syndicated Products, Zap 2 It, Tribune Direct, Chicago Cubs, amNewYork, Classified Ventures, Brass Ring

INVESTMENTS

Adstar (3.4 million shares) EQ, Time Warner (3.2 million shares) EQ, Barings Asia-Pacific Fund (24%) EQ, Dotcast (2%), Legacy.com (40%) EQ, Queztall/Chase Communications Partners (3%), Comcast Sportsnet Chicago (25%) EQ, The WB Network (22%) EQ, TV Food Network (31%) EQ, Brassring (27%) EQ, Careerbuilders (33%) EQ, Classified Ventures (29%) EQ, Cross-Media Services (33%) EQ, Jobscience (10%), Knight-Ridder/Tribune Information Services (50%) EQ, Yellowbox (18%)

NEW VIACOM

TELEVISION

Cable Networks: MTV Networks, including MTV: Music Television, MTV2, Nickelodeon, Nick at Nite, Noggin, The N, Nicktoons Network, VH1, TV Land, Spike TV, CMT: Country Music Television, Logo, Comedy Central, VIVA, TMF, Paramount Comedy; and BET.

DIGITAL MEDIA

Neopets, GameTrailers, IFILM, MTVi Group, Game One.

ENTERTAINMENT

Paramount Pictures, Paramount Home Entertainment, Republic Pictures Corporation, United International Pictures (50%), DreamWorks, MTV Films, Nickelodeon Movies and Famous Music.

VIVENDI UNIVERSAL, S.A.

FILM AND TELEVISION

Canal+ Group Includes: multiThématiques, CinéCinéma, Planète, Jimmy and Seasons, Sport+, CanalSatellite, Ma Planète, Extreme Sports Channel, NBA+, Pilotime, STUDIOCANAL

VIDEO GAMES

Blizzard Entertainment, Coktel, Fox Interactive, Knowledge Adventure, Massive Entertainment, Radical Entertainment, Sierra Entertainment

MUSIC

Universal Music Group, Island Def Jam Music Group, Interscope A&M Records, Geffen Records, DreamWorks Records, Lost Highway Records, MCA Nashville, Mercury Nashville, DreamWorks Nashville, Mercury Records, Polydor, Universal Motown Records Group, Decca, Deutsche Grammophon, Philips, Verve Music Group.

TELECOMMUNICATIONS

SFR Cegetel Group, Maroc Telecom.

WALT DISNEY COMPANY

PUBLISHING

Book Publishing Imprints: Miramax Books, ESPN Books, Theia, ABC Daytime Press, Hyperion Audiobooks, Hyperion East, Disney Publishing Worldwide, Cal Publishing Inc., CrossGen, Hyperion Books for Children, Jump at the Sun, Volo, Michael di Caupa Books, Disney Global Children's Books, Disney Press, Global Retail, Global Continuity. **Magazines:** *Automotive Industries, Biography (with GE and Hearst), Discover, Disney Adventures, Disney Magazine, ECN News, ESPN Magazine (distributed by Hearst), Family Fun, Institutional Investor, JCK, Kodin, Top Famille, US Weekly (50%), Video Business, Quality.*

RADIO STATIONS

Atlanta: WKHX, WYAY, WDWD. **Chicago:** WMVP, WLS, WZZN, WRDZ. **Dallas:** WBAP, KSCS, KMEO, KESN, KMKI. **Detroit:** WDRQ, WJR, WDVD. **Los Angeles:** KABC, KLOS, KDIS, KSPN. **Minneapolis-St. Paul:** KQRS, KXXR, KDIZ, WGVX, WGVY, WGVZ. **New York:** WABC, WPLJ, WQEW, WEVD. **San Francisco:** KGO, KSFO. **Sacramento:** KIID. **Oakland:** KMKY. **Washington DC:** WMAL, WJZW, WRQX. **Wichita:** KQAM. **Seattle:** KKDZ. **St. Louis:** WSDZ. **Cleveland:** WWMK. **Phoenix:** KMIX. **Denver:** KADZ, KDDZ. **Tampa:** WWMI. **Houston:** KMIC. **Miami:** WMYM. **Philadelphia:** WWJZ. **Boston:** WMKI. **Hartford:** WDZK. **Providence:** WDDZ. **Richmond, VA:** WDZY. **Charlotte:** WGFY. **Orlando:** WDYZ. **West Palm Beach:** WMNE. **Pittsburgh:** WEAE. **Louisville:** WDRD. **Albany, NY:** WPPY. **Kansas City, MO:** KPHN. **Mobile, AL:** WQUA. **Jacksonville:** WBML. **Flint:** WFDF. **Fremont, OH:** WFRO. **Damascus, MD:** WDMV. **Norfolk, VA:** WHKT.

Radio Disney, ESPN Radio (syndicated programming)

CABLE TELEVISION

ABC Family, The Disney Channel, Toon Disney, SoapNet, ESPN Inc. (80%—Hearst Corporation owns the remaining 20%) includes ESPN, ESPN2, ESPN News, ESPN Now, ESPN Extreme, Classic Sports Network, A&E Television (37.5%, with Hearst and GE), The History Channel (with Hearst and GE), Lifetime Television (50%, with Hearst), Lifetime Movie Network (50% with Hearst), E! Entertainment (with Comcast and Liberty Media), The Disney Channel UK, The Disney Channel Taiwan, The Disney Channel Australia, The Disney Channel Malaysia, The Disney Channel France, The Disney Channel Middle East, The Disney Channel Italy, The Disney Channel Spain, ESPN INC. International Ventures, Sportsvision of Australia (25%), ESPN Brazil (50%), ESPN STAR (50%)—sports programming throughout Asia, Net STAR (33%) owners of The Sports Network of Canada

OTHER INTERNATIONAL VENTURES

Tele-Munchen (German television production and distribution), RTL-2 (German television production and distribution), Hamster Productions

(French television production), TV Sport of France, Tesauro of Spain, Scandinavian Broadcasting System, Japan Sports Channel, Buena Vista Television, Touchstone Television, Walt Disney Television, Walt Disney Television Animation (has three wholly owned production facilities outside the United States—Japan, Australia, Canada)

TELEVISION

ABC Television Network, WLS (Chicago), WJRT (Flint), KFSN (Fresno), KTRK (Houston), KABC (Los Angeles), WABC (New York), WPVI (Philadelphia), WTVD (Raleigh–Durham), KGO (San Francisco), WTVG (Toledo).

MOVIE PRODUCTION AND DISTRIBUTION

Walt Disney Pictures, Touchstone Pictures, Hollywood Pictures, Caravan Pictures, Miramax Films, Buena Vista Home Video, Buena Vista Home Entertainment, Buena Vista International

FINANCIAL AND RETAIL

Financial: Sid R. Bass (partial interest—crude petroleum and natural gas production), **Retail:** The Disney Store.

MULTIMEDIA

ABC Internet Group, ABC.com, ABCNEWS.com, Oscar.com, Mr. Showbiz, Disney Online (web sites and content), Disney's Daily Blast, Disney.Com, Family.Com, ESPN Internet Group, ESPN.sportzone.com, Soccernet.com (60%), NBA.com, NASCAR.com, Skillgames, Wall of Sound, Go Network, Toysmart.com (majority stake—educational toys), Disney Interactive (develops/markets computer software, video games, CD-ROMs). **Music:** Buena Vista Music Group, Hollywood Records (popular music and soundtracks for motion pictures), Lyric Street Records (Nashville based country music label), Mammoth Records (popular and alternative music label), Walt Disney Records.

THEATER AND SPORTS

Theatrical Productions: Walt Disney Theatrical Productions (productions include stage version of The Lion King, Beauty and the Beast, King David), Professional Sports Franchises, Anaheim Sports, Inc., Mighty Ducks of Anaheim (National Hockey League).

OTHER

TiVo (partial investment).

THEME PARKS AND RESORTS

Disneyland (Anaheim, CA), Disney-MGM Studios, Disneyland Paris, Disney Regional Entertainment (entertainment and theme dining in metro areas), Disneyland Resort, Disney Vacation Club, Epcot, Magic Kingdom, Tokyo Disneyland (partial ownership), Walt Disney World (Orlando, FL), Disney's Animal Kingdom, Walt Disney World Sports Complex (golf course, auto racing track, and basball complex), Disney Cruise Line, The Disney Institute.

CBS CORPORATION

TELEVISION

Networks: CBS network, UPN television network, The Movie Channel, FLIX and Showtime Network. **CBS Stations:** Alexandria, MN: KCCA; Austin, TX: KEYE; Baltimore, MD: WJZ; Boston, MA: WBZ; Chicago, IL: WBBM; Dallas–Fort Worth, TX: KTVT; Denver, CO: KCNC, Detroit, MI: WWJ; Escanaba, MI: WJMN; Green Bay, WI: WFRV; Los Angeles, CA: KCBS; Miami-Ft. Lauderdale, FL: WFOR; Minneapolis, MN: WCCO; New York, NY: WCBS; Philadelphia, PA: KYW; Pittsburgh, PA: KDKA; Sacramento, CA: KOVR; Salt Lake City, UT: KUTV; San Francisco, CA: KPIX; St. George, UT: KUSG; and Walker, MN: KCCW. **UPN Stations:** Atlanta, GA: WUPA; Boston, MA: WSBK; Dallas, TX: KTXA; Detroit, MI: WKBD; Miami, FL: WBFS; New Orleans, LA: WUPL; Norfolk, VA: WGNT; Philadelphia, PA: WPSG; Pittsburgh, PA: WNPA; Providence, RI: WLWC; Sacramento, CA: KMAX; San Francisco, CA: KBHK; Seattle, WA: KSTW; Tampa, FL: WTOG; and West Palm Beach, FL: WTVX. **Others:** Los Angeles, CA: KCAL and West Palm Beach, FL: WWHB, WTCN. **Television Production and Distribution:** King World Productions, CBS Paramount International Television, Paramount Television and Spelling Television.

OUTDOOR

CBS displays advertising through Viacom Outdoor.

PUBLISHING

Simon & Schuster, Pocket Books, Scribner, Free Press, Aladdin Paperbacks, Simon Spotlight and Atheneum Books for Young Readers.

DIGITAL MEDIA

CBS.com, CBSNews.com, CBSSportsLine.com and UPN.com

RADIO

Infinity Broadcasting: Atlanta, GA: WAOK, WVEE, and WZGC; Austin, TX: KAMX, KJCE, KKMJ, and KXBT; Baltimore, MD: WJFK, WLIF, WQSR, WWMX, and WHFS; Boston, MA: WBCN, WBMX, WBZ, WODS, and WZLX; Buffalo, NY: WBLK, WBUF, WECK, WJYE, and WYRK; Charlotte, NC: WBAV, WFNZ, WNKS, WPEG, WSOC, WKQC and WFNA; Chicago, IL: WBBM, WCKG, WJMK, WSCR, WUSN, and WXRT; Cincinnati, OH: WAQZ, WGRR, WKRQ, and WUBE; Cleveland, OH: WDOK, WNCX, WQAL, and WXRK; Columbus, OH: WAZU, WHOK, and WLVQ; Dallas, TX: KLUV, KOAI, KRLD, KLLI, KJKK, and KVIL; Denver, CO: KWLI, KIMN, and KXKL; Detroit, MI: WKRK, WOMC, WVMV, WWJ, WXYT, and WYCD; Fresno, CA: KFJK, KEPT, KMGV, KMJ, KOQO, KSKS, and KWYE; Greensboro/Winston-Salem, NC: WMFR, WSJS, and WSML; Hartford, CT: WRCH, WTIC, and WZMX; Houston, TX: KIKK, KHJZ and KILT; Kansas City, MO: KBEQ, KFKF, KMXV, and KCKC; Las Vegas, NV: KLUC, KMXB, KKJJ, KSFN, KXNT, and KXTE; Los Angeles, CA: KCBS, KFWB, KLSX, KNX, KROQ, KRTH, and KTWV; Memphis,

TN: WMC and WMFS; Minneapolis–St. Paul, MN: WCCO, WLTE, and KZJK; New York, NY: WCBS, WFAN, WINS, WNEW, and WFNY; Orlando, FL: WJHM, WOCL, and WOMX; Palm Springs, CA: KEZN; Philadelphia, PA: KYW, WIP, WOGL, WPHT, and WYSP; Phoenix, AZ: KMLE, KOOL, and KZON; Pittsburgh, PA: KDKA, WRKZ, WDSY, and WZPT; Portland, OR: KINK, KCMD, KLTH, KUFO, KUPL, and KVMX; Riverside, CA: KRAK, KFRG, KVFG, and KXFG; Rochester, NY: WCMF, WPXY, WRMM, and WZNE; Sacramento, CA: KHTK, KNCI, KSFM, KQJK, KYMX, and KZZO; St. Louis, MO: KEZK, KMOX, and KYKY; San Antonio, TX: KTSA and KJXK; San Diego, CA: KSCF and KYXY; San Francisco ,CA: KIFR, KCBS, KFRC, KITS, KLLC, and KYCY; Seattle, WA: KBKS, KZOK, KMPS and, KJAQ; Tampa, FL: WLLD, WQYK, WRBQ, WSJT, and WYUU; Washington, DC: WARW, WJFK, WLZL and WPGC; and West Palm Beach, FL: WEAT, WIRK, WJBW, WMBX, and WPBZ.

THIS MODERN WORLD

by TOM TOMORROW

This week: it's time for another installment of...

It's Just That Simple:

Easy Answers for Your Troublesome Questions!

Q: Why was there an 18-hour delay before the press was informed that the Vice President had shot a man in the face?

A: Because Dick Cheney wanted the story to be as "accurate as possible!"

IF THERE'S ONE THING THE VICE PRESIDENT IS KNOWN FOR, IT IS HIS COMMITMENT TO *ACCURACY!*

THE LAST THING HE WOULD *EVER* WANT TO DO IS *MISLEAD* ANYONE!

It's just that simple!

Q: How did news of warrantless NSA spying hurt national security? Didn't al Qaeda already know their phones might be tapped?

A: Yes--but if the media weren't constantly reminding them about it, they might forget! It's just that simple!

WE ARE SO ABSENT-MINDED--SOMETIMES WE FORGET TO *EAT* FOR DAYS AT A TIME!

IT'S A GOOD THING *BREATHING* IS AN AUTONOMIC FUNCTION, OR ELSE WE'D BE IN *SERIOUS* TROUBLE!

It's just that simple!

Q: The administration was warned about the breached levee the night Hurricane Katrina hit New Orleans. So why was the government so sluggish in its response to the disaster?

A: It was all Brownie's fault!

WHEN PRESIDENT BUSH SAID "HECKUVA JOB, BROWNIE," HE WAS *OBVIOUSLY* BEING *SARCASTIC!*

LIBERALS HAVE *NO* SENSE OF IRONY!

It's just that simple!

Q: Do they really think we're stupid enough to believe these lame excuses--or do they just not care what we think?

A: Both!

HEH, HEH! IT'S *JUST THAT SIMPLE!*

NOW STOP ASKING SO MANY QUESTIONS--BEFORE SOMEBODY ELSE GETS MISTAKEN FOR A PEN-RAISED *GAME BIRD.*

IF YOU KNOW WHAT I MEAN.

TOM TOMORROW©2006... www.thismodernworld.com

CHAPTER 7

The Worst Media Manipulations—and How to Win Against Spin

By Bob Burton and Diane Farsetta, Center for Media and Democracy

The ideal of accurate, accountable, civic-minded news media has been under nearly constant attack of late. Fake news abounds, from Pentagon-planted stories in Iraqi newspapers to corporate- and government-funded video news releases aired by television newsrooms. Pundit after pundit has been outed for undisclosed conflicts of interest. At times, we at the Center for Media and Democracy have to work double-time just to keep up!

In this chapter, we summarize what we think are the most important—and most under-reported—deceptive public relations and propaganda trends of the last year. More importantly, we end with a quick "media self-defense" course, suggesting some concrete ways that you can unspin yourself and your community.

MILITARY PSYCHOLOGICAL OPERATIONS (PSYOP) FORCES CROSS BORDERS

In November 2005, the *Los Angeles Times* revealed that a small, Washington D.C.-based public relations firm was working with the U.S. military to plant propaganda in Iraqi newspapers. At least dozens of stories written by U.S. information operations troops were translated into Arabic and placed in Baghdad newspapers by the Lincoln Group, without any disclosure to readers of the military's involvement. Headlines included "More Money Goes to Iraq's Development" and "Iraqis Insist on Living Despite Terrorism."

"Though the articles are basically factual, they present only one side of events and omit information that might reflect poorly on the U.S. or Iraqi governments," wrote *Los Angeles Times* reporters Mark Mazzetti and Borzou Daragahi. "The arrangement with Lincoln Group is evidence of how far the Pentagon has moved to blur the traditional boundaries between military public affairs—the dissemination of factual information to the media—and psychological and information operations, which use propaganda and sometimes misleading information to advance the objectives of a military campaign."

Indeed, the U.S. government's blurring of propaganda and news could reasonably be considered *the* major underreported story of recent times. While some examples have attracted much-needed scrutiny, the Pentagon's expansion and outsourcing of psychological operations (PSYOP) activities to private firms remains mostly unexamined. The same is true of Defense Department claims that PSYOP and propaganda originally targeted to foreign audiences can reach U.S. domestic audiences legally, as long as domestic consumption was not the government's intent.

For example, U.S. news media overwhelmingly failed to cover the most important issues related to the Lincoln Group's Iraq work. The original revelations about the program were widely reported. A Nexis news database search pulls up nearly 280 stories mentioning both "Lincoln Group" and "Iraq" in the month following the *Los Angeles Times* piece. These reports led nearly three-quarters of Americans to call the program "inappropriate," and two-thirds to be bothered a "fair amount" or "great deal" by it, according to a December 2005 *USA Today* / CNN / Gallup poll. In response to the uproar, the Pentagon promised to investigate and determine the propriety of the Lincoln Group's activities.

A few months later, the top U.S. general in Iraq said such activities would continue, calling them "within our authorities and responsibilities." Also in March 2006, the *New York Times* reported that the Pentagon's investigation had been completed, but not made public. The Pentagon found that "the Lincoln Group committed no legal violations because its actions . . . were not expressly prohibited by its contract or military rules," according to the *New York Times*. In the month following these developments, just fifty-five news stories mentioned both "Lincoln Group" and "Iraq," and many of them failed to mention the green light given the controversial propaganda program. In May 2006, "Several Pentagon officials said the Lincoln Group and other contractors were still involved in placing propaganda messages in Iraqi publications and on television," reported the *New York Times*.

The Lincoln Group is also part of an unprecedented outsourcing of U.S. PSYOP. In mid-2005, the Defense Department awarded five-year contracts worth up to $300 million total to Lincoln and two other firms, SAIC and SYColeman. Officials said the private firms would "inject more creativity" into Pentagon operations and help introduce "cutting-edge types of media," the *Washington Post* reported. Herb Friedman, a retired Army officer, PSYOP instructor and researcher, saw another reason for the move. "The bottom line is, they don't have the manpower," he told the *Media General News Service*, saying that the U.S. military maintains one active duty and two reserve PSYOP units.

If that's accurate, the low level of military personnel devoted to PSYOP is surprising. The goal of a recent, extensive Defense Department planning process, as described in an October 2003 report, was to advance "information operations as a core military competency." That report, titled "Information Operations Roadmap," calls PSYOP "an increasingly powerful means of deterring aggression." PSYOP, it states, can undermine "both senior leadership and popular support for employing terrorists or using weapons of mass destruction." The report was obtained by the nonprofit National Security Archive via a Freedom of Information Act request and made public in January 2006.

In addition to prioritizing PSYOP, the Pentagon report seems to dismiss laws protecting U.S. audiences from being subjected to propaganda campaigns funded with their own tax dollars. "The increasing ability of people in most parts of the globe to access international information sources makes targeting particular audiences more difficult," it notes, adding that "information intended for foreign audiences, including public diplomacy and PSYOP, increasingly is being consumed by our domestic audience and vice-versa."

However, instead of addressing how longstanding restrictions on domestic consumption of government propaganda could be adapted to modern realities, the Pentagon report claims it's not the *exposure* to propaganda that matters—it's whether the government *means* to expose U.S. residents to propaganda. "Today the distinction between foreign and domestic audiences becomes more a question of USG [U.S. Government] intent rather than information dissemination practices," it concludes.

In a similar vein, the Pentagon's inspector general ruled in December 2005 that "U.S. military websites that pay journalists to write articles and commentary supporting military activities in Europe and Africa do not violate U.S. law or Pentagon policies." The two known U.S. military sponsored "news" websites are targeted to audiences in Northern Africa and Southeastern Europe. The sites have sparked concerns because they are so easy to access from the United States, the articles are posted in English and languages widely used in the target regions, and their U.S. military sponsorship is nearly hidden from the public .

Apparently, the U.S. military deems such concerns inconsequential. The Pentagon plans to increase its Internet-based propaganda, with the U.S. Pacific Command in Asia and Central Command in the Middle East developing their own "regional information websites." Unlike the Homeland Security or Justice Departments, the Defense Department believes it lives in a world without borders, where anyone's news is fair game.

PROPAGANDA: NOT JUST FOR FOREIGN AUDIENCES ANYMORE

The long arm of the U.S. government reaches directly into domestic newsrooms, as well.

Over the past few years, the names Karen Ryan, Armstrong Williams and Jeff Gannon have become infamous—at least, in media analyst and activist circles. Ryan is the reporter-turned-flack who produced fake TV news segments called video news releases (VNRs) for the Health and Human Services and Education Departments. Williams is the conservative pundit who was secretly paid by the Education Department to promote the No Child Left Behind law. And Gannon is a partisan activist whose questionably obtained media credentials gave him access to the White House press briefing room for two years, where he routinely praised the Bush administration and asked softball questions.

As it turns out, Ryan, Williams and Gannon were just the tip of the iceberg. As has happened with military PSYOP and international propaganda, the Bush administration has boosted its spending on domestic media programs, increasingly hired private firms to carry out such activities, and eroded the legal and ethical restrictions on the government's influence of domestic media.

In February 2006, the nonpartisan research arm of the U.S. Congress, the Government Accountability Office (GAO), released the most detailed account to date of government media contracts with private firms. Although the GAO looked at only seven federal departments, its report listed contracts with PR firms, advertising agencies, media companies and individual reporters that totaled a whopping $1.6 billion over thirty months (October 2002 through the end of March 2005).

At 160 pages, the GAO report is a treasure trove of information. Unfortunately, it has received little attention. The Nexis news database lists just eighteen mentions of the report in the month following its release. Worse, those articles contained only brief mentions of a few contracts, mostly taken from a press release put out by the members of Congress who requested the report. Moreover, the contracts mentioned by reporters tended towards the whimsical, such as an Air Force-sponsored bowling tournament and Coca-Cola branded "victory T-shirts." More newsworthy examples—such as Food and Drug Administration efforts "to inform Americans about the consequences and potential dangers of buying prescription drugs from non-U.S. sources," or a multi-million dollar contract "for message development that presents the Army's strategic perspective in the Global War on Terrorism"—went unreported, even by alternative media (except for the Center for Media and Democracy's *PR Watch*).

To be fair, much of the federal government's media work is beneficial, alerting citizens to health threats or informing them about major policies. However, the rapid growth in government media spending raises significant questions. In January 2005, the U.S. House Committee on Government Reform minority office released its own study of government PR. Based on procurement records of federal contracts with major PR firms, the House report found that PR spending had doubled, comparing the second term of the Clinton administration with the first term of the George W. Bush administration.

The House Committee's figures are even more disturbing when considered in tandem with those in the GAO report. PR spending didn't just increase because the new boss prioritizes it more than the old one; it keeps on growing, every year. From 1997 through the end of 2000, government PR contracts averaged $32 million per year. From 2001 through 2004, PR spending averaged $62.5 million annually. And from October 2002 through March 2005, an average of $78.8 million went to private PR firms per year—from just seven federal departments.

The rush to outsource government media work is so great that the U.S. General Services Administration (GSA), which acquires products and services on behalf of federal agencies, started "actively soliciting proposals from PR firms to be added to its list of pre-qualified contractors" in early 2006, according to the trade publication *O'Dwyer's PR Daily*. The GSA explained its move by saying there is the "potential for tremendous sales growth" in government purchases of PR and marketing services. One month later, an agency within the Department of Health and Human Services went a step further, asking PR firms for proposals on how they would replace the agency's communications office.

The U.S. government's growing media obsession isn't only expressed through outsourcing. In February 2005, *Newsday* reported that PR positions within federal agencies, usually called public affairs staff, had grown by 9 percent since 2000. That growth rate was "even faster than the federal work force" overall, and represented a cost increase of more than $50 million. The Pentagon "added the greatest number of PR officials," while the Social Security Administration and State, Agriculture and Interior Departments also boosted public affairs staff levels.

And it's not just the federal purse strings that have loosened; the rules of media engagement are also being bent. Over the past few years, the GAO has ruled repeatedly that government VNRs—fake TV news segments produced by or for federal agencies and aired by many TV stations—are illegal covert propaganda unless they make their source clear to viewers. Karen Ryan's VNRs touting the new Medicare drug benefit were the first to trigger the GAO's condemnation. As others followed, the Bush administration took decisive action—by discrediting and ignoring the GAO.

The Justice Department and the Office of Management and Budget (OMB) claimed that disclosure was irrelevant. Unsourced government VNRs are fine, they said, as long as the segments are "informational" and not "persuasional." The administration failed to define those broad terms, though, and did not examine whether the VNRs criticized by the GAO met the "informational" test. What the administration did do, clearly and frequently, was to stress was that their interpretation of the law superseded the GAO's rulings.

The Bush administration's disregard of historical precedent and the GAO extends beyond VNRs. In September 2005, the GAO released a strong report on the Education Department's contract with the PR firm Ketchum. Several aspects of that contract constituted illegal "covert propaganda" or "purely partisan activities," including Karen Ryan's VNRs and Armstrong Williams' commentaries, according to the GAO. Other improprieties included an article on science literacy that ran in "numerous small newspapers and circulars throughout the country," with no disclosure of "the Department's involvement in its writing," and a media analysis which, among other messages, looked to see if news reports presented "the Bush administration / the GOP" as "committed to education." The report was ignored by the administration, as well as by reporters.

Today, the question is not whether the U.S. government is propagandizing its citizens, but how often—and how citizens can fight back.

IT'S A PRO-NUKE WORLD, AFTER ALL

Of course, not all questionable public relations comes from governments or happens in the United States. In many ways, governments are "late adopters," employing media-manipulating techniques pioneered by industry years earlier. One multinational enterprise that has relied heavily on PR is the nuclear power industry.

With its high start-up and liability costs, uneven safety record, generation of radioactive waste, vulnerability to terrorist attack, and historical link to the spread of nuclear weapons, nuclear power should be—by any stretch of the rational mind—a nearly impossible sell job. Yet, governments around the world have increasingly parroted industry talking points in recent years, saying that nuclear power is needed to meet rapidly rising energy demands while reducing greenhouse gas emissions.

There are reasons for the broad reach and strong sway of nuclear power PR, according to the Australian newspaper *The Age*. There is "a persistent, wellfunded [sic] and carefully planned international public relations strategy, selling nuclear power as a 'clean, green and safe' solution to global warming," wrote reporter Liz Minchin.

Environmental consultant Alan Tate told Minchin that part of the nuclear power industry's campaign is outreach at international climate change summits. "At the Buenos Aires negotiations in 1998, it became obvious that the nuclear industry was present for the first time, en masse, and possibly more than any other industry at that conference was lobbying fiercely," he said. "They inundated the international negotiators, including with what appeared to be a number of front groups like Students for Nuclear Power." While that push was "fairly unsophisticated," Tate characterized later industry efforts as "more polished" and more effective.

One sign of the renewed push was a March 2005 international conference on nuclear power in the twenty-first century. At that meeting, International Atomic Energy Agency chief Mohamed ElBaradei "pointed to nuclear energy policy plans in China, Finland, the United States and possibly Poland as proof that nuclear power may be returning to vogue," reported *Reuters*. "Fast growing energy demands, security of energy supply, and the risk of climate change are driving a reconsideration, in some quarters, a need for greater investment in nuclear power," ElBaradei stated.

In June 2005, *Reuters* reported that a draft communiqué for the Group of Eight (G8) summit in Scotland had, compared to previous versions, "removed plans to fund research" on clean energy technologies. The draft also "explicitly endorse[d] the use of 'zero-carbon' nuclear power." The final documents expressed support for the "continued development and commercialization of renewable energy," but didn't mention solar or wind power. The summit's "Climate Change Plan of Action" included nuclear energy, but encouraged G8 members using nuclear power "to develop more advanced technologies that would be safer, more reliable and more resistant to diversion and proliferation."

In Britain, the nuclear industry waged a massive PR effort around the May 2005 general election. In the year leading up to the election the nuclear industry ratcheted up its PR and lobbying, according to *The New Statesman*. One company alone, British Energy, hired Monsanto's former head lobbyist and the former national energy minister, and signed a million pound contract with the PR firm Financial Dynamics.

Shortly after the British election, the government's Director-General of Energy Policy asked incoming ministers to raise the possibility of new nuclear plants, as "it is generally easier to push ahead on controversial issues early in a new parliament." In January 2006,

Prime Minister Tony Blair launched a national energy review that was accompanied by even more industry lobbying—some of it supported by public funds. The review was widely criticized as window dressing for predetermined plans to expand nuclear power. Before the resulting report could even be tabled in mid-2006, Blair announced that nuclear power was back on the drawing board.

Nuclear power has also made major gains in the United States. In early 2005, President Bush's State of the Union address touted nuclear power, while Senate Energy Committee Chair Pete Domenici published a book titled, *A Brighter Tomorrow: Fulfilling the Promise of Nuclear Energy.*

The major U.S. industry group, the Nuclear Energy Institute (NEI), saw years of heavy lobbying pay off when the federal energy bill passed in August 2005 contained up to $13 billion in federal subsidies for nuclear power. In April 2006, NEI hired the former majority staff director of the U.S. Senate Energy and Natural Resources Committee as its new head lobbyist. For PR help, NEI turned to the Hill & Knowlton firm, which launched pro-nuclear ad campaigns and formed an industry-funded front group, the "Clean and Safe Energy Coalition." The group's paid spokespeople are former Environmental Protection Agency head Christine Todd Whitman and Greenpeace co-founder Patrick Moore. Moore's PR firm has a history of working for logging, biotechnology and mining companies, among others desperately seeking green credentials.

The world's energy future certainly looks bleak for environmentalists, public health advocates and others critical of nuclear power. But perhaps the lesson to be learned from the industry's striking international resurgence is that lots of money and persistence can overcome bleak odds, leading to credibility, support—even popularity—not to mention more money.

BIG OIL'S BATTLE TANKS

Where the nuclear industry relies on former environmentalists and regulators for its greenwashing, the major oil company Exxon Mobil sends in think tanks to deliver its message on climate change.

As with many other corporate campaigns to shape public opinion, Exxon's approach relies on the third-party technique; having a seem-

276 | CENSORED 2007

ingly independent individual or group articulate messages that would seem self-interested and not credible if the company were the direct source. Think tanks are, in many ways, the ideal third party. They combine impressive names and scholarly credentials with aggressive media outreach and, often, a willingness to obscure funding sources and funders' impact on their stances.

Based on a trawl through the Nexis news database of 2004 articles, the media watchdog group Fairness and Accuracy in Reporting (FAIR) calculated that think tanks classified as "conservative" or "center-right" received over 15,000 media citations, representing 50 percent of all think tank references in U.S. news. The inclusion of "centrist" groups brought that total up to 83 percent. FAIR defined think tanks that promote changes favored by right-wing groups as "conservative", and think tanks that support the status quo as "centrist". (At the time of writing, FAIR's data for 2005 was not yet available.)

The top ten U.S. think tanks scored over 1,000 mentions each, with the top five accounting for just over half of the total. In the big league are the American Enterprise Institute (AEI, classified as conservative), Brookings Institution (centrist) and Heritage Foundation (conservative), with the Competitive Enterprise Institute and Frontiers of Freedom Institute making a respectable showing.

Over the last decade, there have been numerous exposés of think tanks operating as corporate shills. One example is Citizens for a Sound Economy, which mounted a $700,000 campaign in 1998 opposing a restoration plan for the Florida Everglades. The campaign was covertly funded by three sugar companies that faced the loss of thousands of acres of sugar cane farms.

The Society of Professional Journalists' ethics code also states, "The public is entitled to as much information as possible on sources' reliability." In other words, there's a good reason for the old journalistic mantra, "Follow the money." But when think tanks cover for their corporate benefactors' controversial activities, do mainstream journalists unmask the funding that provides at least the appearance of a conflict of interest?

In Exxon Mobil's case, the oil behemoth almost makes such debunking easy. It voluntarily discloses on its own website who they fund, at what level, and for what programs. But even if journalists miss the PDF file tucked in the back reaches of Exxon's website, most of the same data is more readily available on ExxonSecrets.org, a website from the environmental group Greenpeace.

In 2004, the most recent year for which funding data is available, Exxon contributed $270,000 to the Competitive Enterprise Institute (CEI). Two-thirds of the funding was earmarked for "climate change outreach" and related work, with the remainder going to general support. The Frontiers of Freedom Institute (FoF) received $250,000 for climate change-related work, while Exxon gave the American Enterprise Institute (AEI) $225,000 in general support.

Exxon cut big checks for some relatively little-known groups, too. The New York-based Congress on Racial Equality (CORE) received $135,000 of Exxon shareholders funds, while the Center for the Defense of Free Enterprise (CDFE), based in Washington state, got $130,000.

With more than $1 million of Exxon's readily traceable largesse dispatched to just five think tanks for climate change advocacy, the task of reporting on corporate influence on a major global environmental issue is about as easy as it gets. So how well was the public served by the fourth estate?

Of U.S. news stories from 2004, 305 items mentioned CEI; seventy of those also included a reference to climate change. Yet only one news report mentioned CEI's Exxon funding, and that was a story on the think tank's attack on Morgan Spurlock's film *Super Size Me*, which warned of the health dangers of fast food.

The National Commission on Energy Policy could testify to the importance of disclosing think tanks' funding sources. When this group of corporate executives, academics and union officials called for limits on greenhouse gas emissions, increased auto efficiency standards and more subsidies for nuclear power, CEI smeared them. "The self-appointed, self-styled National Commission on Energy Policy is a lobby for special interests and big government masquerading as an official-sounding panel of unbiased experts," thundered CEI's Myron Ebell. Instead of ferreting out the corporate interests at play, the *Atlanta Journal Constitution* quaintly described Ebell in a December 9, 2004 piece as being from a "pro-business non-profit group."

Unfortunately, Frontiers of Freedom did not receive greater scrutiny. FoF scored 134 media mentions in 2004, fifteen of which referred to climate change. While they may have delivered less bang for Exxon's bucks, they too avoided disclosure. "The whole idea that global warming causes extinctions is really quite nonsensical," Robert Ferguson, the executive director of FoF's Center for Science and Public Policy, told Associated Press. FoF was referred to in the AP story only as a think tank created by former Republican Senator from Wyoming, Malcolm Wallop.

FoF's Center for Science and Public Policy (CSPP) was established in 2002 to alert "policy makers, the media, and the public to unreliable scientific claims and unjustified alarmism which often lead to public harm." While FoF doesn't disclose who funds CSPP, Exxon does. In 2002 the oil company gave FoF a $100,000 grant to launch CSPP and in 2004 they contributed another $70,000. But Associated Press left this vital information out of their reporting.

The same sad pattern held true for the American Enterprise Institute. Of the fifteen stories mentioning AEI and climate change, just two cited Exxon. One of those was a false positive, in which a Greenpeace spokesperson mentioned Exxon, but no reference was made to Exxon's funding of the think tank. The other media hit was a letter in the *Washington Post* from Democratic Senator Frank Lautenberg, who complained that an earlier article failed to disclose the Exxon-AEI conflict of interest.

Among the worst omissions of Exxon-AEI ties was a July 2004 *Christian Science Monitor* story on five state Attorneys-General suing electric utilities for their emissions of carbon dioxide, a factor in climate change. The story quoted AEI's Michael Greve, identifying him as "an environmental expert." Not surprisingly, Greve poured scorn on the lawsuit, saying, "It's easier to gloat about being an environmental steward if the costs are being paid by someone in a different state."

Two other Exxon Mobil grantees received little media attention. CORE, the civil rights group turned rabid anti-environmental outfit, had no climate change-related news hits. And Ron Arnold's Center for the Defense of Free Enterprise didn't get into mainstream newspapers at all in 2004.

The groups mentioned above account for less than one-sixth of the $6.4 million Exxon Mobil gave to dozens of think tanks and groups in 2004, for "public information and policy research." But it's important to note that Exxon's voluntary disclosure doesn't include all of the funding it provides to non-profit groups.

In 2003, a shadowy group by the name of Public Interest Watch (PIW) emerged. Early on, PIW lobbied the U.S. Internal Revenue

Service (IRS) to undertake a tax audit of Greenpeace. Two years later, the IRS launched a three-month long audit.

In March 2006, Greenpeace was informed that it had retained its tax-exempt status. That same month, an insider blew the whistle on PIW's connections to Exxon. From August 2003 to July 2004, Exxon provided PIW with $120,000 of the group's $124,094 in total income. Yet Exxon's public lists of contributions for 2003 and 2004 don't mention Public Interest Watch.

Part of the reason why think tanks so often receive a blank credibility check from journalists is that they're highly trained media manipulators. For example, the Heritage Foundation—whose budget, at $40 million, is larger than the combined funding of the largest "progressive" think tanks—actively builds close relationships with reporters and editors.

For reporters hunting for story leads, Heritage offers an e-mail bulletin on the "hottest topics," complete with contact details of their approved experts. They also feature a "fully equipped Heritage studio" for live broadcasts from Capitol Hill. According to the think tank's annual report, Sean Hannity was just one of twenty-six radio hosts to use their studios in 2005.

Heritage also provides training to reporters. The think tank's Mark Tapscott leads workshops on "computer-assisted research and reporting" (CARR) that have trained 219 editors, reporters and bloggers "from media outlets such as the Associated Press and *Los Angeles Times.*" Heritage says it even "partners with journalists" on CARR work, becoming involved in reporting on "healthcare, homeland security, defense, Social Security and federal spending issues," it reported in 2004.

Heritage even offers to "build computer models for specific news projects, as we did for Cox Newspapers' Washington Bureau." Indeed, its training program has been so successful that in 2005 Heritage started communications skills training programs for Capitol Hill press secretaries, to help them "excel at their jobs."

DON'T DESPAIR—RECLAIM THE MEDIA!

The techniques described above—military PSYOP, government propaganda, high-powered corporate campaigns, and third-party smoke-screens—are powerful manipulators of war and peace, public health, education, public safety, and environmental reporting. When misleading news is filed on such important issues, our democracy is seriously compromised.

What would real disclosure and public interest reporting look like, and how do we get there from here?

Inform yourself. Project Censored is a great resource. For more on the issues in this chapter, see the Center for Media and Democracy's website, www.prwatch.org. CMD also runs SourceWatch, a collaborative online wiki encyclopedia of the people, issues and groups shaping the public agenda, at www.sourcewatch.org. SourceWatch contains detailed profiles of think tanks, PR firms, pundits, lobbyists and more—it's a great media debunking resource. And if you have information to add, you can do so with a few clicks!

Talk back to your media. If your newspaper is referring to corporate-funded think tank fellows as impartial analysts, write a letter to the editor to set them straight. If radio stations are running gung-ho stories about nuclear energy, call them to demand more accurate and balanced coverage. Call your local television stations to ask what their disclosure policy is for VNRs—and how they make sure that policy is observed.

Demand policy solutions, when appropriate. When the controversy around government VNRs was getting lots of media attention, members of Congress pledged to take action. As of this writing, though, no measure requiring on-screen disclosure of government VNRs has been passed. Another very powerful policy reform would be for the IRS to require corporate contributions to non-profit groups to be listed in groups' annual reports to the IRS. (These reports are currently available, via online services like Guidestar, but disclosure of corporate funding is optional.) Call your members of Congress and let them know these issues are important to you!

Support—and become part of—independent media projects. Is there a community radio station, open access TV station, independent weekly paper, or local news blog in your area? If so, why not become the media? Independent local media provide great educational and organizing opportunities, and reporting the news will help you become an even savvier media consumer. You can keep yourself informed on national and international issues by subscribing to quality independent publications.

Spread the message that reclaiming our democracy requires us to reclaim the media. Whichever issue is most important to you, the quality of media coverage determines what others know, don't know, or think they know about it. Bring media literacy and media advocacy ideas into the various groups that you're part of, whether they're focused on human rights, women's rights, the environment, economic or racial injustice, or other issues.

The good news is that more and more people are realizing the importance of media democracy. Together, citizen journalists and media activists can clean up the pollution of our media environment—maybe not as fast as a White House reporter can run to the Heritage Foundation's studio—but the truth will prevail.

Bob Bob Burton is the editor of *SourceWatch* and Diane Farsetta is a senior researcher at the Center for Media Democracy.

THIS MODERN WORLD

by TOM TOMORROW

HOW THE NEWS WORKS NOW

ANOTHER CARTOON SEQUEL YEARS IN THE MAKING

STEP ONE: TRYING TO BUILD A CASE FOR WAR, ADMINISTRATION "LEAKS" STRATEGIC MISINFORMATION TO COOPERATIVE REPORTER.

SADDAM IS BUILDING A **GIANT SPACE LASER** ON THE **MOON**-- AND IT'S AIMED **RIGHT AT US!**

THIS IS OFF THE RECORD, OF COURSE! JUST ATTRIBUTE THE STORY TO AN ANONYMOUS--UM--**CARBON-BASED LIFE FORM!**

ANYTHING YOU **SAY!**

STEP TWO: REPORTER IS GIVEN INEXPLICABLE LATITUDE AT BUREAUCRATICALLY DYSFUNCTIONAL NEWSPAPER.

CHIEF, I JUST GOT A **REAL SCOOP**--

SAY NO MORE! JUST WRITE IT UP AND SEND IT **STRAIGHT** TO THE **COPY DESK!** I'LL READ **TOMORROW**-- ON THE **FRONT PAGE!**

ABOVE THE FOLD?

DUH!

STEP THREE: STORY IS PUBLISHED, GIVING ADMINISTRATION PROPAGANDA A VENEER OF LEGITIMACY.

The New York Times

SADDAM BUILDING LASER CANNON ON MOON

Aimed at Us, Says Anonymous Carbon-Based Life Form

STEP FOUR: ADMINISTRATION TREATS PUBLICATION OF ITS OWN LIES AS PROOF OF THEIR VERACITY.

I DIDN'T **REALIZE** SADDAM WAS SO TECHNOLOGICALLY **ADVANCED!**

WELL--YOU DON'T HAVE TO TAKE **MY** WORD FOR IT! IT'S RIGHT HERE IN **BLACK AND WHITE!**

BONUS STEP: SUBSEQUENT "LEAKS" TURN REPORTER INTO FIRST AMENDMENT MARTYR.

THE ADMINISTRATION'S RIGHT TO **ANONYMOUSLY DECEIVE THE PUBLIC**--

--MUST BE DEFENDED AT **ANY COST!**

IT'S A MATTER OF **JOURNALISTIC INTEGRITY!**

NEXT: ON THE OTHER HAND, WHAT'S A LITTLE TESTIMONY BETWEEN **FRIENDS?**

TOM TOMORROW©2005... www.thismodernworld.com

CHAPTER 8

Fear & Favor 2005
FAIR's Sixth Annual Report

OUTSIDE (AND INSIDE) INFLUENCE ON THE NEWS

By Julie Hollar, Janine Jackson and Hilary Goldstein

In 1896, *New York Times* publisher Adolph Ochs laid out standards by which journalism is still judged today, declaring that his paper would "give the news, all the news . . . impartially, without fear or favor, regardless of party, sect or interest involved."

Unfortunately, mainstream media often fail to live up to that goal; demands from advertisers, government, media owners and other powerful people frequently manage to blur or breach the wall between the editorial and business ends of the newsroom. In survey after survey, journalists report that they feel outside—or inside—pressures to avoid, slant or promote certain stories that might affect those powerful interests. Each year, FAIR compiles a list of some of the most striking examples of such influence. It is by no means comprehensive, but we hope that it sheds some light on those pressures facing journalists and encourages both them and the public to continue to expose threats to independent reporting.

In Advertisers We Trust

Most people are aware that news media rely on corporate advertising dollars—though the fact is rarely discussed, and when it is, editors and producers will generally insist that there's no connection between the companies that buy ads and the content of the news. Each year, however, the line between news and advertising blurs further. Last year the *Fairbanks Daily News-Miner* gave notice to its staff that it was about to hire an "advertorial editor," to be paid half by the newsroom and half by the advertising department (CJR, 9–10/05). While most breaches of the editorial wall are less blatant, they're no less worrying.

The essential conflict of commercial news media was on full display when giant advertisers BP, the oil company, and Morgan Stanley, the financial services company, both issued directives demanding that their ads be pulled from any edition of a publication that included potentially "objectionable" content. BP went so far as to demand advance notice of any stories that mention the company, a competitor of the company or the oil and energy industry in general (AdAge.com, 5/24/05).

While these demands may seem like an egregious intervention into the editorial process, the truth is, as one anonymous editor told *Advertising Age* (5/16/05), there's "a fairly lengthy list of companies that have instructions like this." Another magazine executive, also afraid to talk on the record, told AdAge.com (5/24/05) that "magazines are not in the financial position today to buck rules from advertisers." An *Advertising Age* reporter (5/16/05) who contacted executives at places like *USA Today, Business Week*, the *New York Times* and *Fortune* found them all unwilling to explain how such advertiser demands were handled.

And of course advertisers do not only focus on the news they *don't* want to be associated with. The October 31 issue of *Time Magazine* featured a section labeled "The Future of Energy" about the need to pursue alternatives to oil and to make oil production more efficient. Throughout the feature were full-page ads for BP with taglines like "investing in our energy future" explaining how the company is pursuing alternatives to oil. BP is also mentioned by a source in *Time's* feature article as one of the more innovative energy companies. That, presumably, was free.

U.S. News & World Report featured a similar advertiser-friendly layout in a health column (12/5/05) about Alzheimer's disease, which was interspliced with two full-page ads that seemed more than coincidentally related. One ad was for an Alzheimer's treatment drug called Aricept, and the other was for the MetLife insurance company, touting their foundation's contributions to research on Alzheimer's. "Young Brains, Beware," the magazine's headline read, while the MetLife ad declared, "You'd be surprised how early the effects of Alzheimer's can set in."

Time and *U.S. News* apparently think going to such lengths to serve corporate sponsors is good business. But it's clearly not good business for readers if advertisers are constructing stories that showcase their products.

At least one outlet is shamelessly selling access to its editorial staff to advertisers. When the *Wisconsin State Journal* launched its new *Capital Region Business Journal*, it announced that advertisers who forked over $25,000 would get not only spots in each issue of the *Business Journal* and on its website, but a place on the publication's advisory panel—including at least six meetings a year with top editors of the *State Journal*, which shares staff with the business publication.

State Journal publisher Jim Hopson (*Madison Capital Times*, 3/17/05) claimed that advertisers weren't buying access:

The sponsors who are sitting on our advisory panel are actually doing us a favor. . . . I'm grateful we're getting good sound advice to help make certain we're covering the topics and issues that are important to the business community. If anyone wants access to the *State Journal*, they are welcome to call.

Whether the *State Journal* will consider your advice just as good and sound without $25,000 to back it up, though, was not addressed.

When it comes to blurring the line between the editorial and advertising departments, morning news shows have long been the vanguard. Now some Gannett-owned stations are simply erasing the line, airing so-called "magazine" morning programs on which the majority of guests pay to be on the air—in other words, infomercials.

In Minnesota, Gannett's KARE, an NBC affiliate, announced plans to transform its Today talk show into Showcase Minnesota, on which some segments will be sold to advertisers at the rate of $2,500 for five minutes. The new show will be shifted from the local programming department to the advertising department. KARE's general manager claims the paid segments will be clearly labeled (*Minneapolis Star Tribune*, 11/23/05). In Sacramento, the executive producer of the similar show Sacramento & Co. told the *Sacramento Bee*, (8/17/05): "Our vision for the show is very clear. This is not a news program."

Viewers may not get such a clear vision for these shows, however. It's no secret that advertisers increasingly favor such "advertorial" type programs—with hosts who look like journalists on sets that look like newsrooms—precisely *because* viewers give them more credence than they do late-night spiels about steak knives. The fact that the Sacramento station, Sacramento News10, won't release the names of the companies that have ponied up to be featured on the show isn't much testament to their transparency.

And as for the news value of the paid programming, former Today host Pat Evans—a news department employee—was sanguine, calling the new format "a vehicle for the community to have a voice." That's the "community" that can afford to pay $500 a minute, of course.

Even though public television was created precisely to give citizens media free from corporate pressures, it's not immune to advertisers' demands. Public television plugs for "sponsors" are often indistinguishable from ads on corporate television stations, but at Connecticut Public Television, currying favor with advertisers has gone a giant step further. When producers for CPTV interviewed doctors at Hartford Hospital for a series on women's health, Connecticut Public Broadcasting president and CEO Jerry Franklin demanded they redo the segment at St. Francis Hospital—a major financial sponsor of the series—instead. He told the *Hartford Courant* (8/19/05) that the absence of St. Francis made the segment unbalanced and unfair to the underwriter. And it's not an isolated incident; Franklin has been reaching out to nonprofit funders to "co-produce" CPTV programming for the five years he's been in charge. At least three producers have quit projects at CPTV because of Franklin's pressures (*Hartford Courant,* 8/8/05).

PBS prohibits sponsorships "when there exists a clear and direct connection between the interests or products or services of a proposed funder and the subject matter of the program." Franklin told the *Courant* (8/8/05) that those standards only apply to nationally distributed programming, and that his policy is acceptable because he only partners with nonprofit organizations. Credibility with viewers, apparently, doesn't figure into Franklin's equation.

The Boss's Business

Media companies are so entangled with each other nowadays, it can be hard to keep track of who owns what. But sometimes a media outlet's editorial stance gives you pretty direct clues to that outlet's owners, and their interests. Such was the case with an editorial in the *Dallas Morning News* (2/6/05) weighing in on the current FCC debate about "must carry" rules, which require cable companies to continue to carry local channels as they convert to digital technology.

The *Morning News* argued strongly that "must-carry" rules be maintained. Its editorial spoke urgently of local programming as the "bulwark of a democratic society," the sort of programming that "connects viewers to their community." Nowhere did the paper note, however, that it has another, less high-minded interest in the matter: *The Dallas Morning News* is owned by Belo Corporation, a media company that owns 19 local television stations and is lobbying the FCC in support of "must-carry" rules, which would greatly increase its market power. According to the *Washington Post's* Howard Kurtz (2/14/05), the editorial page editor at the *Morning News* said she regretted the omission, which she blamed on a busy schedule and staff shortages.

Examples of "synergy," the cross-promotion of shows from the same corporate owner, are almost too numerous to count on television these days. Morning shows tend to be the worst offenders: ABC's *Good Morning America* regularly featured interviews and segments devoted to ABC's primetime hit *Desperate Housewives* last year, while CBS's Early Show welcomed cast members booted from that network's popular reality show Survivor. But the practice is even becoming *de rigueur* on what have traditionally been considered "serious" shows—as when ABC's John Stossel hosted a broadcast of *20/20* from the set of *Desperate Housewives*, reporting on "real–life versions of topics covered on the show" (*Variety*, 3/18/05), not long after *Primetime Live* featured (2/3/05) a lengthy interview with the show's star, Teri Hatcher.

Last year, when NBC's Dateline was taking heat for devoting hours of airtime to the finales of Friends and other NBC shows, Jeff Fager, the executive producer of CBS's *60 Minutes* vowed he wouldn't be caught doing that: "We are not going to do the one-hour special for Everybody Loves Raymond's departure," he said, referring to the hit CBS sitcom. Fager explained that "any viewers who tuned in and saw us doing that would leave in a heartbeat."

A year later, when Everybody Loves Raymond went off the air, *60 Minutes* (5/8/05) marked the occasion by interviewing the series' star, Ray Romano. Hypocrisy? No, says Fager—because it wasn't a full hour. This gives us some insight into the ethical reasoning of network news executives: apparently you can turn one-third of your news program into a commercial for your network's shows and still maintain your journalistic integrity.

An activist with Ohio Patients' Rights got a lesson in media self-interest when he tried to place an announcement in the *Cleveland*

Plain Dealer's health calendar for a meeting to discuss the "Cleveland City Council permitting hospitals to ban patients for any complaint." Though he had placed meeting announcements before, this one was rejected with no explanation. Suspecting that the rejection was related to hospitals being a big advertiser in the paper, he submitted a new announcement to a different Cleveland paper, the weekly *Sun News*—owned, like the *Plain Dealer*, by Advance Publications—this time about a meeting to discuss the *Plain Dealer's* censorship of his first meeting announcement. He received an accidental reply from *Sun News* staffer Carol Kovach, who apparently meant to send the message to her executive editor, Linda Kinsey: "Linda: Did you get this? He wants us to publish this. I think it's in poor taste for us to publish the stuff about the PD. A straight meeting notice, OK, but do we really need to bash the PD? Let me know what you think." Needless to say, the announcement never ran.

Though FAIR aims to *promote* journalistic ethics by shining a light on breaches, an item from a past report prompted one paper to commit another breach. The Kingston, N.Y. *Sunday Freeman* published (4/17/05) a syndicated column by Norman Solomon that recounted some of the examples given in FAIR's "Fear & Favor 2004" report (3–4/05)—but with one change. The paper added the following editor's note after an item criticizing the *New Haven Register's* extensive and fawning coverage of a new Ikea store:

Register officials say the news coverage and editorial were warranted because of the positive economic impact Ikea would bring to the New Haven area. *The Register* says it knew prior to the opening that Ikea would be an infrequent advertiser.

What the note failed to mention was that the Register is the flagship publication of the Journal Register Company, the same company that owns the *Freeman*. And in case there is doubt concerning the source of that editorial decision, the journalist who brought the incident to FAIR's attention noted that "everyone in the editorial staff at the *Freeman* is incensed about this breach of ethics (in a journalism ethics column, of all places!)."

Powerful Players & PR

A common complaint about media is that all they care about is money. But there's money, and then there's money. The group People for the

Ethical Treatment of Animals (PETA) had money—they were prepared to pay $5,000 to run an ad in Billboard magazine—and Billboard was happy to take that money. But then, sometime between when Billboard agreed to run the ad and the day it was slated to run, the ad was cancelled. According to the *New York Daily News* (3/29/05), PETA's ad was a direct criticism of Jennifer Lopez, whose new clothing line prominently features real fur. Could it be that the magazine found PETA's money less compelling than the influence of Sony Corporation's Epic Records, which just released Lopez's new album, and that of Lopez's powerful publicist, Nanci Ryder? The *Daily News* couldn't get Billboard to return calls for an explanation of the decision, but Ryder wasn't shy about declaring victory. "I'm doing my job, which is protecting my client," she told the *Daily News*.

If they're not selling interviews to advertisers outright (see In Advertisers We Trust, above), morning news shows are still generally chockablock with soft segments on entertainment, travel and consumer products that don't eschew brand names. Indeed, the only thing distinguishing such popular features from infomercials is that the experts discussing the products don't seem to be paid by the manufacturers.

Take James Oppenheim, technology editor at *Child Magazine*. In November 2004 Oppenheim appeared on a local Austin, Texas news program talking up various toys, including Kodak's new electronic photo album for kids. He also pushed the product in a similar appearance on NBC's Today show (12/21/04). What viewers of neither segment knew was that Oppenheim was paid by Kodak to promote the thing, along with virtually every other product he mentioned (*Wall Street Journal*, 4/19/05). The Austin station says they didn't know about the deal, while NBC says they're looking into it. But these kinds of financial relationships are really open secrets.

The *Wall Street Journal* illustrated how the system works: The companies it interviewed said that disclosure is the responsibility of TV stations, while TV stations claim to be simply shocked when they learn of such relationships, no matter how many times they learn of them.

Since national news shows at least pretend to have standards about such things, companies often don't pay the so-called experts for those spots directly. They just pay the person for appearances on lots and lots of local shows, and then, if they happen to mention the product when they're on, say, *Good Morning America*—that's just "icing."

Of course, journalists should disclose the truth when sources have been paid by the companies they're talking about,but everyone knows why they don't. A spokesperson for Wal-Mart, which pays women to promote their jewelry on TV, spelled it out in the *Wall Street Journal*: If the payments were disclosed, that would make their paid expert's appearances look too much like infomercials.

It's not just morning shows that venture into that gray zone between news and infomercial, though. Newspaper journalists can likewise succumb to the temptation of an easy story provided by PR people. In March 2005, headlines across the country announced a dramatic new study by the National Sleep Foundation showing that half the adult population of the U.S. had trouble falling asleep. But as the *Sacramento Bee's* Dorsey Griffith and Steve Wiegand (6/26/05) pointed out after some digging, the reports largely failed to note this key bit of information: The study and its publicity campaign were funded by pharmaceutical companies that make sleeping pills.

What's more, the *Sacramento Bee* reported that the National Sleep Foundation, though ostensibly an independent nonprofit health advocacy group, gets most of its money from sleeping pill manufacturers, and ten of its twenty-three board members have current or past financial ties to the industry. But reporters didn't have to do this kind of sleuthing to realize that there was a connection between the study and the sleeping pill industry; the fact that the press kit announcing the study also included a pitch for a new sleeping pill, Lunesta, should have been a giveaway.

However, the *Sacramento Bee* looked at eighty-four mainstream news reports on the study and found that only seventeen mentioned the drug industry's sponsorship of the study and the foundation. Those kinds of journalistic gaps, particularly in health reporting, are something worth losing sleep over.

Government Pressures

Media got off to an inauspicious start in 2005 with the revelation that the Bush administration paid journalist Armstrong Williams to plug the No Child Left Behind Act (*USA Today*, 1/7/05). The emergence of similar stories throughout the year showed that the Williams case was hardly an isolated incident of journalistic conflicts between allegiance to the public and to the government (or a government paycheck).

In Florida, the *Sarasota Herald-Tribune* (3/26/05) revealed that Governor Jeb Bush's office used taxpayer dollars to hire the services of Mike Vasilinda, a well-known freelance television reporter in Tallahassee, who also runs his own video production company. The state paid Vasilinda's firm more than $100,000 over four years to produce news spots promoting Bush's policies, as well as those of other Florida government agencies, including the Department of Education and Secretary of State. Meanwhile, Vasilinda was covering those same agencies in his television wire service reports, which aired on CNN and local NBC affiliates.

While some stations, when informed of Vasilinda's dual role, said they'd stop running his reports, others had no qualms. News director Forrest Carr at Tampa's WFLA stated that "[Vasilinda] assures me he has safeguards in place. He would not allow himself to be in a position where he would allow his journalism to be compromised." Presumably, though, Carr won't be attaching notices to Vasilinda's reports to let viewers decide for themselves if they place the same amount of trust in the PR agent–cum–journalist.

The *Boston Globe* (4/8/05) uncovered a similar relationship between Massachusetts Governor Mitt Romney's administration and *Boston Herald* columnist Charles D. Chieppo. In his March 21 column, Chieppo extolled Romney's mass transit plan, which was drawn up by the head of the state's Environmental Affairs office. What he didn't tell readers was that only three days earlier he'd submitted a bid for a $10,000 contract to help promote that office's policies—a contract he won soon after his laudatory column ran.

What's perhaps even more disturbing is that the *Boston Herald* didn't see a problem with Chieppo's deal with the state. Editorial page editor Rachelle Cohen decided to keep him on provided he didn't write about "topics he's consulting on." It wasn't until the *Boston Globe* exposé ran that the paper dropped Chieppo, citing his failure to disclose another contract with a state authority to promote the state's tourism industry (*Boston Globe*, 4/9/05).

On November 2, the *Washington Post* carried a potentially explosive front-page story about "black sites," secret prisons established by the CIA after the September 11 attacks to interrogate terrorism suspects. The *Post* reported that while virtually nothing was known about these sites, concerns about them were increasing in the wake of revelations of prisoner abuse at Abu Ghraib and Guantánamo Bay.

But one crucial thing that the *Washington Post did* know about the sites—their locations—it withheld from the public, at the request of government officials. The *Post* explained that senior officials "argued that the disclosure might disrupt counterterrorism efforts in those countries and elsewhere and could make them targets of possible terrorist retaliation." Of course, keeping the locations secret also offers the government a way to keep their activities out of the public eye. The *Post* article noted that government officials acknowledged that revealing information about the sites would open the U.S. to legal challenges and "increase the risk of political condemnation at home and abroad." In other words, it's just the kind of story that a watchdog press should be digging into.

Other outlets showed less deference to the U.S. government; reports detailing likely locations emerged in the *Financial Times* (11/3/05) and elsewhere. To date, though, the *Washington Post* has kept its pact with the White House.

The Bush administration and its supporters complain regularly about the dearth of positive news stories in Iraq. But a *Washington Post* column by Al Kamen (4/8/05) indicates that at least some journalists are censoring the bad news, not the good news. According to Kamen, an internal army report explained that U.S. forces took an embedded reporter to a school near Mosul to cover the handing out of school supplies to needy students. But when they arrived at the site, the report said, they found not schoolchildren, but an Iraqi family homesteading in the building.

The report continued,

> Fortunately, the reporter elected not to cover the event, which could have made us look bad, since we didn't know what was going on with the school after we funded its construction. . . . [The journalist] understood what had happened and had other good coverage to use . . . rather than airing any of this event.

With journalists, from embedded reporters all the way up to *Washington Post* editors, "electing" not to provide the American public with news that exposes government's failures and wrongdoings, official censorship is apparently no longer even necessary.

STRAIGHT FROM THE SOURCE, NO JOURNALISM REQUIRED

by Janine Jackson

At the beginning of the year, the Armstrong Williams scandal high-lighted the disturbing practice of the Bush administration's using taxpayer dollars to fund media that uncritically promote government policies and programs without disclosing the source of the funding to readers or viewers. Journalist Williams was revealed to have received some $240,000 from the White House to promote George W. Bush's No Child Left Behind Act. But no scandal arose just a short while later, when an inspector general's report found that the Williams deal was just a small part of a pattern of such deals at the Education Department, with some $4.7 million handed out to secretly promote Bush administration policies.

Perhaps that explains why the practice, far from being eliminated by Williams' exposure, appears to be thriving.

As many as eighteen California TV stations aired parts of what looked like a news report but was, in fact, a video press release produced by the state to promote a controversial change in labor laws (*Los Angeles Times*, 2/28/05). The tape, narrated by a former TV reporter who is now a state employee, extols a proposal to change a rule about lunch breaks for hourly workers. The change is opposed by organized labor, but the tape features no dissenting views, only endorsements. These include one from a restaurant owner who, viewers are not told, is currently involved in a lawsuit over the rule in question and was a donor to California Governor Arnold Schwarzenegger's campaign, and another from the deputy secretary of the state agency that is overseeing hearings on the proposed change (leading Democrats to charge that those hearings amount to a kangaroo court). "I don't see it as propaganda," explained the official. Schwarzenegger's office had less trouble with that definition, stating that the tape is "just like any other press release, only it's on video," explained the governor's communications director, Rob Stutzman.

The 6:30 news slot on Portland, Oregon's KOIN-TV on December 25 featured a "presentation" on Portland's progress in cleaning up the polluted Willamette River. Another word for it would be "propaganda," given that the program, introduced by a KOIN news anchor and narrated by Walter Cronkite, was produced for the station free of charge by the city's Bureau of Environmental Services (*Columbia Journalism Review*, 3–4/05). Issues like the EPA's criticisms of the Willamette River Project were nowhere to be found. KOIN might say that there was no intention to confuse viewers about the program's official source, but that wouldn't explain the subsequent repackaged version of the video (also produced at state expense) that allowed the station to add their "KOIN News 6" logo to every frame.

Though the advantages of prepackaged news are evident—it costs little or nothing, and it pleases powerful newsmakers—apparently those enticements are not enough to make some journalists sacrifice their professional integrity. That may be why one PR outfit has sweetened the pot—offering newspaper and radio editors game show-like prizes, including refrigerators and gas grills, for using their material. NewsUSA Inc. produces audio clips, newspaper copy and radio scripts on behalf of paying clients including corporations and associations (*Washington Post*, 12/12/05). In exchange for using these items to fill their pages or airtime, news professionals can enroll in the "Editor Rewards Program" and earn "points" toward products in the company's "prize catalog." Journalism awards, presumably, are not among the goodies on offer.

Reprinted from *Extra!* March/April 2006, Fairness & Accuracy In Reporting (FAIR) http://www.fair.org.

CHAPTER 9

Index on Censorship: Annual Report

By Wendy Ginsberg & Molly Zapp

Global business woke up to the potential rewards offered by China's cyber-media market in 2005. They found themselves in the kind of virtual and real-world environment that quickly drove them to apply the kind of censorship that would never pass at home.

When Microsoft agreed in June 2005 to cater to the Chinese government's web restrictions, the news was hardly groundbreaking. The software giant joined a handful of high-powered Internet service providers—all chomping at the bit to secure a portion of the vast, lucrative Chinese media market—who conceded to proscribe bloggers from using terms including "democracy," "capitalism," "freedom," and "oral sex."

"There are millions of people in China who cannot get to a real newsstand and who secret police have license to vet their mail before delivering it. Many crave the sublime privilege of reading news collected by journalists rather than propagandists," Harvard university professor Jonathan Zitrain wrote in a paper on China's Internet filtering that year. "The free news establishment should take it upon itself to meet them halfway or more."

Though academics and activists tout the Internet as the catalyst to end authoritarianism and expedite democratic transition around the globe, despots have kept pace in the technological arms race. With each new unveiling of software designed to transcend information bans, authoritarian regimes counteract with more secure firewalls.

It's not that the Chinese government was fighting Internet proliferation. In fact, the regime increasingly embraced it, offering pages of information about various government agencies on handfuls of websites.

The state created a transparent facade for its citizens while remaining safely inside its closed fortress. The website proliferation also allowed government to streamline bureaucracies and removed opportunities for graft and dissidence.

In 2005, when one of China's Internet users—the number topped 90 million in 2005—logged on to google.com, everything appeared normal. But the pages available to China-based web surfers were increasingly regulated. Web sites that aroused government hostility, including the BBC, the *Philadelphia Inquirer* and Amnesty International, disappeared off the screen. And Chinese citizens never knew what they were missing.

No explanation was given for the disappearing Web sites. The censors' technology generally replaced the page with a "404—Page not Found" warning, a common enough sight to a regular web browser. In other cases, government-required filters discovered a blocked word on a requested site, and the upload ceased. There is no government agency with which to file complaints. It's as if the sites never existed. With each site restriction and word ban came unintended ramifications, including the elimination of words that reinforce national pride and historical narratives.

"One [such] word [is] pronounced as *cao*, which means "fucking" sometimes; however, it also means "operating," "handling," "exercising" or "practicing," and there was a famous king/hero/tyrant in about the second century called Cao Cao," explained BoingBoing blogger Weizhong Yang. "Therefore you cannot set certain derivations of that word, (for instance, Cao Cao, and Yang Xiu, which is a famous traditional Chinese drama play) as the title of your MSN Space."

To escape the state's grip, many bloggers outside China began a campaign to "Adopt a Chinese Blog." "Web Host Industry Review" reported that the program linked bloggers living in states with less stringent censorship regulations to more vulnerable China-based bloggers and uploaded the Chinese content on to their server, placing it out of the Chinese government's legal reach.

China's authorities responded smartly. A hiring spree commenced in June 2005 aimed to find 4,000 college-educated men and women to skulk the web and erase "unhealthy information" and safeguard "the operating environment of all websites," according to government officials.

The employees dispersed across Beijing's 300 cyber cafes and staked out the country's 3,000 Internet service providers to keep "false information" off screens. Additionally, the government required all China-based websites and Internet cafes to register with the government.

Press freedom organization Reporters sans Frontières (RSF) began a long war of words with the western cyber-media giants over the issue that got increasingly terse as the year rolled on.

"The lack of ethics on the part of these companies is extremely worrying," the organization said of companies like Microsoft and Google. "Their management frequently justifies collaboration with Chinese censorship by saying that all they are doing is obeying local legislation. Does that mean that if the authorities asked Microsoft to provide information about Chinese cyber-dissidents using its services that it would agree to do so, on the basis that it is 'legal'?"

China is not the only country that requires search engines and Internet providers to filter information. France and Germany, where Nazi propaganda and paraphernalia are banned, rely on the software experts to sift them out.

"In the short run, China's filtering remains error-prone and imprecise, so analysts have plenty to criticize," China Internet expert Ben Edelman wrote in the *South China Morning Post*, even as Beijing's fingers closed on the web.

"But in the long run, those who seek to censor online content hold the most important cards: not only can they secretly monitor users' behavior, they can search for circumvention systems and implement filtering that daily becomes more sophisticated, threatening, and punitive."

INDEX INDEX

Index Index is a regularly updated online and print chronicle of free expression violation logged by Index on Censorship. Here are selections from just some of the entries for the more than ninety countries we tracked in 2005.

AFGHANISTAN: Seven people with voter registration cards were murdered by members of the Taliban onSeptember 15, three days before the general election. Human Rights Watch said the killings were consistent with a pre-poll pattern of fear and intimidation by warlords and the Taliban against local politicians and voters (HRW).

AUSTRALIA: Prime Minister John Howard stood by a new anti-terror law's restraints on free speech, rejecting opposition calls on 13 November to drop a sedition clause as it passed through parliament. The law makes it a criminal offence to "promote ill will or hostility between groups," urge violence against the government or assist "an enemy at war" with Australia (The *Advertiser*).

BANGLADESH: The Censorship of Films Amendment Bill 2005 was passed on August 18, aimed at curbing obscene material. Violators of the law face up to three years' imprisonment or fines of 10,000 taka (US$150) a year for three years (*Hindustan Times*).

BELARUS: After the opposition Third Way party posted cartoons criticizing president Lukashenko on the Internet, the KGB raided the homes of five members on sixteen August and confiscated computers. (Cartoonists Rights Network)

BELGIUM: On March 17 Belgium passed a law prohibiting court orders requiring journalists to reveal their sources, unless the required information prevents crimes representing "a serious attack" on a person or persons and there is no other way to obtain it. Journalists are also protected from being sued for retaining stolen documents or complicity in a source's "violation of professional secrecy" (IFEX, IFJ, OSCE).

BRAZIL: Hundreds of gay and lesbian activists staged a mass kiss outside the Brazilian Congress in November to protest against the cutting of the first televised gay kiss in the last episode of the soap opera *America* by Globo, the country's main television network. Protesters also demanded the passing of a long-delayed bill permitting same-sex marriages (BBC Online).

BULGARIA: An Italian parliamentary investigation into communist Bulgaria's role in a 1981 bid to assassinate Pope John Paul II claims that Sofia authorities have censored up to 75 percent of information on the case held in the secret files of its former secret police. Declassified communist East German files suggest the Bulgarian secret service recruited the assassin, Turkish right-wing gunman Mehmet Ali Agca (*Corriere della Sera*).

BURMA: Burma's Information Ministry has laid down new press regulations that ban the use of anonymous sources in all published news reports. According to the ministry's new rules, all sources of the news must be clearly identified or the stories could be deemed unauthorized and subject to penalty. A weekly journal, the *Voice*, was suspended for a month on May 1 because it quoted an unnamed source (SEAPA, mizzima.com).

CANADA: A June exhibition of work by photographer Zahra Kazemi, murdered in Tehran by Iranian secret police, was shut down following complaints that it was too sympathetic to the Palestinian uprising. Authorities in Cote Saint-Luc, Montreal, ordered the removal of five photographs of the Palestinian intifada from a public library exhibition; Kazemi's son Stephan Hachemi then said the borough must either display all the photos or none of them (*Ottawa Citizen*).

CHINA: In October the Ministry of Information stepped up controls on the estimated 550 billion text messages sent yearly in China. Fines will be imposed on people who send messages containing pornography, "provocative language," and that spread "subjects forbidden by the government." The ministry did not reveal how it would monitor the messages (*Asia News*).

COLOMBIA: In the early morning of March 13, the broadcast facilities of Cristalina Este´reo and Esple´ndida Este´reo radio stations in Florencia in southern Colombia were blown up by armed men, demolishing the stations' antennae and taking both off air. Police said the attack was claimed by the Revolutionary Armed Forces of Colombia (FARC). Florencia's mayor, Arnoldo Barrera Cadena, said a special committee would be set up to protect all of the city's media outlets (FLIP).

CUBA: A journalist sentenced to seven months' house arrest was transferred to prison after she defied a court order barring her from reporting. Lamasiel Gutie´rrez Romero of the Nueva Prensa Cubana news agency continued to report from her home in Isla Juventud after being sentenced for crimes of civil disobedience in August. She was transferred to a women's prison near Havana on October 11 (RSF).

DEMOCRATIC REPUBLIC OF CONGO: An association of over 100 community radio stations across the Democratic Republic of Congo stopped all broadcasts on February 23 in protest at state restraints on political broadcasting. The strike follows a recent government order forbidding all "thematic stations" from broadcasting political output because of "persistent excesses" (MONUC).

EAST TIMOR: East Timor's Land and Property Department ordered the country's major and oldest local daily, *Suara Timor Lorosae*, to leave its offices. Salvador J X Soares, the newspaper's publisher and editor-in-chief, said the order is meant to silence his newspaper. "I will resist the order and see what will happen to my newspaper," he said (SEAPA, IFEX).

ERITREA: Imprisoned journalist Dawit Isaac was released by the authorities in Asmara. Isaac, who has Swedish citizenship and was co-owner and reporter on the independent newspaper *Setit*, had been in jail since a 2001 government crackdown on journalists. He had returned to Asmara from Sweden where he fled in 1987 as a refugee from the war with Ethiopia (CPJ).

EGYPT: A new opposition party political daily, *al-Ghad* (the *Future*), was banned as it prepared to publish its first issue on February 8. Party president Ayman Nour has been detained for "forging official documents"—the first issue was due to include an article by Nour describing his arrest, as well as other pieces critical of government policies (al-Ahram).

GABON: The independent *Nku'u Le Messager* newspaper was suspended on August 10 after publishing an editorial by Norbert Ngoua Mezui calling politicians "fat, overpaid and lazy." The government's Media Regulation Council said the ban would be lifted only if the paper changed its editorial board (All Africa).

GAMBIA: Two repressive new media laws were quietly enacted in Gambia. An amendment to the Criminal Code imposed mandatory prison sentences of six months to three years for those convicted of publishing defamatory or "seditious" material, without the option of a fine. In addition, the legislation allows the state to confiscate without judicial oversight any publication deemed "seditious." A second amendment, to Gambia's Newspaper Act raises the bond payable by all Gambian publications from 100,000 dalasis (US$3,578) to 500,000 (US$17,892) and extends it to the broadcast media as well. All media will have to re-register and pay the bond (CPJ).

GERMANY: Police in Berlin have turned to using helicopters with infrared cameras to catch graffiti artists at night, despite criticism that they are grossly overreacting. The high-tech helicopters are borrowed from border police units, usually used to detect illegal immigrants from the air (Reuters).

GREECE: Gerhard Haderer, Austrian author of the comic book "The Life of Jesus," was tried by a court in absentia in Athens for blasphemy alongside his Greek publisher and four booksellers, and given a six months suspended sentence onJanuary 18. His publisher and the booksellers were acquitted. Haderer faces imprisonment if he enters Greece (IFEX, Ananova).

GUATEMALA: After a year of requesting access to a hoard of secret police files, the *New York Times* was granted access to the archive on November 21. The files, documenting thirty-six years of abductions, assassinations and interrogations during the country's civil war, were discovered last year rotting in a disused munitions warehouse in Guatemala City. The U.S. newspaper was allowed access to the estimated 75 million files, but prevented from reporting the names of victims or suspects (*New York Times*).

GUINEA: President Lansana Conté signed an agreement on August 20 allowing private broadcasting for the first time in fourteen years. Religious and political programs are not allowed (IFEX).

INDONESIA: Indonesian President Susilo Bambang Yudhoyono promised that his new government was not trying to curb the independence of Indonesia's media with a bill that would make it a crime to offend top leaders or undermine the country's guiding doctrines. "The government I am leading has no intention at all to limit or curb the freedom of press," Yudhoyono told a Press Day gathering (Jakarta Post).

IRAN: Mokhtar N., twenty-four, and Ali A., twenty-five, were hanged in public on November 13 in the Shahid Bahonar Square of the northern town of Gorgan for homosexual conduct, according to the semi-official Tehran daily *Kayhan* (HRW).

IRAQ: The U.S. military has been paying Iraqi newspapers to publish stories written by a military propaganda unit, according to the *Los Angeles Times*. The articles are translated into Arabic and placed in Baghdad newspapers where they are often presented as unbiased accounts by independent journalists. One military official told the newspaper that the military had also bought an Iraqi newspaper and taken control of a radio station, and that both had been used to channel pro-American messages (*The Guardian*).

JORDAN: Local and international publications, including books, novels and magazines, will no longer be censored in Jordan, the Jordanian Culture Ministry announced in June. Nevertheless, Saddam Hussein's last novel, *Get Out, You Damned* was banned from publication in Jordan after the Jordanian government said that the novel's content could hurt relations between the two countries. The novel is said to be 'a metaphor for a Zionist-Christian plot to overthrow Arabs and Muslims' (Reuters, IRIN).

LATVIA: The Latvian National Opera was banned from performing Sergei Prokofiev's Cinderella in Riga after setting the classic children's story in a brothel. They performed the version only twice, after complaints from Prokofiev's estate. "There was a huge gap between the original music and the new story," Noelle Mann, curator of the Sergei Prokofiev Archive, told the BBC (BBC Online).

MALAYSIA: Police have been ordered to randomly check mobile phones for pornographic images after media reports by a local newspaper that young people were swapping sex videos by mobiles. Officers have been ordered to immediately delete any explicit images they find stored in the phones (*Straits Times*).

MALDIVES: More than 170 people wrote to Maldives' President Mamoun Abdul Gayoom to say that if Jennifer Latheef, an Amnesty International human rights defender, is a terrorist, then they themselves should also be considered terrorists. Latheef was sentenced to ten years imprisonment on October 18 on terrorism charges. The protestors insist that her only crime was to be an observer and photographer during the September 2003 unrest in Male (Minivian News).

MAURITANIA: Mauritanian police detained freelance journalist Mohamed Ould Lamine Mahmoudi on 13 March after he interviewed a woman in the southern town of Mederdra who claimed that she was kept as a slave by a family in another town. Mahmoudi, along with two anti-slavery activists who took down the woman's testimony, were charged with fabricating information and tarnishing Mauritania's image. The three face up to four years in prison if convicted. (AP, CPJ)

MEXICO: Mexican reporter Dolores Guadalupe García Escamilla, who was shot nine times by an unidentified gunman on April 5 in the northern city of Nuevo Laredo, has died of her wounds, IFEX reported. She was attacked a day after the station aired her report about the killing of a local lawyer who represented alleged drug traffickers (IFEX, CPJ).

MOZAMBIQUE: The government announced a draft Freedom of Information Bill on August 2, which media experts hope will pave the way towards greater transparency and government accountability (IRIN).

NIGER: Salifou Soumaila Abdoulkarim was placed in "protective custody" in Niamey on November 12 after his weekly magazine *Le Visionnaire* ran an article claiming State Treasurer Siddo Elhadj had embezzled 17 billion CFA francs (US$30 million) from government coffers. He was denied bail and visitors (CPJ, IFEX).

NEPAL: At a hearing on November 11, the Supreme Court failed to block repressive measures against the media including a October 9 ordinance banning independent radio news broadcasts. A leading human rights group, the Informal Sector Service Centre (INSEC), later announced it was discontinuing its popular human rights education program because of increasing government censorship and pressure (RSF, nepalnews.com).

NORTH KOREA: After CNN broadcast a video of a public execution that had been recorded and smuggled out of the country by an apparent dissident, the government-controlled news agency called CNN "a political waiting maid for the U.S. administration." Otherwise, almost no information regarding human rights conditions is available (Human Rights Watch, CPJ).

PAKISTAN: Rights activists protested in Peshawar against a ban on female local election candidates in the remote Dir district, stronghold of the hardline Islamist Jamaat Islami party. The women protested outside the Peshawar Press Club on July 18, saying the move was unconstitutional. They demanded full representation in polls (BBC Online).

PHILIPPINES: Guillermo Wapile was found guilty of murdering journalist Edgar Damalerio in 2002 and sentenced to life imprisonment by a local court in Cebu City on November 29. This is only the third time a conviction has been made for any of the fifty-five murders of journalists since 1989 in the country regarded as "the most dangerous place for journalists" by international media organizations (IFEX).

RUSSIA: A bill that would ban the work of human rights groups and charities and strictly regulate the activities of domestic organizations was overwhelmingly approved at its first reading in the Russian parliament on November 23. International and Russian pro-democracy and human rights groups condemned the legislation as a Soviet-style assault on freedom of association and expression. The bill was expected to be made law by President Putin before the end of the year (*New Zealand Herald*).

SAUDI ARABIA: A Saudi Arabian court jailed three prominent reformists for up to nine years for challenging the royal family by calling for a constitutional monarchy. The decision deals a blow to tentative reforms in the state's existing absolute monarchy. Judges in Riyadh issued their verdict after a nine-month closed-door trial (*Christian Science Monitor*, Al-Jazeera).

SIERRA LEONE: The editor of Sierra Leone's leading independent daily *For Di People*, Harry Yansaneh, died on July 27 as a result of injuries sustained when he was attacked by six men allegedly acting for a ruling party MP who sought to have the opposition daily closed down (CPJ).

SWEDEN: Controversial Pentecostal pastor Aake Green won an appeal against a month-long prison sentence in June 2004 handed down to him after he compared gay people to "cancer." Green's remarks were his own interpretation of the Bible, the court concluded, and were not intended to incite hatred. Gay rights campaigners described the verdict as "disturbing" (BBC Online, IHT).

THAILAND: A community radio station owned by former rice farmer Satien Chanthorn turned journalist and vociferous government critic was closed down and Satien himself charged with illegally possessing broadcast equipment on November 9. He set up the station, called FM 106.75 MHz, in 2002 under laws providing for community radio broadcasting. But he quickly came into conflict with the government over his reporting of official bungles in the handling of flood relief (CPJ).

TUNISIA: Plain-clothed police physically prevented RSF secretary general Robert Menard from leaving an Air France plane after landing in Tunis on November 17. Menard was told that he did not have accreditation for the WSIS. He did. He was also told that he was banned from Tunisia until he was summoned by Tunis court to answer an official complaint laid against him. Such complaints, buried in courts and beyond legal challenge, are routinely used by the authorities to justify censorship and block free public assembly (Index on Censorship).

TURKEY: Prominent Turkish novelist Orhan Pamuk was charged with insulting the Turkish republic for his claim that 1.5 million Armenians died as a result of genocide by Ottoman troops beginning in 1915. The Turkish authorities claim the death toll was much lower and was caused mainly by hunger and deportation (BBC Online).

TURKMENISTAN: In August Turkmen President Saparmurat Niyazov banned playing of recorded music at all public events, on TV and at weddings in a bid to protect Turkmen culture from "negative foreign influences," as he put it. He has already banned opera and ballet, describing them as "unnecessary" (BBC Online).

UNITED KINGDOM: On January 1 the public got a qualified, but clear legal right of access to information held by over 100,000 public bodies across the United Kingdom. In theory that gives anyone—the right is not limited to UK citizens—to ask any organization covered by the country's new Freedom of Information Act (FOIA) what information it has on any subject they specify, and if the organization has that information, to give them a copy. Some 100,000 public authorities are subject to the Act—but not the security and intelligence services or the courts (Index on Censorship).

UNITED STATES: *Postcards from Buster*, an educational cartoon on the non-profit Public Broadcasting System (PBS), was criticized after Buster the animated rabbit was shown visiting lesbian couples in Vermont, where same sex unions are legal. U.S. Education Secretary Margaret Spellings said the show "exposed" children to gay lifestyles and reminded PBS that it received federal funds. PBS subsequently withdrew the episode and PBS head Pat Mitchell decided not to seek a renewal of her contract (*Washington Post*).

UZBEKISTAN: Nearly 600 Baptist leaflets were confiscated and destroyed in the Tashkent region on August 6. In July other books, including the Bible, were forced to be handed over to the religious affairs committee (HRW).

YEMEN: On November 21 opposition MPs accused the Minister of Information of censoring broadcasts of parliamentary sessions in which ministers were harshly criticized and interrogated. Yemeni TV was broadcasting the debate live, but transmission was stopped during the heated discussion (*Yemen Times*).

ZIMBABWE: News that Zimbabwe's state security had secretly bought a controlling interest in ZMNG, publisher of the *Daily Mirror* and *Sunday Mirror* newspapers triggered a boardroom battle. Dr Ibbo Mandaza, CEO and editor-in-chief, was suspended on October 3. It was previously thought that the newspapers were independent. A judicial inquiry into Mandaza's suspension was postponed on November 21 because the two sides could not agree on the legitimacy of the inquiry (MISA).

Index on Censorship covers news and issues related to freedom of expression throughout the world. www.indexonline.org.

CHAPTER 10

The Global Dominance Group and U.S. Corporate Media

by Peter Phillips, Bridget Thornton, Lew Brown, and Andrew Sloan

The leadership class in the U.S. is now dominated by a neo-conservative group of people with the shared goal of aggressively asserting U.S. military power worldwide. This chapter identifies the key actors supporting a global dominance agenda and examines how this group is interconnected with and supported by the corporate media in the United States. We also examine how the key newsmakers in the U.S. have become affiliated with public relations firms spinning the news for their own benefit and how the corporate media uncritically accepts this new form of American censorship. We review who has benefited from September 11, 2001 and examine how Bush, Cheney, and Rumsfeld, along with interlocking public private partnerships, the corporate media, private foundations, military contractors, policy elites, and government officials, jointly support a U.S. military global domination agenda.

A long thread of sociological research documents the existence of a dominant ruling class in the U.S., which sets policy and determines national political priorities. The American ruling class is complex and inter-competitive, maintaining itself through interacting families of high social standing who have similar life styles, corporate affiliations, and memberships in elite social clubs and private schools. This American ruling class is mostly self-perpetuating, maintaining its influence through policy-making institutions such as the National Manufacturing Association, National Chamber of Commerce, Business Council, Business Roundtable, Conference Board, American Enterprise Institute, Council on Foreign Relations and other business-centered policy groups. C. Wright Mills, in his 1956 book *The Power Elite*, documents how World War II solidified a trinity of power in the U.S., comprised of corporate, military and government elites in a centralized power structure motivated by class interests and working in unison through "higher circles" of contact and agreement. Mills described how the power elite were those "who decide whatever is decided" of major consequence.

FOUNDATIONS OF THE GLOBAL DOMINANCE GROUP (GDG)

Leo Strauss, Albert Wohlstetter, and others at the University of Chicago's Committee on Social Thought receive wide credit for promoting the neo-conservative agenda through their students, Paul Wolfowitz, Allan Bloom, and Bloom's student Richard Perle.

Canadian cultural review magazine Adbusters, defines neo-conservatism as, "The belief that Democracy, however flawed, was best defended by an ignorant public pumped on nationalism and religion. Only a militantly nationalist state could deter human aggression. . . . Such nationalism requires an external threat and if one cannot be found it must be manufactured."

The neo-conservative philosophy emerged as a reaction to the 1960's era of social revolutions. Numerous officials and associates in the Reagan and George H. W. Bush presidencies were strongly influenced by the neo-conservative philosophy including: John Ashcroft, Charles Fairbanks, Richard Cheney, Kenneth Adelman, Elliot Abrams, William Kristol and Douglas Feith.

Within the Ford administration there was a split between Cold War traditionalists seeking to minimize confrontations through diplomacy and detente and neo-conservatives advocating stronger confrontations with the Soviet's "Evil Empire." The latter group became more entrenched when George H.W. Bush became CIA Director. Bush allowed the formation of "Team B" headed by Richard Pipes along with Paul Wolfowitz, Lewis Libby, Paul Nitze and others, who formed the Committee on the Present Danger to raise awareness of the Soviet threat and the continuing need for a strong aggressive defense policy. Their efforts led to strong anti-Soviet positioning during the Reagan administration.

Journalist John Pilger recalls his interview of neo-conservative Richard Perle during the Reagan administration:

I interviewed Perle when he was advising Reagan; and when he spoke about 'total war,' I mistakenly dismissed him as mad. He recently used the term again in describing America's 'war on terror'. 'No stages,' he said. 'This is total war. We are fighting a variety of enemies. There are lots of them out there. All this talk about first we are going to do Afghanistan, then we will do Iraq . . . this is entirely the wrong way to go about it. If we just let our vision of the world go forth, and we embrace it entirely and we don't try to piece together clever diplomacy, but just wage a total war . . . our children will sing great songs about us years from now.'

The 1988 election of George H.W. Bush to the presidency and Cheney's appointment as Secretary of Defense, expanded the presence of neo-conservatives within the government, and the fall of the Berlin Wall in 1989, opened the door to the formal initiation of a global dominance policy.

In 1992 Cheney supported Lewis Libby and Paul Wolfowitz in producing the "Defense Planning Guidance" report, which advocated U.S. military dominance around the globe in a "new order." The report called for the U.S. to prevent any new rivals from raising up to challenge us. Using words like "unilateral action" and military "forward presence," the report advocated that the U.S. dominate friends and foes alike. It concluded that the U.S. could attain this position by making itself "absolutely powerful."

The Defense Policy Guidance report, leaked to the press, came under heavy criticism from many sources. The *New York Times* reported on March 11, 1992 that:

> Senior White House and State Department officials have harshly criticized a draft Pentagon policy statement that asserts that America's mission in the post-cold-war era will be to prevent any collection of friendly or unfriendly nations from competing with the United States for superpower status.

One Administration official, familiar with senior staff's reaction at the White House and State Department, characterized the document as a "dumb report" that "in no way or shape represents U.S. policy." Senator Robert C. Byrd, Democrat of West Virginia, called the draft Pentagon document "myopic, shallow, and disappointing." Many people in the higher circles of government policy making were not yet ready for a unilateral global-dominance agenda. With Bill Clinton's election in 1992, most neo-conservatives were out of direct power during the next eight years.

Both political parties cooperate by encouraging Congress to protect U.S. business interests abroad and corporate profits at home. To maintain defense contractors' profits, Clinton's Defense Science Board called for a globalized defense industry obtained through mergers of defense contractors with transnational companies that would become partners in U.S. military readiness.

The Clinton administration generally stayed away from promoting global dominance as an ideological justification for continuing high defense budgets. Instead, to offset profit declines for defense contractors after the fall of the Berlin Wall, the Clinton administration aggressively promoted international arms sales, raising the U.S. share of world arms exports from 16 percent in 1988 to 63 percent in 1997.

Outside the Clinton administration, neo-conservatives continued to promote a global dominance agenda. On June 4, 1994, some 2,000 regional and national elites attended a neo-conservative 'Lakeside Chat at the San Francisco Bohemian Club's summer encampment. A University of California Berkeley political science professor presented the talk, entitled "Violent Weakness". The speaker argued that increasing violence in society was weakening our social institutions. Contributing to this violence and "decay" of our institutions, he said, is bi-sexualism, entertainment politics, multi-culturalism, Afro-Centrism, and a loss of family boundaries. The professor claimed that to avert further "deterioration," we need to recognize that "elites, based on merit and skill, are important to society and any elite that fails to define itself will fail to survive... We need boundaries and values set and clear! We need an American-centered foreign policy . . . and a President who understands foreign policy." He went on to conclude that we cannot allow the "unqualified" masses to carry out policy, but that elites must set values that can be translated into "standards of authority." The speech received an enthusiastic standing ovation.

During the Clinton administration, neo-conservatives were still active in advocating military global dominance. Many of the neo-conservatives and their global dominance allies found various positions in conservative think tanks and with Department of Defense contractors. They continued close affiliations with each other through the Heritage Foundation, American Enterprises Institute, Hoover Institute, Jewish Institute for National Security Affairs, Center for Security Policy, and several other conservative policy groups.

HCPE advocates for a U.S. led "New World Order," along with Reagan/Bush hard-liners, and other military expansionists, founded Project for the New American Century (PNAC) in June of 1997. Their Statement of Principles set forth their aims as follows:

"We need to increase defense spending significantly if we are to carry out our global responsibilities today and modernize our armed forces for the future

"We need to strengthen our ties to democratic allies and to challenge regimes hostile to our interests and values.

"We need to promote the cause of political and economic freedom abroad.

"We need to accept responsibility for America's unique role in preserving and extending an international order friendly to our security, our prosperity, and our principles."

Such a Reagan-ite policy of military strength and moral clarity may not be fashionable today. But it is necessary if the United States is to build on the successes of this past century and to ensure our security and our greatness in the next.

The signatories of this statement include: Elliott Abrams, Gary Bauer, William J. Bennett, Jeb Bush, Richard Cheney, Eliot A. Cohen, Midge Decter, Paula Dobriansky, Steve Forbes, Aaron Friedberg, Francis Fukuyama, Frank Gaffney, Fred C. Ikle, Donald Kagan, Zalmay Khalilzad, I. Lewis Libby, Norman Podhoretz, Dan Quayle, Peter W. Rodman, Stephen P. Rosen, Henry S. Rowen, Donald Rumsfeld, Vin Weber, George Weigel, and Paul Wolfowitz. Of the twenty-five founders of PNAC, George W. Bush appointed twelve to high-level positions in his administration.

Since its founding, PNAC has attracted numerous others who have signed policy letters or participated in the group. Within PNAC, eight individuals are associated with the number one defense contractor Lockheed-Martin, and seven are linked with the number three defense contractor, Northrop Grumman. PNAC is one of several institutions that connect global dominance neo-conservatives and large U.S. military contractors.

In September 2000, PNAC produced a seventy-six-page report entitled *Rebuilding America's Defenses: Strategy, Forces, and Resources for a New Century*. The report was similar to the *Defense Policy Guidance* document written by Lewis Libby and Paul Wolfowitz in 1992. This is not surprising in that Libby and Wolfowitz were participants in the production of the 2000 PNAC report. Steven Cambone, Doc Zakheim, Mark Lagan, and David Epstein were also heavily involved. Each of these individuals would go on to hold high-level positions in the George W. Bush administration.

Rebuilding America's Defenses called for homeland protection, the ability to wage simultaneous theater wars, perform global constabulary roles, and control space and cyberspace. It claimed that the 1990's was a decade of defense neglect and that the U.S. must increase military spending to preserve American geopolitical leadership as the world's sole superpower. The report claimed that in order to maintain a *Pax Americana*, potential rivals—such as China, Iran, Iraq, and North Korea—needed to be held in check. The report also noted that, "the process of transformation...is likely to be a long one, absent some catastrophic and catalyzing event such as a new Pearl Harbor". The events of September 11, 2001 were exactly the kind of catastrophe that the authors of *Rebuilding America' Defenses* needed to accelerate a global dominance agenda.

Before September 11, members of Congress and liberal HCPE, who continued to hold a detente foreign policy frame, traditionally advocated by the Council of Foreign Relations and the State Department, challenged strategic global dominance policies. September 11 so shocked liberal/moderate HCPE that they immediately gave full support to the Patriot Act, Homeland Security, and legislation to support military action in Afghanistan and later Iraq. The resulting permanent war on terror has led to massive government spending, huge deficits (due also in part to the Bush tax cuts), and the rapid acceleration of the neo-conservative HCPE plans for military control of the world.

GDG ADVOCACY ORGANIZATIONS

Key GDG advocacy groups for the past decade include: Project For The New American Century (PNAC), Hoover Institute (HI), American Enterprise Institute (AEI), Hudson Institute (HI), National Security Council (NSC), Heritage Foundation (HF), Defense Policy Board (DPB), Committee on Present Danger (CPD), Jewish Institute of National Security Affairs (JINSA), Manhattan Institute (MI), Committee for the Liberation of Iraq (CLI), Center for Security Policy: Institute for Strategic Studies (CSP), Center for Strategic and International Studies (CSIS), National Institute for Public Policy (NIPP) and the American Israel Public Affairs Committee (AIPAC).

Core elements of each of these groups in cooperation with major defense contractors have encouraged and supported U.S. military expansion, a powerful U.S. presence in the world, and containment of rivals vis-à-vis policies of detente and statesmanship. Here are key examples of a neo-conservative agenda cited in mainstream news: The Associated Press reported Condoleezza Rice's November 17, 2000 statement, "As the world's leading superpower, the United States has special responsibilities. I like to think about this as a great train that's going down the track, and there's markets and competition for private capital," Rice said. "Clearly the United States is kind of in the conductor's seat. With this position of leadership comes a responsibility to keep the peace, Rice said, and then suggested that the Clinton administration's military policies were not the ideal. "Clearly there has to be a rebalancing of America's military missions and America's military resources," she said, focusing on keeping weapons of mass destruction out of the hands of countries like Iraq and North Korea.

Tom Donnelly of the American Enterprise and PNAC quoted in the *Washington Post* on November 27, 2005, "The Pentagon's restructuring in Asia and the president's trip imply that the administration can be quite sober about what China's rise really means. Make no mistake, the competition already underway with Beijing is critical: America has a vital interest in sustaining its place as the guarantor of Asia's security. Its leadership has led to the region's peace and prosperity. Still there is more at stake. China is an increasingly important player in the Middle East and indeed globally. Ultimately, if the Bush

Doctrine is not successfully applied to East Asia, and China can export its bad behavior to the Middle East, the strategy of promoting democracy will fail there, too."

Richard Perle of American Enterprise Institute, PNAC and Committee to Liberate Iraq, and former Assistant Secretary of Defense, spoke on National Public Radio on June 20, 2000, stating "I think when others have thought this through, it will be recognized that the ability of the United States to defend itself is a stabilizing feature for our security, and depending on what situations we may be concerned, it can be stabilizing for others. For example, suppose we had, as I think we're technologically capable of producing, a ballistic missile defense based on ships. And suppose there was a sharp increase in tension on the Asian subcontinent, the India-Pakistan dispute. Imagine if an American president could say, 'I am dispatching an Aegis cruiser with a ballistic missile defense on it, and we will intercept the first missile fired by either side in this conflict.' Would that be a bad thing for the Indians or the Pakistanis? It seems to me it could very possibly bring stability to a very dangerous situation."

Peter Brooks stated in an NPR interview on October 18, 2005, "Chinese leaders believe that if its economic growth continues apace, China will overcome 150 years of humiliation at the hands of foreign powers, returning to its past glory as the "Middle kingdom", . . . this economic growth will allow it to be able to challenge the world's most powerful nations, including the United States."

In each of the above cases, we see an underlying assumption that the U.S. is the dominant global power and that rivals (China, Iraq, and Iran) need to be contained through expanded military spending and tough U.S. policies. Collectively, these fifteen global dominance advocacy groups in cooperation with the top military contractors have a controlling lock on U.S. military and foreign policy within the current administration and represent a rising power with the traditional higher circles policies elites within the U.S.

WHO PROFITS FROM GDG POLICIES?

Lockheed Martin has benefited significantly from the post-September 11 military expansion promoted by the GDG. The Pentagon's budget for buying new weapons rose from $61 billion in

2001 to over $80 billion in 2004. Lockheed Martin's sales rose by over 30 perecent at the same time, with tens of billions of dollars on the books for future purchases. From 2000 to 2004, Lockheed Martin's stock value rose 300 percent.

New York Times reporter Tim Weiner wrote in 2004, "No contractor is in a better position than Lockheed Martin to do business in Washington. Nearly 80 percent of its revenue comes from the U.S. Government. Most of the rest comes from foreign military sales, many financed with tax dollars."

As of August 2005 Lockheed Martin stockholders had made 18 percent on their stock in the prior twelve months. Northrup-Grumann has seen similar growth in the last three years with DOD contracts rising from $3.2 billion in 2001 to $11.1 billion in 2004.

Halliburton, with Vice-President Richard Cheney as former CEO, has seen phenomenal growth since 2001. Halliburton had defense contracts totaling $427 million in 2001. By 2003, they had $4.3 billion in defense contracts, of which approximately a third were sole source agreements.

Cheney, not incidentally, continues to receive a deferred salary from Halliburton. According to financial disclosure forms, the company paid Cheney $205,298 in 2001; $162,392 in 2002; $178,437 in 2003, and $194,852 in 2004 and his 433,333 Halliburton stock options rose in value from $241,498 in 2004 to $8 million in 2005.

The Carlyle Group, established in 1987, is a private global investment firm that manages some $30 billion in assets. Numerous high-level members of the GDG have been involved in The Carlyle Group including Frank Carlucci, George H. W. Bush, James Baker III, William Kennard, and Richard Darman. The Carlyle Group purchased United Defense in 1997. They sold their shares in the company after September 11, making a $1 billion dollar profit. Carlyle continues to invest in defense contractors and is moving into the homeland security industry.

Profits for defense contractors have been so good that the *New York Times* in May of 2005 described how some $20 to $30 billion is sitting in the coffers of the top military contractors as a result of record Pentagon budgets and robust government spending on homeland security. *The New York Times* reported that Boeing had $6.5 billion in cash on hand.

PUBLIC-PRIVATE PARTNERSHIPS:
MEDIA AND THE GDG

A global dominance agenda includes penetration into the boardrooms of the corporate media in the U.S. A research team at Sonoma State University recently finished conducting a network analysis of the boards of directors of the ten big media organizations in the U.S. The team determined that only 118 people comprise the membership on the boards of director of the ten big media giants. These 118 individuals in turn sit on the corporate boards of 288 national and international corporations. Four of the top ten media corporations in the U.S. have GDG-DOD contractors on their boards of directors including:

> William Kennard: New York Times, Carlyle Group
> Douglas Warner III, GE (NBC), Bechtel
> John Bryson: Disney (ABC), Boeing
> Alwyn Lewis: Disney (ABC), Halliburton
> Douglas McCorkindale: Gannett, Lockheed-Martin

Given an interlocked media network, big media in the U.S. effectively represent corporate America's interests. The media elite, a key component of policy elites in the U.S., are the watchdogs of acceptable ideological messages, the controllers of news and information content, and the decision makers regarding media resources. Corporate media elites are subject to the same pressures as the higher circle policy makers in the U.S., and therefore, equally susceptible to a reactionary response to our most recent Pearl Harbor and continuing threats of terrorism.

As a result, corporate media in the U.S. has shown an expanding dependency on GDG spokespersons as sources for news. Below are the comparative results of mainstream media exposure among a few of the major conservative think tanks in 2000 and 2005:

AEI: American Enterprise Institute
New York Times: 2000: 55, 2005: 99–80 percent increase
Washington Post: 2000: 87, 2005: 157–80.4 percent increase
Transcripts: 2000: 137, 2005: 148–8 percent increase

CSIS: Center for Strategic and International Studies

New York Times: 2000: 25, 2005: 61– 44 percent increase
Washington Post: 2000: 54, 2005: 81– 50 percent increase
Transcripts: 2000: 46, 2005: 98–113 percent increase
Transcripts represented: ABC News Transcripts, CBS News Transcripts, CNN, National Public Radio, and NBC News.

The 24-hour news shows on MSNBC, FOX, and CNN are closely interconnected with various governmental and corporate sources of news. Maintenance of continuous news shows requires a constant supply of entertaining and stimulating events with breaking news bites. Advertisement for mass consumption drives the system and pre-packaged sources of news are vital within this global news process. Ratings demand continued cooperation from multiple-sources for on-going weather reports, war stories, sports scores, business news, and regional headlines. Print, radio, and TV news also engages in this constant interchange with news sources.

The preparation for ongoing wars and terrorism fits well into the visual kaleidoscope of pre-planned news. Government PR specialists and media experts from private interests provide ongoing news feeds to the national media distribution systems. The result is an emerging symbiotic relationship between news dispensers and news suppliers. Examples of this relationship are the press pools organized by the Pentagon both in the Middle East and in Washington D.C., which give pre-scheduled reports on the war in Iraq to selected groups of news collectors (journalists) for distribution through their individual media organizations.

Embedded reporters, working directly with military units in the field must maintain cooperative working relationships with unit commanders to remain in the field. Cooperative reporting is vital to continued access to government news sources. Therefore, rows of news story reviewers back at corporate media headquarters rewrite, soften, or spike news stories from the field that may threaten the symbiotic nature of global news management.

GLOBAL DOMINANCE, IRAN, AND THE MEDIA

Iran as part of the "axis of evil" has long been a target for the Global

Dominance. The corporate media has significantly increased coverage of the danger imposed by a nuclear Iran. Stories linking Iran to a nuclear threat appearing in North American mainstream print media have steadily increased over the last six years from 251 in 2000–2001 to 890 in 2005–2006.

Seymour Hersh in the *New Yorker* detailed the current administration willingness to launch a pre-emptive nuclear strike against Iran. A war on Iran would be a rapid expansion of the GDG military domination agenda and could lead the U.S. into a nuclear showdown with Russia and China. Additionally, Michael Klare wrote in *The Nation* how the administration is pushing military action against Iran and quoted Bush as saying, "This notion that the United States is getting ready to attack Iran is simply ridiculous," Bush declared in Belgium on February 22. He then added, "Having said that, all options are on the table."

The fact is that a policy of first strike aggression against a sovereign nation has long roots in the ground U.S. foreign policy. Plans known as "Global Strike," unveiled by the Air Force in early 2001 by John Jumper and his staff, include details for "imminent" threats from targeted nations, such as Iran, Russia, China, and North Korea. According to globalsecurity.org the Global Strike Task Force is to be the nations "kick-down-the-door force for the new century." Kicking down the door means launching F-22 stealth fighters to destroy any anti-aircraft capabilities quickly followed by the incursion of B-2 stealth Bombers from hangars on Diego Garcia and Royal Air Force, Fairford in the United Kingdom. Those Bombers and fighters represent a massive increase in destructive power. Four B-2s and 48 F-22s have the capability of striking 380 targets in fifty-two sorties. This destructive capacity can be compared with the first twenty-four hours of Desert Storm in which only 203 targets were hit with 1223 strike sorties of a mixed force. Global Strike represents a destructive force thirty-six times greater than the entire combined force of the Desert Storm invasion; a nuclear armed force constantly on alert and ready to be unleashed to any point on the globe within moments notice, but primarily aimed at the axis of evil.

The U.S. corporate media have had no real discussion regarding the long-term implications of a global dominance policy and an attack on Iran. It has been an open secret since the beginning of this administration that the GDG fully intends to use the full military capability of the U.S. to attack a specific set of sovereign states, with or without provocation. In effect, the media have been complicit in controlling public opinion by ignoring the GDG's desire for world military domination.

PUBLIC RELATIONS, THE MEDIA, AND GLOBAL DOMINANCE

The public relations industry has experienced phenomenal growth since 2001 after several years of steady consolidation. There are three publicly traded mega corporations, in order of largesse: Omnicom, WPP, and Interpublic Group. Together, these firms employ 163,932 people in over 170 countries. Not only do these monstrous firms control a massive amount of wealth, they possess a network of connections in powerful international institutions with direct connections to governments, multi-national corporations, and global dominance group policy-making bodies.

Omnicom maintains an enormous group of subsidiaries, affiliates, and quasi-independent agencies such as BBDO Worldwide, DDB Worldwide, and TBWA Worldwide, GSD&M, Merkley Partners, and Zimmerman Partners along with more than 160 firms through Diversified Agency Services division, including Fleishman-Hillard, Integer, and Rapp Collins.

WPP, a U.K. based conglomerate, also touts an impressive list of subsidiaries such as Young and Rubicam, Burson-Marsteller, Ogilvy and Mather Worldwide, and Hill and Knowlton along with numerous other PR, advertising, and crisis management firms.

Before the first Gulf War propaganda spectacle took place courtesy of Hill & Knowlton. They helped create of a national outrage against Iraq by recounting of horrifying events supposedly caused by Iraqi soldiers in Kuwait. A young woman named Nayirah, claimed in Congressional testimony, and before a national audience, that she saw "Iraqi soldiers come into the [Kuwait] hospital with guns, and go into the room where fifteen babies were in incubators. They took the babies out of the incubators, and left the babies on the cold floor to die. What the public was not told is that Nayirah was the daughter of Sheikh Sand Nasir al-Sabah, Kuwait's ambassador to the U.S. The public also wasn't told that her performance was coordinated by the

White House and choreographed by the U.S. public relations firm Hill & Knowlton on behalf of the Kuwait government.

The big PR forms are closely interconnected with corporate media. Four members of the WPP group sit on the Council on Foreign Relations. An Omnicom board member holds a position at Time Warner, one of the largest U.S. media conglomerates, another holds a lifetime trustee position at PBS.

Despite the rapid consolidation and enormity of the top publicly traded firms, several independent firms experienced rapid growth and success. A few notable companies worth attention are 5W Public Relations, The Lincoln Group, and Rendon Group. These firms have experienced explosive growth since September 11.

O'Dwyers named 5W "the fastest growing PR firm in 2005." The company, founded in 2002, recorded an 85 percent increase in their net revenues from 2004 to 2005. 5W's clients include numerous Zionist organizations: Government of Israel, Mayor of Jerusalem, Israel, Likud Party of Israel, Mayor of Tel Aviv, Israel, Israel Ministry of Tourism, Zionist Organization of America, American Jewish Congress, and Heritage Affinity Services (the first-ever Visa Platinum affinity and rewards credit card that supports Israel).

The public relations company Rendon Group is one of the firms hired for the PR management of America's pre-emptive wars. In the 1980s, The Rendon Group helped form American sentiment regarding the ousting of President Manuel Noriega in Panama. They shaped international support for the first Gulf War, and in the 1990s created the Iraqi National Congress from image, to marketing, to the handpicking Ahmed Chalabi.

The Rendon Group created the images that have shaped support for a permanent war on terror include the toppling of the statue of Saddam, Private Jessica Lynch's heroic rescue and dramatic tales of weapons of mass destruction.

The Lincoln Group owes their success directly to the war in Iraq. On their website they state, "Lincoln Group was formed in 2003. After the U.S. Government started asking for support with communications and outreach campaigns in 2004, a government Professional services subsidiary was formed as Iraqex LLC, but we later adopted the parent company name as that subsidiary started to perform marketing and advertising work across the Middle East region." An example of their work was the practice of paying troops and sub-contractors to write articles disguised as freelance journalism. They also develop psyops campaigns in Iraq and Afghanistan.

The Lincoln Group's ability to win huge government contracts, such as the $100,000,000 contract awarded in June 2005, lies in their list of experienced government, military, and defense contractor connections. Topping their cast of players is Vincent Breglio, a pollster for the Reagan and Bush/Quayle administrations followed by PNAC member Devon Cross. Next is Douglas H. Dearth who held a position as course director at the Joint Military Intelligence Training Center and served at the Defense Intelligence Agency. Other advisors include William Zartman of SAIS and retired Col. Charles Dennison Lane.

The public relations industry continues their rapid consolidation of power and influence due in part to the contracts associated with the wars in Iraq and Afghanistan and the contentious relations between Iran, Russia, China, Latin America, and the U.S. as well as domestic issues such as Medicare, Immigration, and Social Security.

The increase of public relations contracts during the Bush compared to the Clinton years increased from the millions to the billions. In 2000, the last full fiscal year of the Clinton Administration, the federal government spent $38.6 million on sixty-four contracts with major public relations agencies. In 2001, the first year of the Bush Administration, the federal government spent $36.6 million on sixty-seven contracts with major public relations agencies. By 2002, the first fully budgeted year of the Bush Administration, federal spending on PR contracts increased to $64.7 million on sixty-seven contracts.

Upon realization that the current administration paid people to represent policy in an unbiased fashion in the "No Child Left Behind" campaign, Rep. Henry Waxman's requested a GAO report into the use of funds for media efforts. The report concluded that during 2003 to 2004 and half of 2005; the administration spent $1.6 billion on 343 contracts with public relations firms, advertising agencies, media organizations, and individual members of the media. The biggest spender was the Department of Defense with $1.1 billion in contracts.

The public relations industry holds significant power. The ease with which the American population accepted the invasion of Iraq was the outcome of a concerted effort involving the government, DoD contractors, public relations firms, and the corporate media. These institutions are the instigators and main beneficiaries of a permanent war on terror. The importance of these connections lies in the fact that powerful segments of the GDG have the money and resources to articulate their propaganda repeatedly to the American people until those messages become self-evident truths and conventional wisdom.

GLOBAL DOMINANCE AND CORPORATE MEDIA

At the beginning of 2006, the Global Dominance Group has well established their agenda within higher circle policy councils and inside the U.S. government. They work hand in hand with defense contractors promoting deployment of U.S. forces in over 700 bases worldwide and have strong inter-locking links with corporate media in the U.S. The Bush administration is paltering to the American public with exaggerated misconceptions of worldwide terrorism to frighten us into supporting a global police state. With a billion dollar PR campaign, seven hundred military bases and a budget bigger than the rest of the world combined, the U.S. military has become the new supreme-power force repressing "terrorism" everywhere.

Vice President Dick Cheney's keynote address at the American Israel Public Affairs Committee (AIPAC) policy conference March 7, 2006 is a telling example of neo-conservative global dominance thought in the current administration. Here are his exact words, "Israel, and the United States, and all civilized nations will win the war on terror. To prevail in this fight, we must understand the nature of the enemy . . . as America experienced on September 11, the terrorist enemy is brutal and heartless. This enemy wears no uniform, has no regard for the rules of warfare, and is unconstrained by any standard of decency or morality. . . . The terrorists want to end all American and Western influence in the Middle East. Their goal in that region is to seize control of a country, so they have a base from which to launch attacks and wage war against governments that do not meet their demands . . . ultimately to establish a totalitarian empire that encompasses a region from Spain, across North Africa, through the Middle East and South Asia, all the way around to Indonesia."

Cheney claims that evil terrorists everywhere are plotting for the ruin of "civilized" nations. In order to stop them we must militarily control all the regions they are threatening in a permanent global war. Cheney's military empire fits in exactly with the GDG's agenda of total military domination of the world. For Cheney and other global dominance neo-conservatives, the terrorist label is so broad that it can be applied to any individual, group, or nation that resists U.S. military occupations, U.S. threats, or U.S. corporate interests anywhere in the world.

In December 2002, Dutch journalist Willem Oltmans speaking at the International Campaign Against U.S. Aggression on Iraq in Cairo, Egypt, described his teen years during World War II in the Dutch resistance movement. "The Nazis called us terrorists," he exclaimed. "Now as the U.S. invades and occupies other countries you do the same thing," he added.

Maintaining a U.S. military global police force enriches defense contractors and enflames resistance. There is no worldwide terrorism threat other than the one fabricated by the corporate media and created when we make war on other peoples.

Challenging the neo-conservative's global dominance agenda is but one part of rebuilding democracy in the U.S.. Also needed is media reform from the bottom up by funding a diversity of independent media operations to challenge the corporate media's top-down propaganda. Needed also is the passing of laws making illegal the creation of false news stories by PR firms.

Addressing world poverty, sickness, and environmental issues will go much further in preventing single acts of terrorism inside the United States than any military actions we can muster. It is time to challenge the neo-conservative global dominance agenda and stand up for human rights and the traditional American values of grass-roots democracy, due process, governmental transparency, and individual freedoms for ourselves and the rest of the world.

INTRODUCTION TO APPENDICES
Understanding Global Dominance Advocates within the HCPE

A group of Department of Defense (DOD) and Homeland Security contractors benefited significantly from expanded military spending after September 11. We include in this study the top seven military contractors who derive at least one third of their income for DOD contracts. We also added the Carlyle Group and Bechtel Group Inc. because of their high levels of political influence and revolving door personnel within the Ronald Reagan, George H. W. Bush, and George W. Bush administrations. These corporations benefited significantly from post-September 11 policies. We seek to understand the sociological phenomena of how, as collective actors, the GDG had the motive, means and opportunity to gain from September 11 and the war on terrorism, and how their most public figures Bush, Cheney, Rumsfeld, and Rice use the U.S. government to expand the GDG agenda.

To establish a GDG parameters list we included the boards of directors of the nine DoD contractors identified below as those corporations earning over one-third of their revenue from the government or having high levels of political involvement. Additionally we have included members of sixteen leading conservative global-dominance-advocating foundations and policy councils.

Connections and associations listed in our GDG are not always simultaneous, but rather reflect links extending for close to two decades inside an increasingly important group within the HCPE. The list includes 237 names of people who have or recently held high-level government positions in the George W. Bush administration, sit on the boards of directors of major DOD contracting corporations, and/or are close associates of the above, serving as GDG advocates on policy councils or advocacy foundations.

Appendix A

COMPANY	DEFENSE CONTRACTS 2004	TOTAL REVENUE 2004	% FROM DOD
Lockheed Martin	$20,690,912,117	$35,526,000,000	58%
General Dynamics	$9,563,280,236	$19,178,000,000	50%
Raytheon	$8,472,818,938	$20,245,000,000	42%
Northrop Grumman	$11,894,090,277	$29,853,000,000	40%
Halliburton	$7,996,793,706	$20,464,000,000	39%
Science Applications Int'l	$2,450,781,108	$7,187,000,000	34%
Boeing	$17,066,412,718	$52,457,000,000	33%
The Carlyle Group	$1,442,680,446	N/A	N/A
Bell Boeing Joint Program	$1,539,815,440	(Boeing)	NA

Note: Figures in Appendix A courtesy of Mergent Online Database.

Appendix B

GLOBAL DOMINANCE GROUP ADVOCACY ORGANIZATIONS

PNAC   Project For New American Century
HO   Hoover Institute
AEI   American Enterprise Institute
HU   Hudson Institute
NSC   National Security Council
HF   Heritage Foundation
DPB   Defense Policy Board
CPD   Committee on Present Danger
JINSA   Jewish Institute of National Security Affairs
MI   Manhattan Institute
CLI   Committee for the Liberation of Iraq
CSP   Center for Security Policy: Institute for Strategic Studies
CSIS   Center for Strategic and Int'l Studies
NIPP   National Institute for Public Policy
AIPAC   American Israel Public Affairs Committee
Team B Presidents Foreign Advisory Board

OTHER IMPORTANT AGENCIES AND ORGANIZATIONS

CIA   Central Intelligence Agency
DoD   Department of Defense
DoS   Department of State
CFR   Council on Foreign Relations
DoJ   Department of Justice
DoC   Department of Commerce
WHOMB   White House Office of Management and Budget
DoE   Department of Energy
DPB   Defense Policy Board
DoT   Department of Transportation
NSA   National Security Agency

Note: In selecting the sixteen important neo-conservative GDG advocacy organizations, we relied mostly on the International Relations Center website, http://rightweb.irc-online.org/, The Center for Public Integrity at: www.publicintegrity.org, and other sources cited in this paper.

Appendix C

PRINCIPLE FUNDERS OF GLOBAL DOMINANCE GROUP ADVOCACY ORGANIZATIONS

1. Scaife—Richard Mellon-Scaife of Pittsburgh inherited the Mellon-Scaife fortune in 1965. He became the preeminent funder of the neo-conservative movement. Through three foundations, he has contributed over $57 million since 1974 directly to GDG organizations.

2. Bradley—the sale of Bradley-Allen to Rockwell for $1.65 billion funded this foundation. Solid neo-conservative activists such as Michael Grebe, President and CEO write the checks, not Bradley family members.

3. Olin—in a 1977 interview, John Olin stated that he created his foundation in an effort "to see free enterprise re-established in this country. Business and the public must be awakened to the creeping stranglehold that socialism has gained here since World War II." Olin Corporation made its fortune from Winchester bullets, copper mining, chlorine, and caustic soda. Through the years over $370 million dollars poured from this foundation into a wide variety of conservative organizations. It closed its doors in 2005.

Appendix D

INDIVIDUALS WITHIN THE GLOBAL DOMINANCE GROUP AND THEIR AFFILIATIONS

1. Abramowitz Morton I.; PNAC, NSC, Asst. Sec. of State, Amb. to Turkey, Amb. To Thailand, CISS, Carlyle
2. Abrams, Elliott; PNAC, Heritage, DoS, HU, Special Asst. to President Bush, NSC
3. Adelman, Ken; PNAC, CPD, DoD, DPB, Fox News, CPD, Affairs, Commander in Chief Strategic Air Command, Northrop Grumman, Arms Control Disarmament Agency
4. Aldrige, E.C. Jr.; CFR, PNAC, NSA, HU, HF, Sec. of the Air Force, Asst. Sec. of State, Douglas Aircraft, DoD, LTV Aerospace, WHOMB, Strategic Systems Group, Aerospace Corp.
5. Allen, Richard V.; PNAC, HF, HO, CFR, CPD, DPB, CNN, U.S. Congress, CIA Analyst,CSIS, NSC
6. Amitay, Morris J.; JINSA, AIPAC

7. Andrews, D.P.; SAIC
8. Andrews, Michael; L-3 Communications Holdings, Deputy Asst. Sec. of Research and Technology, Chief Scientist for the U.S. Army
9. Archibald, Nolan D.; Lockheed Martin
10. Baker, James, III, Caryle, Sec. of State (Bush), Sec. of Tres. (Reagan)
11. Barr, William P.; HF, HO, PNAC, CFR, NSA, U.S. Congress, Asst. to the President (Reagan), Carlyle,
12. Barram, David J.; Computer Sciences Corporation, U.S. DoC
13. Barrett, Barbara; Raytheon
14. Bauer, Gary; PNAC, Under Sec. of Ed.
15. Bechtel, Riley; Bechtel
16. Bechtel, Steve; Bechtel
17. Bell, Jeffrey; PNAC, MI
18. Bennett, Marcus C.; Lockheed Martin
19. Bennett, William J.; PNAC, NSA, HU, Sec. of Education
20. Bergner, Jeffrey; PNAC, HU, Boeing
21. Berns, Walter; AEI, CPD
22. Biggs, John H.; Boeing, CFR
23. Blechman, Barry; DoD, CPD
24. Bolton, John; JINSA, PNAC, AEI, DoS, DoJ, Amb. to UN, Agency Int'l Devel, Under Sec. State Arms Control-Int'l Security
25. Boot, Max; PNAC, CFR
26. Bremer, L. Paul; HF, CFR, Administrator of Iraq
27. Brock, William; CPD, Senator, Sec. of Labor
28. Brooks, Peter; DoD, Heritage, CPD
29. Bryen, Stephen; JINSA, AEI, DoD, L-3 Network Security, Edison Int'l, Disney
30. Bryson, John E.; Boeing
31. Bush, Jeb; PNAC, Governor of Florida
32. Bush, Geroge H. W., President, Carlyle, CIA Dir.
33. Bush, Wes; Northrop Grumman
34. Cambone, Stephen; PNAC, NSA, DoD, Los Alamos (specialized in theater nuclear weapons issues), Ofc. Sec. Defense: Dir. Strategic Def., CSIS, CSP
35. Chabraja, Nicholas D.; General Dynamics
36. Chain, John T. Jr. Northrup Grumman, Sec. of the Air Force, Dir. of Politico-MilitaryAffairs, DoS, Chief of Staff for Supreme Headquarters Allied Powers Europe, Commander in Chief Strategic Air Command
37. Chao, Elaine; HF, Sec. of Labor, Gulf Oil, U.S. DoT, CFR
38. Chavez, Linda; PNAC, MI, CFR
39. Cheney, Lynne; AEI, Lockheed Martin
40. Cheney, Richard; JINSA, PNAC, JINSA, AEI, HU, Halliburton, Sec. of Defense, VP of U.S.

41. Cohen Eliot A.; PNAC, AEI, DPB, DoD, CLI, CPD
42. Coleman, Lewis W.; Northrop Grumman
43. Colloredo-Manfeld, Ferdinand; Raytheon
44. Cook, Linda Z.; Boeing
45. Cooper, Dr. Robert S.; BAE Systems, Asst. Sec. of Defense
46. Cooper, Henry; CPD, DoD, Heritage, Depty Asst. Sec. Air Force, U.S. Arms Control Disarm. Strategic Def. Initiative, Applied Research Assoc, NIPP
47. Cox, Christopher; CSP, Senior Associate Counsel to the President, Chairman: SEC.
48. Crandall, Robert L.; Halliburton, FAA Man. Advisor Bd.
49. Cropsey, Seth; PNAC, AEI, HF, HU, DoD, Under-Sec. Navy
50. Cross, Devon Gaffney; PNAC, DPB, HF, CPD, HO
51. Crouch, J.D.; CSP, Depty. National Security Advisor, DoD, Amb. to Romania
52. Crown, James S.; General Dynamics, Henry Crown and Co.
53. Crown, Lester; General Dynamics, Henry Crown and Co.
54. Dachs, Alan; Bechtel, CFR
55. Dahlburg, Ken; SAIC, DoC, Asst. to Reagan, WHOMB
56. Darman, Richard G.; Carlyle, Dir. of the U.S. Office of Management and Budget, President Bush's Cabinet, Asst. to the President of the U.S., Deputy Sec. of the U.S. Treasury, Asst. U.S. Sec. of Commerce
57. Dawson, Peter; Bechtel
58. Decter, Midge; HF, HO, PNAC, CPD
59. Demmish, W.H.; SAIC
60. DeMuth, Christopher; AEI, U.S. Office of Management and Budget, Asst. to Pres. (Nixon)
61. Derr, Kenneth T.; Halliburton
62. Deutch, John; Dir. CIA, Deputy Sec. of Defense, Raytheon
63. Dine, Thomas; CLI, U.S. Senate, AIPAC, U.S. Agency Int'l Development, Free Radio Europe/Radio Liberty, Prague, Czech Rep., CFR
64. Dobriansky, Paula; PNAC, HU, AEI, CPB, DoS, Army, NSC European/Soviet Affairs, U.S.IA, ISS
65. Donnelly, Thomas; AEI, PNAC, Lockheed Martin
66. Downing, Wayne, Ret. Gen. U.S. Army, NSA, CLI, SAIC
67. Drummond, J.A.; SAIC
68. Duberstein, Kenneth M.; Boeing, WH Chief of Staff
69. Dudley, Bill; Bechtel
70. Eberstadt, Nicholas; AEI, CPD, PNAC, DoS (consultant)
71. Ebner, Stanley; Boeing, McDonnell Douglas, Northrop Grumman, CSP
72. Ellis, James O. Jr.; Lockheed Martin, Retired Navy Admiral and Commander U.S. Strategic Command

73. Epstein David, PNAC, Office of Sec. Defense
74. Everhart, Thomas; Raytheon
75. Falcoff, Mark; AEI, CFR
76. Fautua, David; PNAC, Lt. Col. U.S. Army
77. Fazio, Vic; Northrup Grumman, Congressman (CA)
78. Feith, Douglas; JINSA, DoD, L-3 Communications, Northrup Grumman, NSC, CFR, CPS
79. Feulner, Edwin J. Jr.; HF, HO, Sec. HUD, Inst. European Def. & Strategy Studies, CSIS
80. Foley, D.H.; SAIC
81. Fradkin, Hillel; PNAC, AEI,
82. Frank, Stephen E.; Northrop Grumman
83. Fricks, William P.; General Dynamics
84. Friedberg, Aaron; PNAC, CFR, NSA, DoD, CIA consultant
85. Frost, Phillip (M.D.); Northrop Grumman
86. Fukuyama, Francis; PNAC, CFR, HU
87. Gates, Robert, CIA-dir. NSA, SAIC
88. Gaffney, Frank; CPD, PNAC, Washington Times, DoD
89. Gaut, C. Christopher; Halliburton
90. Gedmin, Jeffrey; AEI, PNAC, CPD
91. Gerecht, Reuel Marc; PNAC, AEI, CIA, CBS
92. Gillis, S. Malcom; Halliburton, Electronic Data Systems Corp
93. Gingrich, Newt; AEI, CFR, HO, DPB, U.S House of Reps., CLI, CPD
94. Goodman, Charles H.; General Dynamics
95. Gorelick, Jamie S. United Technologies Corporation, Deputy attorney general, DoD, Asst. to the Sec. of Energy, National Com. Terrorist Threats Upon the U.S., DoJ, Nat'l Security Adv., CIA, CFR
96. Gouré, Daniel; DoD, SAIC, DoE, DoS (consultant), CSP
97. Haas, Lawrence J.; Communications WHOMB, CPD
98. Hadley, Stephen; NSA advisor to Bush, Lockheed Martin
99. Hamre, John J. ITT Industries, SAIC, U. S. Dep. Sec. of Defense, Under Sec. of Defense, Senate Armed Services Committee
100. Hash, Tom; Bechtel
101. Haynes, Bill; Bechtel
102. Hoeber, Amoretta; CSP, Defense Industry consultant, CPD, CFR, DoD
103. Horner, Charles; HU, CSP, DoS, Staff member of Sen. Daniel Patrick Moyihan
104. Howell, W.R.; Halliburton, Dir. Deutsche Bank
105. Hunt, Ray L.; Halliburton, Electronic Data Systems Corp, President's Foreign Intelligence Advisory Board
106. Inman, Bobby Ray; Ret. Adm. U.S. Navy, CIA-Dep. Dir, CFR, NSA, SAIC

107. Ikle, Fred; AEI, PNAC, CPD, HU, DPB, Under Sec. DoD, Def. Policy Board
108. Iorizzo, Robert P.; Northrop Grumman
109. Jackson, Bruce; PNAC, NSA, AEI, CFR, Office of Sec. of Def., U.S. Army Military Intelligence, Lockheed Martin, Martin Marietta, CLI, CPD
110. Jennings, Sir John, Bechtel
111. Johnson, Jay L.;General Dynamics, Retired Admiral, U.S. Navy
112. Jones, A.K.; SAIC, DoD
113. Joseph, Robert; Under Sec. of State for Arms Control and Int'l Security Affairs, DoD, CSP, NIPP
114. Joulwan, George A.; General Dynamics, Retired General, U.S. Army
115. Kagan, Frederick PNAC, West Point Military Academy
116. Kagan, Robert; PNAC, CFR, DoS (Deputy for Policy), Washington Post, CLI, editor Weekly Standard
117. Kaminski, Paul G. General Dynamics, Under Sec. of U.S. Department of Defense
118. Kaminsky, Phyllis ; JINSA, CSP, NSC, Int'l Pub. Rel. Society,
119. Kampelman, Max M.; PNAC, JINSA, CPD, Sec. Housing and Urban Development, CPD
120. Keane, John M. General Dynamics, Retired General, U.S. Army, Vice Chief of Staff of the Army, DoD Policy Board
121. Kennard, William, Carlyle, NY Times, FCC
122. Kemble, Penn; PNAC, DoS, U.S.IA
123. Kemp, Jack; JINSA, HF, Sec. of HUD, U.S. House of Reps., CPD
124. Keyworth, George; CSP, HU, Los Alamos, General Atomics, NSC
125. Khalilzad, Zalmay; PNAC, Amb. to Iraq
126. King, Gwendolyn S.; Lockheed Martin
127. Kirkpatrick, Jeane; AEI, JINSA, CFR, CPD, NSA, Sec. of Defense Commission, U.S. Rep. to UN, CLI, CPD, Carlyle
128. Kramer, H.M.J., Jr.; SAIC
129. Kristol, Irving; CFR, AEI, DoD, Wall Street Journal Board of Contributors
130. Kristol, William; PNAC, AEI, MI, VP Chief of Staff '89, CLI, Domes. Policy Adv. to VP, '89
131. Kupperman, Charles; CPD, Boeing, NIPP
132. Lagon, Mark; PNAC, CFR, AEI, DoS
133. Lane, Andrew; Halliburton
134. Larson, Charles R.; Retired Admiral of the U.S. Navy, Northrop Grumman
135. Laspa Jude; Bechtel
136. Ledeen, Michael; AEI, JINSA, DoS (consultant), DoD
137. Lehman, John; PNAC, NSA, DoD, Sec. of Navy
138. Lehrman, Lewis E.; AEI, MI, HF, G.W. Bush Oil Co. partner
139. Lesar, Dave; Halliburton

140. Libby, I. Lewis; PNAC, Chief of Staff to Richard Cheney, DoS, Northrup Grumman, RAND, DoD, House of Rep., Team B
141. Livingston, Robert; House of Rep., CSP, DoJ
142. Loy, James M., Lockheed Martin, Retired U.S. Navy Admiral
143. Malone, C.B.; SAIC, Martin Marietta, DynCorp, Titan Corp., CLI, CPD
144. Martin, J. Landis; Halliburton
145. McCorkindale, Douglas H.; Lockheed Martin
146. McDonnell, John F.; Boeing
147. McFarlane, Robert; National Security Advisor (Reagan), CPD, Bush's Transition Advisory Committee on Trade
148. McNerney, James W.; Boeing, 3M, GE
149. Meese, Edwin; HF, HO, U.S. Attorney General, Bechtel, CPD
150. Merrill, Philip; CSP, DoD, Import-Export Bank of U.S.
151. Minihan, Kenneth A.; Ret. General U.S. Air Force, BAE Systems, DoD, Defense Intelligence Agency
152. Moore, Frank W.; Northrop Grumman
153. Moore, Nick; Bechtel
154. Moorman, Thomas S.; CSP, Aerospace Corporation, Rumsfeld Space Commission, U.S. Air Force: Former vice chief of staff
155. Mundy, Carl E. Jr.; General Dynamics, Retired General, U.S. Marine Corps Commandant
156. Muravchik, Joshua; AEI, JINSA, PNAC, CLI, CPD
157. Murphy, Eugene F.; Lockheed Martin, GE
158. Nanula, Richard; Boeing
159. Novak, Michael; AEI, CPD
160. Nunn, Sam; GE, U.S. Senator, Chairman Senate Armed Services Committee
161. O'Brien, Rosanne; Northrop Grumman, Carlyle
162. Odeen, Philip A.; Defense and Arms Control Staff for Henry Kissinger, TRW, Northrop Grumman
163. Ogilvie, Scott; Bechtel
164. Owens, William, Ret. Adm. U.S. Navy, DPB, Joint Chiefs of Staff, SAIC
165. Perle, Richard; AEI, PNAC, CPD, CFR, NSA, JINSA, HU, DoD, DPD, CLI, Carlyle
166. Peters, Aulana L.; Northrop Grumman, SEC
167. Pipes, Daniel; PNAC, CPD, Team B
168. Podhoretz, Norman; PNAC, CPD, HU, CFR
169. Poses, Frederic; Raytheon
170. Precourt, Jay A.; Halliburton
171. Quayle, Dan; PNAC, VP U.S.
172. Ralston, Joseph W.; Lockheed Martin, Retired Air Force Gen., Vice Chairman of Joint Chiefs of Staff

173. Reed, Deborah L.; Halliburton, Pres. Southern CA. Gas & Elec
174. Rice, Condoleezza, Hoover Institute, Foreign Policy Advisor to George H. W. Bush, Secretary State
175. Ridgeway, Rozanne; Boeing, Asst. Sec. of State- Europe and Canada, Amb. German Democratic Republic, Finland, DoD
176. Riscassi, Robert; L-3 Communications Holdings, UN Command/Korea, Army vice chief of staff; Joint Chiefs of Staff
177. Roche, James; Sec. of the Air Force, CSP, Boeing, Northrop Grumman, DoS
178. Rodman, Peter W.; PNAC, NSA, Asst. Sec. of Defense for Int'l Security Affairs, DoS,
179. Rowen, Henry S.; PNAC, HO, CFR, DPB, DoD
180. Rubenstein, David M.; Carlysle, Deputy Asst. to the President for Domestic Policy (Carter)
181. Rubin, Michael; AEI, CFR, Office of Sec. of Defense
182. Rudman, Warren; U.S. Senator, Raytheon
183. Ruettgers, Michael; Raytheon
184. Rumsfeld, Donald; PNAC, HO, Sec. of Defense, Bechtel, Tribune Co.
185. Sanderson, E.J.; SAIC
186. Savage, Frank; Lockheed Martin
187. Scaife, Richard Mellon; HO, HF, CPD, Tribune Review Publishing Co.
188. Scheunemann, Randy; PNAC, Office of Sec. of Defense (consultant), Lockheed Martin, CLI Founder /Dir., CPD
189. Schlesinger, James ; DoE, Atomic Energy Commission, Dir. CIA, CSP
190. Schmitt, Gary; PNAC, CLI, DoD (consultant), CLI
191. Schneider, William, Jr.; BAE Systems, PNAC, DoS, House of Rep./Senate staffer, WHOMB, CSP, NIPP
192. Schultz, George; HO, AEI, CPD, CFR, PNAC, Sec. of State, Sec. of Treasury, Bechtel, CLI, CPD
193. Shalikashvili, John M.; Boeing, Retired Chairman of Joint Chiefs of Staff, DoD, Ret. Gen. U.S. Army, CFR
194. Sharer, Kevin; Northrup Grumman, U.S. Naval Academy, Ret. Lt. Com. U.S. Navy
195. Sheehan, Jack, Bechtel, DPB
196. Shelman, Thomas W.; Northrup Grumman, DoD
197. Shulsky, Abram; PNAC, DoD
198. Skates, Ronald L.; Raytheon
199. Slaughter, John Brooks; Northrop Grumman
200. Sokolski, Henry; PNAC, HF, HO, CIA, DoD
201. Solarz, Stephen; PNAC, HU, DoS, CPD, Carlyle
202. Spivey, William; Raytheon
203. Statton, Tim; Bechtel

204. Stevens, Anne; Lockheed Martin
205. Stevens, Robert J.; Lockheed Martin
206. Stuntz, Linda; Raytheon, U.S. DoE
207. Sugar, Ronald D.; Northrup Grumman, Association of the U.S. Army
208. Swanson, William; Raytheon, Lockheed Martin
209. Tkacik, John; PNAC, HF, U.S. Senate
210. Turner, Michael J.; BAE Systems
211. Ukropina, James R., Lockheed Martin
212. Van Cleave, William R.; Team B, HO, CSP, CPD, DoD, NIPP
213. Waldron, Arthur; CSP, AEI, PNAC, CFR
214. Walkush, J.P.; SAIC
215. Wallop, Malcolm; Heritage, HU, CSP, PNAC, Senate
216. Walmsley, Robert; General Dynamics, Retired Vice-Admiral, Royal Navy, Chief of Defense Procurement for the UK Ministry of Defense
217. Warner, John Hillard; SAIC, U.S. Army/Airforce Assn.
218. Watts, Barry; PNAC Northrop Grumman
219. Weber, John Vincent (Vin); PNAC, George W. Bush Campaign Advisor, NPR
220. Wedgewood, Ruth; CLI, DoD, DoJ, DoS, CFR
221. Weldon, Curt; House of Rep, CSP
222. Weyrich, Paul; HF, PNAC, U.S. Senate
223. White, John P.; L-3 Communications, Chair of the Com. on Roles and Missions of the Armed Forces, DoD
224. Wieseltier, Leon; PNAC, CLI
225. Williams, Christopher A.; PNAC, DPB, Under Sec. for Defense, Boeing (lobbyist), Northrop Grumman (lobbyist), CLI
226. Winter, Donald C; Northrop Grumman
227. Wolfowitz, Paul; PNAC, HF, HU, Team B, Under-Sec. Defense, World Bank, Northrop Grumman, DoS
228. Wollen, Foster; Bectel
229. Woolsey R. James; PNAC, JINSA, CLI, DPB, CIA (Dir.), Under Sec. of Navy, NIPP
230. Wurmser, David; AEI, Office of VP Middle East Adviser, DoS
231. Yearly, Douglas C.; Lockheed Martin
232. Young, A.T.; SAIC
233. Zaccaria, Adrian; Bechtel
234. Zafirovski, Michael S.; Boeing
235. Zakheim, Dov S.; PNAC, HF, CFR, DoD, Northrup Grumman, McDonnell Douglas, CPD
236. Zinni, Anthony C.; Retired General U.S. Marines, BAE Systems, Commander in Chief U.S. Central Command
237. Zoellick, Robert; PNAC, U.S. Trade Representative, DoS, CSIS, CFR, DOJ

THE ISRAEL LOBBY AND THE GLOBAL DOMINANCE GROUP

by Andrew Sloan

*There exists a deep friendship between Israel and the U.S.—
between our peoples and countries. The basis of this friendship is
common values, a commitment to democratic values, freedom,
peace, and common interests, including the drive toward regional
stability and preventing terrorism and violence.*
—Ariel Sharon

*We will speak up for our principles and we will stand up for our
friends in the world. And one of our most important friends is the
State of Israel.* —George W. Bush

Israel's relationship to the United States has been described in many
ways: the U.S.'s pawn, a strategic asset to U.S. interests, a client of
the U.S., the local "cop on the beat" for the U.S. in the Middle East,
an imperialist stooge, a barrier to Soviet penetration of the Middle
East during the Cold War, the U.S.'s protégé, a symbiotic relationship
with the U.S., the dog's tail, the tail's dog, or as the USAID web site
calls it, a "close bilateral relationship." Clearly, the U.S. and Israel
have ties unique to any bi-nation alliance. Determining whether
Israel is the U.S.'s pawn or protégé is a question of Israel's autonomy
and authority of their own foreign and domestic affairs.

What has been especially particular in this relationship is the U.S.'
unwavering support towards Israel, both economically and militaris-
tically. Some argue this support even contradicts the U.S.' self-inter-
ests in the Middle East and beyond. Others juxtapose Israel's
expansionist agenda with the U.S.' neo-conservative global dominance agenda, essentially, as one of the same. This debate of self-
interests (however evident or conspicuous the administration's
agendas really are) has been prompted by the recent eruption of an
even more overarching question: who is responsible for the U.S.'
hyper-generosity towards Israel?

The working paper, "The Israel Lobby and U.S. Foreign Policy" by
John Mearsheimer of the University of Chicago and Stephen Walt of

Harvard's Kennedy School of Government, asserts the Israel Lobby (and yes, they do mean Lobby with a capital L) as being the figurehead in grappling the U.S.' magnificent support. There have been copious amounts of celebratory review articles exalting the duo for their bravery of saying it like it is. What better way to expose such axioms than by individuals at prestigious institutions. Some, however, question whether the Lobby deserves so much credit for the support of the state of Israel, arguing that Washington alone is quite responsible for its choices of USAID allocations. This argument, supported namely by Noam Chomsky, holds that a powerful lobby does indeed exist, but to grant the lobby such influence is to leave the U.S. government "untouched on its high pinnacle of nobility."[1] Despite the paper's criticism or concurrence, all have agreed that Mearsheimer and Walt sparked a much-needed debate into the influence of the Israel Lobby.

The Lobby

As explained by Mearsheimer and Walt, the Israel Lobby has been effective in shaping U.S. foreign policy in a pro-Israel direction. "We use 'the Lobby' as shorthand for the loose coalition of individuals and organizations." They clarify that "this is not meant to suggest the 'the Lobby' is a unified movement with a central leadership, or that individuals within it do not disagree on certain issues." The Lobby, though portrayed as a seemingly concrete entity, is a rather abstract amassing of U.S. sentiments towards Israel, coming from the smallest of synagogues and churches, but also established lobby organizations such as the American Israel Public Affairs Committee (AIPAC) and the Conference of Presidents of Major Jewish Organizations, both of which are run by "hardliners who generally support the Likud Party's expansionist policies."[2] For the purposes of this section, I will focus on think tanks and individuals that are most identifiable and influential, if only to pinpoint entities amongst the vagueness of Mearsheimer and Walt's "Lobby."

The American-Israel Public Affairs Committee alone has a $40 million annual budget. Jeffrey Birnbaum from the Washington Post writes, "It ranked consistently among the five most influential interest groups in *Fortune* magazine's poll of Washington insiders (alongside such better-known lobbies as AARP and the National Rifle

Association). A recent survey by the *National Journal* ranked AIPAC No. 2 among Democratic lawmakers and No. 4 among Republicans."[3] *CNN* reports that in 2000, AIPAC "spent more than $1 million in lobbying. It also directed many of the pro-Israel political action committees, which made $6.5 million in campaign contributions that year, two-thirds to Democrats, and a third to Republicans."[4]

Mearsheimer and Walt argue that there is no match to the Israel Lobby. No other lobby group has such associations and influence. Other critics contend that we overstate the lobby's power because we overlook the benefits Israel and the U.S. share with each other, regardless of any lobby influence.

Besides AIPAC, other pro-Israel lobbies include The Jewish Institute of National Security Affairs (JINSA), the Conference of Presidents of Major Jewish Organizations, Committee for Accuracy in Middle East Affairs (CAMERA), the Zionist Organization of America, and the Washington Institute for Near East Policy (WINEP).

To say that these groups act in isolation amongst other Jewish organizations would be a grave shortcoming. Mearsheimer and Walt explain that major U.S. think tanks that are religiously unaffiliated share common sentiments. "Over the past twenty-five years, [lobby groups] have established a commanding presence at the American Enterprise Institute, the Brookings Institute, the Center for Security Policy, the Foreign Policy Research Institute, the Heritage Foundation, the Hudson Institute, Project for New American Century (PNAC), and the Institute for Foreign Policy Analysis." They write, "These think tanks employ few, if any, critics of U.S. support for Israel."

A letter from PNAC to President Bush in 2002 regarding Israel, Arafat, and the war on terrorism shows quite clearly their neo-conservative and Israel expansionist ideologies:

> . . . No one should doubt that the United States and Israel share a common enemy. We are both targets of what you have correctly called an "Axis of Evil." Israel is targeted in part because it is our friend, and in part, because it is an island of liberal, democratic principles—American principles—in a sea of tyranny, intolerance, and hatred. . . . Mr. President, it can no longer be the policy of the United States

to urge, much less to pressure, Israel to continue negotiating with Arafat, any more than we would be willing to be pressured to negotiate with Osama Bin Laden or Mullah Omar. . . . Israel's fight against terrorism is our fight. Israel's victory is an important part of our victory. For reasons both moral and strategic, we need to stand with Israel in its fight against terrorism."[5]

The letter is signed by such neo-conservative players as Bruce Jackson, Richard Perle, and James Woolsey among others.

Not only does this letter tell the President how to handle Israel's domestic affairs, but it aligns Israel's foreign affairs (as they see them) to our own. Israel's threats are U.S. threats and visa versa.

The Israel Lobby has a significant presence in corporate media. Haim Saban is Chairman and CEO of Fox Family Worldwide, Inc. He says in a 2002 *New York Times* interview, "I'm a one-issue guy and my issue is Israel." Mr. Saban gave millions of dollars to Democratic campaigns, courted John Kerry, and gave tens of millions for a Middle East division at the Brookings Institute, and vacations with Bill Clinton. To say he holds influence over the policies between Israel and the U.S. is not directly known. Yet, Bill Clinton credits him for his dedication to Israel, the support of Mr. Clinton's foundation, and commitment to reconciliation in the Middle East. Perhaps he wants to see peace between Israel and Palestine however, the article mentions his hours long conversations with Ariel Sharon and informal visits. It does not mention any relationship between Mr. Saban and Mr. Arafat.[6]

Examples like Saban are key in understanding how the Lobby works. He is a powerful individual who happens to own one of the top communication companies in the U.S. In this regard, the Lobby is more systemic than specific. The Lobby may work through explicit channels such as an open letter from the PNAC to a president, but more often than not, it is most effective through the channels of private interests, cronyism, and campaign donations. As the most widely accessible mediums of dialogue come from corporations, one can see the Lobby's snowball effect from the executive level down to the home television.

There is no insinuation here that the Jewish Lobby owns the media. Indeed, one need not be Jewish to have a pro-Israel bias just as one may be a deeply religious Jew and renounce the politics of the state of Israel.

It is unclear how much the Israel lobby is responsible for the U.S.' foreign policies with Israel. Nonetheless, there are undeniable correlations that deserve attention. Mearsheimer and Walt note that since 1982, the U.S. has vetoed thirty-two Security Council resolutions critical of Israel, more than the total number of vetoes cast by all the other Security Council members. The U.S. has particularly blocked the efforts of Arab states to put Israel's nuclear arsenal on the International Atomic Energy Agency's (IAEA) agenda, which calls for the disarmament of nuclear weapons and other non-proliferation measures.[7]

The Bush/Cheney administration employs many members of the Lobby including such pro-Israel advocates as Elliot Abrams, John Bolton, Douglas Feith, I. Lewis Libby, Richard Perle, Paul Wolfowitz, and David Wurmser. In 2004, The *New York Times* reported that immediately after September 11, Feith and Wolfowitz pushed for attacks against Iraq and then Iran, a policy AIPAC advocated.[8]

The recent AIPAC scandal clearly shows the Lobby's infiltration into government circles. Lawrence A. Franklin, a veteran Pentagon analyst admitted using his Defense Department position to illegally disclosed classified information to AIPAC employees Steven J. Rosen and Keith Weissman, which later was forwarded to Israel. Franklin was given a prison sentence while Rosen, former director of foreign-policy issues at AIPAC, and Weissman, AIPAC's former senior Iran analyst await trial.[9]

The Israel Lobby has been effective in shaping the media and stifling any public debate critical of Israel and Middle East GDG policies, simply by labeling any type of dissent as anti-Semitic. It is this equating of Israel's foreign policies with Israel's identity as a state of a historically persecuted people that leaves critics tiptoeing around issues. Media analyst Edward Herman, in his paper "The Pro-Israel Lobby," considers that a major manifestation of lobby power "is its ability to keep a lid on public discussion and exposure of Israeli abuses (e.g., torture, aid to terrorist states, cross-border terrorism of its own in Lebanon, illegal buildup of a nuclear arsenal)."[10]

Former Public Editor of the *New York Times*, Daniel Okrent, published an article in April 2005 about how tight of a rope a journal must walk when reporting on the Israel/Palestine conflict. Partisans from each side are quick to criticize any issue having to do with Israel or Palestine. In his postscript, Okrent writes:

> During my research, representatives of If Americans Knew, [an organization that calls into question the media bias towards Israel], expressed the belief that unless the paper assigned equal numbers of Muslim and Jewish reporters to cover the conflict, Jewish reporters should be kept off the beat.
>
> I find this profoundly offensive, but not nearly as repellent as a calumny that has popped up in my e-mail with lamentable frequency—the charge that the *Times* is anti-Semitic. Even if you stipulate that the *Times's* reporters and editors favor the Palestinian cause (something I am not remotely prepared to do), this is an astonishing debasement. If reporting that is sympathetic to Palestinians, or antipathetic to Israelis, is anti-Semitism, what is real anti-Semitism? What word do you have left for conscious discrimination, or open hatred, or acts of intentional, ethnically motivated violence?[11]

Alison Weir and researchers at *If Americans Knew* conducted an analysis of Associated Press coverage of Palestinian and Israeli deaths. The study, conducted for the entire year of 2004, found that AP reported 131 percent of Israeli deaths from the conflict while only 66 percent of Palestinian deaths. Specifically looking at children deaths, the study found 113 percent of Israeli children killed, while a meager 15 percent of Palestinian children killed (see Chapter 11).[12]

The primary newswire in the country is the Associated Press, which provides news feeds to 1,700 daily, weekly, non-English, and college newspapers that serve 121 countries. The Israel bias is more than chilling.[13] The U.S. independent Jewish weekly newspaper, *Jewish Press*, ran an article following up a lecture by Alison Weir at Sonoma State University, sponsored by Project Censored. The article claimed Weir applauding a massacre of Jews standing outside a nightclub, and Project Censored as urging readers to support the International Solidarity Movement, "an organization notorious for its support of Palestinian terror organizations." Alison's research was

340 | CENSORED 2007

never mentioned, and instead, she and Project Censored were dismissed as Jew-haters.[14]

Noam Chomsky has been a leading critic of Mearsheimer and Walt's "Israel Lobby." He is hesitant to grant any lobby such omnipotence, and to do so, is to underestimate the imperialist agendas coming from Washington. He does not blame Israel of malicious treatment towards Palestinians before holding the U.S. up to scrutiny for funding and supporting such maltreatment in the first place.

"In my opinion the Israeli lobby gets its input in large part because it happens to line up with powerful sectors of domestic U.S. power," Chomsky writes.[15]

Indeed, the U.S. and many Arab nations use Israel as a point of contention in inter-Arab matter and U.S.-Middle East matters. There is no doubt that the current and previous administrations use Israel to perpetuate the Global Dominance Agenda (see Chapter 10) and define an "us vs. them" scenario. In a speech to AIPAC, Cheney illustrated the global struggle between "good and evil", reminiscent of Cold War rhetoric and clearly stated the importance of the U.S.-Israel relationship:

> . . . the freedom and security of Israel are vital interests to the United States of America . . . There is no doubt that America's commitment to Israel's security is solid, enduring and unshakeable . . . Israel, and the United States, and all civilized nations will win the war on terror. . . . The terrorists want to end all American and Western influence in the Middle East. . . . ultimately to establish a totalitarian empire that encompasses a region from Spain, across North Africa, through the Middle East and South Asia, all the way around to Indonesia.[16]

It is important to give weight to both sides of the coin. There already exists a strong global dominance agenda in the U.S. government that aligns with Israel's expansionist agendas. The question stands, why must a lobby exist when there is already such a strong relationship? Israel is a geo-political asset to the U.S., in part because of the war on terror as well as its location in an oil rich region. As Israel faces hostility from its neighbors, foreign interests of both countries align. But this does not mean all foreign interests align, which is why the

Lobby's influence is beneficial for Israel in eliminating U.S. contradictions. The Lobby has effectively been stifling debate and allowing a powerful minority to implement brutal foreign policies that go unquestioned. At this point in our geo-political history, the U.S. media must provide accurate, fair, and balanced coverage of the Israeli-Palestinian-U.S. relationship.

Notes

1. Chomsky, Noam. "The Israel Lobby?," *Z Magazine*, March 28, 2006.
2. Mearsheimer and Walt. "The Israel Lobby." *London Review of Books*, March 23, 2006.
3. Birnbaum, Jeffrey H. "Pro-Israel Lobbying Group Holds Meeting Amid Worries." *The Washington Post*, May 19, 2005.
4. "Republicans Launch National Convention in New York City," *Lou Dobbs Tonight* on CNN, August 31, 2004.
5. Project for the New American Century letter to President George W. Bush. April 3, 2002, http://www.newamericancentury.org/Bushletter-040302.htm
6. Sorkin, Andrew Ross. "Schlepping to Moguldomo." *The New York Times*, September 5, 2004.
7. Mearsheimer and Walt. "The Israel Lobby." *London Review of Books*, March 23, 2006.
8. Risen, James and David Johnston. " Spy Case Renews Debate Over Pro-Israel Lobby's Ties to Conservatives at Pentagon."*The New York Times*, September 6, 2004.
9. Seper, Jerry. "Dismiss AIPAC charges, duo asks; Case is called unprecedented." *The Washington Times*, February 16, 2006.
10. Herman, Edward. "The pro-Israel lobby." *Z-Magazine*, July 1994.
11. Okrent, Daniel. "The Hottest Button: How The Times Covers Israel and Palestine." *The New York Times*, April 24, 2005.
12. Weir, Alison. "Deadly Distortion." If Americans Knew, April 26, 2006, http://www.ifamericanknew.org/media/ap-report.html
13. Associated Press. "About AP: Facts and Figures." http://www.ap.org/pages/about/about.html
14. Olshaker, Edward, "Hate Uncensored." *Jewish Press*, February 15, 2006, http://www.jewishpress.com/page.do/18254/Hate_Uncensored.html.
15. Speech by Noam Chomsky at the University of California at Berkeley, "The New World Order," March 16, 1991.
16. Transcript: Vice President Cheney Speaks to *The American Israel Public Affairs Committee 2006 Policy Conference*. Washington D.C Convention Center, Washington, D.C. March 7, 2006, http://www.washingtonpost.com/wpdyn/content/article/2006/03/07/AR2006030700739.html.

THIS MODERN WORLD
by TOM TOMORROW

CHAPTER II

A Study of Bias in the Associated Press

By Peter Phillips, Sarah Randle, Brian Fuch, Zoe Huffman, and Fabrice Romero

On October 25, 2005 the American Civil Liberties Union (ACLU) posted to their website forty-four autopsy reports, acquired from American military sources, covering the deaths of civilians who died while in U.S. military prisons in Iraq and Afghanistan in 2002–2004. A press release by ACLU announcing the deaths resulted from torture was immediately picked up by Associated Press (AP) wire service, making the story available to U.S. corporate media nationwide. A thorough check of LexisNexis and Proquest electronic data bases, using the keywords ACLU and autopsy, showed that at least 95 percent of the daily papers in the U.S. did not to pick up the story nor did AP ever conduct follow up coverage on the issue.

The autopsy reports provide positive proof of widespread torture by U.S. forces. Our research team at Project Censored felt that this story should have been front page news throughout the country. Instead the story was hardly covered and quickly disappeared.

One of forty-four U.S. military autopsy reports reads as follows: "Final Autopsy Report: DOD 003164, (Detainee) Died as a result of asphyxia (lack of oxygen to the brain) due to strangulation as evidenced by the recently fractured hyoid bone in the neck and soft tissue hemorrhage extending downward to the level of the right thyroid cartilage. Autopsy revealed bone fracture, rib fractures, contusions in mid abdomen, back and buttocks extending to the left flank, abrasions, lateral buttocks. Contusions, back of legs and knees; abrasions on knees, left fingers and encircling to left wrist. Lacerations and superficial cuts, right fourth and fifth fingers. Also, blunt force injuries, predominately recent contusions (bruises) on the torso and lower extremities. Abrasions on left wrist are consistent with use of restraints. No evidence of defense injuries or natural disease. Manner of death is homicide. Whitehorse Detainment Facility, Nasiriyah, Iraq."

A second report describes how a twenty-seven-year-old Iraqi male died while being interrogated by Navy SEALs on April 5, 2004 in Mosul, Iraq. During his confinement he was hooded, flex-cuffed, sleep deprived and subjected to hot and cold environmental conditions, including the use of cold water on his body and hood. The exact cause of death was "undetermined" although the autopsy stated that hypothermia may have contributed to his death.

Another Iraqi detainee died on January 9, 2004 in Al Asad, Iraq, while being interrogated. He was standing, shackled to the top of a doorframe with a gag in his mouth, at the time he died. The cause of death was asphyxia and blunt force injuries.

Anthony Romero, Executive Director of ACLU stated, "There is no question that U.S. interrogations have resulted in deaths." ACLU attorney Amrit Sing adds, "These documents present irrefutable evidence that U.S. operatives tortured detainees to death during interrogations."

Our research showed that the *Los Angeles Times* covered the story on page A-4 with a 635-word report headlined "Autopsies Support Abuse Allegations." Fewer than a dozen other daily newspapers including: *Bangor Daily News*, Maine, page 8; *Telegraph-Herald*, Dubuque Iowa, page 6; *Charleston Gazette*, page 5; *Advocate*, Baton Rouge, page 11; and a half dozen others actually covered the story. The *Pittsburgh Post-Gazette* and the *Seattle Times* buried the story inside general Iraq news articles. *USA Today* posted the story on their website. MSNBC posted the story to their website, but apparently did not consider it newsworthy enough to air on television.

Given that nearly every daily newspaper in the United States subscribes to AP wire service and that AP had in fact sent out the torture story led us to question if story selection bias was widespread within U.S. newspapers and if bias was evident within the AP system itself.

ASSOCIATED PRESS

The Associated Press is a not-for-profit cooperative wire service for news at a national and global level. The mission of the AP is "to be the essential global news network." It boasts of "distinctive news services with the highest quality, reliability and objectivity with reports that are accurate, balanced and informed." The AP has 242 bureaus worldwide that delivers news report twenty-four hours a day, seven days a week to 121 countries in five languages including English, German, Dutch, French, and Spanish and has 3,700 employees. In the U.S. alone, 1,700 daily, weekly, non-English, college newspapers, and 5,000 radio and television stations receive the AP. The AP reaches over a billion people every day via print, radio, or television. Internationally, the AP has 8,500 subscribers. To subsidize revenue, the AP has sold selections of text, photo, audio, and video to commercial online operations. Annual revenues in 2004 were $630 million.

There are two types of members in the cooperative: regular and associate. The regular membership is only available to printed newspapers, mainly dailies, published in the U.S. It entails regular exclusive contributions of news to AP and entitles the member to a vote in elections for the AP Board of Directors. Associate membership is available to daily newspapers, some weekly newspaper, and broadcast stations but do not allow a vote in elections for the Board of Directors. Associate members also contribute news to the AP and receive the same services.

Members pay a subscription fee, based on the size of circulation, to have access to the newswire services. The smaller the circulation, the smaller the services and thus the smaller the number of stories available to the newspaper. If a story is run on the state wire, only those in that state will see the story. But if the story is more nationally pertinent then it will be put out on the national wire, and so forth up to the international level. Once the story has been put out on the wire, it is up to the individual member whether the story will go into their newspaper, air on their radio or television station.

The AP Board of Directors is made up of twenty-two newspaper and media executives including the Presidents/CEOs of ABC, Cox News, McClatchy, Gannett, Scripps, Tribune, Hearst, *Washington Post* and several smaller/regional newspaper chains. Two directors are members of conservative policy councils including the Hoover Institute and the Business Round Table. Three are on the board of directors of Mutual Insurance, and one is on the board of the world's largest defense contractor, Lockheed Martin. The AP Board represents a solid corporate media network of the largest publishers in the U.S. and provides a clear tilt towards right-wing conservative perspectives (see appendix for full listing of AP directors).

IMPEACHMENT MOVEMENT AND AP

Impeachment advocates are mobilizing widely in the U.S. Over 1,000 pro-impeachment letters to the editors in major newspapers were published during a six month period from October 2005 to March of 2006. *Pittsburgh Post-Gazette* letter writer George Matus says, "I am still enraged over unasked questions about exit polls, touch-screen voting, Iraq, the cost of the new Medicare . . . who formulated our energy policy, Jack Abramoff, the Downing Street Memos, and impeachment." David Anderson in McMinnville, Oregon pens to the *Oregonian*, "Where are the members of our congressional delegation now in demanding the current president's actions be investigated to see if impeachment or censure are appropriate actions?" William Dwyer's letter in the Charleston Gazette says, "Congress will never have the courage to start the impeachment process without a groundswell of outrage from the people."

Dozens of city councils, boards of supervisors, and local and state level Democrat central committees have voted for impeachment. Arcata, California voted for impeachment on January 6, 2006. The City and County of San Francisco, voted Yes on February 28. The Sonoma County Democrat Central Committee (CA) voted for impeachment on March 16. The city council of Sebastopol California voted for impeachment in May. The townships of Newfane, Brookfield, Dummerston, Marlboro, Rockingham, Battleboro and Putney in Vermont all voted for impeachment in March and April. The New Mexico State Democrat party convention rallied on March 18 for the "impeachment of George Bush and his lawful removal from office." The national Green Party called for impeachment on January 3. New Hampshire Democrats voted for impeachment on June 9. Democrats in Maine called for impeachment June 4. Vermont's Democrat party called for impeachment in April, and an impeachment resolution was introduced into the Illinois Legislature April 24. Brookline, Massachusetts called for impeachment in late May of 2006.

Op-ed writers at the *St. Petersburg Times, Newsday, Yale Daily News, Barrons, Detroit Free Press,* and the *Boston Globe* have called for impeachment. The *San Francisco Bay Guardian* (1/25/06) *The Nation* (1/30/06) and *Harper's* (3/06) published cover articles calling for impeachment. As of March 16, 2006, thirty-two U.S. House of Representatives have signed on as co-sponsors to House Resolution 635, which would create a Select Committee to look into the grounds for recommending President Bush's impeachment.

Polls show that nearly a majority of Americans favor impeachment. In October of 2005, Public Affairs Research found that 50 percent of Americans said that President Bush should be impeached if he lied about the war in Iraq. A Zogby International poll from early November 2005 found that 53 percent of Americans say, "If President Bush did not tell the truth about his reasons for going to war with Iraq, Congress should consider holding him accountable through impeachment." A March 16, 2006 poll by American Research Group showed that 42 percent of Americans favored impeaching Bush.

Despite all this advocacy and sentiment for impeachment, AP has yet to cover this emerging mass movement. While AP has covered most incidental calls for impeachment listed above, they have not evaluated impeachment as a widespread national issue. Instead AP has covered impeachment very much like the *Wall Street Journal*'s editorial on March 16, which said it is the "the loony left" seeking impeachment, and perhaps some Democrats will join in feeding on the "bile of the censure/impeachment brigades."

Along this line AP released a national story by Deborah Hasting on April 29, 2006 critical of former attorney general Ramsey Clark's impeachment efforts. Hasting's writes [Clark] "lives in a reality of his own making . . ." and went on to link Clark to an international "rogues gallery" of criminals including: Slobodan Milosevic, (See Chapter 14 for a discussion of Milosevic's trail) Charles Taylor, Moammar Gadhafi, and Saddam Hussein. Hasting dismisses Clark and impeachment as "gullible and misinformed," leaving out the fact that tens of millions of American agree with Clark's position.

AP's coverage of impeachment leaves one to question—if a national movement calling for the impeachment of the President is rapidly emerging and AP and the corporate media are not covering it, is there really a national movement for the impeachment of the President?

AP BIAS ON THE ISRAEL-PALESTINE CONFLICT

Alison Weir, Joy Ellison, and Peter Weir of the organization If Americans Knew recently conducted research on the AP's reporting of the Israel-Palestine conflict. The study was a statistical analysis of the AP newswire in the year 2004, looking at the number of Israeli and Palestinian deaths reported. Specifically they looked at headlines and the lead paragraph coverage to determine what an average person would actually read.[1]

The study found that there is a strong correlation between the likelihood of a person's death receiving coverage by AP and that person's nationality. In 2004 there were 141 reports of Israeli deaths in AP headlines and lead paragraphs, while in reality there were only 108 Israeli deaths, this difference comes from reporting a death more than once. During this same period, Palestinian deaths were reported as 543 by the AP, but at the time 821 Palestinians had been killed. The ratio of actual number of Israeli conflict deaths to Palestinian deaths in 2004 was 1:7, yet AP reported deaths of Israelis to Palestinians at a 2:1 ratio. In other words, the AP reported 131 percent of Israeli deaths, whereas they only reported 66 percent of Palestinian deaths.

The same could be said of AP's reporting of children's deaths. Nine reports of Israeli children's deaths were reported by the AP in headlines and leading paragraphs in 2004, while eight actually occurred. Only twenty-seven Palestinian children deaths were

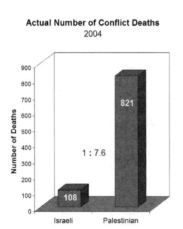

Actual Number of Conflict Deaths
2004

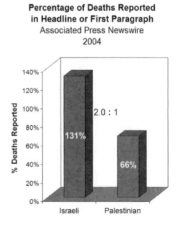

Percentage of Deaths Reported
in Headline or First Paragraph
Associated Press Newswire
2004

reported by AP when actually 179 children died. While there were twenty-two times more Palestinian children's deaths than Israeli children's deaths, the AP reported 113 percent of Israeli children's deaths and 15 percent of Palestinian children's deaths. Israeli children's deaths were reported at a rate seven and one-half times grater than that of Palestinian children.

The report also looked into how often the AP used the words "clash" and "clashes" in AP reports pertaining to the Israeli-Palestinian conflict. They found that of all the conflicts the AP reported in 2004, forty-seven deaths occurred during a clash, and all of these forty-seven deaths were Palestinian. AP covered over 700 news stories on deaths in Israel and Palestine in 2004, showing that while there is plenty of coverage of the conflict, the information given was significantly biased.

AP BIAS ON THE OVERTHROW OF PRESIDENT ARISTIDE IN HAITI

On February 29, 2004 AP widely reported that President Aristide was ousted by Haitian rebels and that the United States provided an escort to take Aristide out of the country to a safe asylum. Within twenty-four hours an entirely different story emerged that placed the U.S. at the center of a forced regime change. Instead of the U.S. being the supportive facilitator of Aristide's safety, independent news sources though Pacifica radio news were reporting that Aristide was kidnapped by U.S. forces.

AP quickly changed their story. On March 1, 2004 an AP report by Deb Riechman said, "White House officials said Aristide left willingly and that the United States aided his safe departure. But in a telephone interview with the Associated Press, Aristide said: 'No. I was forced to leave.' 'They were telling me that if I don't leave they would start shooting and be killing in a matter of time,' Aristide said during the interview, which was interrupted at times by static. It was unclear whether Aristide meant that rebels or U.S. agents would begin shooting. Asked to identify the 'agents,' Aristide said: 'White American, white military.' 'They came at night . . . There were too many. I couldn't count them,' he added."

Another account on March 1, 2004 by AP writer Clive Bacchus

stated that "Aristide said he was being held prisoner at the presidential palace in Bangui, Central African Republic, according to Randall Robinson, former president of TransAfrica, a Washington-based group that monitors U.S. policy toward Africa and the Caribbean and supported Aristide. 'About twenty American soldiers, in full battle gear with automatic weapons, came to the residence . . . took them to the airport, at gunpoint, put them on a plane,' said Robinson, who currently lives on the Caribbean island of St. Kitts. 'He said three times before he hung up 'Tell the world it was a coup, it was a coup.'"

The last AP report of Aristide exclaiming he was kidnapped by the U.S. in a State Department coup was on June 27, 2004. Since then there have been sixty news stories by the AP with Aristide mentioned in the articles. Of these stories none mentioned Aristide's claim that he was kidnapped by the United States military. None mention the U.S. backing of the coup. There have been no articles examining claims that the U.S. government sent 20,000 M-16s to the Dominican Republic, many of which ended up in the hands of the Haitian rebels, nor about how the U.S. blocked arms sales to Haiti during Aristide's presidency. Nor has AP covered that Aristide was elected in 2000 by 92 percent of the vote in an election declared free and fair by the Organization of American States.

Continuing stories about Haiti on AP's wire since June of 2004 say Aristide was ousted by rebel forces with no mention U.S. involvement. AP's bias in favor of the State Department's version of the Aristide's removal is a deliberate re-writing of history and a documented case of AP-sanctioned forgetting.[2]

AP'S CHARACTER ASSASSINATION OF CYNTHIA MCKINNEY

During the morning of March 29, 2006, Congress member Cynthia McKinney (D-GA) allegedly slapped a Capitol Hill police officer who has grabbed her while walking to a congressional session. According to a March 30, 2006 AP account, "McKinney, 51, scuffled with a police officer . . . when she entered a House office building without her identifying lapel pin and did not stop when asked. Several police sources said the officer asked her three times to stop. When she kept going, he placed a hand somewhere on her and she hit him." AP writer Giovanna Dell'Orto in Atlanta, McKinney's home district, quoted DeKalb County commissioner Hank Johnson on March 30, 2006 as saying, "Voters should hold her (McKinney) accountable for her irresponsible and reckless behavior." Dell'Orto went on to include quotes from e-mails sent to the *Atlanta Journal Constitution* say that, McKinney should be "arrested," and "she is a laughing stock because of her continued childish and boorish behavior."

According to John Judge, (McKinney's chief of staff) there have been repeated misidentifications of Cynthia McKinney by the Capital Police for the past year. The police have actually put Mckinney's picture up in their office to make sure officers knew her by sight. While an April 6, 2005 AP report made a significant issue of McKinney's failutre to wear her congressional lapel pin, Judge claims that members of Congress often do not wear their pins, and are recognized by police nonetheless.

On April 1, 2005 AP's Laurie Kellman did report on Black leaders coming to McKinney's defense including Rev. Darrel Elligan, the president of Concerned Black Clergy, and celebrities Danny Glover, and Harry Belafonte. However, AP reports quickly degraded to a piling on of negative comments in multiple succeeding articles, each published in April 2005:

"I don't think it's fair to attack the Capital Police," Patrick McHenry (R-NC)

"I don't think any of it justifies hitting a police office," said House Democratic Leader Nancy Pelosi.

"She (McKinney) has a long history of racism," said Tom Delay, former House majority leader.

"With a grand jury investigation and little support from House of Representative colleagues, Cynthia McKinney reversed course and apologized for an altercation . . ."

"Apology or not, U.S. Rep. Cynthia McKinney (D-GA) should be held fully accountable for what appears to be her inexcusable conduct and attitude toward police authority."

"Congresswomen Cynthia McKinney messed up . . . apparently she realized that; she has since apologized on the House floor."

In a national AP release April 5, Doug Gross (Atlanta) traced McKinney's history as the first Black woman elected to Congress from Georgia in 1992. "Known mostly for her flashy fashions, including braids and gold tennis shoes, McKinney had a brash style that made her a target for conservatives and an embarrassment to some of her more moderate democratic colleagues," Gross writes. "She once said," Gross pens, "that officials in the Bush administration had advance knowledge of the Sept. 11 attacks . . . she had been criticized for her outspoken support of the Palestinian cause in Israel."

In a TV interview on April 24, 2006 McKinney was repeatedly badgered by a WGCL-TV (CBS) Atlanta reporter about the Capital Hill police incident. At the end of the interview an irritated McKinney said while still on film, "Oh crap, now you know what . . ." they lied to Coz and Coz is a fool." Coz Carson is McKinney's communication director. McKinney then immediately stated that her comments at that point were off the record, but the station aired her taped words anyway. CNN joined in the fray by broadcasting her comments, and AP released a wire report with the headline, "TV Station Catches McKinney Bad-mouthing Staffer."

One supporter of Cynthia McKinney stated, "Cynthia is guilty of being in Congress while Black." Undoubtedly racism is a factor in the coverage of this incident. However there seems to be even a bigger factor in AP's coverage. McKinney represents a strong Black congresswomen, who has historically challenged the upper-class white establishment, especially the neo-conservatives in power today. (See Chapter 10.) Her positions on 9/11, Palestine, and social class clearly come from a left progressive perspective, as she openly challenges the status quo. In it coverage of McKinney, AP has demonstrated bias towards the status quo and the powerful in the U.S.

AP AS PROTECTORS OF THE POWERFUL

AP is a massive institutionalized bureaucracy that feeds new stories to nearly every newspaper and radio/TV station in the United States and the world. They are so large that top-down control of single news stories is literally impossible. However, our evidence clearly indicates a built-in bias favoring the powerful. ACLU evidence on torture is ignored by the corporate press and AP never mentions it again. The State Department's position on Haiti becomes established history. Cynthia McKinney is bashed and marginalized. Coverage of the Israel-Palestine situation has a clear pro-Israel bias, and the national impeachment movement is totally ignored. The American people absorb these biases and make political decisions on skewed understandings. Without media systems that provide balanced, fair and accurate reporting democracy is faced with a dismal future.

Peter Phillips is a professor of sociology at Sonoma State University and Director of Project Censored. Sarah Randle, Brian Fuch, Zoe Huffman, and Fabrice Romero undergraduate research interns with Project Censored.

APPENDIX

Associated Press Board of Directors

Burl Osborne

Chairman of the AP Board since 2002

Director since 1993 and member of the Executive Committee of The Associated Press

President, Publishing Division from 1995 to 2001

Director from 1987 to 2002 of the Belo Corp.; Publisher Emeritus since 2001

Director at J. C. Penney Holding Company

R. Jack Fishman

President and CEO of Lakeway Publishers, Inc., that produces the *Citizen Tribune* for the Morristown, Tenn., area, along with the *Tullahoma News*

Dennis J. FitzSimons

Chairman, President and CEO of Tribune, Co.

Member of The Business Council as well as the Civic Committee of The Commercial Club of Chicago

Joe Hladky

President and Publisher of The Gazette Co.

Walter E. Hussman Jr.

Publisher of Arkansas Democrat-Gazette and Hoover Institution Board of Overseers

Julie Inskeep

Publisher of *The Journal Gazette* in Fort Wayne, Indiana

George B. Irish

President of Hearst Newspapers and a senior vice president of Hearst
    Corporation
Past president of the Texas Daily Newspaper Association
Currently serves on the boards of the American Press Institute, the
    Newspaper Association of America, and the Columbia University
    Graduate School of Journalism Millikin University

Boisfeuillet (Bo) Jones

Publisher and chief executive officer of *The Washington Post* Next chairman
    of the Newspaper Association of America Member of the University of
    Maryland School of Journalism Board of Visitors

Mary Junck

CEO and Chairman of the Board of Lee Enterprises Inc. chain of fifty-eight
    mid-West daily newspapers
Former senior executive at Times Mirror Company

David Lord

Board member of PAGE buying cooperative and the Newspaper
    Association of America Current president of the Inland Press
    Association

Kenneth W. Lowe

President, CEO and Director of The E.W. Scripps Company

Douglas H. McCorkindale

Chairman of the board at Gannett Co., Inc. since 2001
CEO and President of Gannet Co., Inc. from 2000 to 2005 Vice Chairman
    of Gannet Co., Inc. from 1984 to 2001
Board of Directors at Lockheed Martin Corp. Continental Airlines, Inc. and
    Mutual Insurance Company Ltd.

R. John Mitchell

Publisher of the *Rutland Herald* and long-time publisher of *The Times Argus*
    in Barre
Charter member of the New England Press Association Hall of Fame

Steven O. Newhouse

Chairman of Advance.net
Editor in Chief at the *Jersey Journal*

Gary Pruitt

Chairman, president, and CEO of The McClatchy Company
Board member of the James Irvine Foundation

Secretary of the Board at the Newspaper Association of America
Board of directors at Mutual Insurance, Co.

Michael E. Reed

CEO at GateHouse Media Inc., formerly known as Liberty Group
    Publishing, Inc.
Board of Directors at the Newspaper Association of America and the Inland
    Newspaper Association

Bruce T. Reese

President and CEO of Bonneville International Corp.
Joint Chairman of the Board of the National Association of Broadcasters
Board of Directors of the Radio Advertising Bureau

Jon Rust

Publisher of the *Southeast Missourian*
Co-President of Rust Communications since 2001

William Dean Singleton

CEO of MediaNews Group Inc.
Former Chairman of the Newspaper Association of America (worked on
    easing FCC regulations on cross ownership)

Jay R. Smith

President of Cox Newspapers, Inc.
Chairman of the Board at the Newspaper Association of America from
    2005–2006
Vice Chairman of the Board at the American Press Institute
Board of Directors for Mutual Insurance, Co. Ltd.

David Westin

President of ABC News since 1996
Board Member at the International Academy of Television Arts and
    Sciences

H. Graham Woodlief

President of the Publishing Division
Vice President of Media General Inc. since 1989
Board Chairman of Southern Production Program Inc.

Notes

1. "*Deadly Distortion: Associated Press Newswire Coverage of Israeli and Palestinian Deaths,*" If Americans Knew, 2005, http://www.ifamericansknew.org/.
2. Duff, Lyn and Dennis Bernstein, *The Other Regime Change: Overthrowing Haiti's President Jean-Bertrand Aristide,* Chapter 13 in *Impeach the President: the Case Against Bush and Cheney,* Edited by Dennis Loo and Peter Phillips, Seven Stories Press: New York, 2006.

THIS MODERN WORLD

by TOM TOMORROW

LANGUAGE IS A VIRUS

AN ONGOING LOOK AT THE MYRIAD WAYS IN WHICH REALLY, REALLY STUPID IDEAS INFECT THE POLITICAL MAINSTREAM

THIS WEEK: THE WAR ON RATIONALITY

STEP ONE: A CONSERVATIVE SCHOOL BOARD OBJECTS TO THE TEACHING OF A COMMONLY ACCEPTED SCIENTIFIC PRINCIPLE.

"HUMAN SEXUAL REPRODUCTION" IS AN INTERESTING *THEORY*--

--BUT MUST OUR CULTURE *ALWAYS* BE SO OBSESSED WITH *SEX*?

STEP TWO: AN ANCIENT *MYTH* IS SPRUCED UP SLIGHTLY AND PRESENTED AS A CREDIBLE SCIENTIFIC *ALTERNATIVE*...

PROPONENTS OF "INTELLIGENT DELIVERY" BELIEVE THAT BABIES ARE DELIVERED BY A *STORK* IN A *MESSENGER CAP*!

DON'T OUR CHILDREN DESERVE TO HEAR *BOTH SIDES* OF THE *CONTROVERSY*?

STEP THREE: SELF-STYLED EXPERTS STRIVE TO INSTILL DOUBT WHERE NONE SHOULD PLAUSIBLY EXIST.

WHAT THE SECULAR REPRODUCTIONISTS BELIEVE IS *ABSURD*, BOYS AND GIRLS! IT WOULD BE LIKE SQUEEZING A *CANTELOUPE* OUT OF YOUR *NOSE*! HA, HA!

HA, HA!

STEP FOUR: THE SCIENTIFIC COMMUNITY IS CHALLENGED TO DEBATE THE ISSUE. IF THEY REFUSE, SO MUCH THE BETTER!

THEY'RE *AFRAID* TO *FACE* US!

THEY *KNOW* THEY DON'T STAND A CHANCE AGAINST OUR RELENTLESS *STORKIST LOGIC*!

STEP FIVE: THE LINE BETWEEN EDUCATION AND IGNORANCE GROWS EVER MORE INDISTINCT.

I *USED* TO THINK I UNDERSTOOD WHERE BABIES CAME FROM--UNTIL I LEARNED ABOUT THE LIES AND DISTORTIONS OF THE *SECULAR REPRODUCTIONISTS*!

WHY DO THEY HATE THE STORK SO MUCH?

TOM TOMORROW©2005 ... www.thismodernworld.com

CHAPTER 12

Heterosexual Anxiety and Gay Media Visibility
Heterosexuals' Perceptions of Gay Images

By James J. Dean

From the Oscar nominated film *Brokeback Mountain* (2005) to hit TV shows like *Will & Grace*, mass media representations of gay and lesbians have been undeniably increasing over the last decade. This new visibility has been the subject of much scholarly debate, particularly since gay and lesbian visibility has not always been such a prominent fixture of the mass media landscape.

For example, as Vito Russo's classic *The Celluloid Closet* (1987) shows, the history of gay and lesbian characters in movies is a story of invisibility, virulent stereotype, and innuendo. From the time of the silent pictures and talkies in the early 1900s to the 1980s, Russo illustrates that gay men and lesbians were often presented as deviant and pathological human types, such as murderers, sociopaths or victims of psychological sickness. However, beginning in the 1980s but most significantly in the 1990s, media scholars noted the salient increase in the number of gay and lesbian images and, more importantly, representational changes from the dominant stereotypes of the past.[1] Recent gay and lesbian media scholarship can consequently be seen as a debate about the meaning of this new gay and lesbian visibility.

Media scholar Larry Gross maintains that, although there has been an increase in gay images, to a large extent these images continue to reinforce stereotypical representations of gays and lesbians as inferior or hyper-visible tokens who are reduced to their homosexuality.[2] Gross writes, "The rules of the mass media game have had a double impact on gay people: not only have they mostly shown them as weak and silly, or evil and corrupt, but they continue for the most part to exclude and deny the existence of normal, unexceptional as well as exceptional lesbians and gay men."[3]

Similarly, Suzanna Walters contends that there are two dominant patterns of gay visibility in the 1990s.[4] Either gays are assimilated into a story's narrative and viewed as just like straights, or gay characters are just commodified ciphers without depth, who are depicted in movies "in order to exhibit a certain hipness but who are insignificant as anything *other* than signs of hipness, and, further, signs of hipness of the lead character."[5] Steven Seidman also argues that the recent gay and lesbian visibility can be seen as creating new boundaries of gay representation.[6] He states that gay images in today's popular cultural representations evidence a shift from the "polluted" to the "normal" gay. Seidman states that "The 'normal' gay is presented as fully human, as the psychological and moral equal of the heterosexual"; however, he observes that "the normal gay is expected to be gender conventional, link sex to love and a marriage-like relationship, defend family values, personify economic individualism, and display national pride."[7]

While Gross, Walters, Seidman and other scholars have documented the shifts in mainstream images of gay and lesbians, they have not examined how heterosexual men and women are reacting to this increase in gay and lesbian representation in the mass media. With the huge success of shows like *Will & Grace, Queer Eye for the Straight Guy* and Ellen DeGeneres' popular talk show, gay and lesbian visibility has not increased but it is part of the mainstream media's regular programming.

In this chapter I examine the responses of heterosexual men and women to this unprecedented level of gay and lesbian media visibility by analyzing the responses of sixty heterosexuals to my interview questions. First, I examine the homophobic anxiety of heterosexuals who find the increased number as well as the new acceptability of gay mass media imagery alarming, uncomfortable and even panic inducing. After discussing some variations in this homophobic anxiety, I turn to heterosexual individuals whose anxiety is less over the increase in gay visibility and more in how they worry that some homosexual media images might reinforce negative stereotypes of gays and lesbians. Specifically, in this essay I use the popular TV show *Will & Grace* as a way to gauge heterosexual anxiety over gay media visibility. This show has been one of the most widely watched primetime sitcoms to feature gay protagonists in the history of TV programming. During the 2004 to 2005 season an average of one million viewers watched the show.

The sixty heterosexual men and women whose voices appear in this chapter live in Albany, New York or in the surrounding region. The study, conducted in 2005, examines the racial and gender character of heterosexual identity and is based on interviews with fifteen Black men, fifteen Black women, fifteen white men and fifteen white women. These heterosexual individuals range in age from twenty to sixty-eight years of age.[8]

Heterosexuals' perceptions of gay and lesbian visibility are not uniform. I sketch the range of anxieties that heterosexuals' responses revealed when I interviewed them about what they thought about gay media visibility. I found that heterosexual anxiety registers not only a sense of homophobic dread or supportive hope, but it also shows that heterosexuals feel a stake in gay visibility and gay and straight relations in general.

HETEROSEXUAL ANXIETY AND GAY MEDIA VISIBILITY

Gay media visibility blurs boundaries between public and private spheres of social life, where the public enters the private home through the omnipresent TV set. The growing number of gay characters and personalities affirms the status of gays as social equals, and the popularity of these characters seems to confirm that gay characters and personalities are interesting for American viewers.

However, how heterosexual men and women actually feel and are responding to these images is another story. For some heterosexual men and women, gay and lesbian visibility produces anxiety. These heterosexuals view gay visibility as not only the promotion of homosexuality for homosexuals, but also as encouragement for heterosexual individuals to "try out" or "experiment" with it. My study showed that some heterosexual men found images of feminine gay men to be a source of discomfort and anxiety, and some straight women worried that young people or children would start to view homosexuality as acceptable and normal on the basis of its newfound visibility.

For example, Nia, a twenty-two-year-old Black college student, talked about her anxiety in relation to the idea of her future children becoming gay as a result of internalizing images of gays and lesbians on TV. Nia explains,

On T.V. now, you're starting to see more and more gay people. People internalize images and I just would hate for my
son or daughter to be that way. That's why I don't think I'm
even gonna have a television in my house when I have a
child. I would hate for them to be flicking through and see
something like that and that image stays in their head and
they internalize that and because of it chose to go that route.

Nia's fear and anxiety was stronger than others. She felt paranoid
about how powerful gay media visibility was, projecting that it could
encourage and even create a homosexual identity. Her feelings point
to the general acceptance of gay characters on television today and
the fact that they're often represented as good, likable and attractive
individuals.

While Nia focused on the idea that gay and lesbian visibility creates the possibility of her children choosing "to go that route," other
heterosexual men and women focused on what they perceived as the
overrepresentation of gays and lesbians on television overall, stating
that their depiction was out of proportion to the actual number of gay
men and lesbians in the U.S.'s population. For example, Milton, a
White thirty-six-year-old self-employed businessman, states that he
thinks that gay and lesbian visibility is a trend in popular culture that
has reached its zenith and is now declining. He says,

Well, I see that gays and lesbians are changing very quickly,
and very rapidly, and very extremely. In the beginning, ten
years ago, fifteen years ago, gay and lesbians were in the
closet, I'll say. And that's probably the threshold of when
things started to change. And then they started to become
outward about their preference. And then, they went too far
overboard with their preference, then, I think it almost
became fashionable for popular culture to be gay or lesbian.
And maybe that's starting to wear off now, and starting to
become a little less extreme.

While Milton knows gays and lesbians and considers some friends,
he still feels uncomfortable with the number of gay representations
in the media. Indicative of the way gay visibility is handled by those

heterosexuals who are less homophobic but still uncomfortable with gays, Milton reasons that gays were trendy for a while but now are becoming less popular, which assuages his anxiety.

Similarly, Joe, a white twenty-seven-year-old waiter, states that he views the number of images of gays on TV as much higher than their actual percentage of U.S. society's population. He says,

> I think that the media image portrays higher percentages, gives the impression that there's a higher percentage of the population that's gay or lesbian than there actually is. I think that the gay and lesbian population is somewhere around 5, maybe 10 percent and I think by watching TV you get the impression it's much higher than that. Because it's certainly not 5 percent of the time that you see gay and lesbians on T.V. It's certainly not the case. It's certainly much greater than that. You definitely get the impression that there are more gays and lesbians than there are.

Joe repeats Milton's sentiment. The number of gay representations in popular media is larger than their actual number in the population. If before heterosexuals took for granted their majority identity status, then gay visibility makes them question how big of a majority they are now.

While some heterosexuals worried that gay images could turn their children gay and others felt a general sense of alarm at the growing number of media images, many heterosexual men registered their anxiety over gay visibility by remarking on Jack, the feminine gay male character on *Will & Grace*. These heterosexual men felt uncomfortable with Jack's male femininity and buffoon-like behavior. For instance, Jeff, a thirty-seven-year-old Jewish accountant, says,

> I liked *Will & Grace*; I thought it was a good show. But I do think that they made Jack a bit of a stereotype, but I think Will cancelled that out a little bit. I thought that [Jack] was kind of stereotypical and is a bit much. But then you have Will to offset it, who was your normal kind of guy for the most part.

For Jeff, gay male representations that are not gender conventional exhibit an abnormal masculinity; that is, they challenge a binary gender order of men as masculine and women as feminine. Acceptable gay images for many heterosexuals are ones that mirror heterosexual gender conventions or conventions of intimate relations by linking sex to love in quasi-marital relationships.

Paul, a white fifty-six-year-old school teacher, is also uncomfortable with the Jack's femininity on *Will & Grace*. However, as a supporter of equal rights for gays and lesbians, he has different concerns. Paul says,

> I think [*Will & Grace* is] okay. I don't know how gays perceive it. The way I've had it [I've] enjoyed parts of it, but other parts are incredibly uncomfortable. So, I might feel uncomfortable. I guess the overly flamboyant gay [Jack] is still uncomfortable to me. And I think a lot of it is learned behavior. In general, I think, 'How do gays react to that type?' for example.

Like Jeff and Paul, Maria, a white twenty-six-year-old policy worker expresses similar sentiments about Jack on *Will & Grace* but without feeling discomfort with Jack's feminine behavior. She says,

> I think it plays on some stereotypes. I think, not Will, Jack, I think Jack is very flamboyant and I know that there are people who are flamboyant, but I just think that the media puts people like that on TV because it's something that the general population will identify with. I think Jack's funny, but I don't know how many people are excited that he's the representative. It's the one show they [gays] have. Will is sort of the contrast in that he's not as a feminine and stuff. So, I like that show in the sense that they put two different types of roles on, but I don't know. I couldn't really say what kind of role models those would be.

Maria is worried about how a stereotypically feminine gay character like Jack will be viewed by others. She thinks in part that media representations should act as role models representing what gay men are "really" like for people who are unexposed to them. She is concerned with stigmatizing stereotypes of gays.

However, Maria's point of view offers only a thin tolerance for homosexual visibility. While she is well-intended, Maria, like Jeff and Paul, unwittingly ends up implying that more "straight acting" characters like Will, not Jack, should be portrayed on TV in order to present gays who are good role models to the American public. It is this logic of wanting to promote gay tolerance and acceptance through the representation of gay role models that presents a thorny problem for sympathetic heterosexuals like Maria. That is, should characters like Jack be excluded from the public eye because they might reinforce stereotypes of gay men as feminine or are they an important part of a growing diversity of homosexual imagery?

If Maria presents the question of what kind of gay imagery is good for gay representation, then Alan, a white forty-year-old English graduate student, offers a sharper critique of *Will & Grace*, pointing out how it fails to portray Will sincerely involved with another man. For Alan, the show is "cynical" since it never openly displays gay male affection without devaluing it with comedic jokes. He says,

> Will on *Will & Grace* is never gay on stage. He says he's a gay character, he has a boyfriend, but we never see the consummation of that. We see all the sort of style codes and what not, he performs them well, but and sometimes quite cynically. I think ultimately it's a very cynical show, but it's not a show where you're gonna have open physical affection between two men, unless it's jokey. It becomes a style thing more than anything else.

Alan's perception of the comedy sitcom seems accurate. Comedy is a conservative genre that typically makes its protagonists buffoons in order for the audience to laugh at them.[9] It seems that America is better able to deal with homosexuality in a comedic genre, precisely because comedy sitcoms don't ask viewers to take them seriously.

While Alan registered an important observation on the lack of serious intimacy between men on the show, other heterosexuals like Erica, a Black twenty-two-year-old restaurant manager, found the show funny but also inauthentic.

> *Will & Grace*, I've considered it a guilty pleasure for a long time because I sometimes laugh at the jokes. Will's my

favorite. He's very dry and I like his character a lot. He's really funny, the way he deals with everybody else, a lot of eye rolling. He seems to be the smartest character on the show. I don't know exactly how I feel because I do laugh at it sometimes. I want to be more self-righteous. I want to say that I don't like it, but I do laugh at the writing. *Will & Grace* is an attempt at being more accurate because they have two gay men, two very distinctly different gay men in terms of how they talk and act or treat people or their dating and things like that. It's like the lesser of the evils. I still feel not completely happy with that TV show. It's too contrived still to me; this wonderful girl living with her gay friend. How sitcom is that? In my lifetime, gay people have not been as easily loved and accepted as these characters on TV. So I guess the reason why it hasn't really changed how I feel is because I'm able to separate fantasy from reality still. I'm just watching a TV show. It's not easy to be the [minority].

Erica feels that the show makes light of the difficulties gays still face in coming out and that the show brushes over the prejudices that are still widely held against gays and lesbians. For her, it's "contrived" and she is critical of the way TV sitcoms obscure homophobia and gays' subordinate status as a minority.

CONCLUSION

In short, media visibility remains a key site for gay men and women's struggle for cultural recognition, respect and civil rights. Heterosexual men and women's perceptions and anxieties run the gamut from feeling threatened and overrun by gay visibility to wanting to protect and assert the need for gays and lesbians to be visible. Gay media visibility walks a cultural tightrope that both shapes and reflects the changing status of gay men and lesbians in U.S. society. At best, gay media visibility promotes an increasing degree of tolerance towards gays and lesbians, helping to promote their integration into a multicultural society. At worst media visibility seems to reinforce negative stereotypes, reinforcing gays' devalued and degraded status. This contradiction characterizes the state of gay and lesbian media visibility today.

James Dean is an Assistant Professor of Sociology at Sonoma State University and a Project Censored evaluator.

I want to especially thank Nick Ramirez for his assistance in this project.

Notes

1. Joshua Gamson, "Sweating in the Spotlight: Lesbian, Gay and Queer Encounters with Media and Popular Culture," *Handbook of Lesbian and Gay Studies*, edited by Diane Richardson and Steven Seidman, Thousand Oaks, CA: Sage Publications, 2002;
    Larry Gross, *Up From Invisibility: Lesbians, Gay Men and Media in America*, New York, NY: Columbia University Press, 2001; Vito Russo, *The Celluloid Closet: Homosexuality in the Movies*, 2nd ed. New York, NY: Harper and Row, 1987; Steven Seidman, *Beyond the Closet: the Transformation of Gay and Lesbian Life*, New York, NY: Routledge, 2002; Suzanna Danuta Walters, *All the Rage: The Story of Gay Visibility in America*, Chicago, IL: University of Chicago Press, 2001.
2. Larry Gross, *Up From Invisibility: Lesbians, Gay Men and Media in America*, New York, NY: Columbia University Press, 2001.
3. Ibid., p. 16.
4. Suzanna Danuta Walters, *All the Rage: The Story of Gay Visibility in America*, Chicago, IL: University of Chicago Press, 2001.
5. Ibid., p. 154.
6. Steven Seidman, *Beyond the Closet: the Transformation of Gay and Lesbian Life*, New York, NY: Routledge, 2002.
7. Ibid., p. 133.
8. James J. Dean, *Straight Trouble: Gendered and Racial Heterosexualities in the Context of Gay and Lesbian Visibility*, Unpublished Ph.D. dissertation, SUNY Albany, 2005 (All respondents' names are pseudonyms).
9. Northup Frye, *Anatomy of Criticism*, Princeton, NJ: Princeton University Press, 1957.

THIS MODERN WORLD

by TOM TOMORROW

CHAPTER 13

Japan's News Media
Voice of the Powerful, Neglecter of the Voiceless

By Tomoomi Mori

Inherent in the mission of journalism the world over is the responsibility of acting as a check on the "centers of power" while also giving a voice to those in society who are excluded from the centers of power. In Japan, however, the news media have it backwards: The media cozy up to and support the powers-that-be, while the voiceless ones in mainstream society are neglected in mainstream coverage. It is no exaggeration to say that the Japanese mainstream press today is all but in a moribund state. As a result, there seems to be less and less tolerance for a diversity of views, with Japanese society as a whole becoming increasingly reactionary in the early years of the twenty-first century.

Traditionally, among the major Japanese vernacular dailies, the *Asahi* and *Mainichi* newspapers have staked out the "liberal" ground while the *Yomiuri* and *Sankei* newspapers took pride in being extremely "conservative"—but this journalistic landscape is rapidly changing. The *Yomiuri* and its cantankerous right-wing chairman, Tsuneo Watanabe, for instance, have recently shifted gears and blasted Prime Minister Junichiro Koizumi's occasional visits to Yasukuni Shrine in Tokyo (where the remains of Japanese Class-A war criminals, among others, are enshrined as gods) as being antagonistic toward China and Korea, former recipients of Japan's wartime colonialist drive.

On the flip side, the "liberal" *Asahi* newspaper, a 2001 editorial approved of the Bush administration's illegal invasion of Afghanistan, claiming: "If possible, the use of force should be avoided. However, we believe that limited armed attacks strictly directed at such facilities as terrorist training camps and military installations are unavoidable to eradicate terrorist organizations that target international society."[1] The *Asahi* has also been hesitant to fundamentally criticize Japanese Prime Minister Junichiro Koizumi, a key Bush administration ally, for the unprecedented measure of sending Japan's military, known as the "Self-Defense Forces," to Iraq in 2004—the first time since World War II that Japanese troops have set foot on foreign soil in a time of war with the protection of heavy weaponry. If this is how Japan's leading "liberal" newspaper acts, where is the hope for an active watchdog press in Japan?

As these "conservative" and "liberal" news organizations in Japan feel out each other's political territory (and readership/viewership markets), blurring the lines between a competitive, diverse news media, the important question arises: How does the public benefit? There are, in fact, a number of problems with the Japanese print and broadcast media in their neglect to monitor the centers of power and contribute meaningfully to the people's right to know, as the media increasingly become an extension of the political regime in power and concern themselves only with circulation figures and viewer rates. Just a few of the problems of Japan's news media are covered here, concluding with signs of change.

THE "KISHA CLUBS"

Project Censored does an excellent job every year of compiling the "top censored stories" of the United States into one 300-page book. If such a list of censored stories in Japan were to be compiled every year, however, that list would no doubt have to be published in the form of an encyclopedia. That's how prevalent censorship is in the Japanese news world. But that censorship does not only come from outside; self-censorship thrives within the Japanese media world itself. Thus, no discussion of censorship in the Japanese media would be complete without acknowledging the "efficiency" of what is known as the *kisha club* (press club) system.[2]

An estimated 800 to 1,000 of these kisha clubs exist throughout Japan, and are attached to various institutions and organizations, ranging from the Imperial Household Agency, the Bank of Japan, government ministries and the prime minister's office, to the courts, the police, city halls, local chambers of commerce and industry, and even local boards of education. The ruling Liberal-Democratic Party and opposition political parties, not to mention some major Japanese corporations, also have their own kisha clubs. The kisha clubs are usually located on the very premises of the institutions or organizations the news media are supposed to monitor, and in the cases of public agencies, the expenses for these kisha clubs are usually borne by the agencies with taxpayer money. Even though these kisha clubs are located on public premises, the clubs are generally off-limits to the ordinary, taxpaying citizen.

Smaller news organizations and freelancers are prohibited from joining the kisha clubs. The bigger news companies can only enter these clubs after approval from the other club members. Being a club member means your news organization gets desk space and a small cubby hole into which the day's news briefings will be filed from the institution's press officer. As may be expected, reporters stationed at these kisha clubs spend a lot of precious time just waiting around for press conferences and the news to be delivered to them. Many Japanese reporters find the kisha clubs a convenient way to do their jobs under the stress of heavy deadlines; other reporters consider kisha clubs a necessary evil at best and a nuisance at worst, and find no choice but to put up with the system's bureaucratic nature.

There are a web of formal and informal rules and regulations that kisha club members are expected to follow. Among the formal ones are *kurabu kiyaku* (written list of regulations) and, more commonly and perhaps more insidiously, *kokuban kyotei* (blackboard agreements).[3] Under the latter system, a schedule of upcoming press conferences and briefings are listed on a blackboard for all kisha club members to see. If no objections are raised by the reporters of the club about the listings on the blackboard, then the postings are fixed and the reporters are automatically not allowed to scoop other reporters on those particular items. It is said in Japan that if you are a reporter who belongs to a kisha club, you won't get the scoop; on the other hand, if you *don't* belong to a kisha club, you won't get the story. That is not much of an exaggeration.

Takao Fujita of rural Kyoto, Japan probably had no idea of the fight he was facing when he first entered this closed media world back in the late 1980s.[4] He put aside some of the chores on his 1.3-hectare farm of rice, turnips and potherb mustard long enough to go to the big city to demand answers from the Kyoto prefectural government's kisha club. Fujita was incensed by a 1987 Kyodo News wire service report, carried in the southern island of Okinawa: Kyodo reportedly quoted the governor of Kyoto Prefecture as saying that the leveling of Okinawan sugar cane fields after a recent typhoon would helpfully deprive anti-emperor "radicals" there from hiding in the brush during a planned sports meet at which then-crown prince Akihito was to appear.

The article caused an uproar down south in Okinawa, and as a farmer up north, Fujita too was offended by it. He wanted to know from the reporters why such an insulting remark toward farmers (traditionally a conservative voting bloc in Japan) could be reported so far away in Okinawa but not in Kyoto, where he lived. The answer, he found after nosing around a bit, was because of the kisha club system.

When he petitioned the Kyoto prefectural kisha club for an audit of its financial records, he was rebuffed; he then decided to take it to the courts. A lengthy series of legal battles followed in which he sued the city and prefecture of Kyoto for misuse of public money in supporting the kisha clubs. The local district court ruled against him, and Japan's Supreme Court rejected his appeal. Not too surprisingly, stories about his anti-kisha club lawsuits rarely made it into the news. After all, who would want to give space or time to an outsider questioning the very foundation of the closed Japanese news community? "The [kisha club] reporters run, practically fly, away when they see me coming," Fujita said at the time, with some amusement. "One reporter sitting in the press club even denied being a reporter when I approached him! Unbelievable. He just didn't want to answer my questions. They won't even talk to me."5

After a few years, Takao Fujita gave up his battle against the Japanese press establishment in the early 1990s and went back to more pressing matters at his farm, which he still owns today. He spent an estimated millions of yen in legal fees fighting the kisha club system and lost every step of the way. Perhaps he never had a chance of success from the beginning. But without such fights against Japan's media system by "outsiders"—be they ordinary, working-class Japanese citizens or the more well-off foreign correspondents based in Tokyo—it is unlikely that the press system in Japan will ever change.

BOWING DOWN TO ROYALTY

On September 26, 1988, the *Mainichi* newspaper's English edition, the *Mainichi Daily News,* published an editorial titled "A Nation Plunged Into Grief."[6] The editorial lamented the death of then-emperor Hirohito (who had cancer) and expressed its "deepest sorrow" for the loss of this historical figure. With only a passing mention of the controversy that had surrounded Hirohito's reign—whether or not he was, in fact, responsible for the deaths of hundreds of thousands of people throughout the Asia-Pacific region during World War II or whether he was merely an observer of the process—the editorial went on to recognize the imperial monarch as "a symbol of national unity" who had been long "supported by the people, institutionalized by the new [postwar] Constitution."

The editorial, like any other obituary, listed the accomplishments of the deceased's eventful life. It praised the human qualities of the man who was once revered by the Japanese as a god but who humbly "renounced the myth of divinity" at the war's end. Hirohito's life had been spared from the gallows, it is now widely believed, by a U.S. government eager to maintain control over the Japanese people and gain its military/industrial/political toehold in Far East Asia. But in the editorial, Emperor Hirohito came across as he always had in the Japanese press: a benevolent father-figure who had cared deeply about his family, "keenly aware of the moral responsibility inherently shouldered by a monarch" and ready to make any sacrifice necessary for the people. The editorial closed with a heartfelt goodbye to one of the twentieth century's most well-known international figures: "With deep emotion we bid farewell to His Majesty the Emperor by saying, 'Your Majesty, it was in a most turbulent age that you were our Emperor.'"[7]

There was only one small problem, however: The emperor wasn't dead yet.

Hirohito was, at that moment, on his deathbed fighting for his life and would go on to live another four months. In a scenario feared by daily newspaper editors the world over, the prepared obit on Hirohito had been mistakenly laid out on the editorial page, run through the printing presses and distributed to newsstands and subscribers in the thousands before anyone at the paper could correct the error.

Japan's powerful Imperial Household Agency, in return, demanded some heads. The result was a terse, two-paragraph apology in the paper the next day, acknowledging "an extremely serious error" and retracting the emperor's premature demise: "The mistake has filled us with great remorse and we offer the profoundest of apologies."[8] Tadao Koike, the vernacular *Mainichi's* editor-in-chief, was relieved of editorial duties and Ken Kondo, the English-language *MDN's* editor/general manager, was fired.[9]

The "dead emperor incident" certainly wasn't the first gaffe by the *Mainichi's* English-language news staff in Tokyo (don't even ask about the time a photo of a speared duck in a Tokyo park was "inadvertently inverted," that is, published upside-down). But it was by far the biggest one—and served as yet another reminder, if one were needed in Japan, of the relationship between Japan's royal family and its press. As one "center of power," the Japanese media establishment is expected to fully respect and uphold the dignity of other centers of power, especially the Japanese monarchy. And the Japanese press has mostly kept to its end of the bargain. It would be simply unimaginable in Japan today to see the Japanese royal family treated by the Japanese press the same way, for instance, that the British media have covered the British royal family and the late Princess Diana. Japan's mainstream news media do not hesitate to print all the salacious details of scandal in overseas countries' dynasties and first families (Bill Clinton and Monica Lewinsky gave the Japanese press a field day), but here in Japan, the staining of the Chrysanthemum Throne is strictly taboo.

After Hirohito finally did die on January 7, 1989 ("X-Day," as it was known), Japanese TV newscasters and program hosts paid tribute by appearing in black clothing and speaking in solemn, subdued tones. It was the ultimate funeral coverage. Out in the streets of some Japanese cities, citizens had protested and demonstrated against the whitewashing of Hirohito's wartime legacy, but of course, it was left up to the overseas press to present those kinds of pictures to the world. The Japanese news media would keep the myth of Emperor Hirohito, now known as Emperor Showa, intact.

Looking back, the overseas press has long covered the Japanese royal family much more openly and aggressively than its Japanese counterpart. Nowhere has that been more obvious than in the reportage of the search for two prospective brides for two prospective Japanese emperors.

In 1958, the U.S. magazine *Newsweek* "scooped" the entire Japanese press corps in first reporting that Michiko Shoda, a "commoner" not from the royal circles, was to be the future wife of then-crown prince Akihito.[10] Of course, the "scoop" was an open secret all along among the Japanese press establishment, which presumably had been pressured by the Imperial Household Agency to keep Shoda's identity confidential until it could be officially announced. History was to repeat itself thirty-five years later when the *Washington Post* newspaper similarly "scooped" the entire Japanese press corps about Masako Owada, also a "commoner," becoming the future wife of emperor Akihito's son, Naruhito: "News of the palace schedule immediately prompted new speculation about who the royal bride will be. Once again, many suggested that the new princess may be Harvard graduate Masako Owada, an official in the Foreign Ministry."[11]

The *Post* turned out to be correct, and the Japanese imperial household officials immediately objected to the revealing of the royal secret. But unlike the case with the early "death" of the emperor, there were no journalistic casualties this time. If the Japanese press happens to violate the imperial codes of conduct, whether in big or small ways, heads roll. When the overseas news media do it, it becomes, well, news. Lest this portion of this essay concerning royal brides become a candidate for a "Junk Food News" ranking by Project Censored, it is important to keep in mind one central point: that the Japanese news mainstream media, given the choice of serving the minority elite or serving the majority public, will always choose the former. That can only be a dangerous course for the future of a free and open press in Japan.

JAPAN BROADCASTING CORPORATION AND "SEX SLAVE" COVERAGE

In the 1930s, as Japan's colonialist sweep through Asia intensified, so did its institutionalized system of sexual slavery. The issues of sexual slavery in Japan's wartime past and the Japanese government's continued denial of its role in establishing that system of slavery are so sensitive that today, seventy years later, they still stand as obstacles to truly amicable relations between Japan and some of its Far East Asian neighbors. How the Japanese media, particularly Japan's public broadcaster, have covered or not covered this issue in recent years has become equally controversial, adding to increasing Japanese distrust of the nation's media.

According to Amnesty International, just one of many organizations around the globe to have taken up the issue in the past couple of decades, the Japanese military established its first "sex station"[12] in Shanghai, China in 1932, and began in earnest to institutionalize the system of sexual slavery throughout Asia around the time of the Nanking Massacre in China in 1937. By the end of World War II in 1945, scores of "sex stations" had been established by the Japanese Imperial Army around China, Korea, Taiwan, the Philippines, Malaysia, Indonesia, Burma, Thailand, Cambodia, Thailand and many other Pacific islands (along with mainland Japan and Okinawa).[13] Up to 200,000 women, possibly more, from those countries had been forced under horrendous conditions to provide sex to Japanese soldiers at the fronts, shattering the women's lives forever.[14]

In 1998, the idea of a people's tribunal to bring justice to the victims of Japan's wartime sexual slavery system was proposed. The idea became reality in 2000 with the holding of "The Women's International War Crimes Tribunal on Japan's Military Sexual Slavery" from December 8–12 in Tokyo.[15] Organized by Asian women and human rights organizations, and supported by international nongovernmental organizations, the Women's Tribunal set out to "bring those responsible for [sexual enslavement] to justice, and to end the ongoing cycle of impunity for wartime sexual violence against women."[16] It was democracy and justice in action.

To top it off, the tribunal was to be taped for a later broadcast and potentially seen by millions of Japanese viewers of the educational television channel of Nippon Hoso Kyokai, or Japan Broadcasting Corporation (NHK), Japan's public broadcaster, as part of an NHK series called *Senso o Do Sabaku Ka?* (How should wars be judged?). For possibly the first time since World War II, the silenced voices of the thousands of Asian victims of rape as a tool of war would be heard by the Japanese people. Although the tribunal had no official legal standing, over the course of the gathering, testimony was given by some of the surviving victims of the Japanese military's system of sexual slavery, along with scholars in various fields and even by former Japanese soldiers.

Largely ignored by Japan's mainstream press, the tribunal was attended by about a thousand people every day and covered in major newspapers in both eastern and western nations.[17] The tribunal's preliminary judgment on the final day? The late Emperor Hirohito, several high-ranking Japanese military officials of that time and indeed the Japanese government itself—all guilty of crimes against humanity, especially the crimes of rape and sexual slavery.[18]

But a funny thing happened to the tribunal on the way to the TV screen: When the series finally aired on NHK on January 29 to February 1, 2001, key parts of the Women's Tribunal appeared to have been unreported, toned down, or deleted altogether. The tribunal's preliminary judgment against the emperor was never mentioned, nor was any footage of the tribunal itself shown. The program instead featured criticism of the tribunal, including by a right-wing scholar who dismissed the tribunal's claims and said the Asian women victims were nothing more than prostitutes working for the Japanese military at the time. The organizers of the tribunal charged that the Japanese public broadcaster's news coverage of their historical event had been "sabotaged," and sued NHK.[19]

And there the matter more or less stayed for four years, until two reporters from the *Asahi* newspaper revived the issue by dropping a bombshell in January 2005: that it was pressure from two leading rightist politicians in the Japanese Diet (parliament) that had led to the "sabotaging" of the tribunal aired on NHK back in 2001. One of the two politicians, Shinzo Abe, then-deputy chief cabinet secretary under prime minister Koizumi (and a neo-conservative who is now favored to succeed Koizumi as prime minister in 2006), admitted meeting NHK executives but denied exerting any political pressure: "I told them the reporting had to be neutral, that opposing views had to be introduced and that there was a need for a neutral distribution of time (to the two sides). I only said what I had to as a Diet member. It was different from political pressure."[20]

In the denials and counter-charges of misreporting that followed from NHK, the background behind what had happened to the tribunal program in the final days before it was broadcast on NHK came to light.[21] A group of ultra-rightists in paramilitary uniforms and traveling in sound trucks had reportedly protested in front of NHK offices just days before the program went on air. One day before the airing of the program, a group of NHK executives—including Takeshi Matsuo, then executive director-general of broadcasting, and Naoki Nojima, an NHK director-general overseeing relations with Diet members—met in government offices with Abe and Shoichi Nakagawa, (the future minister of economy, trade and industry). There, the NHK officials reportedly briefed the politicians on the program to air the following day. In the twenty-four hours between that briefing and the televising of the show, the high-level NHK executives reportedly took the unusual step of getting directly involved in the editing process of the tribunal program. As the clocked ticked down to showtime, the substance of the tribunal that was critical of the Japanese emperor was continually edited out and new material blasting the tribunal was edited in. It was historical revisionism, Japanese media-style.

NHK and the politicians, for their part, have denied that any pressure or wrongdoing took place.[22] And what happened to the two *Asahi* newspaper reporters, Masakazu Honda and Makoto Takada, who investigated and broke open the big NHK censorship scandal? They were banished by their "liberal" newspaper company to a journalistic Siberia: One of the reporters is said to have been transferred to a non-editorial posting in a subscription section of the paper, while the other has been moved from the paper's Tokyo headquarters to a local bureau in Akita, an area of northern Japan known for its long, cold winters. The NHK "sex slave" coverage case stands as a textbook example in Japan as to what can happen when the powerful forces of politics and media meet.

"THE GREAT VIEWERS' FEE REVOLT"

It was also during this same period (late 2004 through summer 2005) that NHK suffered a deepened crisis in public confidence after it was found that NHK employees, including the former producer of a popular annual New Year's Eve program, had embezzled tens of millions of yen in NHK funds in 2000 and 2001. The Japanese public hit NHK right back where it hurt, refusing in waves to pay the "obligatory" subscription fees that NHK charges to television viewers throughout Japan. This resulted in profit losses of billions of yen to the public broadcaster.

On its founding in 1926, NHK was modeled after the British Broadcasting Corporation (BBC) of England, and like the British system today, NHK can legally charge a fee (roughly 1,300 yen or $12 USD dollars per month) to all owners of a television in Japan—regardless of whether or not people actually watch the public television channels. Enforcement, however, is hard to follow up and there is no formal penalty system presently in place for the many Japanese citizens who routinely do not pay the pesky NHK fee collector who comes to the door.

When otherwise loyal paying viewers in the hundreds of thousands, then, suddenly started refusing to hand over their NHK subscription fees in late 2004 to early 2005 to protest the surfacing corruption within the nation's public broadcaster, it was nothing short of a media consumer revolt. The number of new non-payers as of November 2004 stood at 113,000, jumping to 397,000 by February 2005.[23] By August 2005, it had skyrocketed to about 1.17 million viewers, posing losses of around 10 billion yen to the public broadcaster.[24]

NHK touts its duty "to transmit impartial, high-quality programs that are not influenced by the government or private organizations,"[25] but the charges of "sabotage" in the tribunal censorship case would seem to betray that line. Although there appeared to be no clear links between protests over the tribunal censorship issue and "The Great NHK Viewers' Fee Revolt," as I call it, clearly Japanese public trust in the nation's public broadcasting system—just as with the Public Broadcasting System (PBS) in the U.S. and the BBC in the U.K.—has fallen to new lows in recent years. If recent trends are any sign, it may be years before that Japanese public trust is truly recovered.

And just as with PBS and the BBC, this drop in Japanese public trust in NHK comes at a time of financial downsizing and a weakening in the mission of public broadcasting to provide high-quality, commercial-free, independent programming. The latest news is that three of NHK's eight public television and radio channels are to be axed by the Japanese government in the near future.[26] At the same time, NHK is seriously considering changing the current "obligatory" viewer-fee system to a mandatory one, meaning that citizens who do not regularly pay the country's public broadcaster the viewer fee will formally be treated as lawbreakers.[27] Just how the public of Japan is to truly benefit from such a heavy-handed, bare-bones public broadcasting system that is subject to right-wing political pressure is, at this stage, anybody's guess.

SIGNS OF CHANGE

As of this writing (June 2006), there are dark clouds forming on the media horizon in Japan. The administration of Prime Minister Junichiro Koizumi is pushing ahead with a vaguely worded bill that, if passed into law, will make it illegal for people to "conspire" in the planning of crimes.[28] The government insists that the *Kyobozai Hoan* (Conspiracy Law) is necessary to fight organized crime, but there has been some public outcry against the possibility of misuse of the law to silence critics of the government: "People fear the new law would encourage self-censorship or spying in non-profit organizations, churches, labor unions, and political groups. Constitutional guarantees of freedom of speech and assembly, as well as protections against searches and seizures, could be rendered null."[29] Consider it the Japanese version of USA PATRIOT Acts I and II.

Many Japanese citizens who are old enough to remember WWII worry that the proposed "Conspiracy Law" of 2006 is little more than a return to the "Peace Preservation Law" *(Chian-iji Ho)* of 1925. The "Peace Preservation Law" was used by the Japanese state to punish journalists and other critics of the Japanese monarchy of "thought crimes" in the years leading up to Japan's rabid militarization and colonization of Asian nations, and the lethal effects of the 1925 law on freedom of speech are still being heard in the Japanese courts today.[30]

At a time when the United States government, under its "war on terrorism," is pressuring Japan to remilitarize and amend the Japanese constitution's Article 9, which "forever renounce[s] war . . . and the threat of force as a means of settling international disputes"[31]—and at a time when Japanese neo-conservatives are pushing for the teaching of more *aikoku-shin* (patriotism) in public schools and Japanese schoolteachers are being punished for refusing to sing the national anthem or to stand up before the national flag at school ceremonies—this trend toward censorship of free speech and curbing of basic human rights in Japanese society is very worrisome.

It is all the more worrisome because the Japanese mainstream news media, whether "liberal" or "conservative" or a crossover of both, seem unwilling to address or speak out strongly on the public's behalf against the government winds of censorship that are blowing. At least some of the millions of regular Japanese readers of the "liberal" *Asahi* newspaper and the "conservative" *Yomiuri* newspaper must have felt uneasy to recently read of the two chairmen of the "arch-enemy" news companies sitting down to talk with one another and having more to agree than disagree on when it came to politics and unresolved war issues.[32] Lost in the friendly talk over tea was the essential question: What is the Japanese news media doing to stand up for the public's right to know?

That question is being answered not by the corporate-dominated mainstream media of Japan, but by working-class citizens, journalists, academics and other activists who are taking media matters into their own hands. Despite all the bad news about the Japanese news media that we see these days (and there is lots of it), some positive signs of change are worth noting. The crisis in journalism in Japan, as elsewhere in the world, has spawned a movement of media reform and, indeed, new media itself:

➤ In May 2001, Yasuo Tanaka, governor of Nagano Prefecture, Japan, announced that he would shut down the prefectural kisha club, which he said had become a "vested interest" to the tune of 15 million yen in taxpayer money per year.[33] The three rooms formerly occupied by the prefectural kisha club were to be vacated in a month's time, he declared, and in their place a new, open Press Center would be made available to "all citizens active in the media field—whether they write for mainstream periodicals, limited-circulation publications, Web-based journals, or any other media channel—and to freelance writers as well." The revolutionary move has not yet been followed by any other local government in Japan, but it does serve as a solid example for the dismantling of other kisha clubs in the future.

➤ On March 20, 2004—one year to the day after the U.S. launched its illegal invasion of Iraq—Japanese photojournalist and author Ryuichi Hirokawa in Tokyo launched *Days Japan,* a monthly photojournalism magazine focusing on the realities of such social issues as poverty, war, sexual violence and discrimination.[34] In just two years of existence, *Days Japan*, with its mission of "bring[ing] back to the fore a world of journalists who are well aware of their most basic role in society and who will share the same vision of responsible journalism well into the future," has come to stand head and shoulders above its mainstream media counterparts in Japan and the United States in both substance and style.

➤ OhMyNews, an independent news organization founded in 2000 in Seoul, South Korea (motto: "Every Citizen is a Reporter"),[35] has made a positive impact on the Korean news scene; OhMyNews has announced plans to also establish an editorial branch in Japan in 2006.[36] The Japanese-language websites Nikkan Berita (slogan: "Alternative Media in the Hands of Citizens")[37] and JANJAN (acronym for "Japan Alternative News for Justice and New Culture"),[38] not to mention the bilingual "IndyMedia Japan" based in Tokyo,[39] are taking on the corporate news world and making their own unique marks on behalf of the voiceless in Japanese society. What these independent media lack in millions of yen worth of resources, personnel and equipment, they more than make up for in the true spirit of journalism.

Finally, here in Japan we join with many around the world who wish a hearty "Congratulations!" to Project Censored for thirty years of carrying on the good fight—for seeing the corporate writing on the media wall three decades ago and continuing to demand that the censored stories in American society be covered. At the same time, we acknowledge the challenges facing the news media in societies the world over and the hard work that will be needed in the years ahead for people of different cultures, languages and viewpoints to come together and fight a common battle for a free, responsible and open press. News media must strengthen, not weaken, the foundations of democracy wherever we live by providing the information that people need to make wise decisions in their lives. Information is indeed power in the twenty-first century, and if the big media companies around the planet can "globalize" on their terms, so can all of us on ours.

Tomoomi Mori is a doctoral student in the Faculty of Social Studies at Doshisha University in Kyoto, Japan. His research is on the Japanese news media and media systems, with a special focus on the *Hankyore* newspaper and OhMyNews web service in the Republic of Korea. His master's thesis was on "A Comparison of Alternative Media in Japan and the Republic of Korea."

Notes

1. *Asahi Shimbun* (English-language edition), "Some military force necessary in the fight against terrorism," October 10, 2001.

2. Hatta, Naomi, "Kisha Clubs," *Japan Media Review*, May 19, 2005, http://www.japanmediareview.com/japan/wiki/Kishaclubs/

3. Freeman, Laurie Anne, *Closing the Shop: Information Cartels and Japan's Mass Media*, Princeton, NJ: Princeton University Press, 2000, 103-107.

4. Covert, Brian, "Kyoto's 'kisha club' system challenged by gutsy farmer," *Mainichi Daily News*, February 1, 1993.

5. Ibid.

6. *Mainichi Daily News*, "A Nation Plunged Into Grief," September 26, 1988.

7. Ibid.

8. *Mainichi Daily News*, "Profoundest Apologies," September 27, 1988.

9. Koike later served as president of the Mainichi Newspapers, while Kondo went on to become a professor of journalism in the international studies division of International Christian University in Tokyo.

10. Asano, Kenichi, "Japan's media lack bite," *Number 1 Shimbun* (publication of the Foreign Correspondents' Club of Japan) 37, no. 11, 2005.

11. Reid, T.R. and Shigehiko Togo, "Japan Picking Princess: Secrecy Surrounds Crown Prince's Choice," *Washington Post*, January 6, 1993.

12. The widely accepted terms are "military comfort stations" *(jugun ianjo* in Japanese) and "comfort women" *(ianfu)* to describe the facilities and the women, respectively, used to provide sexual services to Japanese soldiers at the battlefronts. But since those euphemisms seem to have strong military origins and connotations in both English and Japanese—and because there is nothing "comforting" about institutionalized rape—those commonly used terms are avoided here and instead replaced with more direct terms: "sex stations," "sex slaves," "sexual slavery," and so on.

13. Hayashi, Hirofumi, "The 'Sex Slave'," International Edition, *Days Japan*, Tokyo, 2, no. 1, winter 2006, 22-23.

14. Amnesty International, "Still Waiting After 60 Years: Justice for Survivors of Japan's Military Sexual Slavery System," October 28, 2005, http://web.amnesty.org/library/Index/ENGASA220122005.

15. Violence Against Women in War—Network Japan (VAWW NET), "What is the Women's Tribunal?" http://www1.jca.apc.org/vaww-net-japan/english/aboutus/aboutus.html.

16. Ibid.

17. Morris-Suzuki, Tessa, "Free Speech—Silenced Voices: The Japanese Media, the Comfort Women Tribunal, and the NHK Affair," *Japan Focus*, August 13, 2005, http://japanfocus.org/article.asp?id=365.

18. Violence Against Women in War—Network Japan (VAWW NET), "Judgments," http://www1.jca.apc.org/vaww-net-japan/english/womenstribunal2000/judgement.html.

19. Violence Against Women in War—Network Japan (VAWW NET), "Why Do We Sue NHK?" http://www1.jca.apc.org/vaww-net-japan/english/backlash/whydowesue.html.

20. Honda, Masakazu and Makoto Takada, "LDP pressure led to cuts in NHK show," *Asahi Shimbun*, January 12, 2005, http://www.asahi.com/english/politics/TKY200501120160.html.

21. Morris-Suzuki, Tessa, "Free Speech—Silenced Voices: The Japanese Media, the Comfort Women Tribunal, and the NHK Affair," *Japan Focus*, August 13, 2005, http://japanfocus.org/article.asp?id=365.

22. Ibid.

23. *Daily Yomiuri*, "Nonpayment of NHK fee spreads," February 4, 2005.

24. *Daily Yomiuri*, "1.17 million subscribers refuse to pay NHK fee," August 3, 2005.

25. NHK Online, "Receiving Fee System: The Structure of Independence," http://www.nhk.or.jp/pr/koho-e.htm.

26. *Asahi Shimbun* (English-language edition), "Major cuts eyed for NHK channel lineup," June 1, 2006.

27. *Asahi Shimbun* (English-language edition), "NHK fees likely to become mandatory, but also lower," June 3–4, 2006.

28. North, Scott, "The return of 'thought crimes' in Japan," *Asia Times* Online, May 12, 2006, http://www.atimes.com/atimes/Japan/HE12Dh01.html.

29. Ibid.

30. Asia Media/UCLA Asia Institute, "Japan: Retrial over wartime free-speech crackdown OK'd" (also published in *Japan Times*), March 11, 2005, http://www.asiamedia.ucla.edu/article.asp?parentid=21661.

31. *Japan Times Weekly* Online, "Article 9 a UNSC-bid hurdle: Powell," August 21, 2004, http://www.japantimes.co.jp/weekly/news/nn2004/nn20040821a7.htm.

32. Asahi.com, "Yomiuri, Asahi editorial chiefs call for a national memorial" (*Ronza* magazine reprint), February 9, 2006, http://www.asahi.com/english/Herald-asahi/TKY200602090272.html.

33. Tanaka, Yasuo, "Declaration of Departure from the Press Club System," Web Site Shinshu (Nagano Prefectural Government), May 15, 2001, http://www.pref.nagano.jp/hisyo/press/kisya_e.htm.

34. *Days Japan*, "The aim of publishing *Days Japan*," September 12, 2005, http://www.daysjapan.net/e/news/050912.html

35. OhMyNews International, http://english.ohmynews.com/

36. Kambayashi, Takehiko, "OhMyNews to Put Down Roots in Japan," *Japan Media Review*, March 30, 2006, http://www.japanmediareview.com/japan/stories/060329kambayashi/

37. Berita, Nikkan, http://www.nikkanberita.com/

38. JANJAN, http://www.janjan.jp/

39. Independent Media Center (IndyMedia) Japan, http://japan.indymedia.org/

CHAPTER 14

Milosevic's Death in the Propaganda System

Edward S. Herman and David Peterson

The March 11, 2006 death of former Yugoslav President Slobodan Milosevic in his prison cell in The Hague was greeted by Western political circles and media alike with an outpouring of venom that reflected the demon role assigned to him in the myth-making of the past fifteen years. Milosevic was a "monster," a "sociopath," and a "war criminal who wrecked southeastern Europe in the latter part of the twentieth century," former U.S. Ambassador to the United Nations Richard Holbrooke told the Cable News Network the very first morning.[1] "Milosevic started four wars. He lost them all. The biggest of them all was the one in Bosnia, where over 300,000 people died, two-and-a-half million homeless. And we bombed him in August and September of 1995. We should have done this much earlier." During this and the ten days following his death terms such as "Butcher of the Balkans" and "Butcher of Belgrade" were used scores of times in the U.S. media alone (and widely used abroad as well).[2]

Milosevic was the demon inserted between the two rounds of demonization of Saddam Hussein (1990–1991 and 2002–2006). Thus, the "Butcher of the Balkans" was elevated to the same pantheon of officially designated monsters as the Butcher of Baghdad, whereas other figures, such as Ariel Sharon, whose 1982 invasion of Lebanon and the subsequent managed killings at Sabra and Shatila were cited by the International Criminal Tribunal for the Former Yugoslavia (ICTY, or Yugoslav Tribunal) as an illustration of "genocide,"[3] remain honored statesmen. Sharon was hailed as a "man of peace"—certainly never the "Butcher of Tel Aviv."

The political basis of these designations is made clear by the fact that Milosevic had been Richard Holbrooke's partner in arriving at the Dayton Peace Accords of 1995, the Bosnian Serb Leaders Ratko Mladic and Radovan Karadzic already having been designated war criminals by the ICTY, hence excluded from the negotiations.

"People keep asking whether Milosevic is going to deliver on the peace agreement," Holbrooke said at Dayton. "It's impossible to answer that question right now. All we know is that he has delivered on everything . . . over the past four months."4 Similarly, Saddam Hussein was a partner of the United States and Britain throughout the 1980s and was given economic and military aid and diplomatic support by this Anglo-American coalition. There were no "butcher" designations then, although it was during this period that Saddam was deadliest and he was actually using "weapons of mass destruction" with Western support. Exemption from charges expressed in invidious language, as well as from sanctions, bombing, and trials in courts of justice are the benefits of offering positive service to the powerful. The same exemptions apply to those able to manipulate these subaltern leaders.

Milosevic's initial indictment for war crimes by the ICTY on May 22, 1999 did not mention Bosnia—it focused solely on his alleged "superior authority" and responsibility for 344 deaths in Kosovo, all but forty-five of which occurred *after* NATO began its bombing war against Yugoslavia on March 24, 1999.5 Croatia and Bosnia were only brought into the picture by the ICTY prosecutor several months after Milosevic's June 28, 2001 kidnapping and transfer to the Hague, surely because the number of bodies found in Kosovo after the end of the bombing war was disappointingly small, and certainly not sufficient to sustain a charge of genocide.6 Croatia and Bosnia also posed a potential numbers problem, and there was a six year delay in charging Milosevic as the lead villain. His constructive role in Dayton and earlier peace efforts also complicated the case. However, the Tribunal could count on the mainstream media not to bring up these awkward matters, and they are not mentioned in the numerous articles on the trial by Marlise Simons in the *New York Times*.7

The mainstream media's protectiveness of this demonizing narrative is illustrated by widespread inaccuracies in the reported number of deaths in Kosovo, Croatia, and Bosnia. The U.S. Defense and State Departments had claimed at various times during the Kosovo bombing war that 100,000, 225,000, and in one press release 500,000 Kosovo Albanians had been killed by the Yugoslav army.8 This was eventually pared to 11,000, although after a uniquely intensive search only some 4,000 bodies were found, including unknown numbers of fighters and victims of NATO and Kosovo Liberation Army actions.

As of early March 2006, only 2,398 people remained listed by the Red Cross as still missing. There has never been any hint of criticism in the mainstream media of the inflated numbers given by U.S. officials, nor have there been any doubts expressed as to the accuracy of the 11,000 figure, although it came from sources of proven unreliability and was 70 percent higher than the official count of the dead and missing (6,398).[9] In the *New York Times*, Michael Ignatieff explained that if the numbers of bodies found was less than 11,000 it must have been because the Serbs moved them out.[10] He never explained why the official count of dead plus missing fell far short of 11,000, but he didn't have to worry: inaccuracies are ignored when a demonized enemy is involved.

By January, 1993, Bosnian Muslim officials were claiming that 200,000 or more Bosnian Muslims had been slaughtered by the Serbs,[11] and although the numbers were unverified and came from a biased source, they were immediately accepted and institutionalized by the mainstream media and journalist campaigners for war such as David Rieff, Ignatieff, Christopher Hitchens, and Ed Vulliamy. Estimates under 100,000 by former State Department official George Kenney and others with intelligence access were simply ignored. However, in 2003, a study by Ewa Tabeau and Jakub Bijak, researchers working for the Demographic Unit of the Office of the Prosecutor at the ICTY, as well as ongoing research by Mirsad Tokaca at the Sarajevo-based and Norwegian and Bosnian government-funded Research and Documentation Center, both came out with estimates of total Bosnian deaths on the order of 100,000.[12] In the Tabeau-Bijak study only 55,000 of these were civilians, including over 16,000 Serbs. These are certainly not negligible numbers, but they are far less satisfactory than 200,000 or more dead Bosnian Muslims, especially if you are eager to make a case for genocide and to justify the intense focus on this killing area as opposed to others that involved numbers running to seven digits.[13]

It should be noted that the claimed number of executions in the Srebrenica massacre, which has been maintained at 8,000 since the events of July 1995, have also been challenged. In this case, as in Kosovo, the number of bodies found in the vicinity—only some 2,600, including unknown numbers who may have been killed in action or before July 1995—fell far short of the initially claimed total. Other evidence in support of the politically correct total has been meager, and despite Madeleine Albright's statement in August 1995 that "we will be watching" via satellite,[14] no satellite evidence of moved or reburied bodies has ever been provided to the public. There is a good case to be made that although there were surely hundreds of executions, and possibly as many as a thousand or more, the 8,000 figure is a political construct and eminently challengeable.[15]

But doubting the Srebrenica narrative is dangerous, and even approving the work of someone who has raised any questions whatsoever can elicit attacks. This was dramatically evident in an interview of Noam Chomsky by Emma Brockes, published in the London *Guardian* on October 31, 2005. The headline of the interview read:

Q: Do you regret supporting those who say the Srebrenica massacre is exaggerated?
A: My only regret is that I didn't do it strongly enough.[16]

The quotes were manufactured by Brockes and *The Guardian*. Brockes also claimed that Chomsky stated that "during the Bosnian war the 'massacre' at Srebrenica was probably exaggerated," after which she sneered at his childish use of quotation marks. Brockes constructed this out of the whole cloth; quotation marks are not used in verbal interviews, and Chomsky did not make the alleged remark or exaggeration.

Chomsky did laud Diana Johnstone's book *Fools' Crusade* and signed a letter assailing a decision not to publish it in Sweden. Johnstone is said by Brockes to have claimed that the Srebrenica numbers executed were "exaggerated." However, Johnstone never used that word, never denied executions, and spent most of her discussion of Srebrenica on its context and the uses to which the massacre claims were put. It is enlightening to see that any suggestion that the 8,000 number was inflated is illicit and to be condemned, without further discussion.

Brockes's misrepresentations were so clear and numerous that *The Guardian* published a set of comments titled "Corrections and clarifications" and removed the interview from their web site.[17] This in turn elicited a furious response from what we may call the "Bosnia Genocide Lobby," a well-organized set of institutions and individuals funded by George Soros, Western governments, and others who attack any challenges to the established narrative. One of the more important responses to the "corrections" was a letter signed by twenty-five writers and analysts, many affiliated with the Lobby's organizations—the Balkan Investigative Reporting Network (publisher of *Balkan Insight*), the Bosnian Institute, and the Institute for War and Peace Reporting—and journalists like David Rieff, David Rohde, and Ed Vulliamy, all of whom challenged the "correction" and called upon *The Guardian* to retract it.[18]

Perhaps the most notable features of this letter are its use of the words "revisionism" and "denial" to refer to any questioning of the established number, and its treatment of any suggestion of doubt as intolerable. The "authority" that determines whether genocide takes place is the ICTY, "an international court established by the United Nations"—hence presumably an independent and authoritative body, despite massive evidence to the contrary (see below). Yet even the ICTY indicated that the 8,000 figure might be exaggerated. Its judges stated that the evidence only "suggests" that a majority of the 7,000–8,000 classed as missing were executed, as opposed to dying in battle, making the possible total of executed only 3,600–4,100—the judges thus falling into the "revisionist" and "denial" categories.[19]

Of course, Tabeau and Bijak's research, as well as that of the Tocaka-led RDC (not yet finalized at the time of this writing), are also clear-cut cases of "revisionism" and "denial" according to the Lobby's peculiar usage of these terms. But given the fact that the Tabeau-Bijak research was supported by the ICTY and the RDC's research was backed by the Norwegian and Bosnian governments, the Lobby could not condemn these organizations. Instead the chosen route was silence, a route also taken by the mainstream media and U.S. officials.[20] A global Nexis database search for articles written during the first eleven days after Milosevic's death[21] discloses that the reported death toll from the wars in the former Yugoslavia[22] was said to be 200,000 or greater in at least 202 different items (such as news reports, obituaries, editorials and op-eds), and 100,000 in only thirteen. The death toll was estimated to be 250,000 in at least ninety-nine different items, and 300,000 in no less than twenty-seven different items. On at least seventy-six different occasions the U.S. media reported a death toll of 200,000 or greater, and only twice used the 100,000 figure. This means that although researchers at the ICTY and the Bosnian Government have concluded that a figure in the vicinity of 100,000 is a more accurate estimate for war-related deaths in Bosnia, that figure was the least often cited in reports and comments on the wars. It is a testimony to the deep-seated bias of the media that the death toll issued by relatively scholarly establishment sources was not able to displace the old and higher figures that were issued by Bosnian Muslim officials who were noted for lack of scruple.[23] The journalists hate to abandon numbers that have backed their biases so well.

THE ICTY AS A POLITICAL ARM OF NATO

Before examining the charges Milosevic faced in his trial, let us look more closely at the body that brought those charges, the "international court established by the United Nations." It is an interesting fact that the United States, which has been a leader in the organization and support of the ICTY, has refused to have anything to do with the recently organized International Criminal Court, allegedly because it poses a threat of "politicization."[24] Unbiased commentators might ask whether the problem with the ICC might be that it was less subject to U.S. control than the ICTY, and whether the merit of the ICTY from the U.S. standpoint might have been its domination by the U.S., and hence politicization in a proper direction. This point is not raised by apologists for the ICTY, such as the twenty-five signers of the pro-Brockes letter to *The Guardian* or to Marlise Simons *et al.*, in good part because dominant U.S. influence is seen as natural and appropriate. The word 'politicization' is not used in such cases of deep internalized bias any more than words like 'aggression' or 'terrorism'.

But the politicization of the ICTY was thorough. The initial organization, staffing, funding, and the vetting of top personnel was conducted by high NATO officials,[25] who provided (or withheld) information and served as the police arm of the ICTY.[26] The ICTY's actions were geared to meet NATO demands.

The political role of the ICTY was openly acknowledged by former State Department lawyer Michael Scharf, who stated in 1999 that the organization was seen in the government as "little more than a public relations tool," useful "to isolate offending leaders diplomatically" and to "fortify the international political will to employ economic sanctions or use force."[27] York University Professor of Law Michael

Mandel makes a convincing case in *How America Gets Away with Murder* that the ICTY was brought into existence "as a way of opposing the peace process and justifying the military solution that they [U.S. leaders] favored."[28] He points out that State Department official Lawrence Eagleburger named the top Serb leaders as war criminals in December 1992, shortly before the ICTY was created in 1993, and that U.S. officials were already using alleged Serb criminality to subvert peace plans that were under consideration in 1992 and 1993. The argument was that "justice" must not give way to political expediency and goals such as ending conflict without more fighting. "In other words, the proposal for a war crimes tribunal was used by the Americans to justify their intention to go to war, collateral damage and all, by branding their proposed enemies as Nazis."[29]

The Mandel charge is proved by history. The United States and Izetbegovic scuttled the important Lisbon peace agreement of February 1992, and they helped prevent peace via the Vance-Owen and Owen-Stoltenberg plans, as is described in Bosnian Peace Plan negotiator David Owen's memoir *Balkan Odyssey.*[30] This peace-prevention program kept the Bosnian wars going for nearly four years, ending with a settlement at Dayton that reduced Bosnia to a NATO colonial province. Leading up to the Kosovo war, the ICTY's work was very closely geared to NATO's (and essentially the U.S.'s) plan for war. As NATO began planning for war in June 1998, the ICTY began a parallel campaign of well-publicized accusations and investigations of Serb actions in Kosovo and denunciations of Serb behavior.[31] The day after the killings at Racak on January 15, 1999, one of the landmark events that propelled the war, ICTY chief prosecutor Louise Arbour quickly declared the incident a "war crime" based solely on a communication with U.S. and OSCE representative William Walker.[32] Two months later, on March 31, 1999, just a week after the bombing war began, Arbour held a press conference to publicize the formerly sealed indictment of Zeljko Raznatovic ("Arkan"). The indictment was prepared as early as September 1997, but its release was timed to meet the propaganda needs of the NATO powers.[33]

The indictment of Milosevic and four others on May 22, 1999 (though not published until May 27),[34] was a high-point in ICTY public relations service to NATO, and was clearly done in collaboration with NATO officials.[35] It occurred in the midst of the seventy-eight-day NATO bombing war against Yugoslavia, and more specifically at a time when NATO had begun bombing Serbian civilian facilities and infrastructure. This last was causing unease and eliciting criticism even in the NATO countries, and the indictment served the public relations function of distracting attention from the new turn in the NATO bombing to the villainy of the leaders of the target country. Clinton, Madeleine Albright and James Rubin quickly called attention to this implication, Albright stating that the indictments "make very clear to the world and the publics in our countries that this [NATO policy] is justified because of the crimes committed, and I think also will enable us to keep moving all these processes [translation: *bombing*] forward."[36]

The indictment was put together hastily, based on information supplied to the ICTY prosecutor by the United States and United Kingdom, information admittedly unverified by the Tribunal itself (despite prosecutor Arbour's statement on April 20, 1999 that "We are subject to extremely stringent rules of evidence with respect to the admissibility and the credibility of the product that we will tender in court, we certainly will not be advancing any case against anybody on the basis of unsubstantiated, unverifiable, uncorroborated allegations"[37]). Its political ties were further revealed by Arbour's statement that she issued the indictment because "the evidence upon which this indictment was confirmed raises serious questions about their [the indictees] suitability to be guarantors of any deal let alone a peace agreement." Milosevic and his indicted colleagues had not been tried and convicted, but although Arbour stated that the indictees were entitled to the presumption of innocence until they were convicted, the "evidence" (unverified by the ICTY) demanded that that rule be set aside.[38]

In July 1995 the ICTY had indicted Mladic and Karadzic for their roles in wartime Bosnia and Herzegovina, including the charge of genocide for the conduct of their subordinates at various detention facilities dating back to 1992. Four months later, in mid-November, the ICTY extended this indictment to cover a second count of genocide at Srebrenica, well before the facts of the case had been collected and verified by the ICTY, but serving to exclude these two Bosnian Serb officials from the Dayton process.[39] Noting that the indictment "marks a fundamental step," then-ICTY President Antonio Cassese explicitly acknowledged its political objective in an interview with the Italian newspaper *L'Unita*. "The indictment means that these gentlemen will not be able to participate in peace negotiations," Cassese emphasized. "Let us see who will sit down at the negotiating table now with a man accused of genocide."[40] As Scharf noted in 1999, one of the aims in the creation of the ICTY was "to isolate enemy leaders diplomatically"—a political aim, not a judicial one.[41]

Arbour was quick to acknowledge the unverified war crime at Racak, but when Michael Mandel presented her with a three-volume dossier on NATO war crimes in May 1999, it took her and her successor Carla Del Ponte an entire year to consider the case. Del Ponte finally declared that a preliminary check had found that this set of allegations did not even provide a basis for opening an investigation. An internal report had declared that with only 495 dead victims "there is simply no evidence of the necessary crime base for charges of genocide or crimes against humanity," although the forty-five deaths at Racak and the 344 victims listed in Milosevic's indictment had been sufficient to spur Arbour's aggressive action.[32] The ICTY's political ties are further clarified by the fact that Del Ponte's leading expert in developing the case for no investigation indicated that he had relied on NATO country press releases as information sources, declaring them "generally reliable and that explanations have been honestly given."[33] We may recall prosecutor Arbour's assurance, cited earlier, that her office employs only "extremely stringent rules of evidence" that exclude "unsubstantiated, unverifiable, uncorroborated allegations," now clearly excluding allegations by her (and Del Ponte's) NATO masters.

These evidences of ICTY political subordination and facilitation of war crimes—the bombing of Serb civilian facilities was stepped up immediately following the ICTY indictment of Milosevic in late May 1999—and its laughable justification for not investigating NATO's war crimes would have discredited the ICTY as a supposedly judicial body, if we were not dealing with a well-oiled propaganda machine that will swallow anything to bring "justice" to a demonized enemy. It is easy to demonize the enemy when dealing with a civil war, where there are many victims with just grievances and political axes to grind. The trick is to choose the right victims,[34] attribute their pain to the demon, allow unlimited use of hearsay evidence, strip away the context, and rewrite history.

THE CHARGES AGAINST MILOSEVIC

Some of the major claims supporting Milosevic's demon status were formulated in the charges spelled out in the several indictments against him,[45] along with the evidence brought in support of those charges. These became premises of the mainstream media and members of the Lobby. Let us turn to those charges and see how they stand up today, the prosecution having completed its case in late February 2004, and Milosevic putting up his defense from late August, 2004, cut short by his death.[46]

1. Author and orchestrator of four wars

Central to the ICTY case and repeated in virtually all the articles on the death of Milosevic is the claim that he was not just personally responsible for the Balkan wars of the 1990s, but that he was perhaps *uniquely* responsible for them as well. Thus the indictments of Milosevic are replete with charges that he participated in a "joint criminal enterprise as co-perpetrator," and that, depending on the territory at issue (Kosovo, Croatia, or Bosnia), the "purpose" of each of these joint criminal enterprises was the "expulsion of a substantial portion of," or the "forcible removal of the majority of," or the "forcible and permanent removal of the majority of" the ethnic non-Serb populations from each territory, either to "ensure continued Serbian control" or to create a "new Serb-dominated state"—the so-called "Greater Serbia" that has so entranced Western commentary.[47] Milosevic "bore chief responsibility for the break-up of Yugoslavia . . . and for the subsequent wars," Misha Glenny maintained throughout a series of obituaries about Milosevic.[48] As Richard Holbrooke summed up the demon theory in an op-ed column, Milosevic's death in his prison cell "knowing he would never see freedom again" was a "fitting end for someone who started four wars (all of which he lost), causing 300,000 deaths, leaving more than 2m people homeless and wrecking the Balkans."[49] Following Milosevic's death, sentiments such as these were an almost uniform refrain in the Western media. The other nationalisms that surfaced in these wars were allegedly responsive; only that of Milosevic and the Serbs was causal.

This evil villain interpretation of recent Balkan history is not merely simple-minded, it is contradicted by massive evidence. For one thing, it falsifies the role of the other nationalisms in the Balkans—Croatian nationalism was strong, and its proponents like President Franjo Tudjman were eager and planning for secession well before Milosevic was in power.[50] Bosnian Muslim President Alija Izetbegovic's drive for Muslim domination in Bosnia dated back at least as far as his *Islamic Declaration* of 1970.[51] Secondly, it overstates Milosevic's nationalism, which was itself responsive to the perceived threats to Serbian interests and nationalist sentiments arising from his constituents; and his famous ultra-nationalist speeches of 1987 and 1989 were not ultra-nationalist at all. At various points, these speeches touted the importance of "brotherhood and unity" to the survival of Yugoslavia; they warned against all forms of "separatism and nationalism" as anti-modern and counter-revolutionary; and they called for mutual toleration and "full equality for all nations" within a multinational Yugoslavia, using language carefully kept out of news reports of those speeches.[52] Among the myths constructed to explain the breakup of Yugoslavia and its incorporation into Western structures, surely the one that accuses Milosevic of having used these two speeches to stoke the nationalistic fires that would accompany Yugoslavia's demise ranks as the most enduring.

This view grossly underrates the role of Germany, the United States and other external powers in producing and underwriting the wars. Germany led the way in encouraging Slovenia and Croatia to secede from Yugoslavia, in violation of the Helsinki agreement and Yugoslav Constitution. Any Yugoslav army action to prevent this illegal secession and protect the integrity of Yugoslavia's common state could be said to be "responsive," with Germany and the leaders of the seceding countries "authors" of the wars that followed.

The great powers were also heavily responsible for these wars by their refusal to allow the "nations" within the seceding artificial republics to remove themselves and stay with Yugoslavia or merge into Serbia or Croatia peacefully. The EU-sponsored Badinter Commission (1991–1992) declared against such separation, although this would have been a plausible right of secession at least as justified as the secession of the republics. This externally imposed declaration was heavily responsible for the ethnic struggles and cleansing that ensued.

Finally, Milosevic was president of Serbia, but not Yugoslavia, at the time of Slovenia's secession in late June 1991, and had nothing to do with the Yugoslav army's response.⁵³ That response was confused and extremely modest, with skirmishes that lasted only ten days. As for Milosevic's responsibility for the Kosovo war, it is now clear that the United States and its allies, including the ICTY, were preparing for a war by April 1998,⁵⁴ the United States eventually helping to arm the KLA and giving the KLA reason to believe that NATO would eventually come to its aid by direct military intervention. It is also well established that the early 1999 Rambouillet peace talks were a fraud, with the bar deliberately raised to assure Yugoslav rejection and justify a military attack.⁵⁵ Milosevic didn't start this war, the U.S. and its NATO allies did, and they did so in plain violation of the UN Charter.

2. Aim to create a "Greater Serbia"

In the series of ICTY indictments of Milosevic, the claim that he was striving to produce a "Greater Serbia" ranks high in the explanation of the Yugoslav wars. Six years ago, Tim Judah wrote that it was a "cruel irony" that it all began with the slogan "All Serbs in One State;" and in an obituary in the *Washington Post* this past March, we read again that Milosevic's "pledge to unify all Serbs in one state turned into an ironic promise."⁵⁶ But in truth this is neither a cruel nor any other kind of irony. Rather, it is a gross misrepresentation of both the dynamics of those cruel conflicts and of Milosevic's language and politics.

In one of the most remarkable developments in the Milosevic trial, on August 25, 2005, after former deputy prime minister of Serbia Vojislav Seselj had given compelling testimony that this notion of a joint criminal enterprise and Milosevic's role in the supposed search for a "Greater Serbia" was incompatible with a wide array of facts, prosecuting counsel Geoffrey Nice acknowledged to the court that Milosevic had never advocated a "Greater Serbia" but rather that he wanted all Serbs to remain living together in one state.⁵⁷ That is, Nice conceded that Milosevic's aim was defensive—that he wanted to prevent the dismantling of Yugoslavia, but as a second line of defense he sought to help the stranded Serb minorities in the exiting republics stay together. This of course was what Abraham Lincoln did after the secession of the Southern states in the run-up to the Civil War—presumably, he was trying to create a "Greater America." This spectacular admission by Nice, which confused the judges, would seem to have removed or rendered innocuous a central ICTY charge.

But it is not even true that Milosevic fought regularly to keep all Serbs in one state. He either supported or agreed to a series of settlements, like Brioni (July 1991), Lisbon (February 1992), Vance-Owen (January 1993), Owen-Stoltenberg (August 1993), the European Action Plan (January 1994), the Contact Group Plan (July 1994), and ultimately the Dayton Accords (November 1995)—none of which would have kept all Serbs in one state. He declined to defend the Krajina Serbs when they were ethnically cleansed from Croatia from May to August 1995. He agreed to an official contraction in the earlier Socialist Federal Republic of Yugoslavia to the Federal Republic of Yugoslavia (comprising Serbia and Montenegro—now undergoing a final breakup), which in effect abandoned the Serbs in Croatia and Bosnia to their fate outside any "Greater Serbia." His aid to Serbs in both Croatia and Bosnia was sporadic, and their leaders felt him to have been an opportunistic and unreliable ally, more concerned with getting sanctions against Yugoslavia removed than making serious sacrifices for the stranded Serbs elsewhere.

In short, Milosevic struggled fitfully to defend Serbs who felt stranded and threatened in hostile secessionist states of a progressively dismantled Yugoslavia; and he wanted but did not fight very hard to preserve a shrunken Yugoslav Federation that would have kept all the Serbs in a successor common state. To call this a drive for a "Greater Serbia" is Orwellian political rhetoric that transforms a weak (and failed) defense into a bold and aggressive offense.

3. Leader with command responsibility of a "joint criminal enterprise" aiming to eliminate Bosnian Muslims

The ICTY has been extremely demanding in applying the concept of command responsibility to Milosevic, and remarkably liberal in finding him leader of a "joint criminal enterprise." During the trial, not one of the 296 prosecution witnesses testified to any instruction to commit actions that constituted war crimes or to his expression of approval of criminal actions, and no documents were entered into the record supporting the prosecution view on these matters (whereas quite a few witnesses testified to his anger at war crimes, and cited cases of prosecution of Yugoslav personnel for war-criminal activities). But still, he should have known, and he was responsible for his subordinates. Needless to say, the same rule was not applied by the ICTY to the top leaders of NATO, Croatia, and Bosnia and Herzegovina.

The "joint criminal enterprise" concept was adopted by the prosecution to extend his indictment responsibilities to warfare in Croatia and Bosnia and Herzegovina, and especially to join Milosevic with Mladic and Karadzic as partners in the more extensive killings in Bosnia.58 It was awkward that the latter two were indicted back in 1995 instead of the "boss," but as noted earlier, the media won't notice. In the indictments of Milosevic issued during 2001, the boss and the Bosnian Serb leaders allegedly had a common goal: to eliminate the Muslims in the interest of that "Greater Serbia." Unfortunately, no common plan was ever uncovered, but the alleged partners did sometimes cooperate and Muslims were killed.

There is much solider evidence of a Croat-U.S. plan to remove Serbs from the Krajina, efficiently implemented in May and August 1995, but somehow this has never been pursued by the ICTY as a "joint criminal enterprise." The one involving Milosevic also runs up against Milosevic's previously mentioned acceptance of a series of peace plans from 1991 onward, sometimes with furious opposition from the Bosnian Serb leaders, efforts by the demon that obviously did not envisage the elimination of Muslims.

4. Guilty of genocide

Milosevic could be indicted for two counts of genocide in 2001 because earlier in that same year the Bosnian Serb General Radislav Krstic had been found guilty of genocide, and Milosevic was the boss of the "joint criminal enterprise." The *Krstic* judgment was based on the events at Srebrenica, but was built on ICTY judges' logic that is not merely untenable, but nonsensical. Can you be aiming to exterminate *all* Bosnian Muslims if you spare the women and children and execute largely if not exclusively military-aged men until then encamped in one of the supposedly demilitarized "Safe Areas"? The court's ruling in the *Krstic* judgment was that actions constitute genocide if the perpetrators regarded "the intended destruction as sufficient to annihilate the group as a distinct entity in the geographic area at issue."59 This made genocide the equivalent of ethnic cleansing, and there would have been literally dozens of cases of genocide in Bosnia on this foolish criterion,60 including many carried out by

Bosnian Muslim leader Naser Oric in 1992–1993 in the villages near Srebrenica. It would clearly make the Croatian removal and killing of the Krajina Serbs (with active U.S. aid) a case of genocide—more clearly than the Srebrenica massacre, as the Croatian cleansing involved the killing of several hundred women and children and covered a much larger geographic area.

The *Krstic* finding of genocide was not only tooled and used selectively by the ICTY, it was a debasement of the meaning of the word and arguably a "revisionist" usage that downplays the significance of policies that aim to wipe out an *entire* people (as Elie Wiesel himself has pointed out).[61] What is more, the Milosevic trial produced not one iota of evidence that Milosevic knew about, approved, or had the power to control the events at Srebrenica, which were rooted in local conditions and carried out by Bosnian Serb forces. Indeed, in a scholarly and exhaustive study, Dutch historian Cees Wiebes writes that the "mood in Belgrade was one of disbelief . . . An interview with [the Bosnian-Serb mining official] Rajko Dukic, who talked to Milosevic after the fall of the enclave, indicates that [Milosevic] was indeed surprised. [Milosevic] asked the group of persons that included Dukic 'which idiot' had taken the decision to attack Srebrenica."[62]

5. The Death—or Killing—of Milosevic

The death of Milosevic was a boon to the ICTY. His defense was going well, and had dealt severe blows to the prosecution claims on his supposed aim of a "Greater Serbia," the Racak massacre, the allegedly close links and common aims of the joint conspirators, the history of the wars for which Milosevic was claimed to be responsible, and the policies of the Yugoslav military and police. Of course his defense was almost entirely unreported in the mainstream media, but it would have made the judges' final decision and report problematic. Given the political role of the ICTY and biases deeply embedded in the carefully chosen judges, as well as the media and culture at large, there is no doubt that Milosevic would have been found guilty—a political court provides a political decision. But their report and decision would have been vulnerable to critical attack, as there is no way that an honest and unbiased court could avoid finding against the prosecution. In fact, it would have thrown the case out a long time ago.

Milosevic's death ends the need to construct a juridical argument for the necessary finding of guilt. His guilt was decided long ago, and the mainstream media have declared him guilty once again in the death denunciations, which have consisted largely of name-calling and repetition of the farcical claims discussed above.

Milosevic thought that he was being poisoned, and the ICTY and media have suggested that he was poisoning himself, either in an attempted suicide or to worsen his condition to justify outside medical treatment. Neither of these is plausible, but what is true is that his treatment by the ICTY surely hastened his death and makes that institution guilty of some form of grave criminal negligence, perhaps even manslaughter.

Milosevic was refused permission to see his family over a four year period, he was treated harshly by the court in session,[63] and he was explicitly denied the right to get medical treatment in Moscow that he had been requesting since last December, which both Russian and independent consultants said was urgently required for his survival. As late as February 23, 2006, the trial judges ruled that they were "not satisfied" that Milosevic, "if released, would return for the continuation of the trial,"[64] despite a Russian assurance that he would be returned and Milosevic's obvious determination to see his defense to its conclusion. This is the same court that recently permitted the Kosovo Albanian "indicted war criminal" Ramush Haradinaj to leave prison and return to Kosovo to engage in a political campaign. The ICTY has maintained a reliable double standard reflecting its political role, and in the case of its treatment of Milosevic, this has proved deadly.

Conclusion

The seizure and trial of Milosevic was the high point in ICTY service to NATO, designed to demonstrate with a show-trial that the long-standing NATO target in Yugoslavia was evil and the NATO war was therefore a justifiable "humanitarian intervention." It worked less well than anticipated, because the patched-together charges were very hard to support and Milosevic put up a vigorous defense. Fortunately for the prosecution, the media featured the charges and parade of victims of war and Milosevic's alleged recalcitrance and defiance, while ignoring the substance of his quite effective defense, and paid no attention whatsoever to the disastrous effects of the "humanitarian intervention" on its supposed beneficiaries. There has not been a word pointing out the contrast between Clinton's alleged Kosovo objective of a "tolerant, multi-ethnic community" and the resulting reality of widespread fear, intolerance, serious and irreversible ethnic cleansing, and a mafia- and terrorist-run state.[65]

A lesson learned by NATO officials and supporters is that even unfair show trials supported by the media can be problematic as some awkward evidence inevitably trickles out. The early death of a defendant like Milosevic makes it easy to ignore reality. Better yet, and possibly to be implemented in the future, would be killing the targeted demon long before a trial becomes necessary, leaving it to the reliable media to find the assassinated victim guilty *in absentia*. NATO did try this in dealing with Milosevic but failed (with a missile attack targeting his residence in Belgrade on April 22, 1999). This was a costly failure, ending with the problematic trial. Given the proclivities of the U.S. foreign policy managers we may expect more aggressive targeting in the future, and, if driven to it, Guantánamo-style trials.

[Earlier versions of this chapter were published in *Z Magazine* (May, 2006) and on the Electric Politics website.]

Notes

1. *CNN Morning News*, 11:00 AM EST, Transcript 031105CN.V28, March 11, 2006.
2. Based on searches of English-language media sources including the wire services (AFP, AP, DPA, Reuters, and many others), European, Canadian, U.S. print, TV and radio, and other regions for mentions of the phrases 'Butcher of the Balkans' or 'Butcher of Belgrade' during the period March 11–21, 2006.
3. *Prosecutor v. Radislav Krstic* (IT-98-33), August 2, 2001, Sect. G, http://www.un.org/icty/krstic/TrialC1/judgement/index.html; also see Michael Mandel, *How America Gets Away With Murder: Illegal Wars, Collateral Damage and Crimes Against Humanity*, New York: Pluto Press, 2004, pp. 152-160.
4. Michael Dobbs, "U.S. Gains Assurances On Troops; Balkan Presidents Promise Security," *Washington Post*, November 24, 1995. Although buried beneath the events of subsequent years, the fact that Milosevic helped the American negotiators secure the Dayton Accords was widely reported at the time.
5. UN International Criminal Tribune for the former Yugoslavia, *Prosecutor Against Slobodan Milosevic et al.*, IT-99-37-I, "Kosovo" (May 22, 1999), http://www.un.org/icty/indictment/english/mil-ii990524e.htm. Under Schedule A – Schedule G, this initial indictment lists a total of 344 persons "known by name killed." Of these 344 persons, no less than 299 are claimed to have been killed on March 25, 1999 or later.
6. UN ICTY, *Prosecutor Against Slobodan Milosevic et al.*, IT-01-50-I, "Croatia" (October 8, 2001), http://www.un.org/icty/indictment/english/mil-ii011008e.htm; and *Prosecutor Against Slobodan Milosevic et al.*, IT-01-51-I, "Bosnia and Herzegovina" (November 22, 2001), *http://www.un.org/icty/indictment/english/mil-ii011122e.htm*.
7. In our earlier study of reporting on the Tribunal by the *New York Times'* Marlise Simons, we described Simons' portrayal of the Tribunal as the epitome of Western justice, and showed

how her reporting for the *Times*, over an extended period of years, replicated the point of view of the Tribunal's prosecutors, which is largely the point of view of the NATO bloc, and the point of view of its American leadership above all.

See Edward S. Herman and David Peterson, the *New York Times on the Yugoslavia Tribunal: A Study in Total Propaganda Service*, ColdType.net, 2004, http://www.coldtype.net/Assets.04/Essays.04/YugoTrib.pdf.

8. See James Rubin, "State Department Regular Briefing," *Federal News Service*, April 19, 1999; "US concerned up to 500,000 missing Kosovar Albanian men may be dead," *Agence France Presse*, April 19, 1999; and Bob Holer and Anne E. Kornblut, "Up to 500,000 unaccounted for in Kosovo; Missing men feared dead, US reports," *Boston Globe*, April 20, 1999. As the State Department asserted in a weekly Fact Sheet released at the time: "[S]ome 150,000 to 500,000 military-age men remain missing in Kosovo." See "Ethnic Cleansing in Kosovo," April 22, 1999, http://www.state.gov/www/regions/eur/rpt_990422_ksvo_ethnic.html.

9. UN ICTY Office of Prosecutor, Carla del Ponte, "Statement to the Press by Carla del Ponte," press release, December 20, 2000, par. 16, http://www.un.org/icty/pressreal/p550-e.htm; "Kosovo: deplores slow progress of working group on missing persons," ICRC, March 9, 2006, http://www.icrc.org/web/eng/siteengo.nsf/iwpList74/0B705A092BFF53FDC125712C0046039C.

10. Michael Ignatieff, "Counting Bodies in Kosovo," *New York Times*, November 21, 1999.

11. While in Geneva for talks on the Vance-Owen peace plan, and later in Washington on a visit arranged by the Carnegie Endowment for International Peace, Bosnian Muslim President Alija Izetbegovic pressed the claim that 200,000 already had been killed. See John A. Callcott, "Bosnia-Herzegovina peace talks break for five days," UPI, January 4, 1993; Barry Schweid, "Bosnian Leader Appeals for U.S. Support," AP, January 8, 1993; "Profile: Happy to Butcher Bosnia," *The Independent*, January 9, 1993; David Binder, "Bosnian Shifts on Geneva Talks To Protest Killing," *New York Times*, January 10, 1993. The month of January, 1993 also witnessed the claim about Bosnian Muslim women suffering the "most massive raping in human history" (Izetbegovic while in Geneva) first placed into mass circulation. On "The Uses of Rape," see Diana Johnstone, *Fools' Crusade: Yugoslavia, NATO, and Western Delusions*, (Monthly Review Press, 2002), pp. 78-90.

12. Jakub Bijak and Ewa Tabeau, "War-related Deaths in the 1992–1995 Armed Conflicts in Bosnia and Herzegovina: A Critique of Previous Estimates and Recent Results," *European Journal of Population* 21 (June 2005): 187-215, http://www.ingentaconnect.com/content/klu/eujp/2005/00000021/F0020002/00006852; Mirsad Tokaca of the Sarajevo-based Research and Documentation Center, as quoted in "Bosnian war 'claimed 100,000 lives'," *Deutsche Presse-Agentur*, November 21, 2005; in Nedim Dervisbegovic, "Research halves Bosnia war death toll to 100,000," *Reuters*, November 23, 2005; in Vesna Peric Zimonjic, "Balkans: How Many Really Died in Bosnia's Wars?" *Inter-Press Service*, December 6, 2005; in "Sarajevo researcher says 99,000 killed in Bosnian war," BBC *Worldwide Monitoring* translation of a HINA news agency report (Zagreb), December 17, 2005; and in Emir Suljagic talks to Mirsad Tokaca, "Genocide is not a matter of numbers," *Bosnia Report*, December - March, 2006, http://www.bosnia.org.uk/bosrep/report_format.cfm?articleid=3055&reportid=170.

13. The "sanctions of mass destruction" imposed on Iraq by the United States and Britain through the UN following the first Persian Gulf War were responsible for the death of a million Iraqis or more, and the wars in the Democratic Republic of the Congo since the last 1990s have caused deaths estimated to run into the millions. For data on Iraq, see, e.g., John Mueller and Karl Mueller, "Sanctions of Mass Destruction," *Foreign Affairs*, May/June, 1999, http://www.foreignaffairs.org/19990501faessay979/john-mueller-karl-mueller/sanctions-of-mass-destruction.html; and Joy Gordon, "Cool War: Economic sanctions as a weapon of mass destruction," *Harper's*, November 2002, http://www.scn.org/ccpi/HarpersJoyGordonNov02.html. And for data on the Democratic Republic of the Congo, B. Coghlan *et al.*, "Mortality in the Democratic Republic of Congo: a nationwide survey," *The Lancet* (367), January 7, 2006, pp. 44-51, http://72.14.203.104/search?q=cache:XNrxID-zHBQJ:www.theirc.org/resources/DRCMortality0106Study.doc+&hl=en&gl=us&ct=clnk&cd=1. According to the *New York Times*, UN Secretary-General Boutros Boutros-Ghali used the phrase "war of the rich" to express how "many Africans describe the conflict in Yugoslavia, arguing that the faces seen on television are well fed compared to the victims in Africa, the

continent whose interests the Secretary General—an Egyptian—has said need more representation." Seth Faison, "U.N. Chief Mired in Dispute With Security Council," July 24, 1992.

14. Steven Lee Meyers, "Making Sure War Crimes Aren't Forgotten," *New York Times*, September 22, 1997.

15. See, e.g., Edward S. Herman, "The Politics of the Srebrenica Massacre," ZNet, July 7, 2005, http://www.zmag.org/content/showarticle.cfm?ItemID=8244; George Pumphrey, "Srebrenica 'Massacre': Is The Hague Hyping A Hoax?" as posted to *The Emperor's New Clothes*, May 8, 2000, http://www.tenc.net/articles/pumphrey/Srebrenica.html; David Peterson, "Srebrenica and the Neocolonial Community," ZNet, October 17, 2004, http://blog.zmag.org/ee_links/bosnia_herzegovina1; Nebojsa Malic, "Silver City: Srebrenica10 years Later," *AntiWar.com*, July 7, 2005, http://antiwar.com/malic/?articleid=6565; David Peterson, "The Srebrenica Massacre," ZNet, July 10, 2005, http://blog.zmag.org/ee_links/srebrenica; Nebojsa Malic, "Smokescreen—Using Srebrenica,"*AntiWar.com*, July 14, 2005, http://www.antiwar.com/malic/?articleid=6646; and Johnstone, *Fools' Crusade*, pp. 109-118.

16. Emma Brockes, "The Greatest Intellectual?" *The Guardian*, October 31, 2005. Subsequently pulled from *The Guardian*'s website. A copy still can be found on the *Chomsky.Info* website under its original title, "The Greatest Intellectual?" http://www.chomsky.info/onchomsky/20051031.htm.

17. Ian Mayes, "Corrections and clarifications: *The Guardian* and Noam Chomsky," *The Guardian*, November 17, 2005, http://www.guardian.co.uk/corrections/story/0,3604,1644017,00.html.

18. Marko Attila Hoare *et al.*, "Srebrenica — defending the truth," *Bosnia Report*, December - March, 2006, http://www.bosnia.org.uk/bosrep/report_format.cfm?articleid=3054&reportid=170.

19. Mandel, *How America Gets Away With Murder*, pp. 155-156.

20. In late December 2005, the U.S. Government acknowledged, we believe for the very first time, that the "official death toll" from the war in Bosnia and Herzegovina was "below 100,000." See U.S. Department of State, "Review of European Security Issues — A Look Ahead For 2006," December 30, 2005, http://usinfo.state.gov/eur/Archive/2006/Jan/03-735048.html. But this same report also noted that, "As recently as November [2005], U.S. officials marking the 10th anniversary of the end of the war said the death toll ranged between 200,000 and 300,000—a range that has been widely cited by government officials and media accounts for a decade."

21. Our media universe consisted of large numbers of English-language sources deriving from the wire services (including AFP, AP, DPA, Reuters, and many others), European, Canadian, U.S. print, TV and radio, and other regions (e.g., Australia, though by no means only).

22. In reporting war-related deaths in the former Yugoslavia, the historical practice through 2005 had been to attach a figure of 200,000 or greater (e.g., Holbrooke's 300,000) to Bosnia and Herzegovina specifically. Thus, editorializing the 10th anniversary of the accords that "put an end to a brutal civil war in Bosnia," the *New York Times* stated that the "war among Bosnian Muslims, Catholic Croats and Orthodox Serbs left 200,000 dead . . ." ("Bosnia, 10 Years Later," November 25, 2005). With Milosevic's death, however, the media began to use these old figures imprecisely, and to attach them sometimes to B-H alone, sometimes to *all* the wars. Our media universe captures this ambiguity in reporting.

23. On this lack of scruple, see Herman, "The Politics of the Srebrenica Massacre," ZNet, July 7, 2005, esp. Sect. 2, "The Serial Lying Before and After Srebrenica," http://www.zmag.org/content/showarticle.cfm?ItemID=8244.

24. As David Scheffer, Clinton's so-called Ambassador at Large for War Crimes, pointed out in the *American Journal of International Law*, without the safety-valve of the U.S. veto on the Security Council, "There will be significant new legal and political risks in such [highly controversial] interventions, which up to this point have been mostly shielded from politically motivated charges." In short, any outcome that Washington controls is free of "politically motivated charges." When ultimate control slips from Washington's grasp, and other states begin to exercise significant influence, *political factors* intervene! Scheffer is quoted in Mandel, *How America Gets Away With Murder*, pp. 213.

25. Mandel, *How America Gets Away With Murder*, pp. 130-133

26. The United States refused to share satellite images of Croatian actions against Krajina Serb

civilians with the ICTY, thus hampering its attempt to build a case against this U.S. ally. See Raymond Bonner, "War Crimes Panel Finds Croat Troops 'Cleansed' the Serbs," *New York Times*, March 21, 1999.

27. Michael Scharf, "Indicted For War Crimes, Then What?" *Washington Post*, October 3, 1999.
28. Mandel, *How America Gets Away With Murder*, p. 125.
29. Ibid., p. 126
30. "The new administration had already made up their mind and were intent on killing off the [Vance-Owen Peace Plan]," David Owen writes of the period in late January and early February, 1993, recounting his first meeting with Secretary of State Warren Christopher, and a series of attacks on the plan in the American media. "They promised to come up with an alternative policy over the next few weeks, but in the meantime seemed intent on killing off a detailed plan backed by all their allies and close to being agreed by the parties. It was by any standard of international diplomacy outrageous conduct." *Balkan Odyssey* (New York: Harcourt Brace and Company, 1995), Ch. 3, "The Vance-Owen Peace Plan," pp. 112-120.
31. Mandel, *How America Gets Away With Murder*, "The ICTY at War," pp. 132–146, esp. pp. 132-134.
32. UN ICTY, "Statement by Justice Louise Arbour," press release, January 16, 1999, http://www.un.org/icty/pressreal/p378-e.htm.
33. As Arbour explained at the time: "In light of recent reports of his alleged involvement in Kosovo, I have decided to make public the existence of an indictment against Zeljko Raznjatovic, also known as Arkan.... [Publicizing his indictment now] will...serve to put on notice those who might be inclined to retain his services, or to obey his orders, that they too will be tainted by their association with an indicted war criminal." UN ICTY "Statement by the Prosecutor," March 31, 1999, http://www.un.org/icty/pressreal/p391e.htm.
34. UN ICTY, *Prosecutor Against Slobodan Milosevic et al.*, IT-99-37-I, "Kosovo" (May 22, 1999), http://www.un.org/icty/indictment/english/mil-ii990524e.htm.
35. Mandel, *How America Gets Away With Murder*, p. 144.
36. CNN Live Event/Special, 1:24PM, Transcript # 99052703V54, May 27, 1999.
37. Arbour was responding to British television reporter Lindsay Hill, who had asked Arbour how she can "ensure that the Tribunal remains independent and impartial and doesn't become part of NATO's war strategy or doesn't become perceived as being part of NATO's war strategy?" See British Ministry of Defense Briefing, April 20, 1999, http://www.kosovo.mod.uk/brief200499.htm. Along with Arbour, British Foreign Secretary Robin Cook and General Sir Charles Guthrie also participated in this news conference.
38. UN ICTY "Statement by Justice Louise Arbour, Prosecutor," May 27, 1999, http://www.un.org/icty/pressreal/p404-e.htm.
39. On July 24, 1995, Karadzic and Mladic became the fifth and sixth veterans of the wars to be indicted overall. See *Prosecutor Against Radovan Karadzic and Ratko Mladic*, IT-95-5-I, "Bosnia and Herzegovina" (July 24, 1995), http://www.un.org/icty/indictment/english/kar-ii950724e.htm. This initial indictment covered events in Bosnia and Herzegovina exclusive of those associated with the July, 1995 evacuation of the "Safe Area" Srebrenica and its aftermath—a subsequent indictment not released until the month of November. See *Prosecutor Against Radovan Karadzic and Ratko Mladic*, IT-95-18 "Srebrenica" (November 14, 1995), http://www.un.org/icty/indictment/english/kar-ii951116e.htm.
40. The *L'Unita* interview was reported in "Karadzic a Pariah, Says War Crimes Tribunal Chief," ANP English News Bulletin, July 27, 1995.
41. Scharf, "Indicted For War Crimes, Then What?" *Washington Post*, October 3, 1999.
42. See UN ICTY Office of the Prosecutor, *"Final Report to the Prosecutor by the Committee Established to Review the NATO Bombing Campaign Against the Federal Republic of Yugoslavia"*, June, 2000, par. 90, http://www.un.org/icty/pressreal/natoo61300.htm. (And the accompanying ICTY Press Statement (PR/P.I.S./510-e), June 13, 2000, http://www.un.org/icty/pressreal/p510e.htm.)
43. Mandel, *How America Gets Away With Murder*, pp. 189-190.
44. Kirsten Sellars reports that in October, 1998, Michael Scharf estimated that "over 90 percent" of the evidence then used by the prosecution derived from hearsay sources. See *The Rise and Rise of Human Rights* (Sutton Publishing, 2002), p. 187.
45. In all, the Tribunal issued indictments of Milosevic on eight different occasions: Three for

Kosovo (http://www.un.org/icty/indictment/english/mil-ii990524e.htm (May 22, 1999); http://www.un.org/icty/indictment/english/mil-aio10629e.htm (June 29, 2001); and http://www.un.org/icty/indictment/english/mil-2aio11029e.htm (October 29, 2001); three for Croatia (http://www.un.org/icty/indictment/english/mil-iio11008e.htm (October 8, 2001); http://www.un.org/icty/indictment/english/mil-aio21023.htm (October 23, 2002); and http://www.un.org/icty/indictment/english/mil-2aio20728e.htm>July 28, 2004); and two for Bosnia and Herzegovina (http://www.un.org/icty/indictment/english/mil-iio11122e.htm (November 22, 2001); http://www.un.org/icty/indictment/english/mil-aio40421-e.htm (November 22, 2002).

46. For a comprehensive online listing of ICTY sources, see The Trial of Slobodan Milosevic: Kosovo, Croatia, and Bosnia-Herzegovina, IT-02-54, http://www.un.org/icty/cases-e/cis/milosevic/menu-e.htm; and Transcripts, http://www.un.org/icty/transe54/transe54.htm.

47. *Inter alia,* see *Second Amended Indictment of Milosevic et al. for Kosovo,* October 29, 2001, http://www.un.org/icty/indictment/english/mil-2aio11029e.htm; *Initial Indictment of Milosevic et al. for Croatia,* October 8, 2001, http://www.un.org/icty/indictment/english/mil-iio11008e.htm; and *Initial Indictment of Milosevic et al. For Bosnia,* http://www.un.org/icty/indictment/english/mil-iio11122e.htm.

48. Misha Glenny, "Just what the Balkans didn't need," *New Statesman,* March 20, 2006.

49. Richard Holbrooke, "Rough justice for Milosevic is as fitting as a tribunal verdict," *Financial Times,* March 14, 2006.

50. Johnstone, *Fools's Crusade,* pp. 23-35; pp. 152-56. See further the January 25, 2006 Milosevic trial testimony of Col. Milan Kotur on the planning for exit and warfare by the Croat government of President Franjo Tudjman well before the war broke out, including a 1990 video in which Croat leaders discuss how they will remove the Serb population, http://www.un.org/icty/transe54/060125ED.htm.

51. Ibid, pp. 55-68

52. The media never quote from these Milosevic speeches, understandably. In his June 28, 1989 speech, Milosevic stated that "Yugoslavia is a multinational community and it can survive only under the conditions of full equality for all nations that live in it," and nothing elsewhere in this speech is in conflict with this sentiment (see "Slobodan Milosevic's 1989 Speech at Kosovo Polje," BBC Summary of World Broadcasts, June 30, 1989, http://emperorsclothes.com/milo/versions.htm). Francisco Gil-White has shown how systematically the Western media have distorted the record in referring to this speech, and how the BBC itself eventually misread the language that it had reported back in 1989 to accord with the new party line (Francisco Gil-White, "How Politicians, the Media, and Scholars Lied about Milosevic's 1989 Kosovo Speech," *Historical and Investigative Research,* September 8, 2005, http://www.hirhome.com/yugo/milospeech.htm).

53. On the Slovene responsibility for this war, citing U.S. Ambassador Warren Zimmerman, see Johnstone, *Fools' Crusade,* pp. 137-138.

54. Mandel, *How America Gets Away With Murder,* pp. 132-138

55. George Kenney reports that in 1999, a U.S. Government official conceded to him that at Rambouillet, U.S. negotiators "deliberately set the bar higher than the Serbs could accept." In Kenney's paraphrase, the "Serbs needed...a little bombing to see reason." "Rolling Thunder: the Rerun," *The Nation,* June 14, 1999.

56. Tim Judah, "Is Milosevic Planning Another Balkan War?" *Scotland on Sunday,* March 19, 2000; Daniel Williams and R. Jeffrey Smith, "Crusader for Serb Honor Was Defiant Until the End," *Washington Post,* March 12, 2006.

57. See UN ICTY *Prosecutor v. Slobodan Milosevic,* IT-02-54-E, pp. 43225-43227, August 25, 2005, http://www.un.org/icty/transe54/050825IT.htm. In a startling concession to the Milosevic defense, and in contradiction of the serial indictments of Milosevic *et al.* for having participated in a "joint criminal enterprise" the alleged purpose of which was to create a "new Serb-dominated state," the "Greater Serbia" of lore, Prosecutor Geoffrey Nice asserted that "The concept that all Serbs should live in one state is different from the concept of the Greater Serbia..." (p. 43225). Shortly thereafter, Nice acknowledged that Milosevic was motivated not by any desire to create a "Greater Serbia" but by the "pragmatic" goal of "ensuring that all the Serbs who had lived in the former Yugoslavia should be allowed for either constitutional or

other reasons to live in the same unit. That meant as we know historically from his perspective first of all that the former Yugoslavia shouldn't be broken up because he argued, well, then, if they all live in the same place one where they can do it in the former Yugoslavia" (p. 43227). As best we can tell, this instance of the prosecution's abandonment of one of the central charges against Milosevic was never reported in the English-language print media.

58. For a superior discussion of the "joint criminal enterprise" concept drafted as an Expert Witness Report on behalf of the defense shortly before Milosevic's death, see David Chandler, *The 'Butcher of the Balkans'? The Crime of 'Joint Criminal Enterprise' and the Milosevic? Indictments at the International Criminal Tribunal at The Hague*, University of Westminster, U.K., 2006, http://www.wmin.ac.uk/sshl/pdf/CSDCHandlerHagueReport0306_5_.pdf.

59. UN ICTY *Prosecutor v. Radislav Krstic*, IT-98-33, August 2, 2001,//www.un.org/icty/krstic/TrialC1/judgement/index.htm

60. In the *Initial Indictment of Milosevic et al. for Bosnia and Herzegovina*, November 22, 2001, http://www.un.org/icty/indictment/english/mil-ii011122e.htm, a large number of population centers in Bosnia are listed in addition to Srebrenica where the genocide criterion would apply, according to the standard used for the judgment in the *Krstic* case.

61. Elie Wiesel, "The Question of Genocide," *Newsweek*, April 12, 1999.

62. Cees Wiebes, *Intelligence and the War in Bosnia 1992 –1995*, London: Lit Verlag, 2003, p. 388.

63. John Laughland, who visited Milosevic in his prison cell in November 2005, writes that "when on Tuesday Milosevic pleaded that he was too sick to continue, presiding judge Patrick Robinson simply barked: 'Are you deaf? I told you to call the next witness'" ("International Law is an ass," *The Spectator*, November 19, 2005). Also, after attending the opening session of the Milosevic trial, Canadian defense attorney Edward L. Greenspan expressed shock at Judge Richard May's attitude toward Milosevic. "May doesn't even feign impartiality or, indeed, interest," Greenspan wrote. "He clearly reviles Milosevic." Greenspan was appalled by May's habit of interrupting Milosevic's cross-examination of witnesses—a practice that only worsened during Milosevic's defense, after May died and was replaced by Judge Patrick Robinson. "It looks like May has forgotten that Milosevic is entitled to due process," Greenspan wrote. "The first two minutes of the Milosevic trial told me all I needed to know. This is a lynching." Edward L. Greenspan, "This is a lynching," *National Post*, March 13, 2002.

64. UN ICTY *Decision on Assigned Counsel Request for Provisional Release*, IT-02-54-T, February 23, 2006, par. 18, http://www.un.org/icty/milosevic/trialc/decision-e/060224.htm.

65. For the role of Kosovo and of the Balkan region more generally within international criminal networks, see, e.g., Barbara Limanowska, *Trafficking in Human Beings in South Eastern Europe*, United Nations Development Program, March, 2005, http://www.unicef.org/ceecis/Trafficking.Report.2005.pdf.

CHAPTER 15

Finding The Openings For Media Democracy

By Robert A. Hackett, NewsWatch Canada, School of
Communication, Simon Fraser University and William K.
Carroll, Department of Sociology, University of Victoria

For thirty years, Project Censored has been one of the most important organizations in what is now a burgeoning movement to democratize the American mediascape—to hold corporate media
accountable, to build alternative media, and to refashion government
communication policies to favor diversity and citizen access over corporate profits and power.

How can such a movement be built in the face of huge obstacles?
Interviews with 150 media activists in the U.S., Britain and Canada,
summarized in a recent book,[1] offer many insights into the openings
for moving towards a just and democratic media system.

To be sure, our respondents were well aware of the sobering challenges they faced. For many Americans, the "national religion" of
free market fundamentalism has helped to "naturalize" the commercial media system: they regard it background wallpaper, rather than a
subject of political debate and democratic decision-making—unless
they think the media are too "left-liberal"!

The tactics and rhetoric of activists themselves are sometimes self-
marginalizing, failing to resonate with dominant values. Sometimes
competing for the same supporters and funders, non-profit groups
become jealously protective of their own turf. Progressive groups
often lack common focus, strategy and coordination. There is no con-
sensus about how to "frame" democratic media activism as a coher-
ent project: is it about freedom of press and expression, media
democracy, media justice, the right to communicate, or the cultural
environment? As well, there are leadership conundrums: on the one
hand, a suspicion towards effective leadership in general; on the
other hand, the "strong founder syndrome," whereby organizations
may fail to grow beyond the vision and energy of their original leader.

In a society that systematically under-rewards public service and over-rewards self-interested profit-oriented behaviour, however socially and environmentally destructive it may be, public interest advocacy groups are constantly under-funded and short-staffed.

Weaknesses in the coalitions for media democracy include the relative absence of journalists and organized labour as potential partners, as well as unresolved internal tensions of race and gender. Add to that the power of the opponents of media democratization—notably large media corporations, and the politically organized conservatives, politicians and regulators who often align with corporate interests.

Sounds pretty grim, doesn't it? But what social justice movement does not face huge obstacles? There is a dialectic between obstacles and openings. Social movements are catalyzed and defined by what they perceive to be obstacles to valued goals. From their experience and reflections, the activists we interviewed pointed to a number of openings and opportunities. These can be divided into five categories: hot pokers, systemic openings, resources, allies, and strategies.

HOT POKERS

"Hot pokers" refers to negative events and trends that galvanize people into action. The apparently fraudulent election of George W. Bush in 2000, and the invasion of Iraq in 2003 on the basis of now-discredited pretexts, infuriated millions of people, in the U.S. and elsewhere. The complicity of U.S. corporate media in these events recruited thousands more people to the idea of media reform. So too have bad media practices and policies. Our respondents cited dozens of issues that have galvanized public response: the wholesale clearcutting of local radio programming by the ClearChannel media empire, corporate abuse of copyright, TV commercials imposed in school classrooms, cutbacks and political pressure on PBS, distribution barriers to alternative magazines, growing media concentration, the FCC's repression of low-power FM radio, and the continued stereotyping and marginalization of people of color in the dominant "machinery of representation". All of the above are examples of the democratic deficit inherent in the current political economy of communication in hyper-capitalist America. Sometimes that democratic deficit can be personified in the form of a (now disgraced) autocratic press baron like Conrad Black, who swallowed a major Canadian newspaper chain in 1996; or former FCC chairman Michael Powell, a right-wing ideologue openly contemputous of public opinion and public interest regulation. Media democrats could hardly ask for better "villains," both of whom unwittingly helped to galvanize major media reform campaigns in Canada and the U.S., respectively. Threats to existing media that people value can spur them to action. Funding cutbacks to the Canadian Broadcasting Corporation, whose radio service has a particularly devoted audience, have fuelled campaigns by the Friends of Canadian Broadcasting for two decades. In the U.S., an apparent corporate-style takeover of the alternative radio network Pacifica sparked resistance in affected cities in the late 1990s. Most especially, protests in Berkeley, California, including sit-ins, on-air confrontations, and an unprecedented demonstration of about 15,000 people, convinced the Pacifica board to retreat.

A major long-term catalyst for media activism is the frustration of social movements in dealing with corporate media. Ethnic minorities have been active for decades due to their marginalization. Mark Lloyd of the Civil Rights Forum argued that media reformers should thus look to diverse ethnic groups searching for equality under the law. For professor Marc Raboy, the many people involved in anti-WTO activism will bolster media democratization as they "come to realize the limitations of the media with respect to those issues."

Those employed by media industries have their own hot pokers—like layoffs and commercially motivated threats to editorial integrity. The advent of the McNewspaper, a management model in which news is driven explicitly by commercial imperatives, catalyzed union organizing in Canadian newsrooms. Even if journalists are reluctant to join explicitly political campaigns, their professional concerns, such as free speech, do overlap with those of media activists.

CRACKS IN THE SYSTEM

If negative events provide an incentive for action, there need to be positive openings in the political, cultural, technological, economic and spatial environment for activism to have an impact.

However deeply flawed American democracy may be, the political system can provide openings. Media scholar and advocate Bob McChesney argues that paradoxically, the non-competitive nature of elections in the many gerrymandered Congressional districts liberates politicians from worrying about negative media coverage. Compared to the British-style parliamentary system, party discipline within American politics is lax. On the one hand, it is very difficult for third parties to break into the system and raise new issues like media reform, as has sometimes happened in Britain and Canada. But on the other hand, individual politicians within the two semi-official parties have greater leeway to pursue their own favored causes. The late Senator Paul Wellstone, and Representatives Jesse Jackson Jr., John Conyers and especially Bernie Sanders are amongst those who took up the cudgels for media reform.[2]

Technological and other changes sometimes upset long-established communication structures and generate "critical junctures" in policy-making. One such juncture, the merger of two of America's largest cable companies in 2002, required the renegotiation of local cable franchises in many cities. San Francisco's Media Alliance and groups elsewhere, backed by the Consumer Federation of America and the Center for Digital Democracy in Washington D.C., seized the opportunity to build local campaigns for more community access programming and other public interest goals.

The dominant media system itself is not monolithic. "It's not the case that nothing critical or progressive ever gets through," says Janine Jackson of the New York-based media watchdog FAIR. Journalists do have a certain amount of autonomy, creating "a lot of give in the system" for groups who know how to use it, adds her colleague Jim Naureckas. Other FAIR veterans point to success in using rivalries between corporate media organizations, and their need for credibility with audiences. And while diversity in a commercial media system is significantly limited by the imperative of profitability, it does provide market niches for alternative media.[3]

Universities should not be overlooked as resources. While they are hardly the radical hotbeds depicted in right-wing mythology or Sixties nostalgia, and while corporatization is affecting them as much as the media, universities have provided important bases for media criticism, and indeed for monitoring projects like Project Censored, and its northern counterpart, NewsWatch Canada.

The cultural ecology of certain cities has nurtured media activism. San Francisco and Vancouver, for instance, have combined rich cultural diversity; strong popular traditions of labour militancy and progressive politics; media production skills and resources; relatively strong alternative media and a poor local mainstream press; and perhaps, sufficient distance from the national power-centres (New York, Toronto) to facilitate political and cultural experimentation.

At a broader level, as speakers like Herbert Chao Gunther of San Francisco's Public Media Center and Texan populist Jim Hightower repeatedly point out, the values of progressives (including on media issues) are not as divorced from "mainstream" America as the vested interests of the status quo want you to believe. As George Lakoff puts it in a much-discussed book:4

> I believe that progressive values *are* traditional American values, that progressive principles are fundamental American principles, and that progressive policy directions point the way to where most Americans really want our country to go.

The spread of higher education, the increasing proportion of the workforce in the 'knowledge industry,' and the general 'mediatization' of economic, social and political processes, are trends likely to nourish future media activism. Writer Barbara Ehrenreich described the corporate media's disconnection from "the great majority of Americans" as "our opportunity." Popular skepticism towards the media is arguably on the rise, even if this has yet to translate into a sophisticated understanding of media's political economy and "what can be done from a citizen's point of view to respond," argues a Vancouver journalist. Project Censored contributes to the important process of citizen education.

Although its capitalist face is often seen as a threat to human welfare and democracy, globalization also has created openings for media democratization. On the one hand, the trend of media globalization may have a liberalizing impact on previously authoritarian societies, though we shouldn't exaggerate either the impact or the benefits of entertainment- and advertising-saturated global media.5 On the other hand, transnational movements *against* corporate-driven top-down globalization have stimulated the development of alternative media, notably the Independent Media Centers.

RESOURCES

In order to take wing, social movements need to mobilize existing resources and/or acquire new ones. How else can they create collective organizations, launch and win campaigns, provide incentives for participation, punish or defeat opponents, and achieve influence in relation to other political and social actors? The activists we interviewed described a variety of economic, psychological and cultural resources already available to them.

Those media democracy groups that have survived have been able to tap funds from philanthropic foundations, subsidies from wealthier allied organizations (such as trade unions, especially in the UK), and membership dues. Some groups have been able to generate revenue streams (and sometimes cross-subsidize more directly political work) through marketable commodities—such as FAIR's magazine *Extra!*, and the Media Alliance's computer classes and (until industry-initiated cancellations this year) health insurance services.

Other valuable movement-building resources include existing communication networks, such as membership lists, internet listserves, and conferences. Campaigns, democratic media, and communication policies—from the Zapatistas use of the internet to the best of European public broadcasting—can provide inspirational models. The most sustainable media democracy groups have developed positive organizational cultures that at their best maintain membership morale and involvement by combining social and material incentives, a good board-staff relationship, participatory decision-making, a clear political vision, and an ongoing public profile. Above all, it is people's energy and commitment that is key to grassroots social change. Many groups have been built or sustained through the talent and commitment of social animators like Granville Williams in Britain's Campaign for Press and Broadcasting Freedom, Andrea Buffa at Media Alliance, and many others who have won the appreciation of their peers.

ALLIES

As The Beatles once sang, "I get by with a little help from my friends." Although as noted above, media democratization has been hampered by weak ties with social forces that should count among its supporters, our respondents identified many partner-groups they have worked with, thus collectively outlining the shape of a potential coalition. Foremost allies included other media activists and communication-oriented groups. Collaborations between them seem to work best when there is a complementary division of labor; groups that are too close functionally and geographically may have "turf issues."

What other allies were mentioned? They included non-media advocacy groups in civil society concerned with progressive social change, particularly non-profit organizations in the fields of the environment, civil rights and women's equality. Examples include the Leadership Conference on Civil Rights; the National Organization of Women; religious organizations (including the U.S. Catholic Conference, the National Council of Churches, and the Unitarian Universalist Church); pediatricians; public health groups; disability advocates; mainstream educational and cultural organizations like the national PTA and National Education Association; Washington-based public interest policy advocates; progressive policy research institutes, like the Center for Policy Initiatives; foundations and institutes seeking investment in childcare, or the prevention of violence and alcohol abuse; associations of Latinos and African-Americans; neighborhood associations and local coalitions; librarians and academics; and the emerging movements for global justice.

While it has been a weak link in media democracy alliances in the U.S., organized labor has several potential motives for supporting them. When they represent workers inside media industries, unions have a stake in promoting job security, working conditions, and the integrity and autonomy of journalism in the face of ownership, commercial and state pressures. Unions outside the media industries have good reason to be frustrated with their mass-mediated image (or invisibility).

Perhaps for understandable historical reasons, American progressives sometimes see the state as a monolithic and repressive force. But governments, political parties and state agencies sometimes have coinciding interests with media democrats. In Canada, the state-funded National Film Board has produced progressive documentaries, and during the 1960s, its Challenge for Change program used media to raise public awareness about the realities of poverty, to give a public voice to those without one, and to "help disadvantaged communities organize themselves and take control of their destinies."[6]

Much more recently, inside-the-Beltway dissidents like FCC commissioners Jonathan Adelstein and especially Michael Copps were crucial sparkplugs for the relatively successful grassroots campaign against the lifting of media ownership ceilings in 2003.[7] And in between, political parties like the New Democrats in Canada and the Greens in the U.S. have advocated the break-up of media monopolies, support for non-commercial media, and other democratic reforms.

Sometimes on specific issues, allies of convenience can be found in surprising quarters. Youthful dot.com millionaires in Seattle helped fund the launching of the IndyMedia Center at the 1999 WTO protests. The Canadian Association of Advertisers has actually opposed the expansion of advertising time on commercial broadcasting: it doesn't want to dilute the intensity of contact with audiences. Social conservatives worry about the excesses of commercial programming, and right-wing groups like the National Rifle Association were amongst the coalition opposing the FCC's media ownership liberalization in 2003.

The social energies for media justice are not confined to organizations with websites and name plates on the door. San Francisco activist and scholar Dorothy Kidd suggests that under the surface, the expansion of communicative skills and awareness amongst subaltern communities and movements is an enormous resource. And in the words of Peter Phillips, editor of this book, potential allies include "anybody concerned with human rights and social justice."

In speaking with media activists, it became clear that they understand "alliances" along a spectrum, from coincidental alignment on the same side of an issue, to short-term cooperation on a single project, to long-term working relationships, to (however rare) mutual solidarity and automatic reciprocal support. One of the most encouraging factors is the widespread recognition of the importance of building flexible coalitions for media change, on the basis of mutual respect and autonomy.

STRATEGIES

Two further encouraging observations conclude this overview of openings. First, media democrats have recognized the need to develop "collective action frames" that define issues, name problems, and offer solutions in ways that resonate with the experience and values of potential supporters. Given the diversity of interests and groups with a stake in media democracy (or is it media justice?), it is unlikely that one frame will fit all. Still, the Free Press conferences, drawing several thousand enthusiastic media activists to Madison in 2003 and St. Louis in 2005, showed that a handful of core themes can crystallize the concerns of a wide range of people. Those themes include a press genuinely free from the lies and propaganda of corporations and governments alike; a progressive and democratic press that can combat the Right's longstanding domination of the political agenda; and even more broadly, media justice, which repositions the problem of the media as just one aspect of social justice in a world organized around globalized capitalism, racism and patriarchy.[8]

Second, through decades of practice, activists have honed a rich repertoire of action-routes and strategies. In many ways, these strategies are complementary. Taken together, they challenge all aspects of the dominant media "field" or system, including the production and distribution of news and other media texts, the provision of access to the means of communication (including the architecture of the internet), the ways in which audiences receive and make sense of media representations, and the framework of government regulation and policies towards media.[9] The diversity of approaches is suggested by the slogan for Vancouver's annual Media Democracy Day—"Know the media, change the media, be the media." When you think about it, each of the following strategies contributes to media democratization in distinct ways:

➤ Alternative media arm their audiences with information to take action on various issues, and also expose and fill the blind spots of currently dominant corporate media. Alternative media can provide models of what a democratic communication system might look like.
➤ Media education, parodies and culture jamming (like the magazine AdBusters) can help audiences acquire critical tools to change how they perceive and interact with media images and institutions.
➤ Some forms of activism take on the messages and practices of corporate media more directly. Some projects, like SPIN in San Francisco, teach community advocacy groups strategic communication skills in hopes of shifting media coverage. Creative confronta-

tions like protest rallies, marches and town hall meetings can force media corporations and governments to pay attention to a grievance. Journalists and their professional associations and unions can work to offset the power of media owners and advertisers.

➤ Many activists use established judicial and political channels to reform the government policies that help shape the architecture of the media system. This may involve lobbying government both to raise the priority of media issues in the legislative agenda, and to promote progressive democratic positions on a range of issues—public service broadcasting, intellectual property regimes, freedom of expression, children's privacy on the internet, public access to cable TV and the internet, and much else. The Campaign for Press and Broadcasting Freedom in Britain, and Free Press in the U.S., are impressive efforts to build broad coalitions focusing on such media reform.

Media activism cannot succeed in a vacuum. If there is to be a "deep media democracy movement," argues Dorothy Kidd, independent media need to follow the lead of social movements rather than vice versa. The point, observed Liza Dichter with the Center for Independent Media Action, is to build a constituency for media democracy by listening to other social movements and figuring out how "the media piece" fits into *their* agenda —a principle embodied in "The Listening Project" (available at www.omgcenter.org/listen/, accessed October 2005).

I conclude simply by noting how important Project Censored has been for thirty years, as one arc of the media democracy rainbow. It spans several of the strategies noted above. It both supports existing alternative media by publicizing its stories, and constitutes an alternative medium in its own right, providing "mobilizing information" about various issues that many people reading this book might not otherwise encounter. Its annual list of under-reported stories functions as media education, highlighting the increasingly glaring omissions of corporate media. It could conceivably be used in "shame the media" campaigns for more accountability and diversity. This book and Project Censored conferences also help to connect progressive advocates and organizations from within and outside the media field.

All the strategies and openings summarized in this chapter, including Project Censored itself, are no more than opportunities.

They are relevant to the extent that people collectively use them in struggles for better media and better democracy.

Robert A. Hackett, professor, School of Communication, Simon Fraser University; Co-director of NewsWatch Canada since 1993. His most recent publications include Democratizing Global Media: One World, Many Struggles (co-edited with Yuezhi Zhao, 2005), and Remaking Media: The Struggle To Democratize Public Communication (with William K. Carroll, 2006).

Bill Carroll is a critical sociologist with research interests in the areas of social movements and social change, the political economy of corporate capitalism, and critical social theory and method. A professor at the University of Victoria, where he teaches in Sociology and in the Interdisciplinary Graduate Program in Cultural, Social and Political Thought, his current projects include a longitudinal investigation of networks of global corporate power and the study of hegemony and counter-hegemony in a global field.

Notes

1. Hackett, Robert A. and William K. Carroll, *Remaking Media: The Struggle to Democratize Public Communication*, London: Routledge 2006. This article draws mainly from Chapters 7 and 8.
2. McChesney, Robert W. and John Nichols, *Our Media, Not Theirs: The Democratic Struggle against Corporate Media*, New York: Seven Stories Press, 2002, p. 115.
3. Benson, Rodney, "Commercialism and critique: California's alternative weeklies," in Nick Couldry and James Curran (eds.), *Contesting Media Power: Alternative Media in a Networked World*, Lanham: Rowman & Littlefield, 2003, pp. 11-127.
4. *Don't think of an elephant! Know your values and frame the debate*, White River Junction, Vermont: 2004, p. 95.
5. McChesney, Robert W. and Robert A. Hackett, "Beyond wiggle room: American corporate media's democratic deficit, its global implications, and prospects for reform," in Robert A. Hackett and Yuezhi Zhao (eds.), *Democratizing Global Media: One World, Many Struggles*, Lanham: Rowman & Littlefield, 2005, pp. 23-35.
6. D. Henaut, "The 'challenge for change/Societe ouvelle' experience," in N. These and A. Ambrosi (eds.), *Video the Changing World*, Montreal and New York: Black Rose, p. 48.
7. McChesney, Robert W., *The Problem of the Media: U.S. Communication Politics in the 21st Century*, New York: Monthly Review Press, 2004, chap. 7.
8. Hackett, Robert A. and William K. Carroll, "Critical social movements and media reform," *Media Development* 1/2004, pp. 17–18; Hackett and Carroll, *Remaking Media*, pp. 78–79.
9. Ibid., p. 56.

Index

About the Editor

Peter Phillips is a Professor of Sociology at Sonoma State University and Director of Project Censored. He teaches classes in Media Censorship, Sociology of Power, Political Sociology, and Sociology of Media. He has published ten editions of *Censored: Media Democracy in Action* as well as *Impeach the President: The Case Against Bush and Cheney* (2006) and *Project Censored Guide to Independent Media and Activism* (2003) with Seven Stories Press.

Phillips writes op-ed pieces for independent media nationwide including dozens of publications, newspapers and websites including *Z Magazine*, Counterpunch, Common Dreams, Buzzflash, Social Policy, and Briarpatch. He frequently speaks on media censorship and various socio-political issues on radio and TV talk shows, including Talk of the Nation, Air America, Talk America, World Radio Network, *Flashpoints*, and the *Jim Hightower Show*.

Phillips earned a B.A. in Social Science in 1970 from Santa Clara University, and an M.A. in Social Science from California State University at Sacramento in 1974. He earned a second M.A. in Sociology in 1991 and a Ph.D. in Sociology in 1994. His doctoral dissertation is entitled *A Relative Advantage: Sociology of the San Francisco Bohemian Club*, available at http://libweb.sonoma.edu/regional/faculty/Phillips/bohemianindex.htm.

Phillips is a fifth generation Californian who grew up on a family-owned farm west of the Central Valley town of Lodi. Phillips lives today in rural Sonoma County with his wife Mary Lia.

How to Support Project Censored

NOMINATE A STORY

To nominate a *Censored* story send us a copy of the article and include the name of the source publication, the date that the article appeared, and page number. For Internet published news stories of which we should be aware please forward the URL to Censored@sonoma.edu. The final deadline period for nominating a Most Censored Story of the year is March of each year.

CRITERIA FOR PROJECT CENSORED NEWS STORIES NOMINATIONS

1. A censored news story is one which contains information that the general United States population has a right and need to know, but to which it has had limited access.

2. The news story is timely, on-going, and has implications for a significant number of residents in the United States.

3. The story has clearly defined concepts and is backed up with solid, verifiable documentation.

4. The news story has been publicly published, either electronically or in print, in a circulated newspaper, journal, magazine, newsletter, or similar publication from either a foreign or domestic source.

5. The news story has direct connections to and implications for people in the United States, which can include activities that U.S. citizens are engaged in abroad.

SUPPORT PROJECT CENSORED BY MAKING A FINANCIAL GIFT

Project Censored is a self-supported 501-C-3 non-profit organization. We depend on tax deductible donations and foundation grants to continue our work. To support our efforts for freedom of information send checks to the address below or call 707-664-2500. Visa and Mastercard accepted. Donations can be made through our website at: www.project-censored.org.

Project Censored
Sonoma State University
1801 East Cotati Avenue
Rohnert Park, CA 94928
e-mail: censored@sonoma.edu